Aristophanes, William Charles Green

Aristophanes

Aristophanes, William Charles Green

Aristophanes

ISBN/EAN: 9783337005504

Printed in Europe, USA, Canada, Australia, Japan

Cover: Foto ©Thomas Meinert / pixelio.de

More available books at **www.hansebooks.com**

CATENA CLASSICORUM

EDITED BY

THE REV.
ARTHUR HOLMES M.A.
SENIOR FELLOW AND DEAN OF CLARE COLLEGE CAMBRIDGE
AND LATE PREACHER AT THE CHAPEL ROYAL WHITEHALL

AND

THE REV.
CHARLES BIGG D.D.
PRINCIPAL OF BRIGHTON COLLEGE
LATE SENIOR STUDENT AND TUTOR OF CHRIST CHURCH OXFORD

RIVINGTONS

London ... ... Waterloo Place
Oxford ... ... High Street
Cambridge ... ... Trinity Street

ARISTOPHANES

EDITED BY

W. C. GREEN, M.A.
LATE FELLOW OF KING'S COLLEGE, CAMBRIDGE
CLASSICAL LECTURER AT QUEENS' COLLEGE

THE WASPS

RIVINGTONS
London, Oxford, and Cambridge
MDCCCLXVIII

INTRODUCTION TO THE WASPS.

The play of *The Wasps* was exhibited in the spring of B.C. 422, in the archonship of Aminias, probably at the Lenaean festival. It gained the second prize, a play called Προάγων being first, and one of Leucon called Πρέσβεις third.

According to the Greek "Didascalies" it was exhibited in the name of Philonides; and these, as Ranke thinks, are upon the whole the safest guides. He therefore infers that Aristophanes on account of his failure with the *Clouds* returned to his old plan of sheltering himself behind another name, and that the *Proagon*, as well as the *Wasps*, was a play of Aristophanes. On the other hand Richter (who has investigated and edited this play with great care) considers the Didascalies untrustworthy, especially this one; and assigns the *Wasps* to the Great Dionysia, the *Proagon* to the Lenaea. Philonides, he thinks, was merely the principal actor. But this is a matter of no great moment as far as the *Wasps* is concerned; since, whether Philonides were nominal author or actor, Aristophanes was doubtless known to be the real author as well as he is now.

In the *Proagon* Euripides was ridiculed: in the *Wasps* the Athenian litigiousness is the object of satire. According to Ranke, with the *Clouds* ends the first period of Aristophanes' dramatic poetry. And this is a convenient division, borne out in a great measure by a change in the poet's style. For though he is still tolerably consistent, attacking Cleon and the litigious spirit which he had before ridiculed (e.g. *Nub.* 208), yet his style seems less strict and severe: there is more of the ludicrous, more broad fun. And therefore naturally there is less completeness and connexion of parts in this play. It is not so political as the *Knights*, not so personal as the *Clouds*. The *Wasps*, in fact, consists of two distinct parts: the first, which contains the madness of the old dicast and the ridiculous means used to cure him, ending with the parabasis; the second, in which he is converted to fashionable life, being as it were an afterpiece, and deemed by some critics unnecessary. Thus Schlegel calls the *Wasps* Aristophanes' feeblest play; and few critics rank it very high. But it may be said in defence of our poet, that the last scenes form a very striking contrast to the early part, and so enhance its effect. They are perhaps drawn out to a somewhat tedious length, but possibly some certain time had to be filled up. And Aristophanes, after exposing the absurdities of a life devoted to the law-courts, may well have meant to shew the evil of the other extreme—probably too common among the young fashionables at Athens—in the tipsy frolics of the old ex-juryman. Weak in connexion and plot the play may be, but it is brilliant and amusing in particular scenes.

The *Wasps* gave to Racine the idea of *Les Plaideurs*, and several whole scenes may be compared with advantage. On the details of Athenian law, with which the play abounds, Schoemann, Richter in his long and elaborate Prolegomena, and the Dictionary of Antiquities, furnish ample information.

ΑΡΙΣΤΟΦΑΝΟΥΣ ΣΦΗΚΕΣ

TABLE OF THE READINGS OF DINDORF'S AND MEINEKE'S TEXTS.

	Dindorf.	Meineke.
3	προύφείλεις	πρώφειλες
7	ταῖν	τοῖν
	ὕπνου	ἤδη
16	καταπτάμενον	καταπτόμενον
21	πῶς δή, προσερεῖ τις	Ξ. πῶς δή; Σ. προερεῖ τις
25	τοιοῦτον	τοιοῦτ'
36	ἐμπεπρημένης	ἐμπεπρημένην
53	οὕτως	οὕτω σ'
55	πρῶτον	πρότερον
68	ἄνω	ἄνω
74	'Αμυνίας	Σ. 'Αμυνίας
75	εἶναι...λέγει	εἶναι φ. ά. Ξ. ἀλλ' οὐδὲν λέγει
76	Σ. μὰ	μὰ
77	Ξ. οὐκ	Ξ. οὐκ post lacunam Sosiani versus
	ἀρχὴ	ἀρχὴ
78	ὁδὶ	Σ. ὁδὶ
79	ἐ. φ. ά. Σ. οὐδαμῶς γ'	ἐ. φ. ά. Ξ. οὐδαμῶς γ'
81	Ξ. Νικόστρατος	Σ. Νικόστρατος
83	Σ. μὰ	Ξ. μὰ
94	γ' ἔχειν	φέρειν
100	ὅς	ὥς
105	προσεχόμενος	προσισχόμενος
121	δῆτα	δὴ δὲ
125	ἐξεφρίομεν	ἐξεφρείομεν
136	ἔχων...τινάς.	post v. 110 locat
136	φρυαγμοσεμνάκους τινάς	φρυαγμοσεμνακουστίνους
147	οὐκ * ἐρρήσεις	οὐ γὰρ ἐρρήσεις
152	* * τὴν θ. ὤθει	ὅδε τὴν θ. ὠθεῖ
154	μοχλοῦ·	μοχλοῦ
160	ἀποσκλῆναι	ἀποσκλῆν' ἂν
176	ταύτῃ γ'	αὕτη γ'
177	ἐξάγειν δοκῶ	ἔξαγ' ἔνδοθεν
183	ἴδωμαι ΞΑ. τουτονί. ΒΔ. τουτί	ἴδω. ναὶ τουτονί. τουτί
190	ἥσυχον	ἡσύχως
198	κεκλεισμένης	κεκλῃμένης
202	προσκύλιέ γ	προσκυλῖσον
217	τἄρ'...νῦν	νῦν...γάρ
220	μελησιδ.	μελισιδ.

4 READINGS OF DINDORF AND MEINEKE.

	Dindorf.	*Meineke.*
234	'νταῦθ' ἢ Χάβης	'νταυθὶ Χάβης θ'
244	ἠδίκησεν	ἠδίκηκεν
247	λαθών τις	λίθος τις
251	μαθών	παθών
259	βόρβορος	μάρμαρος
274	ἀπολώλεκε	ἀπολώλεκεν
282	καὶ λέγων	λέγων ὡς
283	ὡς	καὶ
302	σὺ δὲ	ἒ ἕ. σὺ δὲ
311	ὁπόθεν γε	ὁπόθεν δὴ
312	ἵν'...παρέχῃς	ΧΟ. ἵν'...παρέχῃς
317	ὑπακούων	ἐπακούων
318	ἀλλ' οὐ γὰρ οἷός τ' ἔτ'	ἀλλὰ γὰρ οὐχ οἷός τ'
323	μέγα βροντήσας	μεγαβρόντα
334	ὁ ταῦτά σ'	οὑνταυθά σ'
335	τὰς θύρας	τῇ θύρᾳ
339	τίνα	ἦ τίνα
343	λέγεις τι	λέγεις σύ τι
350	διορύξαι	διαλέξαι
378	τῶν θεῶν	τοῖν θεοῖν
383	ἅπαντες καλέσαντες	ἅπαντ' ἐκκαλέσαντες
384	τὰ τοιαῦτα	τοιαῦτα
396	διαδύεται αὖ	διαδὺς ἔλαθεν
397	μιαρώτατε	μιάρ' ἀνδρῶν
407	ἐντέτατ' ὀξύ	ἐντετάμεθ' ὀξύ
414	ὡς χρὴ	om.
415	κεκράγετε	κεκράγατε
416	ὡς τόνδ'...μεθήσομαι	ΒΔ. ὡς τοῦδ'...μεθήσομαι
418	θεοσεχθρία	θεοισεχθρία
419	ὑμῶν	ἡμῶν
422	αὖθις	αὐτοῖς
	ἀλλ' ἅπας	ἀλλὰ πᾶς
432	κύκλῳ	'ν κύκλῳ
442	δηλαδή· καὶ	δῆλα δ', εἰ καὶ
452	ἄνες	ἄφες
457	σὺ τῦφε	σύ. ΒΔ. τῦφε
458	Σ. οὐχὶ	οὐχὶ
459	Ξ. καὶ σὺ	καὶ σὺ
460	ἆρ' ἐμ.	Σ. ἆρ' ἐμ.
463	αὐτὰ δῆλα	αὐτόδηλα
465	λάθρα γ' ἐλάνθαν' ὑπιοῦσά με	λάθρᾳ μ' ἐλάμβαν' ὑπιοῦσα
472	ἔλθωμεν	ἔλθοιμεν
473	σοὶ	σοὺς
	ἐρῶν	ἐραστά
480	οὐδὲ μέν γ' οὐδ' ἐν	οὐδὲ μὴν οὔπω 'ν
483	ταὐτὰ ταῦτα	ταῦτα ταῦτα
	ξυνωμότας	ξυνωμότην
485	μοι	σοι
486	οὐδέποτέ γ'	οὐδέπω γ'
487	ὧδ' ἐστάλης	ἐξεστάλης
493	θέλῃ	'θέλῃ
504	νῦν	νῦν γ'
522	καὶ ξίφος	ΦΙ. καὶ ξίφος

READINGS OF DINDORF AND MEINEKE.

	Dindorf.	*Meineke.*
524	εἰπέ μοι	ΒΔ. εἰπέ μοι
525	ἀκράτου	ἄκρατον
526	νῦν δὲ	νῦν δὴ
527	λέγειν τι δεῖ	δεῖ τι λέγειν.
530	ΦΙ. ἀτὰρ	ἀτὰρ
532	λέγειν	λέγων
542	δ' ἐν ταῖς ὁδοῖς	δ' ἂν παισὶν ἐν ταῖσιν ὁδοῖς ἁπάσαις
543	καλούμεθ'	καλοίμεθ'
558	ἀπόφυξιν	ἀπόφευξιν
565	ἀνιῶν	ἀνιῶν
570	συγκύπτονθ' ἅμ βλ.	συγκύπτοντα βλ.
577	καὶ...ἄρχειν	om.
578	αἰδοῖα	τᾀδοῖα
588	σεμνὸν	σε μόνον
599	Εὐφημίου	Εὐφημίδου
600	σπόγγον	σφόγγον
601	τῶν...οἵων	τῶνδ'...οἵων μ'
602	χὐπηρεσίαν	καὶ ὑπηρεσίαν
605	'πιλελήσμην	'πελελήσμην
606	εἰσήκονθ' ἅμα	εἰσήκοντά με
608	φιλήσῃ	φιλῇ με
609	παππάζουσ'	παππίζουσ'
612	καὶ μή	κοὐ μή
614	ἄλλην	ἀλλ' ἥν
615—618	τάδε...κατέπαρδεν	om.
620	καὶ τῆς τοῦ	καὶ τοῦ
627	μ'	γ'
634	οὐκ, ἀλλ'	οὔκουν
636	ὡς δ' ἐπὶ πάντ' ἐλήλυθεν	ὡς ὅδε πάντ' ἐπῆλθε κοὐδέν τι παρῆλθεν
637	κοὐδὲν παρῆλθεν	
642	ὥσθ'	ὡς
645	ἀπόφυξιν	ἀπόφευξιν
661	τούτων	τούτου
665	μὰ Δί' οὐ μέντοι· καὶ	μὰ Δί' οὐ μέντοι. ΦΙ. καὶ
666	ΦΙ. ἐς τούτους κ.τ.λ.	ΒΔ. ἐς τούτους κ.τ.λ.
667	ΒΔ. σὺ γὰρ	σὺ γὰρ
671	δώσετε	οἴσετε
674	λαγαρυζόμενον	λαγαριζόμενον
694	πρίων'	πρίονθ'
695	κωλακρέτην	κωλαγρέτην
698	καὶ τοῖσιν ἅπασιν	καὶ τοισίδ' ἅπασιν
701	ἀκαρῆ	ἀκαρές
704	ἐπισίζῃ	ἐπισίξῃ
710	πύῳ	πυῷ
713	ποθ'· ὥσπερ νάρκη μου κατὰ	πέπονθ'; ὥσπερ νάρκη μου
749	πειθόμενος	πιθόμενος
758	μὴ νῦν	μή νυν
765	ἐνθάδε	ἐνθαδὶ
767	ταῦθ'	πρᾶτθ'
770	γε	δὲ
772	εἵλη	ἕλη
773	καθήμενος,	καθήμενος

READINGS OF DINDORF AND MEINEKE.

	Dindorf.	Meineke.
795	καθέψεις	καταπέψεις
	λέγων	γελῶν
808	ἐπὶ	ἀπὸ
813	κἂν γὰρ...λήψομαι	post v. 797 locat
816	ἵνα γ'	ἵν' ἂν
819	εἴ πως ἐκκομίσαις	οὔπω' ξεκόμισας
822	οἷόσπερ κ.τ.λ.	ΒΔ. οἷόσπερ κ.τ.λ.
826	εἰσαγάγω	εἰσάγω
827	τί τις	τί τίς
833, 4	ἔνδοθεν. τί ποτε τὸ χρῆμ';	ἔνδοθεν ὅ τι ποτε χρῆμ
837	ἁρπάσας	ὑφαρπάσας
849	διατρίψεις	διατρίβεις
858	δὴ τίς ἔστιν; οὐχὶ	δή τις ἐστὶν οὐχὶ
867	ξυνέβητον	ξυνεβήτην
868	ΒΔ. εὐφημία κ.τ.λ.	εὐφημία κ.τ.λ.
875	προθύρου προπύλαιε	προπύλου πάρος αὐλᾶς
885	σοι * * κἀπᾴδομεν	ταὐτά σοι κἀπᾴδομεν
888	ᾐσθόμεσθα	ᾐσθήμεσθα
890	τῶν γ. ν.	τῶν γ. ν. ἰήιε παιάν
893	τίς...ἁλώσεται	τίς...ΒΔ. οὗτος. ΦΙ. ὅσον ἁλώσεται
894—7	Ξ. ἀκούετ'...σύκινος	ΒΔ. ἀκούετ'...σύκινος
902	ποῦ δ' ὁ διώκων	ποῦ ποῦ δ' ὁ διώκων
903	ΒΔ. πάρεστιν...Λάβης	ΒΔ. πάρεστιν οὗτος. ΦΙ. ἑ. ὁ. αὖ Λάβης
905	Σ. σίγα	σίγα
907	ἦν	ἦς
917	ΦΙ. οὐδέν μ.; Ξ. οὐδ. τ.κ.ἑ.	ΦΙ. οὐδὲν μ....ἐμοί.
922	ἀφῆτέ γ' αὐτὸν	ἀφῆτ' ἔτ' αὐτὸν
924	θυείαν	θυΐαν
929	κεκλάγχω	κεκλάγγω
935	ὁ θεσμοθέτης. ποῦ' σθ' οὗτος;	ὁ θεσμοθέτης ποῦ' σθ'; οὗτος,
939	προσκεκαυμένα	προσκεκλημένα
957	ὅτι σοῦ	ὅ τι; σοῦ
961	ἐνέγραφ'	ἔγραφεν
967	ἔλει	ἐλέει
968	τραχήλι'	τὰ τραχήλι'
970	οἰκουρὸς	οἰκουρεῖν
973	ΦΙ. αἰβοῖ...μαλάττομαι	ΦΙ. αἰβοῖ. ΒΔ. τί τὸ κακόν; ΦΙ. ἔσθ' ὅ. μ.
974	περιμένει	περιβαίνει
978	αἰτεῖτε	αἰτεῖσθε
981	ἐξηπάτηκεν	ἐξηπάτησεν
983	ἀπεδάκρυσα	ἐπεδάκρυσα
991	'ντευθενί	'νταῦθ' ἔνι.
993	ΒΔ. φερ'..ἠγωνίσμεθα;	ΒΔ. φ. ἑ. ΦΙ. πῶς ἀ. ἠ.
997	ἀπέφυγεν	πέφευγεν
1011	νῦν μὲν τὰ	νῦν τὰ
1029	πρῶτόν γ'	πρώτιστ'
	ἀνθρώποις	ἀνδραρίοις
1030	ἐπιχειρεῖν	ἐπεχείρει
1037	μετ' αὐτοῦ	μετ' αὐτὸν
1062	ἀνδρικώτατοι	ἀλκιμώτατοι
1064	κύκνου τ' ἔτι	κύκνου τε

READINGS OF DINDORF AND MEINEKE.

	Dindorf.	Meineke.
1076	Ἀττικοί...αὐτόχθονες	om.
1085	ἀπωσάμεσθα	ἐσωζόμεσθα
1085	πρὸς ἑσπέρᾳ	πρὸς ἑσπέραν
1087, 8		inverso ordine legit.
1091	πάντα μὴ	πάντας ἐμὲ
1110	πυκνὸν	Πυκνὸς
1114	ἐγκαθήμενοι	οἱ καθήμενοι
1115	οὐκ...φόρου	om.
1116	γόνον	πόνον
1133	καὶ τρέφειν	κἀκτρέπειν
1138	Θυμοιτίδα	Θυμαιτίδα
1142	ἐοικέναι	προσεικέναι
1157	ἀποδύου	ὑπολύου
1158	ὑπόδυθι	ὑποδοῦ τι
1159	ὑποδύσασθαι	ὑποδήσασθαι
1161	πόδ'	ποτ'
1167	γήρᾳ	γήρως
1168	ὑποδυσάμενος	ὑποδησάμενος
1169	διασαλακώνισοι	διασαικώνισον
1172	δοθιῆνι	Δοθιῆνι
1190	ἐμάχετό γ' αὐτίκα	ἆρ' ἐμάχετ' αὐτίκα
1193	λαγόνας τε	καὶ λαγόνα
1195	πῶς δ' ἂν	πῶς ἂν
1208	προσμάνθανε	προμάνθανε
1219	αὐλητρὶς	αὐλητρὶς
1222	σκόλι' ὅπως δέξει καλῶς	σκόλια πῶς δέξει; Φ. καλῶς
1223	ἄληθες, ὡς οὐδεὶς	ΒΔ. ἄληθες; Φ. ὡς οὐδ' εἰ
1225	δέξει	δέξαι
1226	ἐγένετ' Ἀθηναῖος	Ἀθηναῖός γε
1227	κλέπτης	ὡς σὺ κλέπτης.
1228	τουτὶ σὺ δράσεις; π.	τοῦτ' εἰ σὺ δράσεις, π.
1231	ἕτερον ᾄσομαι	ἕτερ' ἀντᾴσομαι
1239	τούτῳ...ἐγώ.	om.
1244	κᾆτ' ᾄσεται	κἀντᾴσεται
1245	βίαν	βίον
1248	δὴ διεκόμισας	νὴ Δί' ἐκόμπασας
1252	μεθυσθῶμεν	μεθύωμεν
	μηδαμῶς	μή, μηδαμῶς
1262	ἀποίχεται	ἀπέρχεται
1268	ῥοιᾶς	ῥοᾶς
1274	ἐλάττων	ἔλαττον
1287	οὐκτὸς	ἐκτὸς
1303	ὑβριστότατος	ὑβρίστατος
1305, 6		inverso ordine legit
1310	ἀχυρῶνας	ἀχυρμὸν
1324	ὁδὶ δὲ δὴ καὶ	ὁδὶ δὲ καὐτὸς
1338	ἀνέχομαι	οὐκέτ' ἀνέχομαι
1339	ἰαιβοῖ αἰβοῖ	αἰβοῖ
1340	* * ποῦ 'στιν	ποῦ 'στιν ἡμῖν
1350	αὖτ'	ταῦτ'
1356	υἵδιον	υἱίδιον
1360	καὐτὸς ἐπὶ	καὐτός· ἐπὶ
1380	νομίσας	νομίσας σ'

8 READINGS OF DINDORF AND MEINEKE.

	Dindorf.	Meineke.
1387	νὴ...Ὀλυμπίαν	om.
1391	κἀπιθήκην	κἀπιθήκας
1414	πρὸς ποδῶν	προσπολῶν
1418	καλέσῃς	καλέσῃ
1423	δευρὶ πρότερον, ἐπιτρέπεις	δευρὶ· πότερον ἐπιτρέπεις
1432	οὕτω...Πιττάλου	post v. 1440 locat.
1434	αὐτὸς	οὗτος
1443	ἐγώ σε	ἔγωγε
1449	ἀπολῶ σ' τοῖσι	ἀπόλοι' τοῖς σοῖς
1454	πείσεταί τι	τι μεταπεσεῖται
1461	μετεβάλλοντο	μετεβάλοντο
1473	κατακοσμῆσαι	κατακομῆσαι
1481	διορχησόμενος	διορχησάμενος
1487	ῥώμης	ῥύμης
1507	οὐδέν γ'	οὐδὲν
1510	πιννοτήρης	πινοτήρης
1514	ὤζυρέ	μοι· σὺ δὲ
1519	θαλασσίοιο	θαλασσίου θεοῦ

ΥΠΟΘΕΣΙΣ.

I.

Φιλοκλέων Ἀθηναῖος φιλόδικος ὢν τὴν φύσιν ἐφοίτα περὶ τὰ δικαστήρια συνεχῶς. Βδελυκλέων δὲ ὁ τούτου παῖς ἀχθόμενος ταύτῃ τῇ νόσῳ καὶ πειρώμενος τὸν πατέρα παύειν, ἐγκαθείρξας τοῖς οἴκοις καὶ δίκτυα περιβαλὼν ἐφύλαττε νύκτωρ καὶ μεθ' ἡμέραν. ὁ δὲ ἐξόδου αὐτῷ μὴ προκειμένης ἔκραζεν. οἱ δὲ συνδικασταὶ αὐτοῦ σφηξὶν ἑαυτοὺς ἀφομοιώσαντες παρεγένοντο, βουλόμενοι διὰ ταύτης τῆς τέχνης ὑποκλέπτειν τὸν συνδικαστήν· ἐξ ὧν καὶ ὁ χορὸς συνέστηκε καὶ τὸ δρᾶμα ἐπιγέγραπται. ἀλλ' οὐδὲν ἤνυον οὐδὲ οὗτοι. πέρας δὲ τοῦ νεανίσκου θαυμάζοντος τίνος ἕνεκα ὁ πατὴρ οὕτως ἥττηται τοῦ πράγματος, ἔφη ὁ πρεσβύτης εἶναι τὸ πρᾶγμα σπουδαῖον καὶ σχεδὸν ἀρχὴν τὸ δικάζειν. ὁ δὲ παῖς ἐπειρᾶτο τὰς ὑποψίας ἐξαιρεῖν τοῦ πράγματος, νουθετῶν τὸν γέροντα. ὁ δὲ πρεσβύτης μηδαμῶς νουθετούμενος οὐ μεθίει τοῦ πάθους· ἀλλ' ἀναγκάζεται ὁ νέος ἐπιτρέπειν φιλοδικεῖν, καὶ ἐπὶ τῆς οἰκίας τοῦτο ποιεῖ, καὶ τοῖς κατὰ τὴν οἰκίαν δικάζει. καὶ δύο κύνες ἐπεισάγονται πολιτικῶς παρ' αὐτῷ κρινόμενοι· καὶ κατὰ τοῦ φεύγοντος ἐκφέρειν συνεχῶς τὴν ψῆφον μέλλων ἀπατηθεὶς ἄκων τὴν ἀποδικάζουσαν φέρει ψῆφον. περιέχει δὲ καὶ δικαιολογίαν τινὰ τοῦ χοροῦ ἐκ τοῦ ποιητοῦ προσώπου, ὡς σφηξὶν ἐμφερεῖς εἰσὶν οἱ τοῦ χοροῦ, ἐξ ὧν καὶ τὸ δρᾶμα. οἱ ὅτε μὲν ἦσαν νέοι, πικρῶς ταῖς δίκαις ἐφήδρευον, ἐπεὶ δὲ γέροντες γεγόνασι, κεντοῦσι τοῖς κέντροις, ἐπὶ τέλει δὲ τοῦ δράματος ὁ γέρων ἐπὶ δεῖπνον καλεῖται, καὶ ἐπὶ ὕβριν τρέπεται, καὶ κρίνει αὐτὸν ὕβρεως ἀρτόπωλις· ὁ δὲ γέρων πρὸς αὐλὸν καὶ ὄρχησιν τρέπεται, καὶ γελωτοποιεῖ τὸ δρᾶμα.

Τοῦτο τὸ δρᾶμα πεποίηται αὐτῷ οὐκ ἐξ ὑποκειμένης ὑποθέσεως, ἀλλ' ὡσανεὶ γενομένης· πέπλασται γὰρ τὸ ὅλον. διαβάλλει δὲ Ἀθηναίους ὡς φιλοδικοῦντας, καὶ σωφρονίζει τὸν δῆμον ἀποστῆναι τῶν δικῶν. καὶ διὰ τοῦτο καὶ τοὺς δικαστὰς σφηξὶν ἀπεικάζει κέντρα ἔχουσι καὶ πλήττουσι. πεπόηται δ' αὐτῷ χαριέντως. ἐδιδάχθη ἐπὶ ἄρχοντος Ἀμεινίου διὰ Φιλωνίδου [ἐν τῇ πθ' ὀλυμπιάδι]. β' ἦν, εἰς Λήναια. καὶ ἐνίκα πρῶτος Φιλωνίδης Προάγωνι, Λεύκων Πρέσβεσι τρίτος.

II.

ΑΡΙΣΤΟΦΑΝΟΥΣ ΓΡΑΜΜΑΤΙΚΟΥ.

Φιλοῦντα δικάζειν πατέρα παῖς εἴρξας ἄφνω
αὐτός τ' ἐφύλαττεν ἔνδον οἰκέται θ', ὅπως
μὴ λανθάνῃ μηδ' ἐξίῃ διὰ τὴν νόσον.
ὁ δ' ἀντιμάχεται παντὶ τρόπῳ καὶ μηχανῇ.
εἶθ' οἱ συνήθεις καὶ γέροντες, λεγόμενοι
σφῆκες, παραγίνονται βοηθοῦντες σφόδρα
ἐπὶ τῷ δύνασθαι κέντρον ἐνιέναι τισὶ
φρονοῦντες ἱκανόν. ὁ δὲ γέρων τηρούμενος
συμπείθεθ' ἔνδον διαδικάζειν καὶ βιοῦν,
ἐπεὶ τὸ δικάζειν κέκρικεν ἐκ παντὸς τρόπου.

ΤΑ ΤΟΥ ΔΡΑΜΑΤΟΣ ΠΡΟΣΩΠΑ

ΣΩΣΙΑΣ } οἰκέται Φιλοκλέωνος.
ΞΑΝΘΙΑΣ
ΒΔΕΛΥΚΛΕΩΝ.
ΦΙΛΟΚΛΕΩΝ.
ΧΟΡΟΣ ΓΕΡΟΝΤΩΝ ΣΦΗΚΩΝ.
ΠΑΙΔΕΣ.
ΚΥΩΝ.
ΑΡΤΟΠΩΛΙΣ.
ΧΑΙΡΕΦΩΝ, κωφὸν πρόσωπον.
ΚΑΤΗΓΟΡΟΣ.

ΣΦΗΚΕΣ.

ΣΩΣΙΑΣ
ΟΥΤΟΣ, τί πάσχεις, ὦ κακόδαιμον Ξανθία;
ΞΑΝΘΙΑΣ
φυλακὴν καταλύειν νυκτερινὴν διδάσκομαι.
ΣΩΣΙΑΣ
κακὸν ἄρα ταῖς πλευραῖς τι πρώφειλες μέγα.
ἆρ᾽ οἶσθά γ᾽ οἷον κνώδαλον φυλάττομεν;
ΞΑΝΘΙΑΣ
οἶδ᾽· ἀλλ᾽ ἐπιθυμῶ σμικρὸν ἀπομερμηρίσαι. 5

1—53. Xanthias and Sosias, who are set to watch Philocleon, tell each other their troubles and their dreams.

2 **φυλακὴν καταλύειν**.] Cf. Arist. *Polit.* v. 8, ἵνα φυλάττωσι καὶ μὴ καταλύωσιν, ὥσπερ νυκτερινὴν φυλακήν, τὴν τῆς πόλεως τήρησιν. As this verb is used in many phrases, with βίον, πόλεμον, εἰρήνην, βουλήν, and other nouns, it may probably have been with φυλακὴν the common word for coming off guard when relieved. Hence Xanthias in his sleepiness says, 'Oh! I am just taking a lesson at coming off guard.' The watchman in Aesch. *Agam.* 12—17, is described as suffering from his long watch, and having a hard task to keep off sleep.

3 **πρώφειλες**.] 'You had then an old score to pay off on your sides (when you allowed yourself to become sleepy, for it is they that will suffer if you sleep).' The imperfect is far preferable to the present tense here. The MSS. have προῦφειλες, and the scholiast says, ἐχρεώστεις τι κακὸν ταῖς πλευραῖς σου καὶ ἀποδοῦναι θέλεις.

4 **κνώδαλον**.] Cf. *Lysistr.* 476, τί ποτε χρησόμεθα τοῖσδε τοῖς κνωδάλοις; said of women. There seems to be hardly an animal to which κνώδαλον cannot be applied; and as no one English equivalent for it as a term of abuse; for we should vary the species of animal to suit the circumstances. Thus, here we might render it 'serpent,' with reference to the dicast's wiliness, and power of wriggling away: in the Lysistrata (looking to the context), 'these very hornets.'

5 **ἀπομερμηρίσαι**.] Only used (as far as lexicons tell) here. μερμηρίζειν is common in Homer. μέρμηρα ἡ μέριμνα καὶ ἡ φροντίς. Schol.

ΑΡΙΣΤΟΦΑΝΟΥΣ

ΣΩΣΙΑΣ
σὺ δ' οὖν παρακινδύνευ', ἐπεὶ καὐτοῦ γ' ἐμοῦ
κατὰ ταῖν κόραιν ὕπνου τι καταχεῖται γλυκύ.

ΞΑΝΘΙΑΣ
ἀλλ' ἦ παραφρονεῖς ἐτεὸν ἦ κορυβαντιᾷς;

ΣΩΣΙΑΣ
οὔκ, ἀλλ' ὕπνος μ' ἔχει τις ἐκ Σαβαζίου.

ΞΑΝΘΙΑΣ
τὸν αὐτὸν ἄρ' ἐμοὶ βουκολεῖς Σαβάζιον.   10
κἀμοὶ γὰρ ἀρτίως ἐπεστρατεύσατο
Μῆδός τις ἐπὶ τὰ βλέφαρα νυστακτὴς ὕπνος·
καὶ δῆτ' ὄναρ θαυμαστὸν εἶδον ἀρτίως.

ΣΩΣΙΑΣ
κἄγωγ' ἀληθῶς οἷον οὐδεπώποτε.

6 σὺ δ' οὖν, κ.τ.λ.] Sosias tells Xanthias to chance it, for that he can sympathize with him, being also sleepy. This wakes up Xanthias to see the madness of going to sleep, and he in turn rouses his comrade.

8 κορυβαντιᾷς.] For the Corybantic rites the curious may consult Lucret. II. 610, &c.
In Timaeus' Lexicon to Plato, παρεμμαίνεσθαι καὶ ἐνθουσιαστικῶς κινεῖσθαι is the explanation. Ruhnken shews that the word is used 'of those who are afflicted with sleeplessness and hear a sound of flutes in their ears,' from Plato, *Legg.* 790, and elsewhere. Hence the answer of Sosias: 'No, it is no sleepless frenzy, no frenzy like that of the Corybantes, who cannot get rid of the din of the flutes, &c. of their orgies, but rather a sleep that takes me.'

9 Σαβαζίου.] A Thracian name of Dionysus, whose priests were called in Thrace Σαβοί. Schol. Sosias goes abroad for his god of sleep, since Xanthias had spoken of a foreign or Phrygian frenzy in κορυβαντιᾷς.

10 βουκολεῖς.] Sc. τρέφεις: not an uncommon use. It is very doubtful whether (as L. and S. suggest) there is any allusion to the god's *tauriform* worship. ποιμαίνειν ἔρωτα (Theocr.) is an analogous phrase. The notion of 'feeding, keeping, tending,' seems to pass into that of 'gently managing,' even with some deceit implied, as in *Eccl.* 81, βουκολεῖν τὸ δήμιον, and (probably) in *Pac.* 153.

11 ἐπεστρατεύσατο.] Cf. Eur. *Med.* 1185, διπλοῦν γὰρ αὐτῇ πῆμ' ἐπεστρατεύσατο, and Eur. *Hipp.* 535, ἔρως, ἔρως, ὃ κατ' ὀμμάτων στάζεις πόθον, εἰσάγων γλυκεῖαν ψυχᾷ χάριν οἷς ἐπιστρατεύσῃ. With which last Bergler compares v. 8, κατὰ ταῖν κόραιν κ.τ.λ.

12 Μῆδος] Median, *i. e.* barbarian and foreign, because the other had talked of Sabazius, a foreign god. But an 'invasion by Medes' would be a natural phrase for a Greek.

νυστακτής.] Probably the pair nod, and act sleepiness. Whether they get their dreams in the intervals of this their dialogue, or had them before the play began, is uncertain.

22]   ΣΦΗΚΕΣ.   13

ἀτὰρ σὺ λέξον πρότερος.

ΞΑΝΘΙΑΣ

ἐδόκουν ἀετὸν   15
καταπτάμενον ἐς τὴν ἀγορὰν μέγαν πάνυ
ἀναρπάσαντα τοῖς ὄνυξιν ἀσπίδα
φέρειν ἐπίχαλκον ἀνεκὰς ἐς τὸν οὐρανόν,
κἄπειτα ταύτην ἀποβαλεῖν Κλεώνυμον.

ΣΩΣΙΑΣ

οὐδὲν ἄρα γρίφου διαφέρει Κλεώνυμος.   20

ΞΑΝΘΙΑΣ

πῶς δή;

ΣΩΣΙΑΣ

προερεῖ τις τοῖσι συμπόταις λέγων,
ὅτι ταυτὸν ἐν γῇ τ' ἀπέβαλεν κἀν οὐρανῷ

16 καταπτάμενον.] Brunck, Meineke, and Hirschig adopt the form καταπτόμενον as stricter Attic. Yet in *Ach.* 865 Meineke retains προσέπτανθ' οἱ κ. ἀ., saying, 'consulto servavi h. l. formam poeticam.' But why there, and not here? especially since (as Richter says) the slave is telling his dream in rather epic or high-flown style. Cobet says, 'In comoedia ἐπτόμην locum habet; ἐκτάμην ubi supra soccum oratio adsurgit.'

18 ἐπίχαλκον.] This is added (as the scholiast says) to make it clear that it is a shield, not a serpent, that is meant; which last would be the more natural sense to take ἀσπίς in, for eagles carry off snakes rather than shields. And the scholiast adds his opinion that the word for shield was derived from the word for snake, because snakes when asleep coil themselves round in many circles, and the ancient shields were circular. But, as far as we can see from the Greek authors that we have, ἀσπίς, 'shield,' seems older than the other ἀσπίς.

19 κἄπειτα ταύτην ἀποβαλεῖν Κ.] 'And then threw this same shield down—becoming Cleonymus.' The dream might have ended at ἀποβα-

λεῖν, but Cleonymus, for the sake of a hit at his cowardice, is suddenly put in the eagle's place.

20 γρίφου.] παροινίου ζητήματος, Schol. 'Cleonymus then turns out for all the world like a riddle.'

21 πῶς δή;] Bentley's arrangement of the speakers here is rightly accepted by most editors.

προερεῖ.] The vulg. προσερεῖ can hardly stand with the dative. Cobet's προτενεῖ would do. προβαλεῖ is rather suggested by the scholiast's τὰ ἐν τοῖς συμποσίοις προβαλλόμενα αἰνιγματώδη ζητήματα. Cf. *Nub.* 757, ἀλλ' ἕτερον αὖ σοι προβαλῶ τι δεξιόν. προφέρει, as closer to MSS. προσερεῖ, might be read.

22 ὅτι.] This need not be ousted in favour of τί. Riddles were put forward in a positive form. See Samson's riddle in Judges xiv. 14, 'Out of the eater came forth meat, and out of the strong came forth sweetness.' In the same way is the riddle of the Sphinx propounded: ἔστι δίπουν ἐπὶ γῆς καὶ τέτραπον, κ.τ.λ. So here one guest propounds (προφέρει) to his fellows, 'that there is one and the same beast which threw away the shield (or snake) in heaven, earth, and ocean.' The alteration to τί is grounded on

κἂν τῇ θαλάττῃ θηρίον τὴν ἀσπίδα;

ΞΑΝΘΙΑΣ

οἴμοι, τί δῆτά μοι κακὸν γενήσεται
ἰδόντι τοιοῦτον ἐνύπνιον;

ΣΩΣΙΑΣ

μὴ φροντίσῃς.   25
οὐδὲν γὰρ ἔσται δεινόν, οὐ μὰ τοὺς θεούς.

ΞΑΝΘΙΑΣ

δεινόν γε τοῦστ' ἄνθρωπος ἀποβαλὼν ὅπλα.
ἀτὰρ σὺ τὸ σὸν αὖ λέξον.

ΣΩΣΙΑΣ

ἀλλ' ἐστὶν μέγα.
περὶ τῆς πόλεως γάρ ἐστι τοῦ σκάφους ὅλου.

ΞΑΝΘΙΑΣ

λέγε νυν ἀνύσας τι τὴν τρόπιν τοῦ πράγματος.   30

ΣΩΣΙΑΣ

ἔδοξέ μοι περὶ πρῶτον ὕπνον ἐν τῇ πυκνὶ
ἐκκλησιάζειν πρόβατα συγκαθήμενα,
βακτηρίας ἔχοντα καὶ τριβώνια·
κἄπειτα τούτοις τοῖσι προβάτοις μοὐδόκει
δημηγορεῖν φάλαινα πανδοκεύτρια,   35

the supposition that the riddle ought to begin in the orthodox English fashion, with a Why or a What. ἀσπὶς would sound ambiguous in the riddle till the answer was seen.

25 τοιοῦτον.] With τοιοῦτ' ἐν. the οι in τοιοῦτ' would have to be scanned long: which is not so well; for the υ in ἐνύπνιον should certainly be short. Cf. *Eq.* 940, and the note there on ἐναποπνιγείης.

27 δεινόν γέ.] Xanthias takes up the word δεινὸν more in its sense of 'monstrous, strange,' than 'to be feared,' as Sosias had meant it. But 'terrible' will tolerably do duty for both senses.

29 σκάφους.] Cf. Aesch. *S. C. Theb.* 2, ὅστις φυλάσσει πρᾶγος ἐν πρύμνῃ πόλεως οἴακα νωμῶν: and Soph. *Antig.* 190, ταύτης ἔπι πλέοντες ὀρθῆς τοὺς φίλους ποιούμεθα. Xanthias, to keep up the metaphor, asks for the 'keel' of the matter. ὡσανεὶ ἔλεγε τὴν ῥίζαν, Schol., because the keel was laid first. If there is allusion to τρόπον (as Bergler thinks), the equivoque might be kept by 'let us get at once to the *bottom* of the matter.'

33 βακτηρίας κ. τριβ.] Apparently the usual equipment of the older men. Cf. vv. 117, 1131, and *Ach.* 184, 343; also *Nub.* 541.

34—36. The Athenians listen like silly sheep to a devouring monster.

35 πανδοκεύτρια.] πάντα δεχομένη, Schol. Cf. *Eq.* 238, φάραγγα καὶ χάρυβδιν ἁρπαγῆς. The word

ἔχουσα φωνὴν ἐμπεπρημένης ὑός.

ΞΑΝΘΙΑΣ

αἰβοῖ.

ΣΩΣΙΑΣ

τί ἔστι;

ΞΑΝΘΙΑΣ

παῦε παῦε, μὴ λέγε·
ὄζει κάκιστον τοὐνύπνιον βύρσης σαπρᾶς.

ΣΩΣΙΑΣ

εἶθ' ἡ μιαρὰ φάλαιν' ἔχουσα τρυτάνην
ἵστη βόειον δημόν.

ΞΑΝΘΙΑΣ

οἴμοι δείλαιος·   40
τὸν δῆμον ἡμῶν βούλεται διιστάναι.

ΣΩΣΙΑΣ

ἐδόκει δέ μοι Θέωρος αὐτῆς πλησίον
χαμαὶ καθῆσθαι, τὴν κεφαλὴν κόρακος ἔχων.
εἶτ' Ἀλκιβιάδης εἶπε πρός με τραυλίσας·

usually means 'hostess' (as in *Ran.* 114); here it is 'receiver general of all bribes,' perhaps 'one who never shuts the door 'gainst those who come and pay their score.'

36 ἐμπεπρημένης.] ἐμπεφυσημένης καὶ παχείας, Schol., 'of a fat, bloated sow.' But MSS. R, V, have ἐμπεπρημένην, ἐμπεπρησμένην. Whether 'inflamed voice' or 'inflated' be better, is doubtful. Either is curious. Richter renders the common text, 'the voice of a singed sow.' But the time after the singeing is an odd one to choose for describing the animal's voice. Cleon's voice Aristophanes elsewhere calls κυκλοβόρου φωνήν, and φωνὴν χαράδρας ὄλεθρον τετοκυίας (*Eq.* 137, *Vesp.* 1034).

38 βύρσης.] With reference to Cleon's trade, see *The Knights*, passim.

40—41 δημόν...δῆμον.] A similar play on the word is in *Eq.* 954, where Demus' seal is δημοῦ βοείου θρῖον ἐξωπτημένον. Whether βόειον here implies ἀναίσθητον, as a scholiast says, is very doubtful. I know of no such use of βόειος. Some pun on 'fat of bull's flesh,' and 'John Bull' might be suggested as a modern equivalent.

41 διιστάναι.] There is no need to fix on any particular disturbance for this 'setting the people by the ears.' The pun on ἱστάναι, 'to weigh,' and διιστάναι is the chief thing aimed at.

44 τραυλίσας.] Alcibiades' lisp is mentioned by Plutarch. οἱ δὲ τραυλοὶ τὸ λ ἀντὶ τοῦ ρ λέγουσιν. Schol. It was perhaps affectation. 'Labdacismum, quem scriptores notant in Alcibiade, deliciis, non naturae tribuendum arbitror.' Erasmus,

16   ΑΡΙΣΤΟΦΑΝΟΥΣ   [45

ὁλᾷς; Θέωλος τὴν κεφαλὴν κόλακος ἔχει.   45

ΞΑΝΘΙΑΣ
ὀρθῶς γε τοῦτ' Ἀλκιβιάδης ἐτραύλισεν.

ΣΩΣΙΑΣ
οὔκουν ἐκεῖν' ἀλλόκοτον, ὁ Θέωρος κόραξ
γιγνόμενος;

ΞΑΝΘΙΑΣ
ἥκιστ', ἀλλ' ἄριστον.

ΣΩΣΙΑΣ
πῶς;

ΞΑΝΘΙΑΣ
ὅπως;
.νθρωπος ὢν εἶτ' ἐγένετ' ἐξαίφνης κόραξ·
οὔκουν ἐναργὲς τοῦτο συμβαλεῖν, ὅτι   50
ἀρθεὶς ἀφ' ἡμῶν ἐς κόρακας οἰχήσεται;

ΣΩΣΙΑΣ
εἶτ' οὐκ ἐγὼ δοὺς δύ' ὀβολὼ μισθώσομαι
οὕτω σ' ὑποκρινόμενον σοφῶς ὀνείρατα;

ΞΑΝΘΙΑΣ
φέρε νυν κατείπω τοῖς θεαταῖς τὸν λόγον,

Colloq. de Rect. Pron. Similar affectation in the way of drawls and lazy slurring of the liquids is not unknown among the Alcibiadeses of our own time.

45 Θέωλος.] As if from Θεὸς and ὄλλυμι: cf. v. 418, Θεώρου θεοισεχθρία.

46 ὀρθῶς γε.] Alcibiades' lisp led him to Theorus' right name, κόλαξ. An epigram is quoted from the Anthology: Ρῶ καὶ λάμβδα μόνον κόρακας κολάκων διορίζει· λοιπὸν ταὐτὸ κόραξ βωμολόχος τε κόλαξ. τοὐνεκά μοι, βέλτιστε, τόδε ζῷον πεφύλαξο, εἰδὼς καὶ ζώντων τοὺς κόλακας κόρακας: which might be freely imitated: ''Twixt *fowls* and *fools* in northern tongue small difference is heard: There's chattering fowls, and prating fools; the man's much like the bird. And those who of this feather be, 'twere best, my friend, to shun, Sure that for any useful end such fowls and fools are one.'

51 ἐς κόρακας.] To the point perhaps is Diogenes' apophthegm: κρεῖττόν ἐστιν ἐς κόρακας ἀπελθεῖν ἢ ἐς κόλακας. 'Better join the fowls than the fools.' Here 'it is plain that we shall lose him, and the *fowls* (pronounced 'fules') will get him.'

53 οὕτω σ' ὑπ.] This (for vulg. οὕτως) commends itself. It is due to Geel and Bergk, and adopted by Richter.

53 ὑποκρινόμενον.] Cf. Hom. *Od.* XIX. 535, 555, for exactly the same use.

54—135. Xanthias lays the mat-

ΣΦΗΚΕΣ. [61] 17

ὀλίγ' ἄτθ' ὑπειπὼν πρῶτον αὐτοῖσιν ταδί, 55
μηδὲν παρ' ἡμῶν προσδοκᾶν λίαν μέγα,
μηδ' αὖ γέλωτα Μεγαρόθεν κεκλεμμένον.
ἡμῖν γὰρ οὐκ ἔστ' οὔτε κάρυ' ἐκ φορμίδος
δούλῳ διαρριπτοῦντε τοῖς θεωμένοις,
οὔθ' Ἡρακλῆς τὸ δεῖπνον ἐξαπατώμενος, 60
οὐδ' αὖθις ἐνασελγαινόμενος Εὐριπίδης·

ter before the audience, praying them not to expect too much, but promising something new. He and his fellow-slave have (he says) to guard for their young master his old father, who is sick of a law fever, is always getting up early, going off to the courts; who dreams of nothing but law-suits, and has a mania for condemning every one. They have tried mild remedies in vain, and now have to shut him up and guard strictly every hole by which he might slip out.

In the opening scene of Racine's *Les Plaideurs* (which indeed is founded on *The Wasps*), Petit Jean's description of his master's doings presents several points of similarity to that of Xanthias.

54 κατείπω τ. θ.] So in *Eq.* 36 the matter is put before the audience.

55 ὑπειπών.] Used nearly as in Dem. *c. Arist.* 637, καὶ γέγραφεν, οὐδὲν ὑπειπὼν ὅπως ἄν τις ἀποκτείνῃ, τὴν τιμωρίαν: where οὐδὲν ὑπ. means 'with no reservation.' Here 'with this short preface or saving clause.' ὑπὸ expresses the quiet insertion of the clause, which is to save them from any after charge of having promised more than they performed.

57 Μεγαρόθεν.] ὡς ποιητῶν ὄντων τινῶν ἀπὸ Μεγαρίδος ἀμούσων καὶ ἀφυῶς σκωπτόντων. Schol. who quotes also from Eupolis τὸ σκῶμμ' ἀσελγὲς καὶ Μεγαρικὸν σφόδρα. Aristotle (*Poet.* c. 3) says that the Megarians claimed the invention of comedy. In the *Acharnians* the Megarian calls the dressing up of his daughters Μεγαρικὰν μηχανάν.

58 κάρυ' ἐκ φορμίδος.] Such scatterings for a scramble among the audience seem to have been common. Cf. *Plut.* 797, οὐ γὰρ πρεπῶδές ἐστι τῷ διδασκάλῳ ἰσχάδια καὶ τρωγάλια τοῖς θεωμένοις προβαλόντ' ἐπὶ τούτοισιν ἐπαναγκάζειν γελᾶν. Cf. also *Pac.* 962, where Trygaeus does something of the sort, perhaps in parody of other comic writers. In *Nub.* 540—552, Aristophanes disclaims such tricks and repetitions, much as he does here.

60 Ἡρακλῆς.] In the *Alcestis* of Euripides Hercules' unseemly eagerness for his meal is described (v. 753—760, 772—802): and Aristophanes afterwards represents him as greedy when in Hades: cf. *Ran.* 549, &c. Hence Ἡρακλῆς ξενίζεται had passed into a proverb of any one impatient. But there is probably a reference here to some particular exhibition of Hercules missing his meal, either by another comedian, or (as Richter thinks) by our poet himself in a former play.

61 αὖθις...Εὐριπίδης.] As in the *Acharnians* (v. 400—478) and, acc. to the Scholiast, in the *Proagon*. Of course the *Thesmophoriazusae* is out of the question, as it was exhibited at a later date than this play.

ἐνασελγαινόμενος.] ὑβριζόμενος. Schol. L. and S. also take it as passive here; but refer to Diodorus Siculus as using it active. It may just as well here mean ἀσελγῶς πράττων, 'acting outrageously.' ἐν means 'in the play.' Aristophanes would hardly call his own chastisement of Euripides ἀσέλγεια.

2

ΑΡΙΣΤΟΦΑΝΟΥΣ

οὐδ' εἰ Κλέων γ' ἔλαμψε τῆς τύχης χάριν,
αὖθις τὸν αὐτὸν ἄνδρα μυττωτεύσομεν.
ἀλλ' ἔστιν ἡμῖν λογίδιον γνώμην ἔχον,
ὑμῶν μὲν αὐτῶν οὐχὶ δεξιώτερον, 65
κωμῳδίας δὲ φορτικῆς σοφώτερον.
ἔστιν γὰρ ἡμῖν δεσπότης ἐκεινοσὶ
ἄνω καθεύδων, ὁ μέγας, οὑπὶ τοῦ τέγους.
οὗτος φυλάττειν τὸν πατέρ' ἐπέταξε νῷν,
ἔνδον καθείρξας, ἵνα θύραζε μὴ 'ξίῃ. 70
νόσον γὰρ ὁ πατὴρ ἀλλόκοτον αὐτοῦ νοσεῖ,
ἣν οὐδ' ἂν εἷς γνοίη ποτ' οὐδ' ἂν ξυμβάλοι,
εἰ μὴ πύθοιθ' ἡμῶν· ἐπεὶ τοπάζετε.
Ἀμυνίας μὲν ὁ Προνάπους φήσ' οὑτοσὶ
εἶναι φιλόκυβον αὐτόν·

ΣΩΣΙΑΣ
ἀλλ' οὐδὲν λέγει 75
μὰ Δί', ἀλλ' ἀφ' αὑτοῦ τὴν νόσον τεκμαίρεται.

62 **ἔλαμψε, τῆς τύχης χάριν.**] Reiske interprets 'si comoedia, in qua Cleo fuit exagitatus, placuit et splendido applausu fuit excepta.' Rather 'if Cleon came out brilliantly, thanks to good luck (rather than to good management).' So the Scholiast: ὡς τοῦ Κλέωνος ἀπὸ δυσγενῶν ἐκλάμψαντος. Though Cleon did owe his name to good luck, the Knights, Aristophanes says, was enough of a dressing for him. In *Nub.* 549, the poet claims credit for not trampling on him when down.

63 **μυττωτεύσομεν.**] Cf. *Eq.* 771, κατακνησθείην ἐν μυττωτῷ μετὰ τυροῦ· and *Pac.* 247, ὡς ἐπιτετρίψεσθ' αὐτίκα ἀπαξάπαντα καταμεμυττωτευμένα.

65—66 **δεξιώτερον ... φορτικῆς.**] In a former parabasis, *Nub.* 524—527, φορτικοί are similarly opposed to δεξιοί.

67 **ἔστιν γάρ.**] This is to be connected in sense with κατεῖπω τὸν λόγον in v. 54. Cf. *Eq.* 40, λέγοιμ'

ἂν ἤδη. νῷν γὰρ ἔστι δεσπότης κ.τ.λ.

74—84. There are various ways of dividing this dialogue. Dindorf's text makes Xanthias collect the guesses of the audience, and Sosias remark upon them. Meineke reverses this, and, following Bergk, supposes that a line spoken by Sosias, telling of another guess, has been lost before οὐκ, ἀλλὰ φ. μ. In Dindorf's text the οὐκ comes rather awkwardly, having nothing in Sosias' μὰ Δί' ἀλλ'... τεκμαίρεται to refer to. Hence Richter's text, beginning Sosias' part with ἀλλ' οὐδὲν λέγει, seems preferable. Everything then follows naturally, and no loss of a line need be supposed. And the Scholiast says (on the word φιλόκυβος) τινὲς ἀμοιβαῖα, which suggests a division of that line.

74 **Ἀμυνίας.**] Satirized by Cratinus as a flatterer, braggart, and informer. Schol. Cf. *Nub.* 686, for a charge of cowardice against him.

ΣΦΗΚΕΣ.

ΞΑΝΘΙΑΣ
οὐκ, ἀλλὰ φιλο μέν ἐστιν ἀρχὴ τοῦ κακοῦ.
ὁδὶ δέ φησι Σωσίας πρὸς Δερκύλον
εἶναι φιλοπότην αὐτόν.

ΣΩΣΙΑΣ
οὐδαμῶς γ', ἐπεὶ
αὕτη γε χρηστῶν ἐστὶν ἀνδρῶν ἡ νόσος   80

ΞΑΝΘΙΑΣ
Νικόστρατος δ' αὖ φησιν ὁ Σκαμβωνίδης
εἶναι φιλοθύτην αὐτὸν ἢ φιλόξενον.

ΣΩΣΙΑΣ
μὰ τὸν κύν', ὦ Νικόστρατ', οὐ φιλόξενος,
ἐπεὶ καταπύγων ἐστὶν ὅ γε Φιλόξενος.

ΞΑΝΘΙΑΣ
ἄλλως φλυαρεῖτ'· οὐ γὰρ ἐξευρήσετε.   85
εἰ δὴ 'πιθυμεῖτ' εἰδέναι, σιγᾶτε νῦν.
φράσω γὰρ ἤδη τὴν νόσον τοῦ δεσπότου.
φιληλιαστής ἐστιν ὡς οὐδεὶς ἀνήρ,
ἐρᾷ τε τούτου, τοῦ δικάζειν, καὶ στένει
ἢν μὴ 'πὶ τοῦ πρώτου καθίζηται ξύλου.   90
ὕπνου δ' ὁρᾷ τῆς νυκτὸς οὐδὲ πασπάλην.

78 Σωσίας.] Some spectator is meant: Sosias was a common name. But our Sosias thinks with Demosthenes (cf. *Eq.* 85, &c.) that tippling is an honest man's failing; and perhaps means to defend himself as well as his namesake; as if of himself it were also implied that ἀφ' αὑτοῦ τὴν ν. τ. Dercylus is another of the same habits.

82 φιλοθύτην.] This probably means 'superstitious,' too much given to sacrifices, omens, and the like. It recals Nicias' character. φιλόξενος is meant by Nicostratus as praise, and might follow rather naturally on φιλοθύτης, sacrifices entailing feasts. But Sosias takes it of Philoxenus an effeminate rascal.

83 κύν'.] One of Socrates' oaths; and his favourite of the three (κύνα, χῆνα, πλάτανον); but perhaps there is not much reference to him here.

88 φιληλιαστής.] He coins a word beginning, as he said at v. 77, with φιλ. The Heliaea was Philocleon's favourite court. Cf. below, v. 772, and for details about the court see *Dict. Ant*

90 τοῦ πρώτου ξύλου.] Cf. *Ach*. 25, ὠστιοῦνται...περὶ τοῦ πρώτου ξύλου. Schömann hence infers that there were wooden seats in the Pnyx, perhaps in the middle of it, though most were of stone. And that there would be benches for the Heliasts seems tolerably certain.

91 πασπάλην.] Analogous is

ἦν δ' οὖν καταμύσῃ κἂν ἄχνην, ὅμως ἐκεῖ
ὁ νοῦς πέτεται τὴν νύκτα περὶ τὴν κλεψύδραν.
ὑπὸ τοῦ δὲ τὴν ψῆφόν γ' ἔχειν εἰωθέναι
τοὺς τρεῖς ξυνέχων τῶν δακτύλων ἀνίσταται, 95
ὥσπερ λιβανωτὸν ἐπιτιθεὶς νουμηνίᾳ.
καὶ νὴ Δί' ἢν ἴδῃ γέ που γεγραμμένον
υἱὸν Πυριλάμπους ἐν θύρᾳ Δῆμον καλόν,
ἰὼν παρέγραψε πλησίον "κημὸς καλός."
τὸν ἀλεκτρυόνα δ', ὃς ᾖδ' ἀφ' ἑσπέρας, ἔφη 100
ὄψ' ἐξεγείρειν αὐτὸν ἀναπεπεισμένον,
παρὰ τῶν ὑπευθύνων ἔχοντα χρήματα.
εὐθὺς δ' ἀπὸ δορπηστοῦ κέκραγεν ἐμβάδας,
κἄπειτ' ἐκεῖσ' ἐλθὼν προκαθεύδει πρῲ πάνυ,

the use of ἄχνη. κέγχρας ἄλευρον Schol. and on ἄχνην the Scholiast refers to Hom. *Il*. ε. 499, ὡς δ' ἄνεμος ἄχνας φορέει ἱερὰς κατ' ἀλωάς. ἄχνη has other significations, but the idea of something fine and light is in all.

93 ὁ νοῦς κ.τ.λ.] So in *Nub*. 27, Phidippides dreams of horses.

95 τοὺς τρεῖς.] i.e. the thumb, forefinger, and middle-finger. Schol.

96 λ. ἐπιτιθείς.] Cf. *Ran*. 888, *Nub*. 426, οὐδ' ἐπιθείην λιβανωτόν.

98 υἱὸν Πυριλάμπους.] Demus son of Pyrilampes was a beautiful youth. Cf. Plat. *Gorg*. 482, λέγω δὲ ἐννοήσας ὅτι ἐγώ τε καὶ σὺ νῦν τυγχάνομεν ταυτόν τι πεπονθότες, ἐρῶντε δύο ὄντε δυοῖν ἑκάτερος· ἐγὼ μὲν Ἀλκιβιάδου τε τοῦ Κλεινίου καὶ φιλοσοφίας, σὺ δὲ δυοῖν, τοῦ τε Ἀθηναίων δήμου καὶ τοῦ Πυριλάμπους. In *Ach*. 142, this lovers' habit of writing up the name of a favourite is mentioned: καὶ δῆτα φιλαθήναιος ἦν ὑπερφυῶς, ὑμῶν τ' ἐραστὴς ἦν ἀληθῶς, ὥστε καὶ ἐν τοῖσι τοίχοις ἔγραφ' Ἀθηναῖοι καλοί.

99 κημός.] The point is in the rhyme. For the word cf. *Eq*. 1150.

100 ἀλεκτρυόνα κ.τ.λ.] Racine in *Les Plaideurs* has 'Il fit couper la tête à son coq, de colère, pour l'avoir éveillé plus tard qu'à l'ordinaire; Il disoit qu'un plaideur, dont l'affaire alloit mal, Avoit graissé la patte à ce pauvre animal.' And Plautus has something similar, *Aul*. 3. 4. 10, 'Obtrunco gallum furem manifestarium, Credo ego edepol illi mercedem gallo pollicitos coquos, Si id palam fecisset.'

ἀφ' ἑσπέρας.] So MS. *Rav*. acc. to Cobet, and it seems preferable to ἐφ' ἑσπ. ἀπὸ ἑσπ. 'from evening' = 'after evening,' towards night-fall,' is a common phrase. This cock-crowing, though much earlier than the usual time, did not content the old man. ἐν ὑπερβολῇ τοῦτο. Schol. The time of cock-crowing (ἀλεκτοροφωνία) is sometimes put with tolerable definiteness for three o'clock in the morning: as in ὀψὲ, ἢ μεσονυκτίου, ἢ ἀλεκτοροφωνίας, ἢ πρωΐ. St Mark xiii. 35. Here ἀφ' ἑσπέρας might perhaps mean about 9 p.m., which seemed late to Philocleon who was ready to start directly after his supper (v. 103). The Latin 'de' seems to answer to ἀπὸ in this use. Cf. Juv. XIV. 190, Media de nocte supinum clamosus juvenem pater excitat.

103 δορπηστοῦ.] So δειπνηστὸς from δεῖπνον Hom. *Odyss*. ρ. 120.

ὥσπερ λεπὰς προσεχόμενος τῷ κίονι.   105
ὑπὸ δυσκολίας δ' ἅπασι τιμῶν τὴν μακρὰν
ὥσπερ μέλιττ' ἢ βομβυλιὸς εἰσέρχεται
ὑπὸ τοῖς ὄνυξι κηρὸν ἀναπεπλασμένος.
ψήφων δὲ δείσας μὴ δεηθείη ποτὲ,
ἵν' ἔχοι δικάζειν, αἰγιαλὸν ἔνδον τρέφει.   110
τοιαῦτ' ἀλύει· νουθετούμενος δ' ἀεὶ
μᾶλλον δικάζει. τοῦτον οὖν φυλάττομεν
μοχλοῖσιν ἐνδήσαντες, ὡς ἂν μὴ 'ξίῃ.
ὁ γὰρ υἱὸς αὐτοῦ τὴν νόσον βαρέως φέρει.
καὶ πρῶτα μὲν λόγοισι παραμυθούμενος   115
ἀνέπειθεν αὐτὸν μὴ φορεῖν τριβώνιον
μηδ' ἐξιέναι θύραζ'· ὁ δ' οὐκ ἐπείθετο.
εἶτ' αὐτὸν ἀπέλου κἀκάθαιρ', ὁ δ' οὐ μάλα.
μετὰ ταῦτ' ἐκορυβάντιζ'· ὁ δ' αὐτῷ τυμπάνῳ
ᾄξας ἐδίκαζεν ἐς τὸ Καινὸν ἐμπεσών.   120

105 τῷ κίονι.] A pillar at the entrance of the court probably, but no other mention of it is noticed. The comparison of a limpet sticking to a rock is found also in *Plut.* 1096, ὥσπερ λεπὰς τῷ μειρακίῳ προσίσχεται.
106 τὴν μακράν.] A long line drawn on the tablet (πινάκιον, cf. v. 167) meant condemnation: a short line acquittal. Schol.
107—108. By his constant habit of drawing the long line he has got his nails permanently stuffed with wax.
110 ἔχοι.] ἔχῃ Bekk. and vulg. ἔχοι R, V, Dind. Mein. &c. This last, being better on critical grounds, is certainly not to be objected to on grounds of sense, the reference being to a past intention, though τρέφει is pres. tense. And indeed δείσας and μὴ δεηθείη make the opt. ἔχοι quite natural. 'And, as he feared he might be short of voting-pebbles some day, that he might have wherewith to give his vote as dicast, he keeps a whole beach of shingle indoors.'
113 ἐνδήσαντες.] Vulg. ἐγκλείσαντες.
118 ἀπέλου.] Cf. *Nub.* 1044, λοῦσθαι. *Plut.* 657, ἐλοῦμεν.
ὁ δ' οὐ μάλα.] 'But he would none of this :' supply ἀπελούετο, or ἐκαθαίρετο. The imperfect of the active expresses here 'he was for doing the washing or cleansing,' the imperf. pass. with οὐ 'he was not for having it done.'
119 ἐκορυβάντιζ'.] A course of Corybantic orgies and phrenzy might drive away his judicial madness.
120 Καινόν.] The Scholiast names four courts, Παράβυστον, Καινόν, Τρίγωνον, Μέσον. Pausanias mentions Παράβυστον and Τρίγωνον: the first as being in an obscure part of the town—perhaps it was a courthouse built on to the side of some building or temple—the second as named from its shape. Καινόν and Μέσον, the 'New Court' and 'Central Court,' are intelligible enough: but of their exact site we know nothing.

ὅτε δῆτα ταύταις ταῖς τελεταῖς οὐκ ὠφέλει,
διέπλευσεν εἰς Αἴγιναν· εἶτα ξυλλαβὼν
νύκτωρ κατέκλινεν αὐτὸν εἰς Ἀσκληπιοῦ·
ὁ δ' ἀνεφάνη κνεφαῖος ἐπὶ τῇ κιγκλίδι.
ἐντεῦθεν οὐκέτ' αὐτὸν ἐξεφρίομεν.   125
ὁ δ' ἐξεδίδρασκε διά τε τῶν ὑδρορροῶν
καὶ τῶν ὀπῶν· ἡμεῖς δ' ὅσ' ἦν τετρημένα
ἐνεβύσαμεν ῥακίοισι κἀπακτώσαμεν·
ὁ δ' ὡσπερεὶ κολοιὸς αὑτῷ παττάλους
ἐνέκρουεν ἐς τὸν τοῖχον, εἶτ' ἐξήλλετο.   130
ἡμεῖς δὲ τὴν αὐλὴν ἅπασαν δικτύοις
καταπετάσαντες ἐν κύκλῳ φυλάττομεν.
ἔστιν δ' ὄνομα τῷ μὲν γέροντι Φιλοκλέων,
ναὶ μὰ Δία, τῷ δ' υἱεῖ γε τῳδὶ Βδελυκλέων,

---

123 Ἀσκληπιοῦ.] Cf. *Plut.* 411, κατακλίνειν αὐτὸν εἰς Ἀσκληπιοῦ κράτιστόν ἐστι. Similar attempts at a cure are made in the Plutus (v. 655, &c.).
124 κνεφαῖος.] Cf. *Ran.* 1350, ὅπως κνεφαῖος εἰς ἀγορὰν φέρουσ' ἀποδοίμαν. The darkness of early morning is meant in both places. In *Les Plaideurs* (Act II. Sc. 1) L'Intimé tells Léandre that his disguise will not be penetrated for that 'He! lorsqu'à votre père ils vont faire leur cour, A peine seulement savez-vous s'il est jour.'
125 ἐξεφρίομεν.] Cf. v. 156, 892. A third compound from the same verb is διαφρέω, used in *Av.* 193, and (acc. to some texts) in Thuc. VII. 32.
126 ἐξεδίδρασκε...ἐξήλλετο.] Imperf. of attempts.
ὑδρορροῶν.] κοῖλοι τόποι, δι' ὧν χωρεῖ τὸ ὕδωρ τὸ ἐξ ὑετῶν. Schol. and on *Ach.* 922, ὑδρορρόα καλεῖται τὸ μέρος τῆς στεφανίδος δι' οὗ τὸ ἀπὸ τοῦ ὄμβρου ὕδωρ συναγόμενον κατέρχεται. Hence it is plain that they were waterpipes forming a regular part of the internal arrangement of the house. Of course it does not follow that they were really large enough to admit of a man's passage through them: for there is an intended absurdity and exaggeration here. In *Ach.* 922 they may be the same as here (not 'canals' as L. and S. say), and the communication may be by them through the roofs of the ship-sheds (νεώσοικοι). But this will depend on the view taken of τίφη there. In *Ach.* 1186 an open channel seems meant, but that passage abounds in absurdities, and is by some editors rejected.
128 κἀπακτώσαμεν.] Cf. Soph. *Aj.* 579, καὶ δῶμα πάκτου. It is of making all fast by closing doors and the like; whereas ἐμβῦσαι is to 'stuff up,' of such holes and ends of pipes, channels, &c. as would usually be open, but now needed stoppers, to keep in the indefatigable dicast.
129 ὁ δ' ὥσπ. κολοιὸς κ.τ.λ.] 'And he, jackdaw-like, was always knocking him pegs into the wall, and so trying to hop out.' Tame jackdaws used (says the Scholiast) to have perches put to hop on to. Of course *they* did not make their own perches, though Philocleon did.
133 Φιλοκλέων......Βδελυκλέων.] Cleon appears as the κηδέμων of the dicasts in v. 242, cf. v. 596, αὐτὸς δὲ Κλέων κ.τ.λ.

ΣΦΗΚΕΣ.

ἔχων τρόπους φρυαγμοσεμνάκους τινάς. 135

ΒΔΕΛΤΚΛΕΩΝ
ὦ Ξανθία καὶ Σωσία, καθεύδετε;

ΞΑΝΘΙΑΣ
οἴμοι.

ΣΩΣΙΑΣ
τί ἔστι;

ΞΑΝΘΙΑΣ
Βδελυκλέων ἀνίσταται.

ΒΔΕΛΤΚΛΕΩΝ
οὐ περιδραμεῖται σφῷν ταχέως δεῦρ᾽ ἅτερος;
ὁ γὰρ πατὴρ ἐς τὸν ἰπνὸν εἰσελήλυθεν
καὶ μυσπολεῖ τι καταδεδυκώς. ἀλλ᾽ ἄθρει, 140
κατὰ τῆς πυέλου τὸ τρῆμ᾽ ὅπως μὴ 'κδύσεται·
σὺ δὲ τῇ θύρᾳ πρόσκεισο.

ΣΩΣΙΑΣ.
ταῦτ᾽, ὦ δέσποτα.

135 **φρυαγμοσεμνάκους.**] Rendered by Florens Christianus 'capero-fronti-pervicos.' It is compounded of φρύαγμα and σεμνός. But φρυαγμοσεμνακουστίνους is one reading: and the Scholiast seems to think ὀφρὺς part of the compound, which would require ὀφρυαγμ., but what the precise elements would then be, is not plain. Meineke (following Hamaker) puts this line after v. 110, αἴγ. ἔνδον τρέφει. This avoids the awkward construction of the nom. ἔχων after υἱεῖ; and it is not plain how Bdelycleon's manners were 'haughty and pretentious,' which appears about the meaning of the word. If φρυαγμοσεμνακουστίνους be put of Philocleon as v. 111, the end of the word might come from ἀκούειν and the meaning be 'having the temper of a proud stern listener,' who was sure to condemn the accused.

136—229. Philocleon makes several attempts to escape: through the outlet of the water from the bath; through the chimney; by holding on under the donkey; by the roof. At last he is quiet; and the two slaves prepare to receive with stones his peppery fellow-dicasts, whom they expect to come and look for their leader.

137 **Βδελυκλέων ἀνίσταται**] Racine borrows a little of what follows for Sc. 2 and 3 of the first Act in *Les Plaideurs:* but with scarcely any of the fun or liveliness of his original.

139 **ἰπνὸν.**] ἰπνὸς κυρίως ἡ κάμινος, νῦν δὲ τὸ μαγειρεῖόν φησιν. Schol. And in v. 837 it seems certainly 'the kitchen.' Here L. and S. take it for the stove by which the bath was heated; and it may well be so, for v. 141 seems to require something of the sort.

140 **μυσπολεῖ.**] If (as L. and S. say) there be reference to μυστιπολεύω, we should render 'is at his *mouse-tricks*' for '*mysteries.*'

141 **τῆς πυέλου τὸ τρῆμ᾽.**] A hole for letting out the hot water. Schol.

ΑΡΙΣΤΟΦΑΝΟΥΣ

ΒΔΕΛΥΚΛΕΩΝ
ἄναξ Πόσειδον, τί ποτ' ἄρ' ἡ κάπνη ψοφεῖ;
οὗτος, τίς εἶ σύ;

ΦΙΛΟΚΛΕΩΝ
καπνὸς ἔγωγ' ἐξέρχομαι.

ΒΔΕΛΥΚΛΕΩΝ
καπνός; φέρ' ἴδω ξύλου τίνος σύ.

ΦΙΛΟΚΛΕΩΝ
συκίνου. 145

ΒΔΕΛΥΚΛΕΩΝ
νὴ τὸν Δί' ὅσπερ γ' ἐστὶ δριμύτατος καπνῶν.
ἀτάρ, οὐ γὰρ ἐρρήσεις γε, ποῦ 'σθ' ἡ τηλία;
δύου πάλιν· φέρ' ἐπαναθῶ σοι καὶ ξύλον.
ἐνταῦθά νυν ζήτει τιν' ἄλλην μηχανήν.
ἀτὰρ ἄθλιός γ' εἴμ' ὡς ἕτερός γ' οὐδεὶς ἀνήρ, 150
ὅστις πατρὸς νῦν Καπνίου κεκλήσομαι.

ΣΩΣΙΑΣ.
* * τὴν θύραν ὤθει· πίεζε νυν σφόδρα,
εὖ κἀνδρικῶς· κἀγὼ γὰρ ἐνταῦθ' ἔρχομαι.

---

145 συκίνου.] With reference to συκοφάντης; but also καπνοποιὸν τὸ σύκινον ξύλον. Schol.
146 δριμύτατος.] This fact is (says the Scholiast) attested by Aristotle. But Philocleon is δριμὺς much as Demus was to be in *Eq.* 808, εἶθ' ἥξει σοι δριμὺς ἄγροικος κατὰ σοῦ τὴν ψῆφον ἰχνεύων.
147 οὐ γὰρ ἐρρήσεις.] So Dindorf (in his notes), Hermann, and Meineke. Vulg. ἐσερρήσεις. MS. Rav. οὐκ ἐρρήσεις. Elmsl. οὐκέτ' ἐρρήσεις. The ἐς does not seem the preposition wanted, but rather ἐξ. Dindorf compares *Ach.* 487, ἀτάρ, φίλοι γὰρ οἱ παρόντες,...τί ταῦτα τοὺς Λάκωνας αἰτιώμεθα;
τηλία.] This seems a general word for any board. σανὶς βαθεῖα ἐν ᾗ ἄλφιτα ἐπίπρασκον. Schol.

Though used to stop the chimney it may be 'flour-tray, flour-board' here, rather than 'chimney-board:' the flour-board being taken as the nearest thing at hand to clap upon the top of the chimney. Then a log was to be put on this to weigh it down and make matters more safe.

151 Καπνίου.] καπνίας was a kind of wine, but the reference to this (if there be any) has not much point. Nor is it plain what preeminent wretchedness there was in being the son of a 'smoky' father.

152 τὴν θ. ὤθει.] Vulg. παῖ, τήν. MSS. R, V, have nothing before τὴν θ. Meineke reads ὅδε τὴν θ. ὠθεῖ. Hirschig gives this line and what follows to Sosias: so does Richter, with σὺ δὲ to fill the gap.

ΣΦΗΚΕΣ.

καὶ τῆς κατακλεῖδος ἐπιμελοῦ καὶ τοῦ μοχλοῦ·
φύλαττέ θ' ὅπως μὴ τὴν βάλανον ἐκτρώξεται. 155

ΦΙΛΟΚΛΕΩΝ
τί δράσετ'; οὐκ ἐκφρήσετ', ὦ μιαρώτατοι,
δικάσοντά μ', ἀλλ' ἐκφεύξεται Δρακοντίδης;

ΒΔΕΛΥΚΛΕΩΝ
σὺ δὲ τοῦτο βαρέως ἂν φέροις;

ΦΙΛΟΚΛΕΩΝ
ὁ γὰρ θεὸς
μαντευομένῳ μοὔχρησεν ἐν Δελφοῖς ποτὲ,
ὅταν τις ἐκφύγῃ μ', ἀποσκλῆναι τότε. 160

ΒΔΕΛΥΚΛΕΩΝ
Ἄπολλον ἀποτρόπαιε, τοῦ μαντεύματος.

ΦΙΛΟΚΛΕΩΝ
ἴθ', ἀντιβολῶ σ', ἔκφρες με, μὴ διαρραγῶ.

ΒΔΕΛΥΚΛΕΩΝ
μὰ τὸν Ποσειδῶ, Φιλοκλέων, οὐδέποτέ γε.

ΦΙΛΟΚΛΕΩΝ
διατρώξομαι τοίνυν ὀδὰξ τὸ δίκτυον.

ΒΔΕΛΥΚΛΕΩΝ
ἀλλ' οὐκ ἔχεις ὀδόντας.

154 **κατακλεῖδος.**] The exact nature of this part of the fastening does not appear. The μοχλὸς and βάλανος we often meet with, e.g. in Thuc. II. 4, a passage which well illustrates the construction and fastening of doors in ancient time. Richter interprets κατακλεῖς to mean the whole apparatus of fastening: but it looks more like a part; perhaps it is the hole into which the βάλανος went.

155 **φύλαττέ θ' ὅπως.**] Nothing seems gained by the change φύλατθ' ὅπως, which, as Dindorf has it, wants a conjunction. Meineke punctuates μοχλοῦ φύλατθ' ὅπως κ.τ.λ.: but, though the βάλανος certainly did go through the μοχλὸς into its socket, there seems no need to change the common text, by which, as Richter notes, the brief and hurried orders of the slave seem better given.

160 **ἀποσκλῆναι.**] The ἂν which Meineke adds seems unnecessary. The infinitive follows χρῆσαι in such sentences as ἔχρησα πέμψαι (Aesch. Eum. 203); and, though this may be rather a telling of 'what shall be' than an ordaining of a thing 'to be,' an oracle is always a sort of decree or command.

161 **Ἄπολλον κ.τ.λ.**] Cf. Av. 61, Ἄπολλον ἀποτρόπαιε, τοῦ χασμήματος.

164 **τὸ δίκτυον.**] Cf. v. 132.

ΦΙΛΟΚΛΕΩΝ
οἴμοι δείλαιος·
πῶς ἄν σ' ἀποκτείναιμι; πῶς; δότε μοι ξίφος
ὅπως τάχιστ', ἢ πινάκιον τιμητικόν.

ΒΔΕΛΥΚΛΕΩΝ
ἄνθρωπος οὗτος μέγα τι δρασείει κακόν.

ΦΙΛΟΚΛΕΩΝ
μὰ τὸν Δί' οὐ δῆτ', ἀλλ' ἀποδόσθαι βούλομαι
τὸν ὄνον ἄγων αὐτοῖσι τοῖς κανθηλίοις·
νουμηνία γάρ ἐστιν.

ΒΔΕΛΥΚΛΕΩΝ
οὐκοῦν κἂν ἐγὼ
αὐτὸν ἀποδοίμην δῆτ' ἄν;

ΦΙΛΟΚΛΕΩΝ
οὐχ ὥσπερ γ' ἐγω.

ΒΔΕΛΥΚΛΕΩΝ
μὰ Δί', ἀλλ' ἄμεινον. ἀλλὰ τὸν ὄνον ἔξαγε.

ΞΑΝΘΙΑΣ
οἵαν πρόφασιν καθῆκεν, ὡς εἰρωνικῶς,
ἵν' αὐτὸν ἐκπέμψειας.

167 πινάκιον τιμητικόν.] On which to draw the long line: cf. v. 106. It occurs to the old dicast as his own peculiar and most deadly weapon.

170 αὐτοῖσι τοῖς κανθηλίοις.] Of such phrases Elmsley has collected instances in his note on Eur. *Med.* 160. The preposition ξὺν is rarely added. The explanation of the phrase seems to be this: ἡ ναῦς διεφθάρη αὐτοῖς ἀνδράσι, 'the ship was lost with the men themselves, with the very men, with even the men,' and, as they would be the last things to be lost if any escape were possible, everything else belonging to the ship was necessarily lost. Hence αὐτοῖς ἀνδράσιν = 'men and all.'

171 νουμηνία.] On which day there would be a fair. Demus bought the Paphlagonian slave on this day (*Eq.* 43). Dr Primrose (in *The Vicar of Wakefield*) sent his son Moses to sell the horse at a neighbouring fair: and Philocleon pretends in v. 172 to distrust his son's powers at a bargain, fearing a result like that in Goldsmith's story.

κἂν...ἄν.] Cf. note on *Nub.* 783 for the repetition of ἄν.

174 καθῆκεν.] This word suggests Bdelycleon's answer, for καθιέναι ἄγκιστρον is an angling term: cf. Theocr. *Id.* XXI. 42, ἐδόκευον ἰχθύας, ἐκ καλάμων δὲ πλάνον κατέσειον ἐδωδάν. Similar is the use κατεῖναι κάλον, κατιεμένην καταπειρητηρίην, of a sounding line. Herod. II. 28.

ΒΔΕΛΥΚΛΕΩΝ
ἀλλ' οὐκ ἔσπασεν 175
ταύτῃ γ'· ἐγὼ γὰρ ᾐσθόμην τεχνωμένου.
ἀλλ' εἰσιὼν μοι τὸν ὄνον ἐξάγειν δοκῶ,
ὅπως ἂν ὁ γέρων μηδὲ παρακύψῃ πάλιν.
κάνθων, τί κλάεις; ὅτι πεπράσει τήμερον;
βάδιζε θᾶττον. τί στένεις, εἰ μὴ φέρεις 180
Ὀδυσσέα τιν';

ΞΑΝΘΙΑΣ
ἀλλὰ ναὶ μὰ Δία φέρει
κάτω γε τουτονί τιν' ὑποδεδυκότα.

ΒΔΕΛΥΚΛΕΩΝ
ποῖον; φέρ' ἴδωμαι.

ΞΑΝΘΙΑΣ
τουτονί.

175—6 οὐκ ἔσπασεν ταύτῃ γ'.] 'He caught nothing with this line.' Cf. *Thesm.* 928, αὕτη μὲν ἡ μήρινθος οὐδὲν ἔσπασεν. In Euripides (*Electr.* 582) ἦν δ' ἐκσπάσωμαι γ' ὃν μετέρχομαι βόλον is of net-fishing. Such metaphors are frequent in Greek. There is no sufficient reason for changing ταύτῃ to αὕτη. Aristophanes was not bound to quote the proverb with exactly the same words.

177 ἐξάγειν δοκῶ.] Elmsley would read ἐξάξειν; Meineke adopts from Cobet, ἔξαγ' ἔνδοθεν. No change is needed. Cf. Aesch. *Agam.* 16, ὅταν δ' ἀείδειν ἢ μινύρεσθαι δοκῶ; also Plat. *Prot.* 340, δοκῶ παρακαλεῖν; in illustration of which Wayte has quoted several other passages for δοκῶ, 'I am minded,' followed by infinitive of present and aorist.

178 παρακύψῃ.] Cf. *Pac.* 982, *Thesm.* 797, *Ach.* 16. To these Aristophanic passages may be added from the Septuagint, Prov. vii. 6, ἀπὸ γὰρ θυρίδος ἐκ τοῦ οἴκου αὐτῆς εἰς τὰς πλατείας παρακύπτουσα, κ.τ.λ.

Cant. ii. 9, παρακύπτων διὰ τῶν θυρίδων. Not very different is 2 Kings ix. 30, Ἰεζάβελ ἐστιμμίσατο τοὺς ὀφθαλμοὺς αὐτῆς, καὶ ἡγάθυνε τὴν κεφαλὴν αὐτῆς, καὶ διέκυψε διὰ τῆς θυρίδος. In this passage Bdelycleon says that the old man will have no excuse (when the ass is brought out) for peeping out again. He had evidently been peeping out of a window through the netting (v. 164). It is probable that in *Ach.* 16 παρέκυψεν is of the sly peeping of Chaeris before entrance; not of any stooping posture afterwards, as the Scholiast takes it.

179 κάνθων, τί κλάεις;] So Polyphemus asks his ram, why, contrary to his wont, he is so slow? This whole scene is a comic parody on Ulysses' escape beneath the ram's belly, and his assumption of the name Οὖτις (*Odyss.* ix. 425, &c.).

183 ἴδωμαι.] Hirschig, to avoid the use of the middle ἴδωμαι in iambic dialogue, reads ἴδω Ξ. ναὶ τουτονί. But ναὶ seems weak. Richter has ἴδωμεν with τουτονί, given to

ΒΔΕΛΥΚΛΕΩΝ
τουτὶ τί ἦν;
τίς εἶ ποτ', ὤνθρωπ', ἐτεόν;
ΦΙΛΟΚΛΕΩΝ
Οὖτις νὴ Δία.
ΒΔΕΛΥΚΛΕΩΝ
Οὖτις σύ; ποδαπός;
ΦΙΛΟΚΛΕΩΝ
Ἴθακος Ἀποδρασιππίδου.   185
ΒΔΕΛΥΚΛΕΩΝ
Οὖτις μὰ τὸν Δί' οὔ τι χαιρήσων γε σύ.
ὕφελκε θᾶττον αὐτόν. ὦ μιαρώτατος,
ἵν' ὑποδέδυκεν· ὥστ' ἔμοιγ' ἰνδάλλεται
ὁμοιότατος κλητῆρος εἶναι πωλίῳ.
ΦΙΛΟΚΛΕΩΝ
εἰ μή μ' ἐάσεθ' ἥσυχον, μαχούμεθα.   190

Xanthias. Meineke follows Hirschig, but gives the whole line to Bdelycleon.
185 Ἴθακος Ἀποδρασιππίδου.] Of Ithaca, because Ulysses was so; but perhaps there may be some idea of a derivation from ἴθι. Ἀποδρ. a name coined from ἀποδρᾶναι; cf. διαδρασιπολίτας, *Ran.* 1014. Imitating Bunyan's coinage of names we might represent these significant Greek titles by ' Mr Nobody, from the land of Go, son of Mr Ready-to-run.'
186 οὖτις...οὔ τι.] He plays on the words; cf. Hom. *Odyss.* ι. 408, ὦ φίλοι οὖτίς με κτείνει δόλῳ, to which his comrades answer, εἰ μὲν δὴ μήτις σε βιάζεται...νοῦσόν γ' οὔπως ἔστι Διὸς μεγάλου ἀλέασθαι.
188 ἵν' ὑποδέδυκεν.] ἵνα is best taken not as an exclamation, but rather in close connexion with μιαρώτατος, 'abominable wretch, in having crept under there!' This use of relatives and relative particles is common in Greek. Cf. *Nub.* v. 1157, 8, οὐδὲν ἐργάσαισθ'...οἷος ἐμοὶ τρέφεται υἱός, and 1206—8, μάκαρ... αὐτὸς ἐφὺς ὡς σοφὸς χοῖον τὸν υἱὸν τρέφεις. But though, in strictness of construction, οἷος, ὡς, &c. are relative, we turn them by a separate definite clause in English; *e.g.* Plat. *Theaetet.* 161, τὸ δὲ δὴ ἐμόν τε καὶ τῆς ἐμῆς τέχνης σιγῶ ὅσον γέλωτα ὀφλισκάνομεν, 'but of myself and my art I say nothing, such utter ridicule do we incur.' Cf. note on *Nub.* 394.
189 κλητῆρος πωλίῳ.] His position suggests that he is a 'sucking foal;' his litigious tastes that he is the foal of a κλητήρ. But κλητῆρος comes in oddly. Is it a comic substitution for κάνθωνος? It answers to it in quantity and in the initial consonant, and that appears to be about what Aristophanes requires when putting one word παρὰ προσδοκίαν for another.

ΣΦΗΚΕΣ.

ΒΔΕΛΥΚΛΕΩΝ
περὶ τοῦ μαχεῖ νῷν δῆτα;

ΦΙΛΟΚΛΕΩΝ
περὶ ὄνου σκιᾶς.

ΒΔΕΛΥΚΛΕΩΝ
πονηρὸς εἶ πόρρω τέχνης καὶ παράβολος.

ΦΙΛΟΚΛΕΩΝ
ἐγὼ πονηρός; οὐ μὰ Δί', ἀλλ' οὐκ οἶσθα σὺ
νῦν μ' ὄντ' ἄριστον· ἀλλ' ἴσως, ὅταν φάγῃς
ὑπογάστριον γέροντος ἡλιαστικοῦ.   195

ΒΔΕΛΥΚΛΕΩΝ
ὤθει τὸν ὄνον καὶ σαυτὸν ἐς τὴν οἰκίαν.

ΦΙΛΟΚΛΕΩΝ
ὦ ξυνδικασταὶ καὶ Κλέων, ἀμύνατε.

ΒΔΕΛΥΚΛΕΩΝ
ἔνδον κέκραχθι τῆς θύρας κεκλεισμένης.
ὤθει σὺ πολλοὺς τῶν λίθων πρὸς τὴν θύραν,
καὶ τὴν βάλανον ἔμβαλλε πάλιν ἐς τὸν μοχλὸν,   200

191 περὶ ὄνου σκιᾶς.] Of this proverb for 'a mere nothing' the Scholiast gives as origin a tale of a man who, having hired an ass to carry his goods, was for shading himself behind the animal at noonday. To this the owner of the ass objected, saying that he had let out the ass, but not its shadow. The cause was brought into court. And, in after times, Demosthenes is said to have used the story to shame his audience into attention.

192 πόρρω τέχνης.] 'Far advanced in craftiness,' very sly. This suits far better with Bdelycleon's tricks and attempts to escape, than 'without art,' as some unaccountably render it.

193—5. Philocleon replies that he is not πονηρὸς, but ἄριστος to the taste; and that, when they come to taste and know him, they will find him so. He is ὑπογάστριον because of his position. The ass that suckles him, which above was κλητὴρ, is now γέρων Ἡλιαστικός. The Athenians ἐχρῶντο τοῖς ὀνείοις, says the Scholiast. Indeed from *Eq.* 1399, τὰ κύνεια μιγνὺς τοῖς ὀνείοις πράγμασιν, we might infer that they ate such food; but then Cleon's sausages were probably not to be of the first order. However, granting that they ate both dog and donkey, the wit of this passage will still sound rather flat to English ears.

197 ὦ ξυνδικασταί, κ.τ.λ.] So Cleon calls the heliasts to his aid in *Eq.* 255.

198 κέκραχθι.] Cf. *Ach.* 335, ὡς ἀποκτενῶ κέκραχθι.

199. Here he turns to the servant with orders to make all fast.

200 βάλανον...ἐς τὸν μοχλόν.]

30   ΑΡΙΣΤΟΦΑΝΟΥΣ   [201

καὶ τῇ δοκῷ προσθεὶς τὸν ὅλμον τὸν μέγαν
ἀνύσας τι προσκύλιέ γ'.

ΣΩΣΙΑΣ
οἴμοι δείλαιος·
πόθεν ποτ' ἐμπέπτωκέ μοι τὸ βώλιον;

ΞΑΝΘΙΑΣ
ἴσως ἄνωθεν μῦς ἐνέβαλέ σοί ποθεν.

ΣΩΣΙΑΣ
μῦς; οὐ μὰ Δί', ἀλλ' ὑποδυόμενός τις οὑτοσὶ   205
ὑπὸ τῶν κεραμίδων ἡλιαστὴς ὀροφίας.

ΞΑΝΘΙΑΣ
οἴμοι κακοδαίμων, στρουθὸς ἀνὴρ γίγνεται·
ἐκπτήσεται. ποῦ ποῦ 'στί μοι τὸ δίκτυον;
σοῦ σοῦ, πάλιν σοῦ.

ΒΔΕΛΥΚΛΕΩΝ
νὴ Δί' ἦ μοι κρεῖττον ἦν
τηρεῖν Σκιώνην ἀντὶ τούτου τοῦ πατρός.   210

ΣΩΣΙΑΣ
ἄγε νυν, ἐπειδὴ τουτονὶ σεσοβήκαμεν,
κοὐκ ἔσθ' ὅπως διαδὺς ἂν ἡμᾶς ἔτι λάθοι,
τί οὐκ ἀπεκοιμήθημεν ὅσον ὅσον στίλην;

Cf. v. 154. The βάλανος went through the μοχλός, and into a socket behind it; and this verse partly justifies, and certainly explains, Meineke's punctuation at v. 154.

201 δοκῷ.] This beam was plainly distinct from the μοχλός, or ordinary bar. It was probably a large wooden beam put across the whole door, only perhaps to be used when the house was to be permanently shut up, or barricaded, as here.

202—210. This dialogue Meineke makes between Xanthias and Bdelycleon to v. 206, giving 207—210 to Bdelycleon.

206 ὀροφίας.] λέγονται μῦς ὀροφίαι καὶ ὄφεις οἱ περὶ τὰς ὀροφὰς διάγοντες καὶ ταύτας περιτρώγοντες. A mouse is rather thought of here than a snake; cf. v. 140: but in India and hot climates a snake dropping from the roof would be natural enough.

209 σοῦ σοῦ.] From the Scholiast's ἀποσοβοῦσι τὸν γέροντα ὡς στρουθὸν we may conclude that this word σοῦ was in use merely as an exclamation to scare away birds.

210 Σκιώνην.] Cf. Thuc. IV. 120. Scione had revolted to Brasidas in the year before this play was exhibited.

213 ἀπεκοιμήθημεν.] 'Why don't we *at once* sleep?' Cf. Plat. *Prot.* 310, τί οὖν οὐ διηγήσω ἡμῖν τὴν

ΒΔΕΛΤΚΛΕΩΝ
ἀλλ᾽, ὦ πονήρ᾽, ἥξουσιν ὀλίγον ὕστερον
οἱ ξυνδικασταὶ παρακαλοῦντες τουτονὶ   215
τὸν πατέρα.
ΣΩΣΙΑΣ
τί λέγεις; ἀλλὰ νῦν ὄρθρος βαθύς.
ΒΔΕΛΤΚΛΕΩΝ
νὴ τὸν Δί᾽, ὀψὲ τἄρ᾽ ἀνεστήκασι νῦν.
ὡς ἀπὸ μέσων νυκτῶν γε παρακαλοῦσ᾽ ἀεί,
λύχνους ἔχοντες καὶ μινυρίζοντες μέλη
ἀρχαιομελησιδωνοφρυνιχήρατα,   220
οἷς ἐκκαλοῦνται τοῦτον.
ΣΩΣΙΑΣ
οὐκοῦν, ἢν δέῃ,
ἤδη ποτ᾽ αὐτοὺς τοῖς λίθοις βαλλήσομεν.
ΒΔΕΛΤΚΛΕΩΝ
ἀλλ᾽, ὦ πονηρέ, τὸ γένος ἤν τις ὀργίσῃ
τὸ τῶν γερόντων, ἔσθ᾽ ὅμοιον σφηκιᾷ.
ἔχουσι γὰρ καὶ κέντρον ἐκ τῆς ὀσφύος   225
ὀξύτατον, ᾧ κεντοῦσι, καὶ κεκραγότες
πηδῶσι καὶ βάλλουσιν ὥσπερ φέψαλοι.

ξυνουσίαν; and Soph. *Oed. Tyr.* 1002, τί δῆτ᾽ ἐγώγ᾽ οὐ τοῦδε τοῦ φόβου σ᾽, ἄναξ, ἐπείπερ εὔνους ἦλθον, ἐξελυσάμην; To these instances Wayte, in his note on the passage first quoted, adds several.
ὅσον ὅσον.] Cf. *Nub.* 1288, πλέον πλέον.
217 τἄρ᾽ ἀνεστήκασι νῦν.] The MSS. have γάρ...νῦν: Porson γ᾽ ἄρ᾽...νῦν: Meineke νῦν...γάρ, which gives a late position to γάρ. The meaning is that ὄρθρος βαθύς is not too early for them, nay, that they are rather late this time; since generally they come soon after midnight, in the small hours.
220 ἀρχαιομελησ.] Whether μέλος or μέλι be the second element in this compound is rather doubtful.

If μέλι, as the Scholiast and Aristarchus say, then Meineke's ἀρχαιομελισιδ. is to be preferred. But Dindorf quotes from *Av.* 750, ἔνθεν, ὥσπερει μέλιττα, Φρύνιχος ἀμβροσίων μελέων ἀπεβόσκετο καρπὸν ἀεὶ φέρων γλυκεῖαν ᾠδάν. Phrynichus wrote a play named the Phoenissae, in which Sidonians were frequently mentioned. Songs from this play are meant here.
225 κέντρον.] Bergler quotes from Phrynichus, the comic poet, ἔστιν δ᾽ αὐτοὺς τὸ φυλάττεσθαι τῶν νῦν χαλεπώτατον ἔργον· ἔχουσι γάρ τι κέντρον ἐν τοῖς δακτύλοις.
227 φέψαλοι.] So the chorus of old Acharnians (*Ach.* 666) invoke their muse to come fiery and sparkling like φέψαλος.

ΣΩΣΙΑΣ
μὴ φροντίσῃς· ἐὰν ἐγὼ λίθους ἔχω,
πολλῶν δικαστῶν σφηκιὰν διασκεδῶ.

ΧΟΡΟΣ
χώρει, πρόβαιν' ἐρρωμένως. ὦ Κωμία, βραδύνεις; 230
μὰ τὸν Δί', οὐ μέντοι πρὸ τοῦ γ', ἀλλ' ἦσθ' ἱμὰς κύνειος·
νυνὶ δὲ κρείττων ἐστὶ σοῦ Χαρινάδης βαδίζειν.
ὦ Στρυμόδωρε Κονθυλεῦ, βέλτιστε συνδικαστῶν,
Εὐεργίδης ἆρ' ἐστί που 'νταῦθ', ἢ Χάβης ὁ Φλυεύς;
πάρεσθ', ὃ δὴ λοιπόν γ' ἔτ' ἐστίν, ἀππαπαῖ παπαιάξ, 235
ἥβης ἐκείνης, ἡνίκ' ἐν Βυζαντίῳ ξυνῆμεν
φρουροῦντ' ἐγώ τε καὶ σύ· κᾆτα περιπατοῦντε νύκτωρ
τῆς ἀρτοπώλιδος λαθόντ' ἐκλέψαμεν τὸν ὅλμον,
κᾆθ' ἥψομεν τοῦ κορκόρου, κατασχίσαντες αὐτόν.

228 ἐὰν ἐγώ.] Dindorf has plainly shewn, in a note on this line, that the second syllable of ἐὰν is long, and that the insertion of γε has been owing to copyists' ignorance of this. Cf. v. 1231 of this play for one of the many examples.

230—315. The Chorus now enter: they are old men, attired in some way to resemble wasps, perhaps in the colour of their dress, but certainly in their stings. They stir each other up, recount their youthful exploits, and look forward to condemning any who are brought before them. Some boys bearing torches attend them, and they carefully pick their way to Strepsiades' house. Surprised at his non-appearance, they halt, and try to rouse him with their song; imagining possible causes for his delay, reminding him of his severity, and calling him to share in the spoil of a rich man who is to be condemned. A short dispute follows between the old men and their young link-bearers, who threaten to strike work if they do not get figs, but soon find that they may be thankful if they get even their breakfast.

231 ἱμὰς κύνειος.] Whether this be 'a thong of dogskin,' or (as Dindorf and Schneider prefer) 'a thong with which dogs are fastened,' or 'a dog whip,' as some think, it is any way meant as a proverb for toughness. Cf. ἱμάντας ἐκ Λεπρῶν (Ach. 724).

232 Χαρινάδης.] One of the name is mentioned in Pac. 1155; but hardly one of the same character, as he is there a rather jovial countryman invited to feast and make merry.

233 Στρυμόδωρε.] Cf. Ach. 272, Lys. 259. Conthyla was an Attic deme.

235—9. As in Ach. 210, &c. the old men recal the deeds of their youth.

236 ἐν Βυζαντίῳ.] Forty-seven years before: cf. Thuc. I. 94.

239 κορκόρου.] Genitive of part: 'some of the pimpernel.' But it is the ordinary case to use of eatables and drinkables. So the French almost always use 'du, de la' in like phrases.

αὐτόν.] Sc. τὸν ὅλμον. They were short of wood; so stole and broke up a wooden mortar. Others, not

ἀλλ' ἐγκονῶμεν, ὦνδρες, ὡς ἔσται Λάχητι νυνί· 240
σίμβλον δέ φασι χρημάτων ἔχειν ἅπαντες αὐτόν.
χθὲς οὖν Κλέων ὁ κηδεμὼν ἡμῖν ἐφεῖτ' ἐν ὥρᾳ
ἥκειν ἔχοντας ἡμερῶν ὀργὴν τριῶν πονηρὰν
ἐπ' αὐτόν, ὡς κολωμένους ὧν ἠδίκησεν. ἀλλὰ
σπεύδωμεν, ὦνδρες ἥλικες, πρὶν ἡμέραν γενέσθαι. 245
χωρῶμεν, ἅμα τε τῷ λύχνῳ πάντη διασκοπῶμεν,
μή που λίθος τις ἐμποδὼν ἡμᾶς κακόν τι δράσῃ.

ΠΑΙΣ
τὸν πηλὸν, ὦ πάτερ πάτερ, τουτονὶ φύλαξαι.

ΧΟΡΟΣ
κάρφος χαμᾶθέν νυν λαβὼν τὸν λύχνον πρόβυσον.

ΠΑΙΣ
οὐκ, ἀλλὰ τῳδί μοι δοκῶ τὸν λύχνον προβύσειν. 250

ΧΟΡΟΣ
τί δὴ μαθὼν τῷ δακτύλῳ τὴν θρυαλλίδ' ὠθεῖς,
καὶ ταῦτα τοὐλαίου σπανίζοντος, ὠνόητε;

so well, take αὐτὸν to be of the κόρκορος. But αὐτὸν would not have been expressed at all if that had been the meaning; ἤψομεν τοῦ κ. κατασχίσαντες, 'we split up and boiled the pimpernel,' would have been sufficient.

240 ἔσται Λάχητι.] ἡ δίκη ἢ τιμωρία ἢ τοιοῦτόν τι. Schol.

241 σίμβλον.] Cf. the use of βλίττειν in *Eq.* 794. Laches had stored up his plunderings like a bee. His peculations in Sicily are further alluded to in v. 895, &c., where the dog Labes is tried.

243 ἡμ. τριῶν.] A military provision was σιτί' ἡμερῶν τριῶν. Cf. *Pac.* 312, *Eq.* 1079. In Racine's play (Act I. Sc. 4) Dandin, when going out, says, 'Je ne veux de trois mois rentrer dans la maison. De sacs et de procès j'ai fait provision.'

244 κολωμένους.] Cf. *Eq.* 456, χὤπως κολᾷ τὸν ἄνδρα. The middle form of the future is the true Attic form.

247 λίθος.] Better than vulg. λαθών: they are looking well to their footsteps, and avoiding mud and stones, in the dark morning. And λίθος is in MS. V.

248. The boys are beside the regular chorus. Dindorf thinks there were perhaps six. They are sent to bear a message to Cleon at v. 408.

248—272. Of these lines the copyists ingeniously made tetrameter iambics, by insertions here and there of σύ, γε, νῦν, τι, που, δή, ὅδ', ἐξ. The lines are called, 'versus asynarteti:' each is composed of a dimeter iambic and a dimeter trochaic catalectic.

251 μαθών.] 'Urit me pruritus emendandi, et nescio quo modo malim hic legere τί δὴ παθών, non μαθών.' Florens Chr. The same complaint takes Meincke, wherever the phrase τί μαθὼν occurs.

οὐ γὰρ δάκνει σ', ὅταν δέῃ τίμιον πρίασθαι.

ΠΑΙΣ

εἰ νὴ Δί᾽ αὖθις κονδύλοις νουθετήσεθ᾽ ἡμᾶς,
ἀποσβέσαντες τοὺς λύχνους ἄπιμεν οἴκαδ᾽ αὐτοί· 255
κἄπειτ᾽ ἴσως ἐν τῷ σκότῳ τουτουὶ στερηθεὶς
τὸν πηλὸν ὥσπερ ἀτταγᾶς τυρβάσεις βαδίζων.

ΧΟΡΟΣ

ἦ μὴν ἐγὼ σοῦ χἀτέρους μείζονας κυλάζω.
ἀλλ᾽ οὑτοσί μοι βόρβορος φαίνεται πατοῦντι·
κοὐκ ἔσθ᾽ ὅπως οὐχ ἡμερῶν τεττάρων τὸ πλεῖστον 260
ὕδωρ ἀναγκαίως ἔχει τὸν θεὸν ποιῆσαι.
ἔπεισι γοῦν τοῖσιν λύχνοις οὑτοιὶ μύκητες·
φιλεῖ δ᾽, ὅταν τοῦτ᾽ ᾖ, ποιεῖν ὑετὸν μάλιστα.
δεῖται δὲ καὶ τῶν καρπίμων ἅττα μή 'στι πρῷα
ὕδωρ γενέσθαι κἀπιπνεῦσαι βόρειον αὐτοῖς. 265
τί χρῆμ᾽ ἄρ᾽ οὐκ τῆς οἰκίας τῆσδε συνδικαστὴς

253 **δάκνει σ᾽.**] For σὲ elided, even when emphatic, cf. *Nub.* 916, and the note there. And Soph. *Oed. Tyr.* 329, ἐγὼ δ᾽ οὐ μήποτε τἀμ᾽ ὡς ἂν εἴπων μὴ τὰ σ᾽ ἐκφήνω κακά is an analogous elision, for the possessive σὰ must there have some stress laid on it, as opposed to τἀμά. There is a similar complaint of wastefulness in oil in *Nub.* 56—9, where the old men enforce their reproof with blows.

254 **κονδ. ν.**] Cf. *Eq.* 1236, κονδύλοις ἡρμοττόμην.

257. When the light is gone, the old men will flounder about in the mud like sand-pipers. For ἀτταγᾶς cf. note on *Ach.* 875.

259 **βόρβορος.**] Meineke takes μάρμαρος from Hermann. MS. Ven. has βάρβαρος. Hermann argues that 'as the old man says there must be rain within four days at most, it is hard and dry ground that he ought to be complaining of.' But then what force have πηλὸς and ἀτταγᾶς above? And μάρμαρος is an uncommon word to admit on conjecture for 'stony ground, &c.' It seems better to take vv. 261, 262 of past rain, and then τὸ πλεῖστον must be taken with ὕδωρ. The prophecy of rain 'within four days at most' from the signs of the lamp-wicks would be curious. The old men's talk will run about thus: 'You talk of mud: why here is mud beneath my feet—enough to shew that heaven has been raining its hardest for four days—and then look too at the lamp-wicks: they have fungi on them: that shews rain is about; and we shall have some more.' Their first inferring from the mud how much rain there has been, and then passing on to the consideration of rain to come, may be a little rambling, but is not out of character with old men.

262 **μύκητες.**] Cf. Virg. *Georg.* I. 391, testa cum ardente viderent Scintillare oleum et putres concrescere fungos.

264 **δεῖται δὲ, κ.τ.λ.**] And this rain (they go on to say) is wanted for the later fruits.

πέπονθεν, ὡς οὐ φαίνεται δεῦρο πρὸς τὸ πλῆθος;
οὐ μὴν πρὸ τοῦ γ' ἐφολκὸς ἦν, ἀλλὰ πρῶτος ἡμῶν
ἡγεῖτ' ἂν ᾄδων Φρυνίχου· καὶ γάρ ἐστιν ἀνὴρ
φιλῳδός. ἀλλά μοι δοκεῖ στάντας ἐνθάδ', ὦνδρες, 270
ᾄδοντας αὐτὸν ἐκκαλεῖν, ἤν τί πως ἀκούσας
τοὐμοῦ μέλους ὑφ' ἡδονῆς ἑρπύσῃ θύραζε.
τί ποτ' οὐ πρὸ θυρῶν φαίνετ' ἆρ' ἡμῖν ὁ γέρων οὐδ' ὑπα-
κούει;
μῶν ἀπολώλεκεν τὰς
ἐμβάδας, ἢ προσέκοψ' ἐν 275
τῷ σκότῳ τὸν δάκτυλόν που,
εἶτ' ἐφλέγμηνεν αὐτοῦ
τὸ σφυρὸν γέροντος ὄντος;
καὶ τάχ' ἂν βουβωνιῴη.
ἦ μὴν πολὺ δριμύτατός γ' ἦν τῶν παρ' ἡμῖν,
καὶ μόνος οὐκ ἂν ἐπείθετ',
ἀλλ' ὁπότ' ἀντιβολοίη
τις, κάτω κύπτων ἂν οὕτω,
λίθον ἕψεις, ἔλεγεν. 280
τάχα δ' ἂν διὰ τὸν χθιζινὸν ἄνθρωπον, ὃς ἡμᾶς διεδύετ'
ἐξαπατῶν, λέγων ὡς
καὶ φιλαθήναιος ἦν καὶ

268 ἐφολκὸς.] Cf. Aesch. *Supp.*
200, καὶ μὴ πρόλεσχος μηδ' ἐφολκὸς
ἐν λόγῳ γένῃ. The Scholiast says
ἐφολκὶς is the boat towed astern of a
ship. This adjective we more often
find active; e.g. in Thuc. IV. 108,
τοῦ Βρασίδου ἐφολκὰ καὶ οὐ τὰ ὄντα
λέγοντος.
269 Φρυνίχου.] Cf. above, v. 220.
270 ἀλλά μοι δοκεῖ στάντας.]
Cf. *Eq.* 1311, καθῆσθαί μοι δοκεῖ ἐς
τὸ Θησεῖον πλευσάς. The Chorus
having picked their way to Philocleon's house halt there, and chant
their summons.
274 ἀπολώλεκεν τὰς.] Hermann
corrected to ἀπολώλεκεν τὰς to agree
with λέγων ὡς as he has it in v. 283.
Richter's ἐξαπατῶν τε λέγων θ' in v.
283 seems as good, retaining here

the vulg. ἀπολώλεκε.
276 δάκτυλον.] Sc. ποδός.
278 δριμύτατός γ'.] Cf. note on
Eq. 808, εἶθ' ἥξει σοι δριμὺς ἄγροικος,
κ.τ.λ.
279 κάτω κύπτων.] To show in-
attention, or to avoid being moved
by the defendant's piteous appearance.
280 λίθον ἕψεις.] The Scholiast
gives similar proverbs: πλίνθον πλύ
νειν, χύτραν ποικίλλειν, εἰς ὕδωρ γρά-
φειν, Αἰθίοπα λευκαίνειν, κατὰ θα-
λάττης σπείρειν.
281. Perhaps grief at the escape
of a defendant has made him ill.
282 φιλαθήναιος.] To be pronounced with the diphthong short,
for the line answers to ἐμβάδας ἢ
προσέκοψ' ἐν.

τὰν Σάμῳ πρῶτος κατείποι,
διὰ τοῦτ' ὀδυνηθεὶς
εἶτ' ἴσως κεῖται πυρέττων.
ἔστι γὰρ τοιοῦτος ἀνήρ. 285
ἀλλ', ὠγάθ', ἀνίστασο μηδ' οὕτως σεαυτὸν
ἔσθιε, μηδ' ἀγανάκτει.
καὶ γὰρ ἀνὴρ παχὺς ἥκει
τῶν προδόντων τἀπὶ Θρᾴκης·
ὃν ὅπως ἐγχυτριεῖς.
ὕπαγ', ὦ παῖ, ὕπαγε. 290

ΠΑΙΣ

ἐθελήσεις τί μοι οὖν, ὦ πάτερ, ἤν σου τι δεηθῶ;

283 τὰν Σάμῳ.] The accused man claimed to have done the state service by early information which enabled them to get a footing in Samos. The Athenians helped Miletus against Samos under Pericles, about twenty years before this play was exhibited. They reduced the island in nine months. Thuc. I. 115—117.
287 ἔσθιε.] Cf. Hom. *Il.* ζ. 202, ὃν θυμὸν κατέδων. It is a favourite metaphor. Bergler quotes from Alcaeus ἔδωδ' ἐμαυτὸν ὡς πολύπους.
288 παχύς.] So *Pac.* 639, τῶν δὲ συμμάχων ἔσειον τοὺς παχεῖς καὶ πλουσίους, αἰτίας ἂν προστιθέντες ὡς φρονεῖ τὰ Βρασίδου. To be a traitor in the matter of the Thrace-ward parts, and to favour Brasidas, a-mount to about the same, since Brasidas took a leading part in the campaigns there. For the operations cf. Thuc. IV. 102.
289 ἐγχυτριεῖς.] 'Put in the pot,' add 'him to the 'stock' for soup. One of our poet's frequent metaphors from cookery. Cf. *Eq.* 745, ἕψοντος ἑτέρου τὴν χύτραν ὑφειλόμην, where χύτρα is plainly the 'stock-pot' boiling on the fire with the meat in it: and *Eq.* 1136—40, τούσδ' ἐπίτηδες...τρέφεις, κᾆθ', ὅταν μή σοι τύχῃ ὄψον ὄν, τούτων ὃς ἂν

ᾖ παχὺς θύσας ἐπιδειπνεῖς. Being plump and fat (παχὺς), he would be a savoury morsel to add to the pot. Our own slang will supply 'pot' or 'dish' as equivalents. The Scholiast's explanation of ἐγχ. as referring to exposure of infants in χύτραι seems to me quite unnecessary here. Being recognized by Hesychius it deserves some respect, but where Aristophanes can be so easily explained from himself, it appears better so to explain him.
290 ὕπαγ', ὦ παῖ.] Hermann supplies this line to the end of the strophe (after v. 280, λ. ἔ. ἔλεγεν) for the sake of symmetry. There seems no strong reason to give why the chorus should not say it only once, after the completion of both parts of their song. Why may not the chorus have halted, and deferred their 'lead on' to the end? Cf. above, v. 270, στάντας ἐνθάδ' ἐκκαλεῖν.
291—302. These lines metrically are answered by 303—315. The metre in the first five lines is 'Ionicum a minore,' ⌣⌣ − − | ⌣⌣ − − |. Instances of this metre are Aesch. *Pers.* 65—112, and in Latin, Hor. *Od.* III. 13, Miserarum est neque amori dare ludum, &c.

ΣΦΗΚΕΣ.

ΧΟΡΟΣ

πάνυ γ', ὦ παιδίον. ἀλλ' εἰπὲ τί βούλει με πρίασθαι
καλόν; οἶμαι δέ σ' ἐρεῖν ἀστραγάλους δήπουθεν, ὦ παῖ. 295

ΠΑΙΣ

μὰ Δί', ἀλλ' ἰσχάδας, ὦ παππία· ἥδιον γάρ.

ΧΟΡΟΣ

οὐκ ἂν
μὰ Δί', εἰ κρέμαισθέ γ' ὑμεῖς.

ΠΑΙΣ

μὰ Δί' οὔ τἄρα προπέμψω σε τὸ λοιπόν

ΧΟΡΟΣ

ἀπὸ γὰρ τοῦδέ με τοῦ μισθαρίου   300
τρίτον αὐτὸν ἔχειν ἄλφιτα δεῖ καὶ ξύλα κὤψον·
σὺ δὲ σῦκά μ' αἰτεῖς.

ΠΑΙΣ

ἄγε νυν, ὦ πάτερ, ἢν μὴ τὸ δικαστήριον ἄρχων
καθίσῃ νῦν, πόθεν ὠνησόμεθ' ἄριστον; ἔχεις ἐλ- 305
πίδα χρηστήν τινα νῷν ἢ πόρον Ἕλλας ἱρὸν εἰπεῖν;

ΧΟΡΟΣ

ἀπαπαῖ, φεῦ, ἀπαπαῖ, φεῦ, μὰ Δί' οὐκ ἔγωγε νῷν οἶδ' 309
ὁπόθεν γε δεῖπνον ἔσται.   311

298 ἥδιον γάρ.] The ι is scanned short, the answering line being μὰ Δί' οὐκ ἔγωγε νῷν οἶδ'.

300 μισθαρίου.] The τριώβολον, which had to find three (husband wife and child) in the necessaries of life. The diminutive μισθάριον expresses the paltriness of the pay.

302. Hermann adds ἒ ἒ here to balance v. 315. But it might be 'extra metrum' there. Cf. note at v. 290.

303—308. Seeing that figs are quite out of the question, the boy begins to be anxious about his breakfast, if the court should not sit.

305 καθίσῃ.] Cf. v. 1441, ἕως ἂν τὴν δίκην ἄρχων καλῇ. It appears that the archon had the power of determining whether the court should sit, and that it was not sure to sit every day. Cf. *Thesm.* 78, ἐπεὶ νῦν γ' οὔτε τὰ δικαστήρια μέλλει δικάζειν οὔτε βουλῆς ἐσθ' ἕδρα.

308 πόρον Ἕλλας ἱρόν.] From Pindar, acc. to Scholiast. Having used πόρον, 'way,' i.e. means of getting money, he adds ridiculously enough the other words which he remembers come with πόρον in Pindar. The sacred πόρος Ἕλλας is there the Hellespont.

ΠΑΙΣ.
τί με δῆτ', ὦ μελέα μῆτερ, ἔτικτες,

ΧΟΡΟΣ
ἵν' ἐμοὶ πράγματα βόσκειν παρέχῃς;

ΠΑΙΣ
ἀνόνητον ἄρ' ὦ θυλάκιόν σ' εἶχον ἄγαλμα.   314
ἒ ἔ.
πάρα νῷν στενάζειν.

ΦΙΛΟΚΛΕΩΝ
φίλοι, τήκομαι μὲν   317
πάλαι διὰ τῆς ὀπῆς
ὑμῶν ὑπακούων.
ἀλλ' οὐ γὰρ οἷός τ' ἔτ' εἴμ'
ᾄδειν. τί ποιήσω;
τηροῦμαι δ' ὑπὸ τῶνδ', ἐπεὶ
βούλομαί γε πάλαι μεθ' ὑ-   320
μῶν ἐλθὼν ἐπὶ τοὺς καδί-

312 τί με, κ.τ.λ.] From the Theseus of Euripides. The Scholiast gives both lines to the boy, and says that in the play they were spoken by those destined to be eaten by the Minotaur. I do not see what good sense can be made of v. 313 thus given to the boy. It seems better to follow Meineke and Cobet, who give v. 313 to the chorus. 'Why,' laments the boy, 'didst thou bear me?' 'To be a plague to me to keep, of course,' replies the old man. However, v. 313 may in some way resemble the line in Euripides that follows τί με κ.τ.λ.

314 ἀνόνητον, κ.τ.λ.] Hippolytus says (in the Theseus), ἀνόνητον ἄγαλμα, πάτερ, οἴκοισι τεκών. The wallet here was to put the meal in, which the dicasts would buy if they got their pay. Cf. Eccl. 380, B. τὸ τριώβολον δῆτ' ἔλαβες; Χ. εἰ γὰρ ὤφελον. ἀλλ' ὕστερος ἦλθον νὴ Δί' ὥστ' αἰσχύνομαι μὰ Δί' οὐδὲν ἄλλο μᾶλλον ἢ τὸν θύλακον. The boy is here carrying the father's wallet.

315 πάρα νῷν στ.] 'We may both make our moan.' Perhaps, as Richter thinks, both young and old unite to say this. It is no doubt another Euripidean scrap.

316—394. Philocleon hears the chorus, and tells them his hard case. They are indignant. After some talk about ways of escape, the old man hits on the plan of gnawing through the net, and letting himself down by a cord.

318 ὑπακούων.] Meineke's ἐπακούων is in no respect better than this. Cf. Nub. 263. Of Philocleon listening at the window ὑπ. seems correctly said, as it is so frequently used of a door-keeper listening to and answering a knock at the door.

321 καδίσκους.] He would fain be off to his dear balloting-urns, and be doing some mischief. Cf. v. 340, οὐκ ἐᾷ με...δρᾶν οὐδὲν κακόν.

σκους κακόν τι ποιῆσαι.
ἀλλ', ὦ Ζεῦ Ζεῦ, μέγα βροντήσας
ἤ με ποίησον καπνὸν ἐξαίφνης,
ἢ Προξενίδην, ἢ τὸν Σέλλου   325
τοῦτον τὸν ψευδαμάμαξυν.
τόλμησον, ἄναξ, χαρίσασθαί μοι,
πάθος οἰκτείρας·
ἤ με κεραυνῷ διατινθαλέῳ
σπόδισον ταχέως·
κᾆπειτ' ἀνελών μ' ἀποφυσήσας   330
εἰς ὀξάλμην ἔμβαλε θερμήν·
ἢ δῆτα λίθον με ποίησον ἐφ' οὗ
τὰς χοιρίνας ἀριθμοῦσιν.

323 ἀλλ' ὦ Ζεῦ, κ.τ.λ.] These wishes are in a sort of half-tragic style. Cf Aesch. *Prom. Vinct.* 1043—1053: which passage Aristophanes possibly had in his mind here. The metre (anapaestic) is the same.

μέγα βροντήσας.] Vulg. μέγα βρόντα, which Meineke reads as one word, Hirschig as imperative, following it by κἀμὲ π. It seems well to commence the anapaestic system with ἀλλ' ὦ Ζεῦ, and therefore Dindorf's text is preferable, for the paroemiac verse should not be at the beginning.

325 Προξενίδην.] Having spoken of smoke, he adds these as beggarly braggarts (πτωχαλαζόνας), called 'smokes,' Proxenides, and Aeschines, son of Sellus. Schol. Cf. *Av.* 1126, Προξενίδης ὁ κομπασεύς, and below, v. 457.

326 ψευδαμάμαξυν.] The ἀμάμαξυς is a kind of vine, whose wood crackles loud in the fire. Hence the whole word means that Aeschines is false and noisy. Schol. ψευδατράφαξυς in *Eq.* 630 is a similar compound, used also metaphorically.

327 τόλμησον χαρίσασθαι.] 'Bring thy heart to grant me the boon.' 'Id est χαρίσαι,' Brunck, from which note not much is gained.

More to the point is Bergler's quotation from Soph. *Trach.* 1070, ἴθ' ὦ τέκνον, τόλμησον, οἴκτειρόν τέ με. τολμᾶν, τλῆναι, τλήμων express 'endurance' of various kinds, from boldness and hardihood' to 'patience and misery.'

328 κεραυνῷ.] Cf. Soph. *Trach.* 1087, ἔνσεισον, ὦναξ, ἐγκατάσκηψον βέλος, πάτερ, κεραυνοῦ.

329 διατινθαλέῳ.] διαπύρῳ Hesych. Suidas quotes τινθαλέοισι κατικμήναντο λοετροῖς. And ποτῷ τινθαλέῳ occurs in Nicand. *Alexipharm.* 445. Hence it seems used of hot liquid: and the thunderbolt may be conceived of as liquid fire.

330 ἀποφυσήσας.] Men blow off the ashes of fish baked on the coals. Schol. The word σπόδισον suggests this culinary metaphor, which is rather a coming down after the tragic style of the preceding lines.

332 λίθον, κ.τ.λ.] 'Or turn me to stone—so it be that whereon they count the voting-shells.' For χοιρίνας cf. *Eq.* 1332. The prayer that he might be turned to stone suggests Niobe: and it is possible that this may have reference to some play of that name. We know that there was a *Niobe* of Aeschylus, and also one of Sophocles. Cf. v. 580.

ΧΟΡΟΣ

τίς γὰρ ἐσθ' ὁ ταῦτά σ' εἴργων
κἀποκλείων τὰς θύρας; λέ-
ξον· πρὸς εὔνους γὰρ φράσεις.   335

ΦΙΛΟΚΛΕΩΝ

οὑμὸς υἱός. ἀλλὰ μὴ βοᾶτε· καὶ γὰρ τυγχάνει
οὑτοσὶ πρόσθεν καθεύδων. ἀλλ' ὕφεσθε τοῦ τόνου.

ΧΟΡΟΣ

τοῦ δ' ἔφεξιν, ὦ μάταιε, ταῦτα δρᾶν σε βούλεται;
ἢ τίνα πρόφασιν ἔχων;

ΦΙΛΟΚΛΕΩΝ

οὐκ ἐᾷ μ', ὦνδρες, δικάζειν οὐδὲ δρᾶν οὐδὲν κακόν,   340
ἀλλά μ' εὐωχεῖν ἕτοιμός ἐστ'· ἐγὼ δ' οὐ βούλομαι.

ΧΟΡΟΣ

τοῦτ' ἐτόλμησ' ὁ μιαρὸς χα-
νεῖν ὁ Δημολογοκλέων ὁδί,

335 πρὸς εὔνους γ. φ.] The chorus sympathize with him in his prison, much as the ocean nymphs do with Prometheus in his strait. Cf. Aesch. *Prom. Vinct.* 128, &c.

337 τόνου.] Met. from ships, says the Scholiast: *i.e.* from their ropes. It might be from stringed instruments: 'loosen the tension,' and so 'lower the tone.' There is the same doubt as to the metaphor in *Eq.* 532. Herodotus uses the word of the tension of the ropes in the bridge across the Hellespont, VII. 36.

338 ἔφεξιν.] For the accusative see note on *Eq.* 783. For the sense, τίνος ἕνεκεν (Schol. R.) is the best Greek comment. ἔφεξις should be taken in the sense of 'aim, intent,' from ἐπέχειν, in such uses as ἐπέχειν τόξον, ἐπέχειν τὸν νοῦν. 'With what aim, aiming at what, does he wish, &c.' It is generally interpreted as =πρόφασις=ἐπισχεσίη (Hom. *Odyss.* φ. 71), 'grounds,' 'something to rest upon.' The gloss of Hesychius χάριν, ἕνεκα, ἐποχήν, πρόφασιν, is not decisive against the sense of 'final aim;' and we get thus some distinction between ἔφεξις and πρόφασις in our text. 'What is his aim in this? What fair grounds has he to go upon?'

339 ἢ τίνα π. ἔ.] This line some would eject. But vv. 334—345 = vv. 365—378, and ἢ—ἔχων answers tolerably to ἀλλ'...γνάθον, if we take Meineke's ἢ τίνα for τίνα.

342 Δημολογοκλέων.] 'Quasi sui oblitus hoc dicit chorus.' Bergl. Dindorf calls this 'inepta interpretatio.' But it seems about right. The chorus probably, in their anger, are meant to use a word that shall end like Bdelycleon, the man's true name, without looking to the force of that termination. They mean δημολόγος in a bad sense, not reflecting that it will apply to their friends more than to their foes. δημοκλονοκλέων or δημογελοκλέων, conj. Reisk. The Scholiast explains by τύραννος καὶ ἀρχοντιῶν.

ὅτι λέγεις τι περὶ τῶν νε- 343
ῶν ἀληθές. οὐ γὰρ ἄν ποθ᾽
οὗτος ἀνὴρ τοῦτ᾽ ἐτόλμη-
σεν λέγειν, εἰ
μὴ ξυνωμότης τις ἦν. 345
ἀλλ᾽ ἐκ τούτων ὥρα τινά σοι ζητεῖν καινὴν ἐπίνοιαν,
ἥτις σε λάθρα τἀνδρὸς τουδὶ καταβῆναι δεῦρο ποιήσει.

ΦΙΛΟΚΛΕΩΝ

τίς ἂν οὖν εἴη; ζητεῖθ᾽ ὑμεῖς, ὡς πᾶν ἂν ἔγωγε ποιοίην·
οὕτω κιττῶ διὰ τῶν σανίδων μετὰ χοιρίνης περιελθεῖν.

ΧΟΡΟΣ

ἔστιν ὀπὴ δῆθ᾽ ἥντιν᾽ ἂν ἔνδοθεν οἷός τ᾽ εἴης διορύξαι, 350
εἶτ᾽ ἐκδῦναι ῥάκεσιν κρυφθείς, ὥσπερ πολύμητις Ὀδυσσεύς;

ΦΙΛΟΚΛΕΩΝ

πάντα πέφρακται κοὐκ ἔστιν ὀπῆς οὐδ᾽ εἰ σέρφῳ διαδῦναι.
ἀλλ᾽ ἄλλο τι δεῖ ζητεῖν ὑμᾶς· ὀπίαν δ᾽ οὐκ ἔστι γενέσθαι.

ΧΟΡΟΣ

μέμνησαι δῆθ᾽, ὅτ᾽ ἐπὶ στρατιᾶς κλέψας ποτὲ τοὺς ὀβελίσκους

345 ξυνωμότης.] Cleon is always charging 'conspiracy' on his enemies. Cf. *Eq.* 236, 257: and below vv. 483, 488, 495, 507.

349 σανίδων.] τῶν περιεχουσῶν τὰ ὀνόματα τῶν εἰσαχθησομένων εἰς τὸ δικαστήριον. Schol. He wants to go the round of these notices, that he may know what suits are coming on, and so may come into court prepared for the business he has to do. Some however (with another explanation of the Scholiast) take σανίδων here = δρυφάκτων, the rails or barriers. But cf. below, 848, where the σανίδες and γραφαὶ are brought out together: which makes for the first interpretation.

350 διορύξαι.] Meineke's διαλέξαι is from Hesychius: who however when he explains διαλέξαι by διορύξαι may only have been referring to *Lysistr.* 720, διαλέγουσαν τὴν ὀπήν, 'widening the hole,' and may not have meant to imply that the exact infinitive διαλέξαι was in Aristophanes.

351 ῥάκεσιν, κ.τ.λ.] Cf. Hom. *Od.* δ. 245, σπεῖρα κάκ᾽ ἀμφ᾽ ὤμοισι βαλών, οἰκῆϊ ἐοικώς, ἀνδρῶν δυσμενέων κατέδυ πόλιν εὐρυάγυιαν, and Eur. *Hec.* 239, οἶσθ᾽ ἡνίκ᾽ ἦλθες Ἰλίου κατάσκοπος, δυσχλαινίᾳ τ᾽ ἄμορφος, ὀμμάτων τ᾽ ἄπο φόνου σταλαγμοὶ σὴν κατέσταζον γένυν. And his later appearance in the beggar character in the *Odyssey* may also be meant.

353 ὀπίαν.] There is a pun on the double derivation from ὀπὸς or ὀπή; and possibly (as Florens thinks) an allusion to the sourness of the dicast in ὀπίας from ὀπός. He cannot get out through the hole; and he cannot be as sharp and sour as he would fain be with those brought before him.

ΑΡΙΣΤΟΦΑΝΟΤΣ

ἵεις σαυτὸν κατὰ τοῦ τείχους ταχέως, ὅτε Νάξος ἑάλω; 355

ΦΙΛΟΚΛΕΩΝ

οἶδ'· ἀλλὰ τί τοῦτ'; οὐδὲν γὰρ τοῦτ' ἐστὶν ἐκείνῳ προσ-
όμοιον.
ἥβων γὰρ κἀδυνάμην κλέπτειν, ἰσχυόν τ' αὐτὸς ἐμαυτοῦ,
κοὐδείς μ' ἐφύλαττ', ἀλλ' ἐξῆν μοι
φεύγειν ἀδεῶς. νῦν δὲ ξὺν ὅπλοις
ἄνδρες ὁπλῖται διαταξάμενοι 360
κατὰ τὰς διόδους σκοπιωροῦνται,
τὼ δὲ δύ' αὐτῶν ἐπὶ ταῖσι θύραις
ὥσπερ με γαλῆν κρέα κλέψασαν
τηροῦσιν ἔχοντ' ὀβελίσκους.

ΧΟΡΟΣ

ἀλλὰ καὶ νῦν ἐκπόριζε 365
μηχανὴν ὅπως τάχισθ'· ἕ-
ως γάρ, ὦ μελίττιον.

ΦΙΛΟΚΛΕΩΝ

διατραγεῖν τοίνυν κράτιστόν ἐστί μοι τὸ δίκτυον.
ἡ δέ μοι Δίκτυννα συγγνώμην ἔχοι τοῦ δικτύου.

ΧΟΡΟΣ

ταῦτα μὲν πρὸς ἀνδρός ἐστ' ἄνοντος ἐς σωτηρίαν.

355 **Νάξος ἑάλω.**] By Cimon (cf. Thuc. I. 98), about fifty years before this play. Cf. v. 283. From such references we may infer the chorus to be old men of about seventy years.

357 **ἰσχυόν τ' αὐτὸς ἐμαυτοῦ.**] Either 'I had my own proper strength,' was not the weakling I now am; or 'was lord of my own limbs and body.' Mitchell. In this latter case ἰσχύειν would govern a genitive after the analogy of ἄρχειν, κρατεῖν, and such verbs. That ἰσχυον=ἰσχυρότερος ἦν (as L. and S. say) is unlikely. Besides, would not ἰσχυρότερος ἦν αὐτὸς ἐμαυτοῦ mean naturally, 'I was stronger than my former self, than I was *before* that time,' not 'than my present self, than I am *now*'?

363 **γαλῆν.**] Cf. *Pac.* 1151, where the wife is bidden to bring out the meat, εἴ τι μὴ 'ξήνεγκεν αὐτῶν ἡ γαλῆ τῆς ἑσπέρας. For the arrangement ὥσπερ με γαλῆν cf. *Nub.* 257, ὥσπερ με τὸν 'Αθάμανθ' ὅπως μὴ θύσετε.

364 **τηροῦσιν ἔχοντ'.**] For dual with plural cf. *Nub.* 1506, παθόντε... ὑβρίζετε.

368 **Δίκτυννα, κ.τ.λ.**] May the patroness of nets excuse me for tearing this net.

369 **ἄνοντος.**] Cf. Aesch. *Fr.* 145, οὔτ' ἄν τι θύῳς οὔτ' ἐπισπένδων ἄνοις; and Eur. *Andr.* 1132, ἀλλ' οὐδὲν ἦνεν.

ἀλλ' ἔπαγε τὴν γνάθον. 370

ΦΙΛΟΚΛΕΩΝ
διατέτρωκται τοῦτό γ'. ἀλλὰ μὴ βοᾶτε μηδαμῶς,
ἀλλὰ τηρώμεσθ' ὅπως μὴ Βδελυκλέων αἰσθήσεται.

ΧΟΡΟΣ
μηδὲν, ὦ τᾶν, δέδιθι. μηδέν·
ὡς ἐγὼ τοῦτόν γ', ἐὰν γρύ-
ξῃ τι, ποιήσω δακεῖν τὴν
καρδίαν καὶ τὸν περὶ ψυ- 375
χῆς δρόμον δραμεῖν, ἵν' εἰδῇ
μὴ πατεῖν τὰ
τῶν θεῶν ψηφίσματα.
ἀλλ' ἐξάψας διὰ τῆς θυρίδος τὸ καλώδιον εἶτα καθίμα
δήσας σαυτὸν καὶ τὴν ψυχὴν ἐμπλησάμενος Διοπείθους 380

ΦΙΛΟΚΛΕΩΝ
ἄγε νυν, ἢν αἰσθομένῳ τούτῳ ζητητόν μ' ἐσκαλαμᾶσθαι
κἀνάσπαστον ποιεῖν εἴσω, τί ποιήσετε; φράζετε νυνί.

ΧΟΡΟΣ
ἀμυνοῦμέν σοι τὸν πρινώδη θυμὸν ἅπαντες καλέσαντες,
ὥστ' οὐ δυνατόν σ' εἴργειν ἔσται· τοιαῦτα ποιήσομεν ἡμεῖς.

374 δακεῖν τ. κ.] 'To gnaw his heart' in vexation. Cf. *Nub.* 1369.
378 τῶν θεῶν.] Vulg. ταῖν θεαῖν; which would mean Ceres and Proserpine. ψηφίσματα seems by way of surprise for μυστήρια. The Scholiast has the dual. Meineke, Cobet, and some others τοῖν θεοῖν. Probably whether dual or plural be in the text, Ceres and Proserpine are specially meant. Schömann (*De Com. Ath.* p. 249) says, 'τὰ ταῖν θεαῖν ψηφίσματα dicit facete pro τοὺς τ. θ. νόμους, de pietate erga parentes, quae ideo earum dearum Cereris atque Proserpinae, lex dici poterat, quoniam omnem in vita et moribus iis acceptam referebant, mysteriaque iis etiam in hujus rei memoriam celebrabant.'
380 Διοπείθους.] The Scholiast on *Av.* 989, ὁ μέγας Διοπείθης, quotes from Phrynichus ἀνὴρ χορεύει, καὶ τὰ τοῦ θεοῦ καλά. βούλει Διοπείθη μεταδράμω καὶ τύμπανα; and from Amipsias Διοπείθει τῷ παραμαινομένῳ. Hence it is plain that ψυχὴν ἐμπλ. Δ. means 'having filled your soul with raging fury.' Cf. *Ach.* 484, καταπιὼν Εὐριπίδην. The Scholiast further says that Diopithes was an orator; and in the *Knights* (v. 1085) he, or a namesake, is spoken of as maimed (κυλλὸς), or as bribed.
381 ἐσκαλαμᾶσθαι.] Below, at v. 609, ἐκκαλαμᾶται is used, but not so literally. 'arundo' in Latin bears the same sense as κάλαμος in this use.
383 πρινώδη.] Cf. *Ach.* 180, στιπτοὶ γέροντες, πρίνινοι, ἀτεράμονες.

ΑΡΙΣΤΟΦΑΝΟΥΣ

ΦΙΛΟΚΛΕΩΝ

δράσω τοίνυν ὑμῖν πίσυνος· καὶ μανθάνετ'· ἤν τι πάθω
'γώ,   385
ἀνελόντες καὶ κατακλαύσαντες θεῖναί μ' ὑπὸ τοῖσι δρυ-
φάκτοις.

ΧΟΡΟΣ

οὐδὲν πείσει· μηδὲν δείσῃς. ἀλλ', ὦ βέλτιστε, καθίει
σαυτὸν θαρρῶν κἀπευξάμενος τοῖσι πατρῴοισι θεοῖσιν.

ΦΙΛΟΚΛΕΩΝ

ὦ Λύκε δέσποτα, γείτων ἥρως· σὺ γὰρ οἷσπερ ἐγὼ κε-
χάρησαι,
τοῖς δακρύοισιν τῶν φευγόντων ἀεὶ καὶ τοῖς ὀλοφυρμοῖς· 390
ᾤκησας γοῦν ἐπίτηδες ἰὼν ἐνταῦθ', ἵνα ταῦτ' ἀκροῷο,
κἀβουλήθης μόνος ἡρώων παρὰ τὸν κλάοντα καθῆσθαι.
ἐλέησον καὶ σῶσον νυνὶ τὸν σαυτοῦ πλησιόχωρον·
κοὐ μή ποτέ σου παρὰ τὰς κάννας οὐρήσω μηδ' ἀποπάρδω.

ΒΔΕΛΥΚΛΕΩΝ

οὗτος, ἐγείρου.

ΣΩΣΙΑΣ

τί τὸ πρᾶγμ';

386 δρυφάκτοις.] Even in death he would be in the court. Cf. *Eq.* 675 for δρύφακτοι.

387 οὐδὲν πείσει.] 'You'll come to no harm = you'll not die:' ἤν τι πάθω 'γὼ above is the common euphemism, 'If anything should happen to me' = 'If I should die.'

389 Λύκε.] The hero Lycus, son of Pandion, had a statue close to the court, and appears to have been a patron of the courts generally. Cf. below, v. 819. Also Pollux names a special court as τὸ ἐπὶ Λύκῳ δικαστήριον.

390 τοῖς δακρύοισιν, κ.τ.λ.] Generally tears and wailings were thought out of place and displeasing at shrines and temples: but Lycus, he argues, must delight in such, as he has settled himself there.

394 κάννας.] 'reed-mats,' ψιάθους. Schol. Others think it simply means 'a wattled fence.' And a protecting enclosure round the statue of Lycus, whether of mats hung up, or of lattice work, seems to suit the passage.

395—470. Bdelycleon discovers his father escaping, raises the alarm, and they keep him back. The Chorus come to his rescue; Bdelycleon summons more slaves; and, after a scuffle, the Chorus are beaten back, exclaiming loudly at the conspiracy and tyranny.

ΣΦΗΚΕΣ.

ΒΔΕΛΥΚΛΕΩΝ
ὥσπερ φωνή μέ τις ἐγκεκύκλωται, 395
ΣΩΣΙΑΣ
μῶν ὁ γέρων πη διαδύεται αὖ;
ΒΔΕΛΥΚΛΕΩΝ
μὰ Δί᾽ οὐ δῆτ᾽, ἀλλὰ καθιμᾷ
αὑτὸν δήσας.
ΣΩΣΙΑΣ
ὦ μιαρώτατε, τί ποιεῖς; οὐ μὴ καταβήσει;
ΒΔΕΛΥΚΛΕΩΝ
ἀνάβαιν᾽ ἀνύσας κατὰ τὴν ἑτέραν καὶ ταισιν φυλλάσι παῖε,
ἤν πως πρύμνην ἀνακρούσηται πληγεὶς ταῖς εἰρεσιώναις.
ΦΙΛΟΚΛΕΩΝ
οὐ ξυλλήψεσθ᾽ ὁπόσοισι δίκαι τῆτες μέλλουσιν ἔσεσθαι, 400
ὦ Σμικυθίων καὶ Τισιάδη καὶ Χρήμων καὶ Φερέδειπνε;
πότε δ᾽, εἰ μὴ νῦν, ἐπαρήξετέ μοι, πρίν μ᾽ εἴσω μᾶλλον
ἄγεσθαι;
ΧΟΡΟΣ
εἰπέ μοι, τί μέλλομεν κινεῖν ἐκείνην τὴν χολήν,
ἥνπερ, ἡνίκ᾽ ἄν τις ἡμῶν ὀργίσῃ τὴν σφηκιάν;
νῦν ἐκεῖνο νῦν ἐκεῖνο 405

395 ἐγκεκύκλωται.] Rather a curious use of this verb. Euripides uses it of the ether, τοῦ χθόν᾽ ἐγκυκλουμένου αἰθέρος. *Bacch.* 292. Perhaps Aristophanes took it from some poet, Euripides or another, who had spoken of 'a circum-ambient voice.'

396 διαδύεται αὖ.] Dindorf adds the αὖ for the metre. Brunck added οὐ before μὰ Δί᾽. Porson reads διαδὺς ἔλαθεν for διαδύεται: this last Meineke and Hirschig admit.

397 μιαρώτατε, τί ποιεῖς;] μιαρ᾽ ἀνδρῶν, Porson, to avoid the sequence of anapaest after dactyl. It is a nice point to settle whether such a sequence was so utterly inadmissible to an Athenian that we are justified in leaving MSS. in order to avoid it. Cf. notes on *Nub.* 663 and 1407.

398 ἑτέραν.] Sc. θυρίδα. Philocleon was getting down from a window.

399 εἰρεσιώναις.] For these cf. Scholiast on *Eq.* 729.

400—403. He calls on several of his fellow dicasts by name. The names Τισιάδης, from τίσασθαι, and Φερέδειπνος (v. 311, ὁπόθεν τὸ δεῖπνον ἔσται) are significant.

403, 4 τί μέλλομεν.] 'Why do we delay to rouse, &c.' After ἥνπερ supply κινοῦμεν.

405—414. These lines probably

46   ΑΡΙΣΤΟΦΑΝΟΥΣ   [406

τοὐξύθυμον, ᾧ κολαζό-
μεσθα, κέντρον ἐντέτατ' ὀξύ.
ἀλλὰ θαἰμάτια βαλόντες ὡς τάχιστα, παιδία,
θεῖτε καὶ βοᾶτε, καὶ Κλέωνι ταῦτ' ἀγγέλλετε,
καὶ κελεύετ' αὐτὸν ἥκειν   410
ὡς ἐπ' ἄνδρα μισόπολιν
ὄντα κἀπολουμενον, ὅτι
τόνδε λόγον ἐσφέρει,
[ὡς χρὴ] μὴ δικάζειν δίκας.

ΒΔΕΛΥΚΛΕΩΝ

ὦγαθοί, τὸ πρᾶγμ' ἀκούσατ', ἀλλὰ μὴ κεκράγετε.   415

ΧΟΡΟΣ

νὴ Δί' ἐς τὸν οὐρανόν γ'· ὡς τοῦδ' ἐγὼ οὐ μεθήσομαι.

ought to correspond metrically to vv. 463—470: but they do not do so exactly, and it is hardly safe to alter the text to produce a strict agreement.

406 κολαζόμεσθα.] Cf. Plat. *Prot.* 324 C, τιμωροῦνται καὶ κολάζονται. A rare use of the middle form in the present, though in the future tense the middle is the proper Attic form. Cf. above, v. 244.

407 ἐντέτατ' ὀξύ.] This does not content Dindorf, but as the antistrophic verse is also uncertain, he offers no correction. Hermann reads ἐντέταται ὀξύ. Meineke makes this agree with v. 465, by ἐντετάμεθ' ὀξύ here and ἐλάμβαν' ὑπιοῦσα there.

414 ὡς χρή.] Most editors throw these words out; and so the verse would answer to αὐτὸς ἄρχων μόνος.

415 ὦγαθοί, κ.τ.λ.] This scene between Bdelycleon and the enraged Chorus is rather like that between Dicaeopolis and the Acharnian colliers, *Ach.* 284, &c.

416 ὡς τοῦδ' ἐγὼ οὐ μεθήσομαι.] Whether this be given to Bdelycleon, or to the Chorus (and it will make tolerable sense either way, though perhaps the actual holder is more correctly said 'to loose his hold of,' than is he who will not give up his attempt to seize a person), it seems certain that τοῦδε for τόνδε is a proper correction. Dawes pointed out that μεθιέναι, 'to set loose, send from you,' governed the accusative—μεθίεσθαι, 'to loose oneself from, let go one's hold of,' a genitive. The passages which some have brought to support the accus. after μεθίεσθαι are: Soph. *El.* 1277, μή μ' ἀποστερήσῃς τῶν σῶν προσώπων ἡδονὰν μεθέσθαι. Eur. *Med.* 736, τούτοις...ἄγουσιν οὐ μεθεῖ' ἄν ἐκ γαίας ἐμέ. In neither of these passages is the accusative governed by the verb in question (see Elmsley and Porson on the *Medea*, and Jebb on the *Electra*). Brunck also brings Eur. *Iph. in Aul.* 309, ἄφες δὲ τήνδ' ἐμοί. ΜΕ. οὐκ ἄν μεθείμην; which proves nothing; and Eur. *Phoen.* 519, where no doubt ἐκείνου should be read for ἐκεῖνον. The principle of Dawes' rule is so plain, that a few copyists' errors need not weigh against it.

ἐγὼ οὐ.] Cf. *Nub.* 901, ἐγὼ αὐτά: which Dindorf there writes in one word, as by crasis. Editors have not been thoroughly consistent in

ΣΦΗΚΕΣ.

ταῦτα δῆτ' οὐ δεινὰ καὶ τυραννίς ἐστιν ἐμφανής;
ὦ πόλις καὶ Θεώρου θεοισεχθρία,
κεί τις ἄλλος προέστηκεν ὑμῶν κόλαξ.

ΞΑΝΘΙΑΣ

Ἡράκλεις, καὶ κέντρ' ἔχουσιν. οὐχ ὁρᾷς, ὦ δέσποτα; 420

ΒΔΕΛΥΚΛΕΩΝ

οἷς γ' ἀπώλεσαν Φίλιππον ἐν δίκῃ τὸν Γοργίου.

ΧΟΡΟΣ

καὶ σέ γ' αὖθις ἐξολοῦμεν· ἀλλ' ἅπας ἐπίστρεφε
δεῦρο κἀξείρας τὸ κέντρον εἶτ' ἐπ' αὐτὸν ἵεσο,
ξυσταλεὶς, εὔτακτος, ὀργῆς καὶ μένους ἐμπλήμενος,
ὡς ἂν εὖ εἰδῇ τὸ λοιπὸν σμῆνος οἷον ὤργισεν.   425

ΞΑΝΘΙΑΣ

τοῦτο μέντοι δεινὸν ἤδη νὴ Δί', εἰ μαχούμεθα·
ὡς ἔγωγ' αὐτῶν ὁρῶν δέδοικα τὰς ἐγκεντρίδας.

ΧΟΡΟΣ

ἀλλ' ἀφίει τὸν ἄνδρ'· εἰ δὲ μή, φήμ' ἐγὼ

their manner of writing such combinations of vowel sounds: and possibly the original writers were no more so; a rigid uniformity in orthography being a modern refinement.

418 θεοισεχθρία.] The reproachful expression, θεοῖς ἐχθρός, had almost come to be considered one adjective; and from it was formed a noun in -ία. Other readings are θεοσεχθρία, θεοσχθρία, but they do not seem so good; nor do they appear to suit the metre. The lines are composed of four cretics.

421 ἐν δίκῃ.] ἀντὶ τοῦ δικάζοντες. Schol. The prevailing sense of ἐν δίκῃ in Aristophanes (as elsewhere) is 'justly.' Cf. Eq. 257, ἐν δίκῃ γ', ἐπεὶ τὰ κοινὰ πρὶν λαχεῖν κατεσθίεις. And it is not quite certain that here, if the Philippus mentioned was, as the Scholiast says, a traitor and barbarian, Bdelycleon may not mean to hint that his judicial punishment served him right. When this man was condemned does not appear. A passage in The Birds (v. 1700), βάρβαροι δ' εἰσὶν γένος, Γοργίαι τε καὶ Φίλιπποι, apparently refers to the same person.

422 αὖθις.] 'In another trial, as a second instance.' Holden reads αὐτοῖς, which Meineke adopts.

423 ἵεσο ξυσταλεὶς.] Cf. Eccl. 93, ξυστειλάμεναι θαἰμάτια, and 486, πρὸς ταῦτα συστέλλου σεαυτήν. Not very unlike this use, though more specially nautical, is Eq. 432, ἐγὼ δὲ συστείλας γε τοὺς ἀλλᾶντας εἶτ' ἀφήσω κατὰ κῦμ' ἐμαυτὸν οὔριον κλάειν σε μακρὰ κελεύσας.

424 ἐμπλήμενος.] For the form cf. Eccl. 51, τριχίδων ἐμπλήμενος.

428. The metre is the same as that of 418, 419, each line being composed of four cretics. In v. 425 -νας μακαρι- is an equivalent for a

τὰς χελώνας μακαριεῖν σε τοῦ δέρματος.

ΦΙΛΟΚΛΕΩΝ

εἶἐν νυν, ὦ ξυνδικασταί, σφῆκες ὀξυκάρδιοι, 430
οἱ μὲν ἐς τὸν πρωκτὸν αὐτῶν ἐσπέτεσθ' ὠργισμένοι,
οἱ δὲ τὠφθαλμὼ 'ν κύκλῳ κεντεῖτε καὶ τοὺς δακτύλους.

ΒΔΕΛΥΚΛΕΩΝ

ὦ Μίδα καὶ Φρὺξ βοήθει δεῦρο καὶ Μασυντία,
καὶ λάβεσθε τουτουὶ καὶ μὴ μεθῆσθε μηδενί·
εἰ δὲ μή, 'ν πέδαις παχείαις οὐδὲν ἀριστήσετε. 435
ὡς ἐγὼ πολλῶν ἀκούσας οἶδα θρίων τὸν ψόφον.

ΧΟΡΟΣ

εἰ δὲ μὴ τοῦτον μεθήσεις, ἕν τί σοι παγήσεται.

ΦΙΛΟΚΛΕΩΝ

ὦ Κέκροψ ἥρως ἄναξ, τὰ πρὸς ποδῶν Δρακοντίδη,

cretic in time, two short syllables being in place of one long.

429 χελώνας, κ.τ.λ.] This prophecy is fulfilled later on in the play, when Xanthias comes in (at v. 1292) exclaiming, ἰὼ χελῶναι μακάριαι τοῦ δέρματος, after being beaten by his master.

432 τὠφθαλμὼ 'ν.] Cf. *Nub.* 943, τὠφθαλμὼ κεντούμενος ὥσπερ ὑπ' ἀνθρηνῶν...ἀπολεῖται. Elmsley's 'ν κύκλῳ for κύκλῳ seems worthy of acceptation, because MS. Rav. has τὠφθαλμῶν: otherwise the simple dative κύκλῳ might be confirmed by many examples, and would be satisfactory.

433 Μίδα.] Midas, Phryx, and Masyntias are names of slaves.

435 εἰ δὲ μή.] 'Else,' if you do not (obey me and not let him go). Instances like this are frequent, where, a prohibition having gone before, we cannot render εἰ δὲ μή literally without some ambiguity, because of the preceding negative.

οὐδὲν ἀριστήσετε.] Breakfast seems to have been the meal on the absence of which the Greeks most comment as a hardship. Cf. Theocr. *Idyll.* I. 51, πρὶν ἢ 'κράτιστον ἐπὶ ξηροῖσι καθίξῃ, where some read 'νάριστον (ἀνάριστον), 'breakfastless,' and the sense comes out much the same with either reading. Cf. also Aesch. *Ag.* 351, πόνος νῆστις πρὸς ἀριστοισιν ὧν ἔχει πόλις τάσσει.

436 θρίων.] There was a proverb, πολλῶν ἐγὼ θρίων ψόφους ἀκήκοα. Fig-leaves crackle loudly when burnt: hence the proverb, of empty and noisy threats. Schol.

437 τοῦτον μεθήσεις.] See above, at v. 416, for μεθεῖναι and μεθέσθαι.

ἕν τί σοι.] For the tmesis cf. *Nub.* 792, ἀπὸ γὰρ ὀλοῦμαι. *Ach.* 295, κατά σε χώσομεν.

438 Δρακοντίδῃ.] The fable of Cecrops' serpent shape below is found in Ov. *Met.* 255, and elsewhere. But Richter explains Δρακ. differently: 'the poet compares the oft invoked god to the oft accused Dracontides,' for whom cf. v. 157. But the older explanation seems the better; and the reference to Dracontides very doubtful.

454]   ΣΦΗΚΕΣ.   49

περιορᾷς οὕτω μ' ὑπ' ἀνδρῶν βαρβάρων χειρούμενον,
οὓς ἐγὼ 'δίδαξα κλάειν τέτταρ' ἐς τὴν χοίνικα;   440

ΧΟΡΟΣ

εἶτα δῆτ' οὐ πόλλ' ἔνεστι δεινὰ τῷ γήρᾳ κακά;
δηλαδή· καὶ νῦν γε τούτω τὸν παλαιὸν δεσπότην
πρὸς βίαν χειροῦσιν, οὐδὲν τῶν πάλαι μεμνημένοι
διφθερῶν κἀξωμίδων, ἃς οὗτος αὐτοῖς ἠμπόλα,
καὶ κυνᾶς· καὶ τοὺς πόδας χειμῶνος ὄντος ὠφέλει,   445
ὥστε μὴ ριγῶν ἑκάστοτ'· ἀλλὰ τούτοις γ' οὐκ ἔνι
οὐδ' ἐν ὀφθαλμοῖσιν αἰδὼς τῶν παλαιῶν ἐμβάδων.

ΦΙΛΟΚΛΕΩΝ

οὐκ ἀφήσεις οὐδὲ νυνί μ', ὦ κάκιστον θηρίον;
οὐδ' ἀναμνησθεὶς ὅθ' εὑρὼν τοὺς βότρυς κλέπτοντά σε
προσαγαγὼν πρὸς τὴν ἐλάαν ἐξέδειρ' εὖ κἀνδρικῶς,   450
ὥστε σε ζηλωτὸν εἶναι, σὺ δ' ἀχάριστος ἦσθ' ἄρα.
ἀλλ' ἄνες με καὶ σὺ καὶ σύ, πρὶν τὸν υἱὸν ἐκδραμεῖν.

ΧΟΡΟΣ

ἀλλὰ τούτων μὲν τάχ' ἡμῖν δώσετον καλὴν δίκην,
οὐκέτ' ἐς μακράν, ἵν' εἰδῆθ' οἷόν ἐστ' ἀνδρῶν τρόπος

439 βαρβάρων.] He calls to the national hero to aid him against the foreign slaves, Mida, Phryx, and the rest.

440 κλάειν τέτταρ' ἐς τὴν χοίνικα.] 'To weep four times to the choenix,' that is, while kneading four loaves to the choenix of flour, which the Scholiast says was the regular proportion. The slave worked at kneading four loaves to the choenix, bemoaning his hard labour the while with a gush of tears for each loaf. But χοῖνιξ also means a kind of stocks, cf. *Plut.* 276, τὰς χοίνικας καὶ τὰς πέδας ποθοῦσαι. A pun on the two senses may possibly be intended; but the exact meaning of 'weeping four times (when put) into the stocks' is not clear. With κλάειν, τέτταρα, *Ach.* 2, ᾔσθην τέτταρα, may be compared.

442 δηλαδή.] Cobet's δῆλα δ', εἰ καὶ νῦν γε (accepted by Meineke), if not necessary, is very neat.

443 οὐδὲν κ.τ.λ.] The Chorus upbraid the slaves with want of gratitude for clothes given to them. Their master afterwards reckons even the beatings that they got as grounds for gratitude.

444 κἀξωμίδων.] ἱμάτια δουλικὰ καὶ ἑτερομάσχαλα. Schol.

445 πόδας ὠφέλει.] Cf. *Eq.* 874, εὐνούστατόν τε τῇ πόλει καὶ τοῖσι δακτύλοισιν, of the sausage-seller, after his gift to Demus of a pair of shoes.

450 προσαγαγὼν κ.τ.λ.] The culprit was tied up to an olive-tree, and received such a thrashing as any one might envy. εὖ κἀνδρικῶς occurs in the same collocation in *Eq.* 379.

451 ἀχάριστος ἦσθ' ἄρα.] 'You *after all* were thankless:' I was not earning the gratitude I had a right to expect, and thought at the time I should get.

ΑΡΙΣΤΟΦΑΝΟΥΣ [455

ὀξυθύμων καὶ δικαίων καὶ βλεπόντων κάρδαμα. 455

ΒΔΕΛΥΚΛΕΩΝ

παῖε παῖ', ὦ Ξανθία, τοὺς σφῆκας ἀπὸ τῆς οἰκίας.

ΞΑΝΘΙΑΣ

ἀλλὰ δρῶ τοῦτ'· ἀλλὰ καὶ σὺ τῦφε πολλῷ τῷ καπνῷ.

ΣΩΣΙΑΣ

οὐχὶ σοῦσθ'; οὐκ ἐς κόρακας; οὐκ ἄπιτε; παῖε τῷ ξύλῳ.

ΞΑΝΘΙΑΣ

καὶ σὺ προσθεὶς Αἰσχίνην ἔντυφε τὸν Σελλαρτίου.
ἆρ' ἐμέλλομέν ποθ' ὑμᾶς ἀποσοβήσειν τῷ χρόνῳ. 460

ΒΔΕΛΥΚΛΕΩΝ

ἀλλὰ μα Δί', οὐ ῥᾳδίως οὕτως ἂν αὐτοὺς διέφυγες,
εἴπερ ἔτυχον τῶν μελῶν τῶν Φιλοκλέους βεβρωκότες.

ΧΟΡΟΣ

ἆρα δῆτ' οὐκ αὐτὰ δῆλα
τοῖς πένησιν, ἡ τυραννὶς
ὡς λάθρα μ' ἐλάμβαν' ὑπιοῦσα; 465

---

455 **βλεπόντων κάρδαμα.**] So νᾶπυ βλέπειν, πυρρίχην βλέπειν (*Av.* 1169), ναύφρακτον βλέπειν (*Ach.* 95), &c.

456. Bdelycleon has been away for a short time, and now comes out again, encouraging the slaves to drive away the assailants.

457 **ἀλλὰ καὶ σύ.**] To Sosias. Meineke arranges the dialogue differently, without Sosias.

458 **σοῦσθ'.**] Nearly as σοῦ σοῦ above at v. 209. But Aeschylus and Sophocles both use this word of 'haste,' without any notion of driving away: *e.g.* Aesch. *S. c. Theb.* 31, σοῦσθε σὺν παντευχίᾳ: and Soph. *Aj.* 1414, σούσθω, βάτω.

459 **Αἰσχίνην.**] The same as the son of Sellus mentioned above at v. 325. He was καπνώδης διὰ τὴν ἀλαζονείαν. Also the Scholiast finds a reference to σέλας, 'blaze,' in the altered name of the man's father (which he spells Σελάρτιος): ὁ γὰρ καπνὸς τοῦ σέλαος γέννημα, 'smoke is born of blazing fire:' and therefore the smoky Aeschines is fitly ' son of Blazius.'

460 **ἆρ' ἐμέλλομεν.**] Cf. *Ach.* 347, *Nub.* 1301.

462 **Φιλοκλέους.**] ὡς Φιλοκλέους ἀγρίου ὄντος ἐν τῇ μελοποιίᾳ. εἴπερ τὴν πικρίαν αὐτοῦ εἶχον, οὐκ ἂν ῥᾳδίως αὐτοὺς διέφυγες. Schol. The phrase καταπιὼν Εὐριπίδην, *Ach.* 484, expresses the same idea of imbibing a poet's spirit. Cf. also above, v. 380. And Homer's δράκων βεβρωκὼς κακὰ φάρμακ' (*Il.* χ. 94) may be added in illustration: as the serpent 'got venom from his food, and bitter fury within him,' so were this company to be bitter and keen on Philoclean diet. For Philocles cf. *Thesm.* 168, ταῦτ' ἆρ' ὁ Φιλοκλέης αἰσχρὸς ὢν αἰσχρῶς ποιεῖ.

465 **ὡς λάθρα μ' ἐλάμβαν' ὑπιοῦσα.**] This line has to agree with v. 407 in metre. MSS. and editors

εἰ σύ γ', ὦ πόνῳ πονηρὲ καὶ κομηταμυνία,
τῶν νόμων ἡμᾶς ἀπείργεις ὧν ἔθηκεν ἡ πόλις,
οὔτε τιν' ἔχων πρόφασιν
οὔτε λόγον εὐτράπελον,
αὐτὸς ἄρχων μόνος. 470

ΒΔΕΛΥΚΛΕΩΝ
ἔσθ' ὅπως ἄνευ μάχης καὶ τῆς κατοξείας βοῆς
ἐς λόγους ἔλθοιμεν ἀλλήλοισι καὶ διαλλαγάς;

ΧΟΡΟΣ
σοὺς λόγους, ὦ μισόδημε καὶ μοναρχίας ἐρῶν,
καὶ ξυνὼν Βρασίδᾳ, καὶ φορῶν κράσπεδα 475
στεμμάτων, τὴν θ' ὑπήνην ἄκουρον τρέφων;

ΒΔΕΛΥΚΛΕΩΝ
νὴ Δί' ἦ μοι κρεῖττον ἐκστῆναι τὸ παράπαν τοῦ πατρὸς
μᾶλλον ἢ κακοῖς τοσούτοις ναυμαχεῖν ὁσημέραι.

vary in the details: the above is Meineke's. λάθρᾳ γ' ἐλάνθανε, the common reading, seems tautological.
466 πόνῳ πονηρέ.] Cf. *Lys*. 350, ὦνδρες πόνῳ πονηροί. Such alliterations pleased the Greek ear. Cf. note on *Nub*. 6.
κομηταμυνία.] κομᾶν = μέγα φρονεῖν: of Amynias we shall have more at v. 1267.
469 εὐτράπελον.] 'Ready, ingenious,' and so 'plausible.' Possibly the chorus of dicasts would have borne resignedly being tyrannized over, had their enemy defeated them by some dexterous plea, such as they were wont to admire in court. But εὐτράπελος is not always used in a bad sense: cf. Thuc. II. 41, where it is Pericles' boast that to the Athenian beyond all the world it belongs ἐπὶ πλεῖστα εἴδη μάλιστ' εὐτραπέλως τὸ σῶμα αὔταρκες παρέχεσθαι.
470—547. Bdelycleon proposes a conference, to settle matters amicably. At first the chorus will have no compromise with conspirators;

but after some talk it is agreed that Philocleon shall advocate the cause of the dicasts, and shew that their life is the most desirable. The chorus encourage him to do his best in their defence.
473 ἐρῶν.] With the vulg. ἐραστὰ this line did not correspond to the trochaic v. 417. Yet, for the sense, ἐραστὰ comes better after μισόδημε, and the correction in these cases to perfect the metrical correspondence is often a doubtful matter.
475 ξυνὼν Βρασίδᾳ.] Cf. *Pac.* 640, φρονοῖ τὰ Βρασίδου. Hems or edgings of wool were worn, says the Scholiast, by the Laconians. The beard and moustache they also allowed to grow in some manner peculiar to themselves. Hence all these particulars denote τὸ λακωνίζειν.
479 κακοῖς τ. ναυμαχεῖν.] 'Face such a broadside of troubles' we might say. Naval metaphors are of course rife at Athens.

52   ΑΡΙΣΤΟΦΑΝΟΥΣ   [480

ΧΟΡΟΣ

οὐδὲ μέν γ' οὐδ' ἐν σελίνῳ σοὐστὶν οὐδ' ἐν πηγάνῳ· 480
τοῦτο γὰρ παρεμβαλοῦμεν τῶν τριχοινίκων ἐπῶν.
ἀλλὰ νῦν μὲν οὐδὲν ἀλγεῖς, ἀλλ' ὅταν ξυνήγορος
ταὐτὰ ταῦτά σου καταντλῇ καὶ ξυνωμότας καλῇ.

ΒΔΕΛΤΚΛΕΩΝ

ἆρ' ἄν, ὦ πρὸς τῶν θεῶν, ὑμεῖς ἀπαλλαχθεῖτέ μου;
ἦ δέδοκταί σοι δέρεσθαι καὶ δέρειν δι' ἡμέρας.   485

ΧΟΡΟΣ

οὐδέποτέ γ', οὐχ, ἕως ἄν τι μου λοιπὸν ᾖ,
ὅστις ἡμῶν ἐπὶ τυραννίδ' ὧδ' ἐστάλης.

480 σελίνῳ.] Parsley and rue were planted as a border to gardens; those who had not advanced beyond them were only at the entrance or threshold: hence 'you are only at the parsley,' or 'not yet at the parsley,' is a proverb meaning 'you have only just begun,' or 'you have not yet begun.'

481 τοῦτο γὰρ ... τριχοινίκων ἐπῶν.] 'For this three-quart phrase will we throw in,' *i.e.* the phrase οὐδὲ μέν γ'...πηγάνῳ. Cf. *Pac.* 521, ῥῆμα μυριάμφορον. The expressions in the former verse may have been taken from some bad poet. Archippus the Scholiast thinks is here attacked. τριχοίνικος evidently means 'capacious, big;' and the chorus are probably led to use their fine phrase by Bdelycleon's expressions before, ναυμαχεῖν ὁσημέραι, and (perhaps) ἐκστῆναι τοῦ πατρός. Richter thinks all these may have been phrases used by Archippus. This poet wrote a play called ὄνου σκιά, which some think is referred to above at v. 191.

482 ἀλλ' ὅταν.] 'But (you will feel it) when.'

483 καταντλῇ.] Cf. Plat. *Rep.* 344 A. ταῦτα εἰπὼν ὁ Θρασύμαχος ἐν νῷ εἶχεν ἀπιέναι, ὥσπερ βαλανεὺς ἡμῶν καταντλήσας κατὰ τῶν ὤτων ἀθρόον καὶ πολὺν τὸν λόγον.

483 ξυνωμότας.] So MS. V; MS. Rav. has an abbreviation which might equally stand for plural or singular. But, on the score of sense, the plural seems better. The orator would use the word in the plural, ξυνωμόται, associating Bdelycleon with accomplices; cf. v. 488, ξυνωμόται, and *Eq.* 628, ξυνωμότας λέγων πιθανώταθ', in a very similar case.

484 ἀπαλλαχθεῖτέ μου.] 'Will you or won't you keep clear of me?' The leading idea of course is that he is to be rid of them rather than they rid of him, though the Greek at first sight looks as if the reverse were the case.

485 σοι.] Thus Bergk reads for vulg. μοι. The Chorus are addressed in the singular in the person of their leader. δ. μοι means 'is it decreed *for* me?' A curious use of the dative after such a verb.

485 δέρεσθαι καὶ δέρειν.] Bergler compares *Ran.* 861, δάκνειν, δάκνεσθαι.

487 ὧδ' ἐστάλης.] The deficient syllable in MSS. before ἐστάλης is supplied in various ways. ἐπὶ τυραννίδι διεστάλης Bentl. ὧδ' is due to Hermann. Either this or Meineke's ἐξεστάλης makes the line agree with v. 429.

ΒΔΕΛΤΚΛΕΩΝ

ὡς ἅπανθ' ὑμῖν τυραννίς ἐστι καὶ ξυνωμόται,
ἤν τε μεῖζον ἤν τ' ἔλαττον πρᾶγμα τις κατηγορῇ,
ἧς ἐγὼ οὐκ ἤκουσα τοὔνομ' οὐδὲ πεντήκοντ' ἐτῶν· 490
νῦν δὲ πολλῷ τοῦ ταρίχους ἐστὶν ἀξιωτέρα·
ὥστε καὶ δὴ τοὔνομ' αὐτῆς ἐν ἀγορᾷ κυλίνδεται.
ἢν μὲν ὠνῆταί τις ὀρφὼς, μεμβράδας δὲ μὴ θέλῃ,
εὐθέως εἴρηχ' ὁ πωλῶν πλησίον τὰς μεμβράδας·
οὗτος ὀψωνεῖν ἔοιχ' ἄνθρωπος ἐπὶ τυραννίδι. 495
ἢν δὲ γήτειον προσαιτῇ ταῖς ἀφύαις ἡδύσματα,
ἡ λαχανόπωλις παραβλέψασά φησι θατέρῳ·
εἰπέ μοι, γήτειον αἰτεῖς; πότερον ἐπὶ τυραννίδι;
ἢ νομίζεις τὰς Ἀθήνας σοὶ φέρειν ἡδύσματα;

488 τυραννίς.] The Athenians, remembering the Pisistratids, were ever on their guard against 'tyranny.' The mutilation of the Hermae in Alcibiades' time was thought ἐπὶ ξυνωμοσίᾳ νεωτέρων πραγμάτων καὶ δήμου καταλύσεως γεγενῆσθαι. Thuc. VI. 27. And Demosthenes (*de Syntaxi*, p. 170) rebukes this suspiciousness, giving instances which, though of course not so absurd as those of Aristophanes, are absurd enough.

490 πεντήκοντ' ἐτῶν.] Fifty years is put as a round number for a long time. The expulsion of the Pisistratids would be considerably more than fifty years before this play; later disturbances and anti-democratical movements would be less than fifty years ago.

491 ἀξιωτέρα.] Cf. *Eq.* 645, 672, for this market sense of ἄξιος.

493—5. If any purchaser prefer one kind of anchovy to another, an absurd political charge is made out of it. The ὀρφὼς was the more delicate kind.

496 ταῖς ἀφύαις ἡδύσματα.] Various are the readings adopted here: ταῖς ἀφ. ἥδυσμά τι, ταῖς ἀφ. ἥδυσμά τις, ταῖς ἀφ. ἡδύσματα, τις ἀφ. ἡδύ-σμά τι, τις ἀφ. ἡδύσματα. The substitution of τις for ταῖς is to avoid the dactyl in the fifth place; for which, however, cf. *Ach.* 318, τὴν κεφαλὴν ἔχων λέγειν: which some editors alter there. ταῖς ἀφύαις ἡδύσματα seems to square best with *Eq.* 678, ἔπειτα ταῖς ἀφύαις ἐδίδουν ἡδύσματα. Of course τις is not necessary as subject to προσαιτῇ; for the same purchaser may be supposed to go on from the fish stall to the vegetable stall. Indeed, the πρὸς in the compound verb rather implies that it is a further demand of the man who has just bought his anchovies.

497 θατέρῳ.] τῷ ἑτέρῳ ὀφθαλμῷ χαλεπῶς ὑποβλεψαμένη, ὡς οὐκ ἄξιον ἡγουμένη τὸν τυχόντα φαγεῖν γήτειον. Schol. Leeks were, the herb-seller meant, a dish for a king; it was not for the like of him to be wanting them, or to expect Athens to supply him therewith. Perhaps in the next line φέρειν contains a notion of paying as tribute (φόρον), and the line might be paraphrased, 'are you a king, and is Athens bound to pay you tribute of leeks to relish your anchovies?'

ΞΑΝΘΙΑΣ

κἀμέ γ' ἡ πόρνη χθὲς εἰσελθόντα τῆς μεσημβρίας, 500
ὅτι κελητίσαι 'κέλευον, ὀξυθυμηθεῖσά μοι
ἤρετ' εἰ τὴν Ἱππίου καθίσταμαι τυραννίδα.

ΒΔΕΛΤΚΛΕΩΝ

ταῦτα γαρ τούτοις ἀκούειν ἡδέ', εἰ καὶ νῦν ἐγω
τὸν πατέρ' ὅτι βούλομαι τούτων ἀπαλλαχθέντα τῶν
ὀρθροφοιτοσυκοφαντοδικοταλαιπώρων τρόπων 505
ζῆν βίον γενναῖον ὥσπερ Μόρυχος, αἰτίαν ἔχω
ταῦτα δρᾶν ξυνωμότης ὢν καὶ φρονῶν τυραννικά.

ΦΙΛΟΚΛΕΩΝ

νὴ Δί' ἐν δίκῃ γ'· ἐγὼ γὰρ οὐδ' ἂν ὀρνίθων γάλα
ἀντὶ τοῦ βίου λάβοιμ' ἂν οὗ με νῦν ἀποστερεῖς·
οὐδὲ χαίρω βατίσιν οὐδ' ἐγχέλεσιν, ἀλλ' ἥδιον ἂν 510
δικίδιον σμικρὸν φάγοιμ' ἂν ἐν λοπάδι πεπνιγμένον.

502 Ἱππίου.] Aristophanes does not fall into the mistake about Hippias, which Thucydides remarks on (I. 20). He mentions Hippias as the tyrant in *Eq.* 447—9, Α. τὸν πάππον εἶναί φημί σου τῶν δορυφόρων. Κ. ποίων; φράσον. Α. τῶν Βυρσίνης τῆς Ἱππίου.

505 ὀρθροφ.] His life was wretched and toilsome (ταλαίπωρος), with early rising and trudging to the courts (ὀρθροφοιτία), and with pettifogging and suits (συκοφαντία, δίκαι). Mitchell calls him 'a home-forsaker, morning-trudger, a suit and cause-distracted man.' The ταλαιπωρία of his present life is contrasted with the joviality of that proposed.

506 Μόρυχος.] Of course it is only in irony that Morychus' life is termed γενναῖος. For this luxurious gourmand cf. *Ach.* 887, *Pac.* 1008, and below, v. 1142. Bdelycleon had promised εὐωχία to his father, cf. above, v. 341.

508 ὀρνίθων γάλα.] A proverb for the utmost luxury. It is promised as such in *Av.* 733, by the chorus of birds (who ought to know all about it), and again at v. 1673.

510 βατίσιν.] Cf. *Pac.* 810, βατιδοσκόποι. Eels (in the next line) were the delight of Morychus, cf. *Ach.* 887, where the Copaic eel is welcomed as φίλη Μορύχῳ.

511 πεπνιγμένον.] The operation of πνῖξις is best described by Herodotus, II. 92, when he is telling how the Egyptians prepare the edible byblus: οἱ δὲ ἂν καὶ κάρτα βούλωνται χρηστῇ τῇ βύβλῳ χρᾶσθαι, ἐν κλιβάνῳ διαφανεῖ πνίξαντες οὕτω τρώγουσι. It is plain that the operation was performed *without water*, in a close-covered vessel, of earthenware probably, and was nearly what cooks now call 'braising,' and was not 'stewing' or 'seething.' There is also a further metaphorical sense in πεπνιγμένον, because, as Bergler says, 'in judiciis innocentes saepe misere vexarentur et paene enecarentur.' The λοπὰς is the dish in which the meat is served after the cooking: but has not apparently any judicial meaning.

ΒΔΕΛΤΚΛΕΩΝ

νὴ Δί᾿ εἰθίσθης γὰρ ἤδεσθαι τοιούτοις πράγμασιν·
ἀλλ᾿ ἐὰν σιγῶν ἀνάσχῃ καὶ μάθῃς ἁγὼ λέγω,
ἀναδιδάξειν οἴομαί σ᾿ ὡς πάντα ταῦθ᾿ ἁμαρτάνεις. 515

ΦΙΛΟΚΛΕΩΝ

ἐξαμαρτάνω δικάζων;

ΒΔΕΛΤΚΛΕΩΝ

καταγελώμενος μὲν οὖν
οὐκ ἐπαΐεις ὑπ᾿ ἀνδρῶν, οὓς σὺ μόνον οὐ προσκυνεῖς.
ἀλλὰ δουλεύων λέληθας.

ΦΙΛΟΚΛΕΩΝ

παῦε δουλείαν λέγων,
ὅστις ἄρχω τῶν ἁπάντων.

ΒΔΕΛΤΚΛΕΩΝ

οὐ σύ γ᾿, ἀλλ᾿ ὑπηρετεῖς
οἰόμενος ἄρχειν· ἐπεὶ δίδαξον ἡμᾶς, ὦ πάτερ,
ἥτις ἡ τιμή ᾿στί σοι καρπουμένῳ τὴν Ἑλλάδα. 520

ΦΙΛΟΚΛΕΩΝ

πάνυ γε· καὶ τούτοισί γ᾿ ἐπιτρέψαι θέλω.

ΒΔΕΛΤΚΛΕΩΝ

καὶ μὴν ἐγώ.

ἄφετε νῦν ἅπαντες αὐτόν.

512. It is all habit, says the son; I can easily shew you that you are quite wrong, and are making yourself a miserable slave.

516 καταγ. μὲν οὖν.] Nay, to say you are wrong is not enough; you are, though you don't see it, a laughing-stock to the demagogues and orators.

518 ἄρχω.] See the passage in *The Knights* (1111—1150), where the Chorus chide Demus for being duped by the orators and demagogues, and he strives to shew that he is not such a fool as he looks.

They allow, however, at the outset ὦ Δῆμε καλὴν γ᾿ ἔχεις ἀρχὴν, ὅτι πάντες ἄνθρωποι δεδίασί σ᾿ ὥσπερ ἄνδρα τύραννον.

520 καρπουμένῳ.] What good do you, as a dicast, get (asks the son) from the revenues coming in from Greece? you only have your paltry three-obol piece: the demagogues take the lion's share.

521 πάνυ γε.] An assent to δίδαξον: 'with all my heart (I will inform you).'

522 ἄφετε.] Spoken to the slaves, who were still guarding him.

ΑΡΙΣΤΟΦΑΝΟΥΣ

ΦΙΛΟΚΛΕΩΝ

καὶ ξίφος γέ μοι δότε·
ἢν γὰρ ἡττηθῶ λέγων σου, περιπεσοῦμαι τῷ ξίφει.

ΒΔΕΛΤΚΛΕΩΝ

εἰπέ μοι, τί δ' ἢν τὸ δεῖνα τῇ διαίτῃ μὴ 'μμένῃς;

ΦΙΛΟΚΛΕΩΝ

μηδέποτε πίοιμ' ἄκρατον μισθὸν ἀγαθοῦ δαίμονος.   525

ΧΟΡΟΣ

νῦν δὴ τὸν ἐκ θἠμετέρου
γυμνασίου δεῖ τι λέγειν
καινόν, ὅπως φανήσει

καὶ ξίφος γέ.] This line is wrongly given to Bdelycleon in some editions. Bergler corrected the arrangement of speakers. Cf. v. 714, where Philocleon has the sword now asked for. And the καὶ ξίφος γέ μοι δότε, 'Ay, and give me a sword,' plainly shews that it is the beginning of another person's speech. Philocleon will, in tragic fashion, like Ajax, fall on his sword, if defeated.

524 **τὸ δεῖνα.**] Cf. *Lys.* 921, καίτοι τὸ δεῖνα ψίαθός ἐστ' ἐξοιστέα, 926, καίτοι τὸ δεῖνα προσκεφάλαιον οὐκ ἔχεις. Also *Pac.* 268, τὸ δεῖνα γὰρ ἀπόλωλ' Ἀθηναίοισιν ἀλετρίβανος. From all these passages it is plain that τὸ δεῖνα is used when a speaker, suddenly recollecting something that hinders or affects the matter in hand, cannot at once in his hurry find words for it, but explains his meaning in the following clause. Thus in the *Lysistrata* we might render it: 'And yet there's what's-its-name still wanted—a mat, I mean, must be brought;' and so too in the other passage. In the *Peace* it is: 'You don't bring the pestle? No, for what's-its-name prevented —I mean, the Athenians' pestle is dead.' And so here, 'And what if what's-its-name were to happen— if, I mean, you were not to abide by the arbitration.' This explanation appears better than that of L. and S., who take τὸ δεῖνα to be a vocative of address to the person; an explanation which seems not applicable satisfactorily to any of the Aristophanic passages, and impossible in some. *Lys.* 1168 may be added, and will be found to be like those above quoted.

525 **ἄκρατον μισθόν.**] Cf. *Eq.* 85, ἄκρατον οἶνον ἀγαθοῦ δαίμονος. The dicast's mind thinks of 'wage' rather than 'wine.' I have not hesitated with Meineke to accept ἄκρατον for ἀκράτου, due to Richter. The confusion of υ and ν is frequent in MSS. The converse change from πεντώβολον to πεντωβόλου is to be accepted in *Eq.* 798. Cf. also *Pac.* 254.

526 **νῦν δή, κ.τ.λ.**] To vv. 526 —545 correspond metrically vv. 631 —647; but some words have been lost near the end of the antistrophe.

528 **φανῆσει.**] This is to be taken with μὴ κατὰ τ. ν. τ. λέγειν. Bdelycleon interrupts to ask for his desk (κίστην), that he may take notes: he then says to the chorus, with reference apparently to their words 'that you may appear' 'But what sort of a man will you appear, if

ΣΦΗΚΕΣ.

ΒΔΕΛΤΚΛΕΩΝ

ἐνεγκάτω μοι δεῦρο τὴν κίστην τις ὡς τάχιστα.
ἀτὰρ φανεῖ ποῖός τις ὤν, ἢν ταῦτα παρακελεύῃ; 530

ΧΟΡΟΣ

μὴ κατὰ τὸν νεανίαν
τόνδε λέγειν. ὁρᾷς γὰρ ὡς
σοὶ μέγας ἐστὶν ἀγὼν
καὶ περὶ τῶν ἁπάντων,
εἴπερ, ὃ μὴ γένοιθ᾽, οὗ- 535
τός σ᾽ ἐθέλει κρατῆσαι.

ΒΔΕΛΤΚΛΕΩΝ

καὶ μὴν ὅσ᾽ ἂν λέξῃ γ᾽ ἁπλῶς μνημόσυνα γράψομαι 'γώ.

ΦΙΛΟΚΛΕΩΝ

τί γὰρ φάθ᾽ ὑμεῖς, ἢν ὁδί με τῷ λόγῳ κρατήσῃ;

ΧΟΡΟΣ

οὐκέτι πρεσβυτῶν ὄχλος 540
χρήσιμος ἔστ᾽ οὐδ᾽ ἀκαρῆ·
σκωπτόμενοι δ᾽ ἂν παισὶν ἐν
ταῖσιν ὁδοῖς ἁπάσαις

you urge him on in this way?' meaning probably that the chorus, as well as their champion, will cut a very different figure after the contest from what they expect. Then the chorus, ignoring his interruption, go on with their directions to Philocleon.

532 λέγειν.] Meineke adopts Hirschig's λέγων. ὅπως φανήσει λέγων, 'that you may appear speaking, be proved to speak,' is perhaps a little better than φ. λέγειν, 'you may appear to speak:' but the construction with infinitive seems admissible, and has all the MS. authority.

533, 4 ἀγών...περὶ τῶν ἁπάντων.] A kind of phrase frequent in exhortations, e.g. Thuc. VII. 61, ὁ μὲν ἀγὼν ὁ μέλλων ἔσται περί τε σωτηρίας καὶ πατρίδος ἑκάστοις.

535 ὃ μὴ γένοιθ᾽.] This refers only to κρατῆσαι, not to the whole phrase, ἐθέλει κρατῆσαι.

537 ὅσ᾽ ἂν λέξῃ γ᾽ ἁπλῶς.] 'Of every word he says.'

541 ἀκαρῆ.] Cf. Av. 1649, τῶν γὰρ πατρῴων οὐδ᾽ ἀκαρῆ μέτεστί σοι. The word is used of time in Nub. 496. The singular is found in Plut. 244, ἐν ἀκαρεῖ χρόνῳ (or χρόνου). And below, at v. 701, ἀκαρὲς is read by many editors, as countenanced by Suidas.

542—5. The very gamins in the street will mock at us. Street boys seem to have been an institution in all lands. Cf. Horace's 'vellunt tibi barbam lascivi pueri.' Meineke's text has been adopted: for Dindorf's is as far from the MSS. by omission as is Meineke's by the conjectural insertion of παισίν.

58 ΑΡΙΣΤΟΦΑΝΟΥΣ [544

θαλλοφόροι καλοίμεθ', ἀν-
τωμοσιῶν κελύφη. 545
ἀλλ' ὦ περὶ τῆς πάσης μέλλων βασιλείας ἀντιλογήσειν
τῆς ἡμετέρας, νυνὶ θαρρῶν πᾶσαν γλῶτταν βασάνιζε.

ΦΙΛΟΚΛΕΩΝ

καὶ μὴν εὐθύς γ' ἀπὸ βαλβίδων περὶ τῆς ἀρχῆς ἀποδείξω
τῆς ἡμετέρας ὡς οὐδεμιᾶς ἥττων ἐστὶν βασιλείας.
τί γὰρ εὔδαιμον καὶ μακαριστὸν μᾶλλον νῦν ἐστὶ δικα-
στοῦ, 550
ἢ τρυφερώτερον, ἢ δεινότερον ζῷον, καὶ ταῦτα γέροντος;
ὃν πρῶτα μὲν ἕρποντ' ἐξ εὐνῆς τηροῦσ' ἐπὶ τοῖσι δρυφάκτοις
ἄνδρες μεγάλοι καὶ τετραπήχεις· κἄπειτ' εὐθὺς προσιόντι
ἐμβάλλει μοι τὴν χεῖρ' ἁπαλήν, τῶν δημοσίων κεκλοφυῖαν·

544 θαλλοφόροι.] Old men were employed to carry branches of olive at the Panathenaic procession, as being useless for any other service. Schol.

545 ἀντωμοσιῶν κελύφη.] For ἀντ. cf. *Dict. Antiq.* p. 55. κελύφη, 'mere husks, empty shells:' their kernel, force, and virtue being now gone.

547 βασάνιζε.] 'Test your full powers of tongue;' *i.e.* do all you know in the way of speech.

548—649. Philocleon describes how he is courted and flattered by the powerful, that they may ensure acquittal when brought before him as a dicast: how he receives all kinds of presents and indulgences; how he and his fellows do what they will, and give account to none: how he is quite worshipped and petted at his own home, and is a very Zeus to the multitude. When he has ended this speech, during which Bdelycleon takes a few notes, and throws in a few remarks, the Chorus, and Philocleon himself, think that the day is won.

548 βαλβίδων.] A favourite metaphor. Cf. *Eq.* 1159, ἄφες ἀπὸ βαλβίδων ἐμέ τε καὶ τουτονί: also *Lys.* 1000, ἀπὸ μιᾶς ὑσπλαγίδος.

551 τρυφερώτερον.] 'Better found in all luxuries, means of gratifying appetite, &c.' The Scholiast's τρυφῆς δεόμενον is a curious mistake. The word is illustrated in detail in vv. 607—619.

δεινότερον.] 'More feared.' Cf vv. 622—630. The more frequent sense perhaps of δεινὸς in Attic Greek when used of persons, is 'clever, cunning:' but the context is decisive for the other meaning here. δεινὸς is first 'fearful,' then by easy transition 'wonderful;' then, of persons, such fear or wonder at them is grounded on their possession of great powers, especially knowledge or cunning.

κ. τ. γέροντος.] 'Even though he be old,' and the old (as the Scholiast notes) are generally incapable of pleasure, and weak.

553 τετραπήχεις.] Used by way of praise in *Ran.* 1014, γενναίους καὶ τετραπήχεις: here rather of great hulking fellows, who have to cringe to the (probably) insignificant-looking little judge. In Theocr. *Id.* xv 17, ἀνὴρ τρισκαιδεκάπηχυς is contemptuous. Persius' 'Fulfennius ingens' (*Sat.* v. 190) is of this six-foot type.

554 τὴν χεῖρ' ἁπαλήν.] Meineke

ἱκετεύουσίν θ' ὑποκύπτοντες, τὴν φωνὴν οἰκτροχοοῦντες· 555
οἴκτειρόν μ', ὦ πάτερ, αἰτοῦμαί σ', εἰ καὐτὸς πώποθ' ὑφείλου
ἀρχὴν ἄρξας ἢ 'πὶ στρατιᾶς τοῖς ξυσσίτοις ἀγοράζων·
ὃς ἔμ' οὐδ' ἂν ζῶντ' ᾔδειν, εἰ μὴ διὰ τὴν προτέραν ἀπόφυξιν.

ΒΔΕΛΥΚΛΕΩΝ
τουτὶ περὶ τῶν ἀντιβολούντων ἔστω τὸ μνημόσυνόν μοι.

ΦΙΛΟΚΛΕΩΝ
εἶτ' εἰσελθὼν ἀντιβοληθεὶς καὶ τὴν ὀργὴν ἀπομορχθείς, 560
ἔνδον τούτων ὧν ἂν φάσκω πάντων οὐδὲν πεποίηκα,
ἀλλ' ἀκροῶμαι πάσας φωνὰς ἱέντων εἰς ἀπόφυξιν.
φέρ' ἴδω, τί γὰρ οὐκ ἔστιν ἀκοῦσαι θώπευμ' ἐνταῦθα δι-
καστῇ;
οἱ μέν γ' ἀποκλάονται πενίαν αὑτῶν καὶ προστιθέασιν
κακὰ πρὸς τοῖς οὖσιν, ἕως ἀνιὼν ἂν ἰσώσῃ τοῖσιν ἐμοῖσιν·

doubtingly proposes τις for τήν. But surely ἀπαλὴν is an indirect predicate: 'he puts his hand in mine (so as to be) soft,' or 'he puts his hand in mine softly.' For the sense, it is much the same as if the adverb had been used. The transition from plural to singular need cause no difficulty: cf. vv. 564, 565, and *Pac.* 639, ἔσειον...τοὺς παχεῖς, αἰτίας ἂν προστιθέντες ὡς φρονοῖ τὰ Βρασίδου. To illustrate the general sense of this passage, Bergler quotes from Xen. *de Rep. Ath.* I. 18, νῦν δ' ἠνάγκασται τὸν δῆμον κολακεύειν τῶν Ἀθηναίων εἷς ἕκαστος τῶν συμμάχων ...καὶ ἀντιβολῆσαι ἀναγκάζεται ἐν τοῖς δικαστηρίοις καὶ εἰσιόντός του ἐπιλαμβάνεσθαι τῆς χειρός. διὰ τοῦτο οὖν οἱ σύμμαχοι δοῦλοι τοῦ δήμου τῶν Ἀθηναίων καθεστᾶσι μᾶλλον.

557 στρατιᾶς.] For thefts on service cf. above, v. 354: also vv. 236—8. But here is rather meant a fraudulent embezzlement of money entrusted to the soldier to purchase provisions for the mess; as ὑφείλου and ἀγοράζων prove: the ὑπὸ denoting a quietness and secrecy in the transaction.

558 ᾔδειν.] For the form cf. *Nub.* 380, ἐλελήθειν.

560 εἰσελθὼν κ.τ.λ.] 'Then, having gone into court and taken my seat as dicast, after these entreaties, &c.' The ἀντιβολίαι came before the going into court. For εἰσελθὼν compare εἰσιόντος in the passage of Xenophon quoted above.

ἀπομορχθείς.] No other metaphorical use of this word is given. ἀποβαλὼν Schol. but it seems to mean 'having had my anger smoothed away,' having been stroked, patted, &c. into lenity.

562. The defendants will say anything and everything to gain acquittal.

565 ἕως ἀνιών.] Dindorf supplies ἀνιών from MS. V, in which the syllable ων is written. But the ι is long in ἀνιῶν in *Eq.* 349, which makes for Meineke's view, who (with Hermann) writes ἀνιών: 'till, ascending in the scale of miseries, (= making his woes ever greater and greater) he makes his equal to mine.' In illustration of this, in connection with προστιθέασιν in v. 564, may be quoted from Thuc. III. 45, ἐπεὶ διεξεληλύθασί γε διὰ πασῶν τῶν ζημιῶν οἱ ἄνθρωποι προστιθέντες,

οἱ δὲ λέγουσιν μύθους ἡμῖν, οἱ δ' Αἰσώπου τι γέλοιον· 566
οἱ δὲ σκώπτουσ', ἵν' ἐγὼ γελάσω καὶ τὸν θυμὸν κατά-
θωμαι.
κἂν μὴ τούτοις ἀναπειθώμεσθα, τὰ παιδάρι' εὐθὺς ἀνέλκει,
τὰς θηλείας καὶ τοὺς υἱεῖς, τῆς χειρὸς, ἐγὼ δ' ἀκροῶμαι·
τὰ δὲ συγκύψανθ' ἅμ βληχᾶται· κᾄπειθ' ὁ πατὴρ ὑπὲρ
αὐτῶν 570
ὥσπερ θεὸν ἀντιβολεῖ με τρέμων τῆς εὐθύνης ἀπολῦσαι·
εἰ μὲν χαίρεις ἀρνὸς φωνῇ, παιδὸς φωνὴν ἐλεήσαις·
εἰ δ' αὖ τοῖς χοιριδίοις χαίρω, θυγατρὸς φωνῇ με πιθέσθαι.
χἠμεῖς αὐτῷ τότε τῆς ὀργῆς ὀλίγον τὸν κόλλοπ' ἀνεῖμεν.
ἆρ' οὐ μεγάλη τοῦτ' ἔστ' ἀρχὴ καὶ τοῦ πλούτου καταχήνη;

εἴπως ἧσσον ἀδικοῖντο ὑπὸ τῶν κακούργων. καὶ εἰκὸς τὸ πάλαι τῶν μεγίστων ἀδικημάτων μαλακωτέρας κεῖσθαι αὐτὰς, παραβαινομένων δὲ τῷ χρόνῳ ἐς τὸν θάνατον αἱ πολλαὶ ἀνήκουσιν, 'Men have gone through the whole list of punishments, ever adding punishment to punishment (= with continual increase in severity) if by any means they might less suffer from evil-doers. And punishments enacted in old time were milder, naturally enough, even for heinous offences, but, as these in time were defied by transgressors, the more part have now reached the severity of death.' The use of προστιθέναι is similar, also ἀνήκουσι may be compared with ἀνιῶν here.

566 Αἰσώπου.] A tragic actor of the name is meant, says the Scholiast; and this would make the Αἰσώπου τι γέλοιον more distinct from the 'fables' just mentioned. Yet Αἰσωπικὸν γέλοιον is supposed to refer to a different Aesop, namely the writer of fables, in v. 1259: whence it does not seem certain that the fable-writer is not meant here as well. The μῦθοι first mentioned might be longer and more elaborate apologues, and so considered distinct from Aesop's short and funny fables about birds, beasts, &c.

570 ἅμ βληχᾶται.] Dindorf says: 'formam monosyllabam restitui, annotatam ab Hesychio.' συγκύπτοντα βληχᾶται Porson. Richter reads συγκύψανθ' from MSS. R and V: and the aorist participle is quite as good as the present, if not better: cf. Herod. III. 42, συγκύψαντες ποιεῦσι.

κᾄπειθ' ὁ πατὴρ κ.τ.λ.] Cf. Demosth. c. Mid. 574, where Midias is said to intend thus to excite commiseration.

574 κόλλοπ' ἀνεῖμεν.] Cf. v. 337, ὑφέσθε τοῦ τόνου. The κόλλοπες are the small pegs of the lyre to which the strings are fastened, and by turning which they can be tightened. Schol. This passage rather supports the interpretation of v. 337 as a metaphor from a stringed instrument.

575 πλούτου καταχήνη.] Cf. Eccl. 631, καταχήνη τῶν σεμνοτέρων ἔσται πολλή. It seems to strike Bdelycleon as a curious phrase, for he at once jots it down. ἐγχανεῖν is a common word for 'to mock at, have the laugh against,' but the noun καταχήνη, as thus used, hardly finds a literal English equivalent. 'Am I not herein a mighty king, and cannot I snap my fingers at your wealthy men?' is the sense.

ΣΦΗΚΕΣ.

ΒΔΕΛΥΚΛΕΩΝ

δεύτερον αὖ σου τουτὶ γράφομαι, τὴν τοῦ πλούτου κατα-
χήνην· 576
καὶ τἀγαθά μοι μέμνησ' ἄχεις φάσκων τῆς Ἑλλάδος ἄρχειν.

ΦΙΛΟΚΛΕΩΝ

παίδων τοίνυν δοκιμαζομένων αἰδοῖα πάρεστι θεᾶσθαι.
κἂν Οἴαγρος εἰσέλθῃ φεύγων, οὐκ ἀποφεύγει πρὶν ἂν ἡμῖν
ἐκ τῆς Νιόβης εἴπῃ ῥῆσιν τὴν καλλίστην ἀπολέξας. 580
κἂν αὐλητής γε δίκην νικᾷ, ταύτης ἡμῖν ἐπίχειρα
ἐν φορβειᾷ τοῖσι δικασταῖς ἔξοδον ηὔλησ' ἀπιοῦσιν.
κἂν ἀποθνῄσκων ὁ πατὴρ τῳ δῷ καταλείπων παῖδ' ἐπίκληρον,
κλάειν ἡμεῖς μακρὰ τὴν κεφαλὴν εἰπόντες τῇ διαθήκῃ

579 Οἴαγρος.] A tragic actor; whether of Aeschylus or Sophocles is doubtful, and matters little. Aeschylus and Sophocles wrote each a play called *Niobe:* that of Aeschylus is mentioned in *Ran.* 912.
580 ῥῆσιν.] Cf. *Nub.* 1371, Εὐριπίδου ῥῆσίν τιν'. The dicasts get something out of both actor and flutist, before giving them a verdict.
582 φορβειᾷ.] The object of the mouth-piece was, according to the Scholiast, ὅπως ἂν σύμμετρον τὸ πνεῦμα πεμπόμενον ἡδεῖαν τὴν φωνὴν τοῦ αὐλητοῦ ποιήσῃ, to make the stream of breath through the instrument regular and even, and so sweeten the tone. φορβειᾶς ἄτερ came to be a proverb for 'without regulation or control.' Hence Cicero to Atticus (*Epist.* II. 16) says of Pompey, 'Cnaeus quidem noster jam plane quid cogitet nescio; φυσᾷ γὰρ οὐ σμικροῖσιν αὐλίσκοις ἔτι, ἀλλ' ἀγρίαις φύσαισι φορβειᾶς ἄτερ:' quoting what we know to be a fragment of Sophocles. A crow is ridiculously introduced in *The Birds* (v. 861) with such a mouthpiece on.
ἔξοδον ηὔλησ' ἀπιοῦσιν.] 'Plays us out of court.' But the playing out was perhaps to be with the concluding piece of music from some well-known play: the end of a tragedy being called ἔξοδος.
583—6. If a father die, leaving one daughter sole heiress, and have betrothed her already, we set the will aside, and take upon ourselves to give away the bride to our favourite.
583 ἐπίκληρον.] The later name, according to the Scholiast, was μονοκληρονόμος: and it is curious that ἐπίκληρος should in Attic Greek have come to be so specially used of a *daughter* inheriting, and that too an *only* daughter and child. Such an heiress was also called πατροῦχος παρθένος (Herod. VI. 57), and it was a matter to settle by law, who, as next of kin, should have her to wife, if her father had not, before his death, betrothed her.
584 κλάειν...τὴν κεφαλήν.] The construction is curious. In *Plut.* 612, σὲ δ' ἐᾶν κλάειν μακρὰ τὴν κεφαλήν, the second accusative τὴν κ. appears to be in apposition to σέ: 'and to let you—your head (= your person, yourself) go weep.' Here the construction probably is 'having told the will that its head (= itself)

62   ΑΡΙΣΤΟΦΑΝΟΥΣ   [585

καὶ τῇ κόγχῃ τῇ πάνυ σεμνῶς τοῖς σημείοισιν ἐπούσῃ, 585
ἔδομεν ταύτην ὅστις ἂν ἡμᾶς ἀντιβολήσας ἀναπείσῃ.
καὶ ταῦτ' ἀνυπεύθυνοι δρῶμεν· τῶν δ' ἄλλων οὐδεμί' ἀρχή.

ΒΔΕΛΤΚΛΕΩΝ

τουτὶ γάρ τοί σε μόνον τούτων ὧν εἴρηκας μακαρίζω·
τῆς δ' ἐπικλήρου τὴν διαθήκην ἀδικεῖς ἀνακογχυλιάζων. 589

ΦΙΛΟΚΛΕΩΝ

ἔτι δ' ἡ βουλὴ χὠ δῆμος ὅταν κρῖναι μέγα πρᾶγμ' ἀπορήσῃ,
ἐψήφισται τοὺς ἀδικοῦντας τοῖσι δικασταῖς παραδοῦναι·
εἶτ' Εὔαθλος χὠ μέγας οὗτος κολακώνυμος ἀσπιδαποβλὴς
οὐχὶ προδώσειν ἡμᾶς φασίν, περὶ τοῦ πλήθους δὲ μαχεῖσθαι.
κἂν τῷ δήμῳ γνώμην οὐδεὶς πώποτ' ἐνίκησεν, ἐὰν μὴ
εἴπῃ τὰ δικαστήρι' ἀφεῖναι πρώτιστα μίαν δικάσαντας· 595
αὐτὸς δ' ὁ Κλέων ὁ κεκραξιδάμας μόνον ἡμᾶς οὐ περιτρώγει,

may go weep;' but there may be (as Florens supposes) another meaning implied in κεφαλήν, 'the head or beginning of the will,' *prima cera et caput testamenti*. The passages quoted by Bergler with κλάειν μακρὰ do not help us in explaining the construction of κεφαλὴν either in the *Plutus* or here. The explanation of one Scholiast on the *Plutus*, that τύπτουσαν is understood, is not satisfactory.

585 καὶ τῇ κόγχῃ.] Supply εἰπόντες κλάειν. They used to put shells over the seals for greater security. Schol.

πάνυ σεμνῶς.] 'Most pretentiously,' with a great fuss, and show of care.

587 καὶ ταῦτ'...ἀρχή.] And we do all this with no account to render afterwards: which is more than any other magistrate can do, since he has to submit to the εὐθύνη on going out of office.

588 σε μόνον.] Reiske, Porson, Dindorf, Meineke, read it thus. σεμνὸν vulg., σεμνῶν MS. Rav. σεμνῶν might do, 'Why on this point of your grand privileges I do congratulate you.' τουτὶ refers to τὸ ἀνυπευθύνους δρᾶν.

590. Philocleon goes on with his tale, regardless of his son's remark; shewing how the most important public matters are referred to the dicasts, and how the demagogues all court them.

592 Εὔαθλος.] Cf. *Ach.* 210, and the note there. The comic writers, Plato and Cratinus, both mention him. Schol.

κολακώνυμος.] For Cleonymus cf. *Nub.* 353, and above, vv. 20—23. His name is slightly changed so as to include the word (κόλαξ) that best describes his nature.

593 οὐχὶ προδώσειν.] Cf. below, v. 666. In *Eq.* 1048 Cleon represents himself by a lion, ὃς περὶ τοῦ δήμου πολλοῖς κώνωψι μαχεῖται.

595 ἀφεῖναι κ.τ.λ.] Cf. *Eq.* 50, ὦ Δῆμε, λοῦσαι πρῶτον ἐκδικάσας μίαν.

596 κεκραξιδάμας.] Cf. *Eq.* 137, κεκράκτης. His voice is often remarked on as loud: cf. above, v. 36. A φωνὴ μιαρὰ (*Eq.* 218) was one of the requisites for a demagogue.

ἀλλὰ φυλάττει διὰ χειρὸς ἔχων καὶ τὰς μυίας ἀπαμύνει.
σὺ δε τὸν. πατέρ' οὐδ' ὁτιοῦν τούτων τὸν σαυτοῦ πώποτ'
ἔδρασας.
ἀλλὰ Θέωρος, καίτούστὶν ἀνὴρ Εὐφημίου οὐδὲν ἐλάττων,
τὸν σπόγγον ἔχων ἐκ τῆς λεκάνης τἀμβάδι' ἡμῶν περικωνεῖ.
σκέψαι δ' ἀπὸ τῶν ἀγαθῶν οἵων ἀποκλείεις καὶ κατερύκεις,
ἣν δουλείαν οὖσαν ἔφασκες χὐπηρεσίαν ἀποδείξειν.

ΒΔΕΛΥΚΛΕΩΝ
ἔμπλησο λέγων· πάντως γάρ τοι παύσει ποτὲ κἀναφανήσει
πρωκτὸς λουτροῦ περιγιγνόμενος τῆς ἀρχῆς τῆς περισέμνου.

ΦΙΛΟΚΛΕΩΝ
ὃ δέ γ' ἥδιστον τούτων ἐστὶν πάντων, οὗ 'γὼ 'πιλελή-
σμην,   605
ὅταν οἴκαδ' ἴω τὸν μισθὸν ἔχων, κᾆτ' εἰσήκονθ' ἅμα πάντες
ἀσπάζωνται δια τἀργύριον, καὶ πρῶτα μὲν ἡ θυγάτηρ με

597 τὰς μυίας ἀπαμύνει.] As is said in *Eq.* 59, δειπνοῦντος ἑστὼς ἀποσοβεῖ τοὺς ῥήτορας. Homer (*Il.* δ. 130) has a curious simile about Athene keeping off the arrow from Menelaus: ἡ δὲ τόσον μὲν ἔεργεν ἀπὸ χροὸς ὡς ὅτε μήτηρ παιδὸς ἐέργει μυῖαν, ὅθ' ἡδέϊ λέξεται ὕπνῳ.

599 Εὐφημίου.] Euphemius and Theorus were evidently of the same stamp. Of the former we know nothing; the latter is frequently ridiculed.

600 περικωνεῖ.] κυρίως τὸ πισσῶσαι τὰ κεράμια. Schol.

602 χὐπηρεσίαν.] καὶ ὑπηρεσίαν MS. Rav., which Bentley and Meineke also read. Dindorf rather approves it, but notes that the Ravenna MS. has καὶ οὐδὲν for κοὐδὲν in v. 741, and other similar readings, 'crasi non raro neglecta.' It is difficult to lay down any invariable rule how such sequences or blendings of vowel-sounds were written. Possibly the Greeks themselves had no fixed rule. They were pronounced so as to satisfy the requirements of metre, &c., and the audience would be in no doubt about them, while the language was living and in its prime: the method of writing them was for later grammarians to settle and reduce to uniformity.

603, 4. Bdelycleon thinks that his father will turn out but a sorry figure, for all his grand 'empire,' as he calls it : a sow will return to her wallowing in the mire.

606 ὅταν οἴκαδ' ἴω.] All the conjunctives depend on ὅταν: so either the sentence is not strictly regular, having no apodosis to ὃ δέ γ' ἥδιστόν ἐστιν; or the apodosis must be at once supplied before οὗ 'γὼ 'πιλελήσμην: 'what is most sweet (is that) which I had well-nigh forgot; viz. when I go home, &c.' But there is most probably an anacoluthon: the sentence was first meant to run thus: ὃ δέ γ' ἥδιστόν ἐστιν, ὅταν οἴκαδ' ἴω, πάντες ἀσπάζονται: then the verbs were put in the subordinate clause introduced by ὅταν, and, owing to the length of this clause, the regular apodosis required by strictness of grammar was forgotten.

ἀπονίζῃ καὶ τὼ πόδ' ἀλείφῃ καὶ προσκύψασα φιλήσῃ,
καὶ παππίζουσ' ἅμα τῇ γλώττῃ τὸ τριώβολον ἐκκαλαμᾶται,
καὶ τὸ γύναιόν μ' ὑποθωπεῦσαν φυστὴν μᾶζαν προσε-
νέγκῃ,   610
κἄπειτα καθεζομένη παρ' ἐμοὶ προσαναγκάζῃ, φάγε τουτὶ,
ἔντραγε τουτί· τούτοισιν ἐγὼ γάνυμαι, κοὐ μή με δεήσῃ
ἐς σὲ βλέψαι καὶ τὸν ταμίαν, ὁπότ' ἄριστον παραθήσει
καταρασάμενος καὶ τονθορύσας. ἀλλ' ἢν μή μοι ταχὺ μάξῃ...
τάδε κέκτημαι πρόβλημα κακῶν, σκευὴν βελέων ἀλεωρήν·
κἂν οἶνόν μοι μὴ 'γχῇς σὺ πιεῖν, τὸν ὄνον τόνδ' ἐσκεκό-
μισμαι   616
οἴνου μεστὸν, κᾆτ' ἐγχέομαι κλίνας· οὗτος δὲ κεχηνὼς
βρωμησάμενος τοῦ σοῦ δίνου μέγα καὶ στράτιον κατέπαρδεν.
ἆρ' οὐ μεγάλην ἀρχὴν ἄρχω
καὶ τῆς τοῦ Διὸς οὐδὲν ἐλάττω,   620
ὅστις ἀκούω ταῦθ' ἅπερ ὁ Ζεύς;
ἢν γοῦν ἡμεῖς θορυβήσωμεν,

609 ἐκκαλαμᾶται.] Cf. v. 381.
610 φυστήν.] ἐξ ἀλφίτων καὶ οἴνου. Schol.
612—14. He does not depend for his supplies on his son or the steward who will grumble all the while.
612 κοὐ μή.] Vulg. καὶ μή; which is hardly defensible, 'and let me not need to look, &c.' Elmsley proposed κεἰ μή με δεήσει. The correction κοὐ is Hermann's, approved by Meineke and Richter.
614 ἀλλ' ἢν μή μοι.] This is Meineke's reading, adopted by Holden. It is best understood as an aposiopesis, 'and if he do not—woe be to him.' Or, as Hirschig punctuates, we may make τάδε κέκτημαι, κ.τ.λ. the apodosis to ἢν μή. Meineke rejects the four lines 615—618. The vulg. ἄλλην μή, 'lest he may soon have to knead me another,' is not satisfactory.
615 πρόβλημα...ἀλεωρήν.] Homeric: cf. Hom. Il. μ. 57, δηΐων ἀνδρῶν ἀλεωρήν.
616 ὄνον.] There is probably a play on the similarity of sound in οἶνος and ὄνος; and on the double sense of ὄνος. The vessel may have been so named from having two long ears; being a sort of 'diota.'
617 κεχηνώς.] 'Wide-mouthed;' applicable both to the wine-vessel, and to the animal, when braying out his contempt.
618 βρωμησάμενος.] Of the vessel this might refer to the noise of the wine as it was poured in; as Bergler suggests. The general sense of the passage is that Philocleon gets his wine-vessel, fills it for himself, and with his ὄνος laughs to scorn his son's δίνος.
στράτιον.] τὸ εἰς πολλοὺς διῆκον. Schol. πολεμικὸν ἢ φοβερόν. Hesych. The shout of Ares in Homer (Il. ε. 859), ὁ δ' ἔβραχε χάλκεος Ἄρης ὅσσον τ' ἐννεάχιλοι ἐπίαχον ἢ δεκάχιλοι ἀνέρες ἐν πολέμῳ, was decidedly στράτιον.
620—25. A dicast is as sovereign as Zeus: the thunders of the court are spoken of, and feared.

ΣΦΗΚΕΣ.

πᾶς τίς φησιν τῶν παριόντων,
οἷον βροντᾷ τὸ δικαστήριον,
ὦ Ζεῦ βασιλεῦ·
κἂν ἀστράψω, ποππύζουσιν,
κἀγκεχόδασίν μ' οἱ πλουτοῦντες
καὶ πάνυ σεμνοί.
καὶ σὺ δέδοικάς με μάλιστ' αὐτός·
νὴ τὴν Δήμητρα, δέδοικας. ἐγὼ δ'
ἀπολοίμην, εἰ σὲ δέδοικα. 630

ΧΟΡΟΣ

οὐπώποθ' οὕτω καθαρῶς
οὐδενὸς ἠκούσαμεν οὐ-
δὲ ξυνετῶς λέγοντος.

ΦΙΛΟΚΛΕΩΝ

οὐκ, ἀλλ' ἐρήμας ᾤεθ' οὗτος ῥᾳδίως τρυγήσειν·
καλῶς γὰρ ᾔδειν ὡς ἐγὼ ταύτῃ κράτιστός εἰμι. 635

ΧΟΡΟΣ

ὡς δ' ἐπὶ πάντ' ἐπῆλθε κοὐδέν τι παρῆλθεν, ὥστ' ἔγωγ'
ηὐξανόμην ἀκούων,

626 **ποππύζουσιν.**] This sound is here meant by way of charm against evil: cf. Plin. *Hist. Nat.* XXVIII. 5, fulgetras poppysmate adorare consensus gentium est. There are various other uses of the word, which is evidently onomatopoetic.
629 **νὴ τ. Δ.**] The old man probably repeats his assertion thus strongly, not only to impress it on his son (who perhaps makes some gesture of dissent), but to convince and assure himself.
631 **καθαρῶς.**] 'Clearly;' the adverb is to be taken with λέγοντος.
634 **οὐκ, ἀλλ'.**] The proverbial phrase ἐρήμας (ἀμπέλους) τρυγήσειν is again used in *Eccl.* 885. It is from those who guard vines carelessly, according to the Scholiast: and a somewhat similar proverb seems γλυκεῖ' ὀπώρα φύλακος ἐκλε-

λοιπότος. For the watching of vines, see a pleasing picture in Theocritus (*Id.* I. 45—51) of a boy set to watch the ripe grapes, from whom a fox successfully manages τρυγᾶν ἐρήμας. But to the dicast ἔρημος would also suggest δίκη, 'a case undefended'; where judgment goes by default. The whole sense of the speech is 'No (you never did hear any speak better), yet this man thought to win an easy victory, (absurd!) for he knew forensic argument to be my strong point.' Or the ellipse before γὰρ may be rendered by 'why, he knew, &c.'
636—641. In these lines Meineke's readings square better with the corresponding verses 531—536 and are about as near to MSS.
638 **ηὐξανόμην.**] 'Felt myself bigger.' Cf. Plat. *Menex.* 235, ὥστ'

5

κἂν μακάρων δικάζειν
αὐτὸς ἔδοξα νήσοις, 640
ἡδόμενος λέγοντι.

ΦΙΛΟΚΛΕΩΝ

ὡς οὗτος ἤδη σκορδινᾶται κἄστιν οὐκ ἐν αὑτοῦ.
ἦ μὴν ἐγώ σε τήμερον σκύτη βλέπειν ποιήσω.

ΧΟΡΟΣ

δεῖ δέ σε παντοίας πλέκειν
εἰς ἀπόφυξιν παλάμας. 645
τὴν γὰρ ἐμὴν ὀργὴν πεπᾶ-
ναι χαλεπὸν . . .
. . . .
μὴ πρὸς ἐμοῦ λέγοντι.
πρὸς ταῦτα μύλην ἀγαθὴν ὥρα ζητεῖν σοι καὶ νεόκοπτον,
ἢν μή τι λέγῃς, ἥτις δυνατὴ τὸν ἐμὸν θυμὸν κατερεῖξαι.

ΒΔΕΛΤΚΛΕΩΝ

χαλεπὸν μὲν καὶ δεινῆς γνώμης καὶ μείζονος ἢ 'πὶ τρυ-
γῳδοῖς, 650
ἰάσασθαι νόσον ἀρχαίαν ἐν τῇ πόλει ἐντετοκυῖαν.
ἀτάρ, ὦ πάτερ ἡμέτερε Κρονίδη

ἔγωγε γενναίως διατίθεμαι... ἡγούμε-
νος ἐν τῷ παραχρῆμα.μείζων καὶ καλ-
λίων γεγονέναι,... τέως δὲ οἶμαι μόνον
οὐκ ἐν μακάρων νήσοις οἰκεῖν.
639 **δικάζειν.**] They cannot
imagine, even in the isles of the
blessed, life without lawsuits.
642 **σκορδινᾶται.**] Yawning or
gaping is a token of weariness in
Ach. 39. Here the dicast takes it
to mean confusion and loss of presence of mind. The Scholiast explains it as ὃ ποιοῦσιν ἐξ ὕπνου ἀνι-
στάμενοι καὶ μετὰ χάσμης τὰ μέλη
ἐκτείνοντες.
643 **σκύτη βλέπειν.**] A proverb,
used also in Eupolis, according
to the Scholiast: εἴρηται δὲ ἐπὶ τῶν
ὑποψιαστικῶς διακειμένων πρὸς τὰ
μέλλοντα κακά. If so, it is not quite
analogous to βλέπειν νᾶπυ and the
like: for it then ought to mean 'to

look as if going to whip,' rather than
'to be whipt.'
647 **χαλεπὸν.**] Some syllables
have been lost here: the amount
will differ, as we take Dindorf's text
or Meineke's.
649 **κατερεῖξαι.**] Cf. *Ran.* 505,
κατερικτῶν χύτρας ἔτνους δύ' ἢ τρεῖς.
650—724. Bdelycleon in reply
gives some account of the state revenues; shews how large a part of
these is absorbed by self-interested
demagogues, while the people get
but little, and follow blindly and
slavishly these leaders.
651 **ἐντετοκυῖαν.**] ἐγγεννηθεῖσαν.
Schol.
652 **πάτερ.**] Cf. Hom. *Od.* a.
45, ὦ πάτερ ἡμέτερε Κρονίδη, ὕπατε
κρειόντων. Philocleon was led to
use the phrase by his father's boast
that he and his fellow dicasts had

ΦΙΛΟΚΛΕΩΝ

παῦσαι καὶ μὴ πατέριζε.
εἰ μὴ γὰρ ὅπως δουλεύω 'γώ, τουτὶ ταχέως με διδάξεις,
οὐκ ἔστιν ὅπως οὐχὶ τεθνήξεις, κἂν χρῇ σπλάγχνων μ'
ἀπέχεσθαι.

ΒΔΕΛΤΚΛΕΩΝ

ἀκρόασαί νυν, ὦ παππίδιον, χαλάσας ὀλίγον τὸ μέτωπον·
καὶ πρῶτον μὲν λόγισαι φαύλως, μὴ ψήφοις, ἀλλ' ἀπὸ
χειρός, 656
τὸν φόρον ἡμῖν ἀπὸ τῶν πόλεων συλλήβδην τὸν προσιόντα·
κἄξω τούτου τὰ τέλη χωρὶς καὶ τὰς πολλὰς ἑκατοστάς,
πρυτανεῖα, μέταλλ', ἀγοράς, λιμένας, μισθοὺς καὶ δημιόπρατα.
τούτων πλήρωμα τάλαντ' ἐγγὺς δισχίλια γίγνεται ἡμῖν. 660
ἀπὸ τούτων νυν κατάθες μισθὸν τοῖσι δικασταῖς ἐνιαυτοῦ,
ἐξ χιλιάσιν, κοὔπω πλείους ἐν τῇ χώρᾳ κατένασθεν,
γίγνεται ἡμῖν ἑκατὸν δήπου καὶ πεντήκοντα τάλαντα.

the titles of Zeus: vv. 620—25. The father stops him with 'don't be fathering me,' and brings him to the point.

654 σπλάγχνων μ' ἀπέχεσθαι.] Cf. *Eq.* 410, ἦ μήποτ' ἀγοραίου Διὸς σπλάγχνοισι παραγενοίμην. He would be excluded from the sacrifices, if stained with the crime of homicide.

656 λόγισαι φαύλως.] 'Do an easy sum:' one that needs no pebbles or counters, but can be done on the fingers, off-hand. This is of course the sense of φαύλως, as indeed the Scholiast and Suidas explain it. Florens not so well explains it 'do the sum badly,' inexactly, 'quia certior computatio per calculos quam digitos.' But the sum is done exactly enough in what follows.

658 τὰ τέλη, κ.τ.λ.] Schömann *de Com. Athen.* p. 286 explains these items. τέλη are taxes paid by aliens and freedmen, by particular trades, &c.: ἑκατοσταί, harbour dues in the Piraeus: ἀγοραί, λιμένες represent duties paid on exports, imports, and wares sold: μισθοί probably are rents from public lands or houses let out to private individuals: πρυτανεῖα, court-fees, equivalent nearly to the Roman 'sacramenta:' δημιόπρατα, confiscated goods, or the money produced by their sale.

660—663. These make up in all 2000 talents. But each dicast is to have 3 obols a day, or half a drachma: therefore 15 drachmae in a month of 30 days, 150 drachmae in a year of ten months. Then 6000 × 150 dr. = 150 × 60 × 100 dr. = 150 talents. As the Scholiast remarks, the judicial year had but 10 months, 2 months being spent in holiday.

ΦΙΛΟΚΛΕΩΝ
οὐδ' ἡ δεκάτη τῶν προσιόντων ἡμῖν ἄρ' ἐγίγνεθ' ὁ μισθός.

ΒΔΕΛΥΚΛΕΩΝ
μὰ Δί' οὐ μέντοι.

ΦΙΛΟΚΛΕΩΝ
καὶ ποῖ τρέπεται δὴ 'πειτα τὰ χρήματα τἄλλα; 665

ΒΔΕΛΥΚΛΕΩΝ
ἐς τούτους τοὺς, οὐχὶ προδώσω τὸν Ἀθηναίων κολοσυρτὸν,
ἀλλὰ μαχοῦμαι περὶ τοῦ πλήθους ἀεί. σὺ γὰρ, ὦ πάτερ,
αὐτοὺς
ἄρχειν αἱρεῖ σαυτοῦ, τούτοις τοῖς ῥηματίοις περιπεφθείς.
κᾆθ' οὗτοι μὲν δωροδοκοῦσιν κατὰ πεντήκοντα τάλαντα
ἀπὸ τῶν πόλεων, ἐπαπειλοῦντες τοιαυτὶ κἀναφοβοῦντες, 670
δώσετε τὸν φόρον, ἢ βροντήσας τὴν πόλιν ὑμῶν ἀνατρέψω.
σὺ δὲ τῆς ἀρχῆς ἀγαπᾷς τῆς σῆς τοὺς ἀργελόφους περι-
τρώγων.
οἱ δὲ ξύμμαχοι ὡς ᾔσθηνται τὸν μὲν σύρφακα τὸν ἄλλον

664 δεκάτη.] Being but 150 out of 2000.
665 καὶ ποῖ.] Meineke's and Bothe's arrangement of the speakers seems preferable. Philocleon says, 'Then after all we don't get a tenth of the whole. Bd. No, that you don't. Phi. What then becomes of the rest? Bd. Oh! it goes to those braggart demagogues, who cajole you with such fine promises.' The phrase τοὺς οὐχὶ πρ. κ.τ.λ. is much better as said in scorn by Bdelycleon, than as a serious confession on Philocleon's part.
666 κολοσυρτὸν.] Of the lowest rabble: cf. *Plut.* 536. It is a word rather supplied by Bdelycleon to express what the stump-orators virtually meant, than the real word that they would have used, when thus making their showy professions of republicanism.
668 περιπεφθείς.] A peculiar use. In *Plut.* 159, ὀνόματι περιπέττουσι τὴν μοχθηρίαν, as also in Plat. *Legg.* 886 E, λόγοισιν εὖ πως εἰς τὸ πιθανὸν περιπεπεμμένα, the word is of conduct or theories made plausible and smooth to outward view by specious words; but of its application to a person deceived by such means, this seems to be the only instance. But there is something rather analogous in *Eq.* 215, τὸν δῆμον προσποιοῦ ὑπογλυκαίνων ῥηματίοις μαγειρικοῖς: for there the 'sugaring' or 'sweetening' would, strictly, be applied to the viands, but the participle governs the person won over by such skill in cookery.
672 ἀργελόφους.] τὰ περιττὰ καὶ ἄχρηστα, ἀργέλοφοι γὰρ τῆς μηλωτῆς οἱ πόδες. Schol. 'refuse, leavings.'
673—77. These rascals get the best of everything: and the allies soon find that out, and court them, but scorn you.

ἐκ κηθαρίου λαγαριζόμενον καὶ τραγαλίζοντα τὸ μηδέν, 674
σὲ μὲν ἡγοῦνται Κόννου ψῆφον, τούτοισι δὲ δωροφοροῦσιν
ὕρχας, οἶνον, δάπιδας, τυρὸν, μέλι, σήσαμα, προσκεφάλαια,
φιάλας, χλανίδας, στεφάνους, ὅρμους, ἐκπώματα, πλουθυ-
γίειαν·
σοὶ δ᾽ ὧν ἄρχεις, πολλὰ μὲν ἐν γῇ πολλὰ δ᾽ ἐφ᾽ ὑγρᾷ πιτυλεύσας,
οὐδεὶς οὐδὲ σκορόδου κεφαλὴν τοῖς ἑψητοῖσι δίδωσιν.

ΦΙΛΟΚΛΕΩΝ
μὰ Δί᾽ ἀλλὰ παρ᾽ Εὐχαρίδου καὐτὸς τρεῖς γ᾽ ἄγλιθας μετέ-
πεμψα. 680
ἀλλ᾽ αὐτήν μοι τὴν δουλείαν οὐκ ἀποφαίνων ἀποκναίεις.

673 σύρφακα.] Bergler quotes from Euphron, ὅταν μὲν ἔλθῃς εἰς τοιοῦτον συρφετὸν, Δρόμωνα καὶ Κέρδωνα καὶ Σωτηρίδην. It is much the same as κολοσυρτὸς, v. 666.
674 ἐκ κηθαρίου.] πλέγμα ἐστὶ κανισκῶδες ἐπιτιθέμενον τῇ κληρωτρίδι τῶν ψήφων. Schol. It was also called κήθιον: and the κημὸς seems to have been a similar vessel. The word here stands for law-business generally.
λαγαριζόμενον.] The explanation of this word, from λαγαρὸς, seems certainly preferable to that of the Scholiast, τὰ λάγαρα ἐσθίοντα, ὅ ἐστιν εὔθραυστα καὶ εὐτελῆ ὄντα. The general sense then will be: 'when the allies see that you, as a result of your lawsuits, become thin and starved.'
675 Κόννου ψῆφον.] That this means 'a mere cipher,' is tolerably certain; but the origin of the phrase is doubtful. A Connas is mentioned in *Eq.* 534, a worn out musician probably. The Connus, or Connas, of this passage may be the same, or he may be some other man of no account. The Scholiast tells us that Κόννου θρῖον was the proverb; where θρῖον is by Florens taken to mean 'inanis sonus,' cf. v. 436, πολλῶν... οἶδα θρίων τὸν ψό-

φον. And ψῆφος seems used because a dicast is the subject: but it is uncertain whether K. ψῆφος is 'the vote given by Connus,' (of no use or validity we may suppose,) or whether it means 'they think that you are but of the account of Connus,' you, as an item in the reckoning, are but of the value of Connus, viz. worth nothing.
676 ὕρχας.] κεράμινα ἀγγεῖα, ὑποδεκτικὰ ταρίχων, δύο ὦτα ἔχοντα. Schol. Cf. Pers. *Sat.* III. 76, Maenaque quod prima nondum defecerit orca: where the satirist is speaking of presents given by provincial clients to their legal advocates.
676 σήσαμα.] Cakes made of this were favourites at Athens: cf. *Ach.* 1092, σησαμοῦντες.
678 πιτυλεύσας.] πίτυλος ἡ καταβολὴ τῆς κώπης. Schol. πιτυλεύσας here belongs properly to ἐφ᾽ ὑγρᾷ, some ordinary word = πονήσας being understood with ἐν γῇ. A similar zeugma is in *Eq.* 545, σωφρονικῶς κοὐκ ἀνοήτως ἐσπηδήσας ἐφλυάρει. References to the Athenians' labours on the sea are frequent, *e.g.* in *Eq.* 785, τὴν ἐν Σαλαμῖνι.
681 αὐτήν τ. δ.] 'You do not exactly make out the slavery (that you spoke of).' Cf. v. 518.

ΑΡΙΣΤΟΦΑΝΟΥΣ

ΒΔΕΛΥΚΛΕΩΝ

οὐ γὰρ μεγάλη δουλεία 'στὶν τούτους μὲν ἅπαντας ἐν ἀρχαῖς
αὐτοὺς τ' εἶναι καὶ τοὺς κόλακας τοὺς τούτων μισθοφο-
ροῦντας ;
σοὶ δ' ἤν τις δῷ τοὺς τρεῖς ὀβολούς, ἀγαπᾷς οἷς αὐτὸς
ἐλαύνων
καὶ πεζομαχῶν καὶ πολιορκῶν ἐκτήσω, πολλὰ πονήσας. 685
καὶ πρὸς τούτοις ἐπιταττόμενος φοιτᾷς, ὃ μάλιστά μ' ἀ-
πάγχει,
ὅταν εἰσελθὸν μειράκιόν σοι καταπῦγον, Χαιρέου υἱός,
ὡδὶ διαβὰς, διακινηθεὶς τῷ σώματι καὶ τρυφερανθείς,
ἥκειν εἴπῃ πρῲ κἂν ὥρᾳ δικάσονθ', ὡς ὅστις ἂν ὑμῶν
ὕστερος ἔλθῃ τοῦ σημείου τὸ τριώβολον οὐ κομιεῖται· 690
αὐτὸς δὲ φέρει τὸ συνηγορικόν, δραχμὴν, κἂν ὕστερος ἔλθῃ·
καὶ κοινωνῶν τῶν ἀρχόντων ἑτέρῳ τινὶ τῶν μεθ' ἑαυτοῦ,
ἤν τίς τι διδῷ τῶν φευγόντων, ξυνθέντε τὸ πρᾶγμα δύ' ὄντε
ἐσπουδάκατον, κᾆθ', ὡς πρίων', ὁ μὲν ἕλκει, ὁ δ' ἀντενέδωκε·

οὐκ ἀποφ. ἀποκναίεις.] The negative belongs only to the participle.
684—5 ἐλαύνων—πεζομαχῶν—πολιορκῶν.] An explanation of v. 678.
686—90. Then too you are at the beck and call of dissolute young striplings. Chaereas was attacked by Eupolis (says the Scholiast) as of foreign extraction.
686 ἀπάγχει.] A favourite Greek metaphor to express what annoys one, what one cannot away with, cannot swallow. Cf. *Ach.* 125, ταῦτα δῆτ' οὐκ ἀγχονή ;
688 ὡδί.] He imitates the youth's gait.
690 σημείον.] Those who came late were shut out: cf. below, 775, 891. We find in *Thesm.* 277, τὸ τῆς ἐκκλησίας σημεῖον ἐν τῷ Θεσμοφορείῳ φαίνεται: and in Andocides, *De Mysteriis*, p. 6, ἐπειδὴ τὴν βουλὴν εἰς τὸ βουλευτήριον ὁ κῆρυξ ἀνείπῃ ἰέναι καὶ τὸ σημεῖον καθέλῃ. Whence it is rightly inferred by Schömann (*De Com. Ath.* pp. 149—153), that the 'signal' was something plainly visible, of the nature of a standard, set up to denote when it was time to meet, and taken down when all were assembled, or when enough were assembled; and that after it was taken down no late comers were admitted. It is of the σημεῖον for the βουλὴ that Andocides is speaking, but the signals whether for council or law-courts were probably of the same nature.
691 συνηγορικὸν.] 'Counsel's fee:' double of the three-obol piece; but not so very large. However, his gains do not end here, for he and some other make more by a bribe from the defendant.
694 ἐσπουδάκατον.] 'Make a job of it,' have settled it all between them κατὰ σπουδήν. Cf. *Eq.* 1370, κατὰ σπουδάς; and note on *Eq.* 926, where this use of σπουδὴ is illustrated from Demosthenes.
πρίων'.] *i.e.* πρίονε, 'a pair of sawyers.' There is a sort of mock

ΣΦΗΚΕΣ.

σὺ δὲ χασκάζεις τὸν κωλαγρετην· τὸ δὲ πραττόμενόν σε
λέληθεν. 695

ΦΙΛΟΚΛΕΩΝ

ταυτί με ποιοῦσ'; οἴμοι, τί λέγεις; ὥς μου τὸν θῖνα ταράττεις,
καὶ τὸν νοῦν μου προσάγεις μᾶλλον, κοὐκ οἶδ' ὅ τι χρῆμά
με ποιεῖς.

ΒΔΕΛΤΚΛΕΩΝ

σκέψαι τοίνυν ὡς, ἐξόν σοι πλουτεῖν καὶ τοισίδ' ἅπασιν,
ὑπὸ τῶν ἀεὶ δημιζόντων οὐκ οἶδ' ὅπῃ ἐγκεκύκλησαι·
ὅστις πόλεων ἄρχων πλείστων, ἀπὸ τοῦ Πόντου μέχρι Σαρ-
δοῦς, 700
οὐκ ἀπολαύεις πλὴν τοῦθ' ὃ φέρεις, ἀκαρῆ. καὶ τοῦτ' ἐρίῳ σοι

contest between the opposite parties, but they are really in collusion, and agree like a pair of sawyers, one yielding as the other pulls, πρίονθ' Hirschig and Mein. πρίον, πρίονες, πρίων, MSS. Dindorf infers the declension πρίων, -ωνος from Photius, who remarks that Cratinus uses the plural πρίονες διὰ τοῦ ο, as if that were *not* the usual form.

695 **κωλαγρέτην.**] This officer was, among other things, paymaster to the dicasts. The derivation given by the Scholiast seems probable; though quite unconnected with the duty of the office which is here treated of: ὁ ταμίας τοῦ δικαστικοῦ μισθοῦ καὶ τῶν εἰς θεοὺς ἀναλωμάτων. νόμος δὲ ἦν τὰ ὑπολειπόμενα τοὺς ἱερέας λαμβάνειν ἃ εἰσιν οἷον δέρματα καὶ κωλαί.

696 **θῖνα ταράττεις.**] 'You stir my very depths.' Here θίς is of the sand at the bottom, compare Virgil's 'nigrasque alte subjectat arenas.'

698 **καὶ τοισίδ.**] Meineke first proposed κἀστοῖσιν, 'when you and all the citizens might be wealthy:' but afterwards acquiesced in Hermann's καὶ τοισίδ'. Bentley proposed ἀγαθοῖσιν; Reiske ἴσα τοῖσιν ἄπαισιν, 'because the childless are courted by legacy-hunters.'

699 **δημιζόντων.**] This word is referred to by Ruhnken on δημοῦσθαι, in Timaeus' Platonic Lexicon. The two words may have been of much the same force: but in the passages we have for δημοῦσθαι and δήμωμα (Plat. *Theaet.* 161, and Aristoph. *Pac.* 796) scarcely any notion of δῆμος survives.

ἐγκεκύκλησαι.] 'A re venatoria ducta videtur metaphora.' Conz. And this seems right: 'you are encircled, hemmed in, confined, brought to bay.' The Latin version in Bekker's edition gives 'involutus sis nescio quibus angustiis.' Mitchell translates, 'Into corners you're driving (= driven, *metri gratia*), by the men who are thriving on the love, &c.'

701 **ἐρίῳ, κ.τ.λ.**] What they do give is dealt out drop by drop, like oil through wool into a man's ear. Bergler compares Dem. *Olynth.* III. p. 37, ἴσως ἂν ἴσως, ὦ ἄνδρες Ἀθηναῖοι, τελειόν τι καὶ μέγα κτήσαισθε ἀγαθόν, καὶ τῶν τοιούτων λημμάτων ἀπαλλαγείητε, ἃ τοῖς ἀσθενοῦσι παρὰ τῶν ἰατρῶν σιτίοις διδομένοις ἔοικε· καὶ γὰρ οὔτε ἰσχὺν ἐκεῖνα ἐντίθησιν, οὔτ' ἀποθνήσκειν ἐᾷ, καὶ ταῦτα ἃ

ἐνστάζουσιν κατὰ μικρὸν ἀεί, τοῦ ζῆν ἔνεχ', ὥσπερ ἔλαιον.
βούλονται γάρ σε πένητ' εἶναι· καὶ τοῦθ' ὧν οὕνεκ', ἐρῶ σοι,
ἵνα γιγνώσκῃς τὸν τιθασευτήν· κᾆθ' ὅταν οὗτός γ' ἐπισίζῃ,
ἐπὶ τῶν ἐχθρῶν τιν' ἐπιρρύξας, ἀγρίως αὐτοῖς ἐπιπηδᾷς. 705
εἰ γὰρ ἐβούλοντο βίον πορίσαι τῷ δήμῳ, ῥᾴδιον ἦν ἄν.
εἰσίν γε πόλεις χίλιαι, αἳ νῦν τὸν φόρον ἡμῖν ἀπάγουσιν·
τούτων εἴκοσιν ἄνδρας βόσκειν εἴ τις προσέταξεν ἑκάστῃ,
δύο μυριάδ' ἂν τῶν δημοτικῶν ἔζων ἐν πᾶσι λαγῴοις.

νέμεσθε νῦν ὑμεῖς οὔτε τοιαῦτά ἐστιν ὥστε ὠφέλειαν ἔχειν τινὰ διαρκῆ, οὔτ' ἀπογνόντας ἄλλο τι πράττειν ἐᾷ.

703 τοῦθ' ὧν οὕνεκ', ἐρῶ.] 'And this they do, I will tell you why, 'tis that you may.' Meineke, omitting the comma after οὕνεκα, leaves it doubtful whether the sense might not be 'and this for a reason which I will tell you, viz. that, &c.' ὧν οὕνεκ' ἐρῶ being = οὕνεκα τούτων ἃ ἐρῶ.

704 τιθασευτήν.] Demosthenes says (Olynth. III. 37) of certain statesmen τιθασεύουσι χειροηθεῖς αὐτοῖς ποιοῦντες. Indeed there is much in that speech that illustrates Aristophanes' strictures here.

ἐπισίζῃ.] You are kept quiet like a dog till your master urges you on at any one. Ruhnken's ingenious conjecture in Theocr. Id. VI. 29, σίξα δ' ὑλακτεῖν νιν καὶ τὰν κύνα is referred to by Brunck in illustration of this.

705 ἐπιρρύξας.] ἐπιρύζειν κύνας· ἐπαφιέναι καὶ παρορμᾶν. Hesych. ῥύζω is 'to growl, snarl' = Lat. hirrire: cf. 'canina litera,' (Pers. Sat. I. 109) for the letter R. The hound would be set on by a kind of imitative growl, as well as by a hiss (σισμός).

708 προσέταξεν.] Dawes' alteration προσέταττεν is not necessary. With the common text the general sense is: 'If the statesmen chose to feed the people, it would be easy. For if each one of our thousand cities had been (some time ago) ordered to feed twenty men, twenty thousand of our citizens would be now living in clover;' and this plan our statesmen might now adopt. The imperfect προσέταττεν 'were each city ordered, &c.' makes the passage rather neater; but it is intelligible and correct as it stands.

709 μυριάδ' ἄν.] Dobree's correction for μυριάδες. The particle ἄν can hardly be dispensed with. Richter's passages to countenance such omission are not satisfactory. Thuc. III. 74, ἡ πόλις ἐκινδύνευσε διαφθαρῆναι, εἰ ἄνεμος ἐπεγένετο, is plainly not analogous. It means 'the city was in danger of being destroyed (ay, and had been destroyed) if a wind had arisen.' Nor could ἄν have been used with ἐκινδύνευσε without a plain absurdity: the risk was actual and real. Nearly the same may be said of Eur. Hec. 1111, εἰ δὲ μὴ Φρυγῶν πύργους πεσόντας ᾖσμεν Ἑλλήνων δορί, φόβον πάρεσχεν οὐ μέσως ὅδε κτύπας. The noise actually did cause some alarm, we may suppose. If any correction be needed there, the imperf. παρεῖχεν, of the incipient fear so soon to be checked, seems to me better than παρεσχ' ἄν, ὅδ' ἄν, the corrections of Porson and Elmsley. And it will be found that, in all such cases where the past indic. without ἄν is put, either part of the action had taken place (or was taking place), while the condition applies to the completion and effect of the whole; or, by a rhetorical emphasis of expression, what might have occurred is represented as if it had already

717]   ΣΦΗΚΕΣ.   73

καὶ στεφάνοισιν παντοδαποῖσιν καὶ πυῷ καὶ πυριάτῃ,   710
ἄξια τῆς γῆς ἀπολαύοντες καὶ τοῦ Μαραθῶνι τροπαίου.
νῦν δ' ὥσπερ ἐλαολόγοι χωρεῖθ' ἅμα τῷ τὸν μισθὸν ἔχοντι.

ΦΙΛΟΚΛΕΩΝ

οἴμοι, τί ποθ' ὥσπερ νάρκη μου κατὰ τῆς χειρὸς καταχεῖται,
καὶ τὸ ξίφος οὐ δύναμαι κατέχειν, ἀλλ' ἤδη μαλθακός εἰμι;

ΒΔΕΛΥΚΛΕΩΝ

ἀλλ' ὁπόταν μὲν δείσωσ' αὐτοί, τὴν Εὔβοιαν διδόασιν   715
ὑμῖν καὶ σῖτον ὑφίστανται κατὰ πεντήκοντα μεδίμνους
ποριεῖν· ἔδοσαν δ' οὐπώποτέ σοι, πλὴν πρώην πέντε μεδίμνους,

occurred. The same condensed and graphic construction is common in Latin; *e.g.* Pons sublicius iter paene hostibus dedit ni unus vir fuisset, Liv. II. 10, Si per Metellum licitum esset, matres...veniebant, Cic. *Verr.* v. 49, Prope in proelium exarsere, ni Valens imperii admonuisset, Tac. *Hist.* I. 64. See Madvig, *Lat. Gr.* § 348. But no such explanation suits this passage, which is entirely a supposed case. The other correction by Dawes, ἔξων ἂν is unsatisfactory, because ἐν is wanted to make the phrase ἐν π. λ. a proper parody on ἐν πᾶσιν ἀγαθοῖς.

709 ἐν πᾶσι λαγῴοις.] ἐν πᾶσιν ἀγαθοῖς, ἐν τρυφῇ. Schol. A more comical parody is the ἐν πᾶσι βολίτοις of *Ach.* 1026.

710 πυῷ.] For this cf. *Pac.* 1150, ἦν δὲ καὶ πυός τις ἔνδον καὶ λαγῷα τέτταρα.

πυριάτῃ.] A pudding made from the πυός, they say: and the other name for it, πυρίεφθον, as well as the appearance of this word, suggests that it was made by scalding. 'Colostra' is the Latin term, Mart. XIII. 38, 2.

711 τοῦ Μ. τρ.] Cf. *Eq.* 1334. Isocrates in his Panegyric oration is fluent on the Athenians' Marathonian glories.

712 ἐλαολόγοι.] These, as the Scholiast tells us, got small pay: and apparently kept close to the master who was to pay them to see that that same was forthcoming. The dicasts are similarly bound to their paymaster, the κωλαγρέτης mentioned above.

713 τί ποθ' ὥσπερ.] The alterations adopted by many critics in this line are to suit Suidas, who on νάρκη has τί πέπονθα· ὥσπερ νάρκη.

715. They make fine promises, which they never perform. For Euboea, cf. *Nub.* 211—13. Athens was chiefly dependent upon foreign countries for her corn. Hence (as Mitchell remarks) we find her courted by presents of it. And there were rigorous laws to ensure an adequate supply of it, as may be seen from Demosthenes' speeches against Leptines, Phormio, Lacritus, Dionysodorus.

717 ἔδοσαν.] The aorist expresses the completed action, the pres. διδόασιν only the beginning of it, 'they offer.'

πρώην.] This refers to some more recent largess of corn than that sent from Egypt by Psammetichus, twenty-three years before this play. On that occasion some four thousand aliens were found among the fifteen thousand citizens. A strict enquiry into the genuineness of the claim-

74 ΑΡΙΣΤΟΦΑΝΟΥΣ [718

καὶ ταῦτα μόλις ξενίας φεύγων ἔλαβες κατὰ χοίνικα, κριθῶν.
ὧν οὕνεκ᾽ ἐγώ σ᾽ ἀπέκλειον ἀεί,
βόσκειν ἐθέλων καὶ μὴ τούτους   720
ἐγχάσκειν σοι στομφάζοντας.
καὶ νῦν ἀτεχνῶς ἐθέλω παρέχειν
ὅ τι βούλει σοι,
πλὴν κωλαγρέτου γάλα πίνειν.

ΧΟΡΟΣ

ἦ που σοφὸς ἦν ὅστις ἔφασκεν, πρὶν ἂν ἀμφοῖν μῦθον ἀ-
κούσῃς,   725
οὐκ ἂν δικάσαις. σὺ γὰρ οὖν νῦν μοι νικᾶν πολλῷ δεδό-
κησαι·
ὥστ᾽ ἤδη τὴν ὀργὴν χαλάσας τοὺς σκίπωνας καταβάλλω.
ἀλλ᾽ ὦ τῆς ἡλικίας ἡμῖν τῆς αὐτῆς συνθιασῶτα,
πιθοῦ πιθοῦ λόγοισι, μηδ᾽ ἄφρων γένῃ,
μηδ᾽ ἀτενὴς ἄγαν ἀτεράμων τ᾽ ἀνήρ.   730
εἴθ᾽ ὠφελέν μοι κηδεμὼν ἢ ξυγγενὴς
εἶναί τις ὅστις τοιαῦτ᾽ ἐνουθέτει.
σοὶ δὲ νῦν τις θεῶν

ants' citizenship was held, in cases of such distribution. Hence ξενίας φεύγων in the next line. ~~Bdelycleon~~ got his corn, but not without some trouble in establishing his true Athenian birth.

721 στομφάζοντας.] Cf. *Nub.* 1367, στόμφακα, κρημνοποιόν, of Aeschylus.

722 ἀτεχνῶς.] Cf. note on *Ach.* 37.

724 κωλαγρέτου γάλα.] His pay, the three obol piece, is meant: but there is also allusion to ὀρνίθων γάλα, cf. v. 508.

725—759. The Chorus join their persuasion to Bdelycleon's, but the old man cannot bring himself to do without law.

725 ἦ που σοφός.] Cf. Aesch. *Prom. Vinct.* 886, ἦ σοφὸς, ἦ σοφὸς, ὃς πρῶτος ἐν γνώμᾳ τόδ᾽ ἐβάστασε κ.τ.λ. The maxim that follows was from Phocylides: μηδὲ δίκην δικάσῃς

πρὶν ἂν ἀμφοῖν μῦθον ἀκούσῃς. Euripides in *Heracl.* 180, *Androm.* 957 adopts it. It was in the oath of the dicasts, as Bergler shews from Dem. *c. Timocr.* 746, and is urged on our dicast below at v. 919. The Chorus are now converted to Bdelycleon's (and the poet's) view. In the Clouds the chorus veer round in a somewhat similar way, and taking the honest side turn against Strepsiades.

729—36. To this correspond vv. 743—49.

730. ἀτεράμων.] ἀτέραμνος is the commoner form, *e.g.* Theocr. *Id.* x. 7, πέτρας ἀπόκομμ᾽ ἀτεράμνω, of an untiring mower.

731—36. The Chorus wish they had had the advantage of such advice, and counsel Philocleon to take it, as there is evidently some divine inspiration in Bdelycleon's words.

733 σοί.] To Bdelycleon.

παρὼν ἐμφανὴς
ξυλλαμβάνει τοῦ πράγματος,
καὶ δῆλός ἐστιν εὖ ποιῶν·   735
σὺ δὲ παρὼν δέχου.

ΒΔΕΛΤΚΛΕΩΝ

καὶ μὴν θρέψω γ' αὐτὸν παρέχων
ὅσα πρεσβύτῃ ξύμφορα, χόνδρον
λείχειν, χλαῖναν μαλακὴν, σισύραν,
πόρνην, ἥτις τὸ πέος τρίψει
καὶ τὴν ὀσφῦν.   740
ἀλλ' ὅτι σιγᾷ κοὐδὲν γρύζει,
τοῦτ' οὐ δύναταί με προσέσθαι.

ΧΟΡΟΣ.

νενουθέτηκεν αὐτὸν ἐς τὰ πράγμαθ', οἷς
τότ' ἐπεμαίνετ'· ἔγνωκε γὰρ ἀρτίως,
λογίζεταί τ' ἐκεῖνα πάνθ' ἁμαρτίας   745
ἃ σοῦ κελεύοντος οὐκ ἐπείθετο.
νῦν δ' ἴσως τοῖσι σοῖς
λόγοις πείθεται,
καὶ σωφρονεῖ μέντοι μεθι-
στὰς ἐς τὸ λοιπὸν τὸν τρόπον
πειθόμενός τέ σοι.   749

736 σύ.] To Philocleon. Burges proposed τὸ δ' εὖ παρὸν δέχου; Seager παρόν, 'while you may,' which seems worthy of consideration, for σὺ δὲ παρὼν is of doubtful meaning, and comes awkwardly after παρὼν in v. 733.
738 χόνδρον.] Mentioned along with other like things in Ar. *Fr.* 364, δράκους, πυροὺς, πτισάνην, χόνδρον, ζειὰς, αἴρας, σεμίδαλιν.
742 προσέσθαι.] Cf. *Eq.* 359, ἐν δ' οὐ προσίεταί με.
743—6. He is meditating and repenting, say the Chorus.
744 τότ' ἐπεμ.] The metre of this line is not satisfactory, to correspond with v. 730 exactly. ⌈But changes to bring the metre into order are not always safe or worth the making.⌉
748 καὶ σ. μέντοι.] 'And indeed he's wise in such change and compliance.' I can see no reason for changing (with Hirschig) to μεθεστὼς τῶν τρόπων, merely because μεθέστηχ' ὧν εἶχε τρόπων occurs in *Plut.* 365. μεθίστησι is used in *Eq.* 398. The correction of πειθόμενος to πιθόμενος, 'metri gratia,' against all MSS. seems unsafe, as the present participle is better for the sense.

ΦΙΛΟΚΛΕΩΝ

ἰώ μοί μοι.

ΒΔΕΛΤΚΛΕΩΝ

οὗτος, τί μοι βοᾷς;

ΦΙΛΟΚΛΕΩΝ

μή μοι τούτων μηδὲν ὑπισχνοῦ. 750
κείνων ἔραμαι, κεῖθι γενοίμαν,
ἵν' ὁ κῆρυξ φησὶ, τίς ἀψήφι-
στος; ἀνιστάσθω.
κἀπισταίην ἐπὶ τοῖς κημοῖς
ψηφιζομένων ὁ τελευταῖος. 755
σπεῦδ', ὦ ψυχή. ποῦ μοι ψυχή;
πάρες, ὦ σκιερά. μὰ τὸν Ἡρακλέα,
μὴ νῦν ἔτ' ἐγὼ 'ν τοῖσι δικασταῖς
κλέπτοντα Κλέωνα λάβοιμι.

ΒΔΕΛΤΚΛΕΩΝ

ἴθ' ὦ πάτερ, πρὸς τῶν θεῶν, ἐμοὶ πιθοῦ. 760

ΦΙΛΟΚΛΕΩΝ

τί σοι πίθωμαι; λέγ' ὅ τι βούλει, πλὴν ἑνός.

ΒΔΕΛΤΚΛΕΩΝ

ποίου; φέρ' ἴδω.

750—59. The old man is in despair, and will have none of his son's gruel, &c., but in tragic pathos sighs for the law-courts.

751 κείνων ἔραμαι.] Cf. Eur. *Alcest.* 866, κείνων ἔραμαι, κεῖν' ἐπιθυμῶ δώματα ναίειν.

755 τελευταῖος.] Some would find a pleasure in keeping back their votes to the last. Schol.

757 πάρες, ὦ σκιερά.] Again from Euripides, parodied from the *Bellerophon;* of which the Scholiast gives us the following: πάρες, ὦ σκιερὰ φυλλάς, ὑπερβῶ | κρηναῖα νάπη· τὸν ὑπὲρ κεφαλῆς | αἰθέρ' ἰδέσθαι σπεύδω, τίν' ἔχει | στάσιν Εἰνοδία. What Philocleon addresses by σκιερά is not very definite, nor meant to be so.

759 Κλέωνα.] The dicastic character is attacked as harsh and faithless, since Philocleon keeps no faith even with Cleon, from whom his name is formed. Schol. It may however be added that now Cleon and his tribe have been exposed by Bdelycleon; whose words have had their weight (cf. v. 713), though the old dicast is not quite convinced.

760—834. As the old man cannot entirely give up law, Bdelycleon proposes that he shall hold a court at home, and points out the advantages of this plan. Philocleon consents: due preparations are made; and he takes his seat.

761 πίθωμαι.] Conjunctive of deliberation: cf. *Nub.* 87, τί δὲ πίθωμαι δῆτά σοι;

ΦΙΛΟΚΛΕΩΝ
τοῦ μὴ δικάζειν. τοῦτο δὲ
"Αιδης διακρινεῖ πρότερον ἢ 'γὼ πείσομαι.

ΒΔΕΛΥΚΛΕΩΝ
σὺ δ' οὖν, ἐπειδὴ τοῦτο κεχάρηκας ποιῶν,
ἐκεῖσε μὲν μηκέτι βάδιζ', ἀλλ' ἐνθάδε   765
αὐτοῦ μένων δίκαζε τοῖσιν οἰκέταις.

ΦΙΛΟΚΛΕΩΝ
περὶ τοῦ; τί ληρεῖς;

ΒΔΕΛΥΚΛΕΩΝ
ταῦθ' ἅπερ ἐκεῖ πράττεται·
ὅτι τὴν θύραν ἀνέῳξεν ἡ σηκὶς λάθρα,
ταύτης ἐπιβολὴν ψηφιεῖ μίαν μόνην.
πάντως γε κἀκεῖ ταῦτ' ἔδρας ἑκάστοτε.   770

763 *Ἅιδης διακρινεῖ.*] 'Death will part us sooner than I will comply in this.' It seems a mixed construction of, (1) Death only shall part us (myself and the law-courts), and (2) Death shall take me (=I will die) ere I give in to this.' The Scholiast says there is reference to a passage in the *Cressae* of Euripides, where κρινεῖ ταῦτα is used. Aristophanes is indeed perpetually taking fragments from Euripides, but there is perhaps nothing in this phrase to necessitate its being a quotation.
764 κεχάρηκας.] His only joy and pleasure had come to be in courts. In *Les Plaideurs* the same plan is adopted: Act II. Sc. 13. 'Hé doucement! Mon père, il faut trouver quelque accommodement. Si pour vous sans juger la vie est un supplice, Si vous êtes pressé de rendre la justice, Il ne faut pas sortir pour cela de chez vous; Exercez le talent et jugez parmi nous.'
767 ταῦθ' ἅπερ.] *i.e.* ταῦτα δίκαζε ἅπερ ἐ. π. Meineke reads πρᾶτθ' ἅπερ, perhaps because ταῦθ' ἅπερ does not fit in so well with Philocleon's interruption, περὶ τοῦ; τί

ληρεῖς; But the change is needless. Nor is it important whether ταῦθ' or ταῦθ' is read. In *Eq.* 213, ταῦθ' ἅπερ ποιεῖς ποίει is a similar phrase, where the sausage-seller is told that the new trade of politics is but a continuation of his old trade of mincing up sausage-meat. Racine continues in imitation of this part. '*Dandin*. Ne raillons point ici de la Magistrature, Vois-tu je ne veux point être juge en peinture. *Léandre.* Vous serez, au contraire un juge sans appel, Et juge du Civil comme du Criminel. Vous pourrez tous les jours tenir deux audiences: Tout vous sera chez vous matière de sentences. Un valet manque-t-il à rendre un verre net; Condamnez-le à l'amende; et s'il le casse, au fouet. *Dandin.* C'est quelque chose; encor passe quand on raisonne. Et mes vacations, qui les payera? personne? *Léandre.* Leurs gages vous tiendront lieu de nantissement. *Dandin.* Il parle, ce me semble, assez pertinemment.'
769 μίαν.] Sc. δραχμήν: that being the unit of Attic money.
770 πάντως γε, κ.τ.λ.] And the

καὶ ταῦτα μέν νυν εὐλόγως, ἢν ἐξέχῃ
εἴλη κατ' ὄρθρον, ἡλιάσει πρὸς ἥλιον·
ἐὰν δὲ νίφῃ, πρὸς τὸ πῦρ καθήμενος·
ὕοντος, εἴσει· κἂν ἔγρῃ μεσημβρινός,
οὐδείς σ' ἀποκλείσει θεσμοθέτης τῇ κιγκλίδι.   775

ΦΙΛΟΚΛΕΩΝ
τουτί μ' ἀρέσκει.

ΒΔΕΛΥΚΛΕΩΝ
πρὸς δὲ τούτοις γ', ἢν δίκην
λέγῃ μακράν τις, οὐχὶ πεινῶν ἀναμενεῖς,
δάκνων σεαυτὸν καὶ τὸν ἀπολογούμενον.

ΦΙΛΟΚΛΕΩΝ
πῶς οὖν διαγιγνώσκειν καλῶς δυνήσομαι
ὥσπερ πρότερον τὰ πράγματ' ἔτι μασώμενος;   780

causes you dealt with there (says his son) were not much better. This is in contempt: but the old man would probably see nothing in it but a promise that he should have what he had before.
771—74 καὶ ταῦτα...εἴσει.] 'And these cases you will (as reason is) judge out in the sun, if the morning is fine; by the fire, if it snows; you will go indoors, if it rains.' Such appears the best way of punctuating the present text. The common punctuation gives 'if it snows, sitting by the fire, while it rains, you will take cognizance of the case,' if we take εἴσει from εἴσομαι, as the Scholiast does, who explains it by γνώσῃ τὴν δίκην. This is hardly sense. But it is, with the punctuation adopted above, rather a curious order of weather; sunshine—snow —rain: and a conjunction is wanted with ὑ. ἐ. Meineke says that in the reading of MS. V. ὕοντας 'latet aliud quid quam ὕοντος:' but what it could have been, it seems vain to conjecture: nor indeed is there enough ground for rejecting our text as corrupt.

771 ἐξέχῃ.] Cf. Ar. *Fr.* 346, Λέξεις ἆρα, ὥσπερ τὰ παιδί', ἔξεχ' ὦ φίλ' ἥλιε.
772 ἡλ. πρὸς ἥλιον.] The derivation for ἡλιαία suggested here is countenanced by Scholiasts, though ἀλίζεσθαι is doubtless the correct origin of the word.
775 οὐδείς σ' ἀπ.] You may be as late as you like. Cf. above, v. 690.
776 τουτί μ' ἀρέσκει.] This accusative, in place of the usual dative, with such verbs, is called by grammarians an Attic construction. It seems worth while to compare as analogous the use in English of the directly objective case in many phrases, *e.g.* 'Shoot me that bird,' 'Give him the book,' and the like. And in French, 'Donnez-moi,' but 'Il m'a donné, il me donne,' when the case precedes the verb.
778 δάκνων, κ.τ.λ.] For self-biting cf. v. 374. Snappishness towards the defendant often resulted (says the Scholiast) with a hungry juror.
780—83 μασώμενος...ἀναμασώμενοι.] We may infer that ἀναμα-

ΒΔΕΛΥΚΛΕΩΝ

πολλῷ γ' ἄμεινον· καὶ λέγεται γὰρ τουτογί,
ὡς οἱ δικασταὶ ψευδομένων τῶν μαρτύρων
μόλις τὸ πρᾶγμ' ἔγνωσαν ἀναμασώμενοι.

ΦΙΛΟΚΛΕΩΝ

ἀνά τοί με πείθεις. ἀλλ' ἐκεῖν' οὔπω λέγεις,
τὸν μισθὸν ὁπόθεν λήψομαι.

ΒΔΕΛΥΚΛΕΩΝ

παρ' ἐμοῦ.

ΦΙΛΟΚΛΕΩΝ

καλῶς, 785
ὑτιὴ κατ' ἐμαυτὸν κοὐ μεθ' ἑτέρου λήψομαι.
αἴσχιστα γάρ τοί μ' εἰργάσατο Λυσίστρατος
ὁ σκωπτόλης. δραχμὴν μετ' ἐμοῦ πρώην λαβών,
ἐλθὼν διεκερμάτιζ' ἐν τοῖς ἰχθύσιν,
κἄπειτ' ἐπέθηκε τρεῖς λοπίδας μοι κεστρέων· 790
κἀγὼ 'νέκαψ'· ὀβολοὺς γὰρ ᾠόμην λαβεῖν·
κᾆτα βδελυχθεὶς ὀσφρόμενος ἐξέπτυσα·
κᾆθ' εἷλκον αὐτόν.

σᾶσθαι had an analogous use to the Lat. 'ruminare,' and to our own 'to chew the cud,' though this last would hardly be used of judicial reflexion. ἐκ μεταφορᾶς τῶν ἀναπεμπαζόντων τὴν τροφὴν ζώων, καὶ αὖθις ἀναμασωμένων. Schol.

784 ἀνά τοί με πείθεις.] Cf. *Nub.* 792, ἀπὸ γὰρ ὀλοῦμαι.

787 Λυσίστρατος.] Cf. *Ach.* 854, οὐδ' αὖθις αὖ σε σκώψεται Παύσων ὁ παμπόνηρος, Λυσίστρατός τ' ἐν τἀγορᾷ. Also in *Eq.* 1265 he is mentioned. He seems to have been a poor hungry parasite, who probably earned his dinner by his jokes. He is one of Philocleon's companions at the banquet (below, v. 1302, 1308), and we have a specimen there of his style of wit and buffoonery.

788 δραχμὴν.] That the κωλαγρέται might not have to give change, they gave a drachma (=six obols) to a pair of dicasts.

789 ἐν τοῖς ἰχθύσιν.] So ἐν τῷ μύρῳ, 'in the perfume market,' in *Eq.* 1375: ἐν ταῖς μυρρίναις, *Thesm.* 448: κἄν ταῖσι χύτραις καὶ τοῖς λαχάνοισιν ὁμοίως, *Lys.* 557.

790 τρεῖς λοπίδας.] The three mullet scales would look like small coins at first sight.

791 κἀγὼ 'νέκαψ'.] To put coins in the mouth appears to have been a common practice. Alexis (in Athenaeus) has this very word, ὁ δ' ἐγκάψας τὸ κέρμ' εἰς τὴν γνάθον. And in *Eccl.* 818, μεστὴν ἀπῆρα τὴν γνάθον χαλκῶν ἔχων, is said by one who has just been marketing.

793 εἷλκον.] 'I was dragging him off (into court).'

ΒΔΕΛΤΚΛΕΩΝ

ὁ δὲ τί πρὸς ταῦτ' εἶφ';

ΦΙΛΟΚΛΕΩΝ

ὅ τι;
ἀλεκτρυόνος μ' ἔφασκε κοιλίαν ἔχειν·
ταχὺ γοῦν καθέψεις τἀργύριον, ἦ δ' ὃς λέγων.   795

ΒΔΕΛΤΚΛΕΩΝ

ὁρᾷς ὅσον καὶ τοῦτο δῆτα κερδανεῖς;

ΦΙΛΟΚΛΕΩΝ

οὐ πάνυ τι μικρόν. ἀλλ' ὅπερ μέλλεις ποίει.

ΒΔΕΛΤΚΛΕΩΝ

ἀνάμενέ νυν· ἐγὼ δὲ ταῦθ' ἥξω φέρων.

ΦΙΛΟΚΛΕΩΝ

ὅρα τὸ χρῆμα· τὰ λόγι' ὡς περαίνεται.
ἠκηκόη γὰρ ὡς Ἀθηναῖοί ποτε   800

794 **ἀλεκτρυόνος.**] ἐπεὶ πάντα πέττουσιν οἱ ἀλεκτρυόνες, θερμοτάτην κοιλίαν ἔχοντες. An ostrich is our proverbial bird for tough digestion: hence Mitchell renders it 'Health to your ostrich-coats quoth he! Hard cash, I see, disturbs not your digestion.'
795 **ταχὺ γοῦν καθέψεις.**] Hirschig reads καταπέψεις. But how the future tense is to be explained here, is not clear. With the usual text it is 'At all events you make short work of digesting money.' Lysistratus ignores the fact that he had given him fish-scales, and that he had got rid of the contents of his mouth 'exspuendo' not 'digerendo.'
ἦ δ' ὅς.] ἀντὶ τοῦ ἔφη, καὶ ἔστιν ἀπὸ τοῦ ἡμί. κέχρηται δὲ αὐτῷ συνεχῶς ὁ Πλάτων. Schol.
797 **οὐ πάνυ τι μικρόν.**] 'It is not so very small a gain.' For a thorough discussion of οὐ πάνυ see an appendix upon this phrase at the end of Cope's *Gorgias*. The irony of the speaker, the tone of the voice &c., often make οὐ πάνυ, which strictly is 'not altogether, not quite,' a polite equivalent for 'not at all:' but there seems to me no strong reason for the rule laid down by some, that οὐ πάνυ means 'altogether not,' οὐ παντάπασι 'not altogether;' the former a negation of the whole in all its parts, the latter a negation of some one or more parts in the whole. Some passages in Plato and Aristotle are (it appears) decisive against this rule, and there are none which cannot be well explained with οὐ πάνυ = 'not quite,' which seems its natural meaning.
798 Bdelycleon goes in to fetch all that is needed to constitute a court.
799 **λόγι'.**] Frequent recourse is had to oracles, cf. *Eq.* 109 sqq., 195—201, 1030—4. Philocleon speaks these lines to himself: the slaves probably having left the stage with Bdelycleon.

δικάσοιεν ἐπὶ ταῖς οἰκίαισι τὰς δίκας,
κἂν τοῖς προθύροις ἐνοικοδομήσοι πᾶς ἀνὴρ
αὑτῷ δικαστηρίδιον μικρὸν πάνυ,
ὥσπερ Ἑκάτειον, πανταχοῦ πρὸ τῶν θυρῶν.

ΒΔΕΛΥΚΛΕΩΝ
ἰδού, τί ἔτ' ἐρεῖς; ὡς ἅπαντ' ἐγὼ φέρω   805
ὅσαπέρ γ' ἔφασκον, κἄτι πολλῷ πλείονα.
ἁμὶς μέν, ἢν οὐρητιάσῃς, αὑτηὶ
παρὰ σοὶ κρεμήσετ' ἐγγὺς ἐπὶ τοῦ παττάλου.

ΦΙΛΟΚΛΕΩΝ
σοφόν γε τουτὶ καὶ γέροντι πρόσφορον
ἐξεῦρες ἀτεχνῶς φάρμακον στραγγουρίας.   810

ΒΔΕΛΥΚΛΕΩΝ
καὶ πῦρ γε τουτί, καὶ προσέστηκεν φακῆ,
ῥοφεῖν ἐὰν δέῃ τι.

ΦΙΛΟΚΛΕΩΝ
τοῦτ' αὖ δεξιόν·
κἂν γὰρ πυρέττω, τόν γε μισθὸν λήψομαι.
αὐτοῦ μένων γὰρ τὴν φακῆν ῥοφήσομαι.

801 **ἐπὶ ταῖς οἰκίαισι.**] 'At their several homes.'
804 **Ἑκάτειον.**] There were numerous chapels of Hecate about Athens: ὡς τῶν Ἀθηναίων πανταχοῦ ἱδρυομένων αὐτήν, ὡς ἔφορον πάντων καὶ κουροτρόφον. Schol. And probably they were near the entrances of the houses.
805 Bdelycleon comes out with his judicial apparatus.
808 **ἐπὶ.**] The German editors change this to ἐκ or ἀπό. Though these prepositions are more natural with κρεμ., yet the vessel might surely be said to rest *on* its peg.
811 **φακῆ.**] ὥσπερ τὸ συκῆ ἀπὸ συκέα περισπῶσι, καὶ τὸ ἀμυγδαλῆ ἀπὸ ἀμυγδαλέα, οὕτω καὶ φακῆ ἀπὸ τοῦ φακέα. Schol. The plant itself is φακός.
813 **κἂν γὰρ πυρέττω.**] Even though he might be ill and sick of a fever, he might get his pay while sitting comfortably at home by the fire and swallowing his gruel. For οἱ νοσοῦντες χυλὸν πτισάνης ῥοφοῦσι. Schol. And in a fragment of Aristophanes found in Athenaeus (Fr. 201) we have **πτισάνην διδάσκεις αὐτὸν ἕψειν ἢ φακῆν.** This explanation seems so satisfactory that I cannot understand Hermann's transposition of the line to follow v. 797.
815 A cock is brought out, to wake up the dicast, should he go to sleep; a result not improbable. In *Les Plaideurs* L'Intime, in proof of his qualifications for an advocate, says 'J'endormirai, Monsieur, tout aussi bien qu'un autre.' And Dandin accordingly does go to sleep under the effect of the advocate's pleadings.

ΑΡΙΣΤΟΦΑΝΟΥΣ

ἀτὰρ τί τὸν ὄρνιν ὡς ἔμ' ἐξηνέγκατε; 815

ΒΔΕΛΤΚΛΕΩΝ
ἵν' ἄν, ἢν καθεύδῃς ἀπολογουμένου τινός,
ᾄδων ἄνωθεν ἐξεγείρῃ σ' οὑτοσί.

ΦΙΛΟΚΛΕΩΝ
ἓν ἔτι ποθῶ, τὰ δ' ἄλλ' ἀρέσκει μοι.

ΒΔΕΛΤΚΛΕΩΝ
τὸ τί;

ΦΙΛΟΚΛΕΩΝ
θηρῷον εἴ πως ἐκκομίσαις τὸ τοῦ Λύκου.

ΒΔΕΛΤΚΛΕΩΝ
πάρεστι τουτί, καὐτὸς ἄναξ οὑτοσί. 820

ΦΙΛΟΚΛΕΩΝ
ὦ δέσποθ' ἥρως, ὡς χαλεπὸς ἄρ' ἦσθ' ἰδεῖν.

ΒΔΕΛΤΚΛΕΩΝ
οἷόσπερ ἡμῖν φαίνεται Κλεώνυμος.

ΦΙΛΟΚΛΕΩΝ
οὔκουν ἔχει γ' οὐδ' αὐτὸς ἥρως ὢν ὅπλα.

ΒΔΕΛΤΚΛΕΩΝ
εἰ θᾶττον ἐκαθίζου σύ, θᾶττον ἂν δίκην
ἐκάλουν.

ἐξηνέγκατε.] Plural, because one of the slaves helped to bring out the things.

817 **ἄνωθεν.**] The cock was placed on a perch above Philocleon's head. Below at v. 932 he appeals to the bird to confirm his judgment.

819 **εἴ πως.**] This, the common text, is in every way as good as Meineke's alteration. 'If you would manage to bring out Lycus' statue' is a natural way of asking for it.

Λύκου.] Cf. above, v. 389.

820 **πάρεστι τουτί.**] He brings a picture of Lycus, Schol. And apparently it was a stern countenance (χαλεπός), and (the Scholiast says) ill-looking (δύσμορφος). This leads to a comparison with Cleonymus; upon which it is remarked that he is like Cleonymus in not having defensive armour, with allusion to Cleonymus casting away his shield. A hero was commonly represented in full panoply.

823 **οὔκουν κ.τ.λ.**] Sosias is unnecessary here; to whom the line is commonly given. Bergk and Meineke corrected the arrangement. The dialogue runs thus, BD. 'Here is Lycus'. PH. 'What an ugly stern fellow he is.' BD. 'He's something like Cleonymus, methinks.' ΓH. 'Ay, and that's why, hero though he is, he has no shield.'

825 **ἐκάλουν.**] This verb is used of the presiding judge, cf. below v.

ΦΙΛΟΚΛΕΩΝ
κάλει νυν, ὡς κάθημαι 'γὼ πάλαι.   825

ΒΔΕΛΥΚΛΕΩΝ
φέρε νυν, τίν' αὐτῷ πρῶτον εἰσαγάγω δίκην;
τί τίς κακὸν δέδρακε τῶν ἐν τῷκίᾳ;
ἡ Θρᾷττα προσκαύσασα πρώην τὴν χύτραν—

ΦΙΛΟΚΛΕΩΝ
ἐπίσχες οὗτος· ὡς ὀλίγου μ' ἀπώλεσας.
ἄνευ δρυφάκτου τὴν δίκην μέλλεις καλεῖν,   830
ὃ πρῶτον ἡμῖν τῶν ἱερῶν ἐφαίνετο;

ΒΔΕΛΥΚΛΕΩΝ
μὰ τὸν Δί' οὐ πάρεστιν.

ΦΙΛΟΚΛΕΩΝ
ἀλλ' ἐγὼ δραμὼν
αὐτὸς κομιοῦμαι τό γε παραυτίκ' ἔνδοθεν.

ΒΔΕΛΥΚΛΕΩΝ
τί ποτε τὸ χρῆμ'; ὡς δεινὸν ἡ φιλοχωρία.

1441, ἕως ἂν τὴν δίκην ἄρχων καλῇ. Similar is the use of εἰσάγειν in the next line.

827 τί τίς.] The double interrogative is quite after Greek use, and better than the common text τί τις, though 'Who has done what?' is in English very colloquial.

828 προσκαύσασα.] 'Burning the pot' must here mean 'burning or singeing the contents of it;' for the pot would be on the fire in the regular way of business, and would (with the other cooking vessels) become προσκεκαυμένα, cf. below v. 939.

829 ὀλίγου.] Cf. *Nub.* 722, ὀλίγου φροῦδος γεγένημαι.

830 δρυφάκτου.] The only instance of the singular of this word.

831 ἱερῶν.] Cf. *Thesm.* 629, σὺ δ' εἰπέ μοι, ὅ τι πρῶτον ἡμῖν τῶν ἱερῶν ἐδείκνυτο. To the old dicast all appertaining to the law-courts is sacred.

832 ἀλλ' ἐγὼ κ.τ.λ.] Philocleon posts off to fetch something for δρύφακτοι; his son exclaims in surprize at the old man's quickness τί ποτε κ.τ.λ. Then Xanthias runs in, with the tale of the dog's theft: this is at once seized on as the first case for the decision of this home circuit: then, as the old man re-enters, his son exclaims τουτὶ τί ἐστι; The arrangement of the speakers in Dindorf's Poetae Scenici is absurd. The text above follows the arrangement of Richter and Meineke. The adoption of ὅ τι ποτὲ χρῆμ' from Hermann, to end Philocleon's speech in v. 834, seems unnecessary. The meaning of that would be 'I will run in and get whatever we want' or 'whatever article I can lay my hands on'. The common reading τί ποτε τὸ χρῆμ' is 'Why, what ever ails the man? (he runs off so fast). A wonderful thing is the love of place!'

834 φιλοχωρία.] Philocleon has a cat-like attachment to the law-courts.

84   ΑΡΙΣΤΟΦΑΝΟΥΣ   [835

ΞΑΝΘΙΑΣ

βάλλ' ἐς κόρακας. τοιουτονὶ τρέφειν κύνα.   835

ΒΔΕΛΥΚΛΕΩΝ

τί δ' ἔστιν ἐτεόν;

ΞΑΝΘΙΑΣ

οὐ γὰρ ὁ Λάβης ἀρτίως
ὁ κύων παράξας ἐς τὸν ἰπνὸν ἀναρπάσας
τροφαλίδα τυροῦ Σικελικὴν κατεδήδοκεν;

ΒΔΕΛΥΚΛΕΩΝ

τοῦτ' ἆρα πρῶτον τἀδίκημα τῷ πατρὶ
εἰσακτέον μοι· σὺ δὲ κατηγόρει παρών.   840

835—890. The first criminal to be tried is found in a dog who has stolen and eaten a cheese. His fellow dog is to prosecute. After due sacrifices and prayers from Bdelycleon and the chorus that their artifice may succeed, the trial begins.

835 βάλλ' ἐς κ.] Said to the dog. τρέφειν.] Infinitive of exclamation: cf. *Nub.* 268, τὸ δὲ μηδὲ κυνῆν ...ἐλθεῖν ἔχοντα. The explanation of such a construction seems to be that the infinitive of the verb may stand for a noun, and then, the noun having been expressed, the rest of the sentence is left unsaid, the tone of the speaker plainly enough indicating what it would be. Thus, 'that I didn't even put a cap on before I came (was foolish):' and here, 'To keep such a dog (is absurd).'

836 Λάβης.] 'Griper, Nipper, Holdfast;' a natural name for a dog: the Scholiast quotes Δάκης as a dog's name used by Teleclides. But there is evident allusion to Laches and his peculations in Sicily. Cf. above, v. 240, ἔσται Λάχητι νυνί (ἡ δίκη). Laches went with the first Athenian expedition to Sicily, in B.C. 427. Cf. Thuc. III. 86, 88, 90. He was superseded by Pythodorus (Thuc. III. 115). The facts of the deme of Aexone being given to the dog (Laches' real deme, cf. Plat. *Lach.* 197), and of the theft being a *Sicilian* cheese, leave no doubt that Laches is here alluded to.

837 ἰπνόν.] 'The kitchen:' for the limited sense of 'oven' will not suit. Cf. v. 139.

838 τροφαλίδα.] 'fresh curd-cheese,' from τρέφειν. Cf. Theocr. *Id.* XXV. 106, ἄλλος ἀμόλγιον εἶχ', ἄλλος τρέφε πίονα τυρόν. One Scholiast appears to interpret it 'a round cheese;' and that the cheese was round is likely: but the explanation perhaps arises from some confusion between τρέπειν and τρέφειν. The dairy sense of τρέφειν is quite established enough to make the meaning of τροφαλὶς certain.

Σικελικήν.] πολυθρέμμων δὲ ἡ Σικελία, διὸ τυρὸν πολὺν καὶ κάλλιστον ἔχει. Schol.

839 τοῦτ' ἆρα, κ.τ.λ.] Racine has a dog-trial in imitation of this. But there is not very much similarity between Aristophanes and the French dramatist here. The latter makes the tediousness and bombast of the advocates the chief feature in the trial, which ends in the judge being sent to sleep, and, on being awakened, hastily condemning the accused to the galleys.

840 εἰσακτέον.] The technical

ΞΑΝΘΙΑΣ

μὰ Δί' οὐκ ἔγωγ'· ἀλλ' ἅτερός φησιν κύων
κατηγορήσειν, ἥν τις εἰσάγῃ γραφήν.

ΒΔΕΛΥΚΛΕΩΝ

ἴθι νυν, ἄγ' αὐτὼ δεῦρο.

ΞΑΝΘΙΑΣ

ταῦτα χρὴ ποιεῖν.

ΦΙΛΟΚΛΕΩΝ

τουτὶ τί ἔστι;

ΒΔΕΛΥΚΛΕΩΝ

χοιροκομεῖον Ἑστίας.

ΦΙΛΟΚΛΕΩΝ

εἶθ' ἱεροσυλήσας φέρεις;

ΒΔΕΛΥΚΛΕΩΝ

οὔκ, ἀλλ' ἵνα 845
ἀφ' Ἑστίας ἀρχόμενος ἐπιτρίψω τινά.

ΦΙΛΟΚΛΕΩΝ

ἀλλ' εἴσαγ' ἀνύσας· ὡς ἐγὼ τιμᾶν βλέπω.

ΒΔΕΛΥΚΛΕΩΝ

φέρε νυν, ἐνέγκω τὰς σανίδας καὶ τὰς γραφάς.

word of the judge: cf. note on v. 8?5.

844 τουτί.] Philocleon returns, with a pig-sty fence, ἀγγεῖόν τι κανωτόν, to serve for δρύφακτοι. It is called 'of Hestia,' because (says the Scholiast) they kept pigs close to their homes (if that be the meaning of ἐπὶ τῆς ἑστίας τρέφουσι χοίρους), the pig-stye adjoining the house probably. In an Irish cabin indeed the pig is more literally ἐπὶ τῆς ἑστίας. Also, at libations, they began with the goddess Hestia; hence Philocleon, when charged with temple-robbing, replies, 'No, it's all in the regular course; I begin with Hestia, as our wont is, and go on to despatch my victim.' Cf. Plat. *Euthyphr*. 3, ἀφ' Ἑστίας ἄρχεσθαι κακουργεῖν τὴν πόλιν. The phrase passed into a proverb for beginning at the very beginning.

847 τιμᾶν βλέπω.] Cf. *Ach*. 375, οὐδὲν βλέπουσιν ἄλλο πλὴν ψήφῳ δακεῖν. The infinitive takes the place of the noun: hence such phrases as βλέπειν νᾶπυ may be compared with this.

848 σανίδας.] These are certainly here what they most probably are at v. 349, tablets with notices of the suits upon them; containing in fact a programme of the dicastic business

ΑΡΙΣΤΟΦΑΝΟΥΣ

ΦΙΛΟΚΛΕΩΝ

οἴμοι, διατρίβεις κἀπολεῖς τριψημερῶν·
ἐγὼ δ' ἀλοκίζειν ἐδεόμην τὸ χωρίον.   850

ΒΔΕΛΥΚΛΕΩΝ

ἰδού.

ΦΙΛΟΚΛΕΩΝ

κάλει νυν.

ΒΔΕΛΥΚΛΕΩΝ

ταῦτα δή.

ΦΙΛΟΚΛΕΩΝ

τίς οὑτοσὶ
ὁ πρῶτός ἐστιν;

ΒΔΕΛΥΚΛΕΩΝ

ἐς κόρακας, ὡς ἄχθομαι,
ὁτιὴ 'πελαθόμην τοὺς καδίσκους ἐκφέρειν.

ΦΙΛΟΚΛΕΩΝ

οὗτος σὺ ποῖ θεῖς;

ΒΔΕΛΥΚΛΕΩΝ

ἐπὶ καδίσκους.

to be done. There was no strong necessity for them perhaps, when only one suit, and that a known one, was coming on; but Philocleon will insist in having all the minutest particulars of law-court furniture.

850 ἐγὼ δ'...τὸ χωρίον.] Meineke thinks this line corrupt. It is commonly interpreted, 'And I wanted to furrow up the ground,' *i. e.* to trace the line on the πινάκιον τιμητικόν. He was in a hurry to be at his work, and to condemn his man. And *Thesm.* 777—786 is brought to support such a metaphor; where Mnesilochus, meaning to write, says, ἄγε δὴ πινάκων ξεστῶν δέλτοι, δέξασθε σμίλης ὁλκούς, κήρυκας ἐμῶν μόχθων· οἴμοι τουτὶ τὸ ῥῶ μοχθηρόν· χώρει, χώρει. ποίαν αὔλακα; βάσκετ' ἐπείγετε πάσας καθ' ὁδοὺς κεῖνα ταῦτα·

ταχέως χρή. But is it not possible that Philocleon, who, though a dicast, is in some respects a rough old-fashioned fellow, has a farm? and that he counted on getting away to it, after despatching his law business, and doing a little farmer's work. 'You will keep me here all day,' he says, 'and I wanted to do a bit of ploughing on my farm.' χωρίον is frequently used in this sense: cf. *Ach.* 226, *Pac.* 1146, 1148. The delay of these preparations wearies him, though he is anxious to have everything correct: hence at v. 855 he will not have κάδισκοι fetched, but at once produces something to serve for them. Of course there is a little inconsistency in his wanting thus to get it over, but that is not unnatural in an old man of his sort.

ΦΙΛΟΚΛΕΩΝ

μηδαμῶς.
ἐγὼ γὰρ εἶχον τούσδε τοὺς ἀρυστίχους. 855

ΒΔΕΛΥΚΛΕΩΝ

κάλλιστα τοίνυν· πάντα γὰρ πάρεστι νῷν
ὅσων δεόμεθα, πλήν γε δὴ τῆς κλεψύδρας.

ΦΙΛΟΚΛΕΩΝ

ἡδὶ δὲ δὴ τίς ἐστιν; οὐχὶ κλεψύδρα;

ΒΔΕΛΥΚΛΕΩΝ

εὖ γ' ἐκπορίζεις αὐτὰ κἀπιχωρίως.
ἀλλ' ὡς τάχιστα πῦρ τις ἐξενεγκάτω 860
καὶ μυρρίνας καὶ τὸν λιβανωτὸν ἔνδοθεν,
ὅπως ἂν εὐξώμεσθα πρῶτα τοῖς θεοῖς.

ΧΟΡΟΣ

καὶ μὴν ἡμεῖς ἐπὶ ταῖς σπονδαῖς
καὶ ταῖς εὐχαῖς
φήμην ἀγαθὴν λέξομεν ὑμῖν, 865
ὅτι γενναίως ἐκ τοῦ πολέμου
καὶ τοῦ νείκους ξυνεβήτην.

ΒΔΕΛΥΚΛΕΩΝ

εὐφημία μὲν πρῶτα νῦν ὑπαρχέτω.

---

855 ἀρυστίχους.] ἀγγεῖον ᾧ ἔστιν ἀρύσασθαι, κοτύλη ἢ κύαθος. Schol.
859—62. Myrtle boughs and frankincense are brought out. On μυρρίναι the scholiast says μυρρίναις γὰρ ἐστεφανοῦντο οἱ ἄρχοντες: and at most festivals these boughs appear to have been used. Cf. the well-known song on Harmodius and Aristogiton, ἐν μύρτου κλαδὶ τὸ ξίφος φορήσω. And at the merry-making in *The Peace* (v. 1154) myrtle-boughs are sent for. Cf. also *Ran.* 871 for fire and frankincense thus called for: ἴθι νυν λιβανωτὸν δεῦρό τις καὶ πῦρ δότω, ὅπως ἂν εὔξωμαι πρὸ τῶν σοφισμάτων.

863—67. This is a system of anapaests. A strophe follows, vv. 868—873, εὐφημία...πλάνων, to which correspond vv. 885—890, ξυνευχόμεσθα...νεωτέρων.

868 εὐφημία.] Constantly called for on similar occasions; cf. *Eq.* 1316, *Nub.* 263, *Thesm.* 295. This line is given by Meincke to the chorus. Richter gives the following line to Bdelycleon, making the chorus resume with τὸ πρᾶγμ' ὃ κ.τ.λ.

869—74. The Chorus pray that

ΧΟΡΟΣ

ὦ Φοῖβ' Ἄπολλον Πύθι', ἐπ' ἀγαθῇ τύχῃ
τὸ πρᾶγμ' ὃ μηχανᾶται 870
ἔμπροσθεν οὗτος τῶν θυρῶν,
ἅπασιν ἡμῖν ἁρμόσαι
παυσαμένοις πλάνων.
Ἰήιε Παιάν. 874

ΒΔΕΛΤΚΛΕΩΝ

ὦ δέσποτ' ἄναξ, γεῖτον ἀγυιεῦ τοὐμοῦ προθύρου προπύλαιε,
δέξαι τελετὴν καινὴν, ὦναξ, ἣν τῷ πατρὶ καινοτομοῦμεν·
παῦσόν τ' αὐτοῦ τοῦτο τὸ λίαν στρυφνὸν καὶ πρίνινον ἦθος,
ἀντὶ σιραίου μέλιτος μικρὸν τῷ θυμιδίῳ παραμίξας·
ἤδη δ' εἶναι τοῖς ἀνθρώποις
ἤπιον αὐτὸν,
τοὺς φεύγοντάς τ' ἐλεεῖν μᾶλλον 880
τῶν γραψαμένων,
κἀπιδακρύειν ἀντιβολούντων,
καὶ παυσάμενον τῆς δυσκολίας
ἀπὸ τῆς ὀργῆς
τὴν ἀκαλήφην ἀφελέσθαι.

Bdelycleon's device may turn out well, and suit them all, giving them rest from their wanderings and errors in legal matters.

872 ἁρμόσαι.] Infinitive, as frequently in prayers, dependent on δὸς, or some word of the kind.

875—885. Bdelycleon puts up his special prayer that his father may be turned to a milder mood.

875 προθύρου προπύλαις.] Readings vary here. The MSS. are corrupt: MS. R. has προθύρου πρόσθ' πύλας: MS. V. προπύλου προσπύλας: the rest προθύρου πρὸς πύλας. The correction in the text is Bentley's; Bergk reads πρόσθεν προπυλαίου: Meineke προπύλου πάρος αὐλᾶς. The sense does not vary much, whichever correction we take as most probable. Meineke thinks his nearest to the Ven. MS., and that the expression is probably a fragment from Euripides.

876 καινοτομοῦμεν.] Cf. *Eccl.* 584, εἰ καινοτομεῖν ἐθελήσουσιν, καὶ μὴ τοῖς ἤθάσι λίαν τοῖς τ' ἀρχαίοις ἐνδιατρίβειν.

877 στρυφνὸν.] From στύφειν, 'astringere:' χείλεα στυφθεὶς, Anth. The next word πρίνινος is applied to old men in *Ach.* 179, coupled with στιπτοί.

878 σιραίου.] τὸ ἡψημένον γλεῦκος, βραχὺ δ' ἔχον παράπικρον ὅταν καθεψηθῇ. Schol. Instead of bitter a little sweet is to be put into the old man's composition.

880 φεύγοντάς τ' ἐλ.] He had been always ready to condemn, and inexorable to piteous appeals. Cf. above, 560—70.

884 ἀκαλήφην.] 'The nettle, the sting.' Crates in the *Phoenissae* used the word in the same way. Schol.

ΣΦΗΚΕΣ.

ΧΟΡΟΣ

ξυνευχόμεσθά σοι * * κἀπᾴδομεν 885
νέαισιν ἀρχαῖς, ἕνεκα τῶν προλελεγμένων.
εὖνοι γάρ ἐσμεν ἐξ οὗ
τὸν δῆμον ᾐσθόμεσθά σου
φιλοῦντος ὡς οὐδεὶς ἀνὴρ
τῶν γε νεωτέρων. 890

ΒΔΕΛΥΚΛΕΩΝ

εἴ τις θύρασιν ἠλιαστής, εἰσίτω·
ὡς ἡνίκ᾽ ἂν λέγωσιν, οὐκ ἐσφρήσομεν.

ΦΙΛΟΚΛΕΩΝ

τίς ἄρ᾽ ὁ φεύγων οὗτος; ὅσον ἁλώσεται.

ΞΑΝΘΙΑΣ

ἀκούετ᾽ ἤδη τῆς γραφῆς. ἐγράψατο

885 **ξυνευχόμεσθά σοι**] ταῦτά or ταὐτά before σοι is generally accepted to fill the gap.
888 **ᾐσθόμεσθα.**] Corrected from ᾐσθόμεθα of MSS. In what way ᾐσθήμεσθα, the reading of Cobet and Meineke, is better, it is hard to say.
890 **τῶν γε νεωτέρων.**] τῶν γενναιοτέρων. R. V. And the Scholiast recognizes both readings. But the common text suits the metre, corresponding with v. 873, παυσαμένοις πλάνων; and is better for the sense. 'You love the people as no man does of the nobler sort,' is a sentiment hardly intelligible. But, 'as no man does, at least of the younger men, of men now-a-days,' fits well with the character of the chorus who are approvers of an older generation. After this line Meineke adds ἴῃε παιάν, to balance the same in v. 874; unnecessarily perhaps; cf. above, v. 281.
891—994. The trial begins. There is a dog plaintiff, and a dog defendant. The charge is set forth; the damages laid. Philocleon is eager to condemn, before he has heard half the case. Xanthias is spokesman for the prosecuting dog; shews how the accused stole the cheese and gave him no share. The old dicast will hardly hear any defence, but Bdelycleon makes him do so, and sets forth piteously the case of the accused, brings witnesses to shew that the accuser is just as bad; produces the children of the accused as a last resource to move pity. Philocleon is a little melted, but yet means to condemn. Bdelycleon, however, deceives him, and makes him put his vote into the wrong urn, and Labes is acquitted.
891 **εἴ τις θύρασιν.**] Bdelycleon acts as thesmothetes: cf. above, v. 775, οὐδείς σ᾽ ἀποκλῄσει θεσμοθέτης τῇ κιγκλίδι. The signal for the gathering we may suppose now to be taken down: cf. note on σημείου at v. 690.
893 **τίς ἄρ᾽ ὁ φ.**] Philocleon is eager for his work; predetermined that the defendant shall be well trounced.
ὅσον.] Exclamatory, 'how finely, how thoroughly!'
894—97. Bdelycleon introduces the suit, ἀκούετ᾽ ἤδη, 'Oyes, Oyes,'

90 ΑΡΙΣΤΟΦΑΝΟΥΣ [895

κύων Κυδαθηναιεὺς Λάβητ' Αἰξωνέα,   895
τὸν τυρὸν ἀδικεῖν ὅτι μόνος κατήσθιεν
τὸν Σικελικόν. τίμημα κλῳὸς σύκινος.

ΦΙΛΟΚΛΕΩΝ
θάνατος μὲν οὖν κύνειος, ἢν ἅπαξ ἁλῷ.

ΒΔΕΛΥΚΛΕΩΝ
καὶ μὴν ὁ φεύγων οὑτοσὶ Λάβης πάρα.

ΦΙΛΟΚΛΕΩΝ
ὦ μιαρὸς οὗτος· ὡς δὲ καὶ κλέπτον βλέπει,   900
οἷον σεσηρὼς ἐξαπατήσειν μ' οἴεται.
ποῦ δ' ἔσθ' ὁ διώκων, ὁ Κυδαθηναιεὺς κύων;

Mitch. Cf. the usual ἀκούετε λέῳ, Ach. 1000.
895 Κυδαθηναιεύς.] The deme of the parties concerned is mentioned in all such formulae. Here the deme of Cydathenus is given to the dog, because that was (it is said) the deme of Cleon. Cleon compares himself to a dog in *Eq.* 1023, and is compared to one by his adversaries.
Λάβητ' Αἰξωνέα.] Labes is (as we have seen at v. 836) to represent Laches. This deme of Aexone was noted for the scurrilous language to which its inhabitants were addicted, says Stephanus; and Plato (*Laches*, 197) seems to confirm this, where Laches says, 'I will say nothing in reply, though I have plenty to say, lest you should assert that I am Aexonian not only in name but in nature.'
897 Σικελικόν.] Bergler quotes from Antiphanes in Athenaeus, τυρὸς Σικελὸς, μύρον ἐξ 'Αθηνῶν, ἐγχέλεις Βοιώτιαι. For Laches' peculations in Sicily cf. note on v. 836.
τίμημα.] The damages were first laid by the plaintiff, who was said τιμᾶσθαι. Against this the opponents might ἀντιτιμᾶσθαι. The judge finally decided the amount (ἐτίμα).
κλῳός.] περιτραχήλιος δεσμός.

Schol. It is of fig-wood with allusion probably to συκοφαντία: of which Aristophanes never tires.
898 θάνατος μὲν οὖν.] The mild penalty does not content Philocleon. All his interpolations in the trial scene are severe, and against the defendant.
900 κλέπτον βλέπει.] 'He carries thief in his face.'
901 σεσηρώς.] The 'grin,' expressed by this word, is generally in mockery or malice, but not always so, as Theocr. *Id.* VII. 19, εἶπε σεσαρὼς ὄμματι μειδιόωντι, proves. Hence Richter's alteration σεσηνὼς (a form perhaps not elsewhere found) is needless. The Scholiast's explanation, κεχηνώς, διηνοιγμένον ἔχων τὸ στόμα, further confirms the text. And the broad grin would be more immediately striking as the dog came in, than would the wagging of his tail. Richter quotes, *Eq.* 1029, ὃς κέρκῳ σαίνων σ', ὁπόταν δειπνῇς, ἐπιτηρῶν ἐξέδεταί σου τοὔψον ὅταν σύ που ἄλλοτε χάσκῃς.
902 ποῦ δ' ἔσθ' ὁ διώκων.] Dindorf in the old Poetae Scenici had ποῦ δ' ὁ δ., which manifestly was wrong. In his larger edition he approves ποῦ μοῦ διώκων, *i. e.* ποῦ μοι ὁ διώκων, which is a curious crasis. ποῦ ποῦ δ' ὁ δ. Mein., ποῦ δ' οὖν ὁ δ.

ΣΦΗΚΕΣ.

ΚΥΩΝ

αὖ αὖ.

ΒΔΕΛΤΚΛΕΩΝ
πάρεστιν.

ΦΙΛΟΚΛΕΩΝ
ἕτερος οὗτος αὖ Λάβης.

ΒΔΕΛΤΚΛΕΩΝ
ἀγαθός γ᾽ ὑλακτεῖν καὶ διαλείχειν τὰς χύτρας.
σίγα, κάθιζε· σὺ δ᾽ ἀναβὰς κατηγόρει.   905

ΦΙΛΟΚΛΕΩΝ
φέρε νυν, ἅμα τήνδ᾽ ἐγχεάμενος κἀγὼ ῥοφῶ.

ΞΑΝΘΙΑΣ
τῆς μὲν γραφῆς ἠκούσαθ᾽ ἣν ἐγραψάμην,
ἄνδρες δικασταί, τουτονί. δεινότατα γὰρ
ἔργων δέδρακε κἀμὲ καὶ τὸ ῥυππαπαῖ.
ἀποδρὰς γὰρ ἐς τὴν γωνίαν τυρὸν πολὺν   910

Hotib. The reading of the text is in Hirschig and Richter.
903 αὖ αὖ.] μιμεῖται τὴν φωνήν. Schol. This line is variously divided. To give πάρεστιν to Bdelycleon, ἕτερος—χύτρας to Philocleon, as Dobree does, seems best. On the dicast asking for the prosecutor, he is brought forward, and barks, and Bdelycleon says, 'He is here.' The dicast remarks that he looks like a second Labes. The son rejoins that he is good at barking, &c.: and then bids his father listen in silence, while Xanthias gets up and speaks for the prosecutor.
904 διαλείχειν.] The prosecuting dog is about as bad as the other. In *Eq.* 1030—34 Cleon is described as a dog Cerberus, of whom Demus is to beware, and who will escape notice κυνηδὸν νύκτωρ τὰς λοπάδας καὶ τὰς νήσους διαλείχων. The χύτραι here mean subject states or islands, as there νήσους is by way of surprise for χύτρας.
906 τήνδ᾽.] Sc. φακῆν. Cf. above, v. 811.

907 ἦν.] It is a question whether we ought against nearly all MSS. to change this to ἧς, though this latter is certainly the more Attic construction. Richter and Meineke do, following Brunck.
909 ῥυππαπαῖ.] 'The seamen,' because ῥυππαπαῖ was the seamen's cry; for which cf. *Ran.* 1073; also *Eq.* 602, for a rhyming imitation, ἱππαπαῖ. The scholiast adds that the sailors were aggrieved by this cheese theft, ὡς τῶν ἐρετῶν καὶ ναυτῶν περὶ πλείστου ποιουμένων τὸν τυρόν. However this may be, the sailors are mentioned naturally enough, since Laches was in command of a fleet in Sicily.
910 γωνίαν.] This and ἐν τῷ σκότῳ the Scholiast explains ἐπειδὴ ἐν μέρει τῆς δύσεως ἡ Σικελία. Sicily (as regards Greece) was out of the way and in a corner westward. Perhaps this is striving too much for a double meaning in all the details of the dog's theft.

ΑΡΙΣΤΟΦΑΝΟΥΣ

κατεσικέλιζε κἀνέπλητ' ἐν τῷ σκότῳ,
νὴ τὸν Δί', ἀλλὰ δῆλός ἐστ'· ἔμοιγέ τοι
τυροῦ κάκιστον ἀρτίως ἐνήρυγει
ὁ βδελυρὸς οὗτος.

ΞΑΝΘΙΑΣ
κοὐ μετέδωκ' αἰτοῦντί μοι.
καίτοι τίς ὑμᾶς εὖ ποιεῖν δυνήσεται,   915
ἢν μή τι κἀμοί τις προβάλλῃ τῷ κυνί;

ΦΙΛΟΚΛΕΩΝ
οὐδὲν μετέδωκεν;

ΞΑΝΘΙΑΣ
οὐδὲ τῷ κοινῷ γ' ἐμοί.

ΒΔΕΛΥΚΛΕΩΝ
θερμὸς γὰρ ἀνὴρ οὐδὲν ἧττον τῆς φακῆς.
πρὸς τῶν θεῶν, μὴ προκαταγίγνωσκ', ὦ πάτερ,
πρὶν ἄν γ' ἀκούσῃς ἀμφοτέρων.

ΦΙΛΟΚΛΕΩΝ
ἀλλ', ὠγαθέ,   920
τὸ πρᾶγμα φανερόν ἐστιν· αὐτὸ γὰρ βοᾷ.

911 κατεσικέλιζε.] 'He si-sliced away.'
914 κοὐ μετέδωκ'.] That he gave no share to the other dog (Cleon's representative) is the chief crime. Xanthias' complaint, as the aggrieved dog, has an ironical meaning.
915 καίτοι κ.τ.λ.] Who can benefit you, without a previous sop to your Cerberus? It must be, 'love me, love my dog.' Cf. the note above at v. 904, and *Eq.* 1030—34.
917 οὐδὲν κ.τ.λ.] Meineke with Bergk gives this and the following line to Philocleon. Neither thus, nor with Dindorf's arrangement, is the connexion of θερμὸς γὰρ ἀνήρ with the preceding plain. Florens says, that Philocleon, while speaking, tries whether his lentil porridge is ready; and, finding it hot, says that the accused is 'as hot (meaning 'as bold') as the lentil porridge.' But the direct mention of him as ἀνήρ, 'the man' (instead of 'the dog') is curious. Nor is θερμότης a natural reason for withholding a share of anything. ἀνήρ may indeed be compared with ἄνδρα in v. 923; but the sense of the line as applied to Labes or Laches is not satisfactory. The line is better given to Bdelycleon, with reference to some gesture of anger and eagerness to condemn shewn by Philocleon. Thus Bdelycleon would say, seeing his father's hot haste, 'Why, the man's as hot as his lentil porridge! Pray, father, in heaven's name don't condemn too soon.'
920 ἀμφοτέρων.] Cf. note at 725.

ΣΦΗΚΕΣ.

ΞΑΝΘΙΑΣ

μή νυν ἀφῆτέ γ' αὐτόν, ὡς ἔντ' αὖ πολὺ
κυνῶν ἁπάντων ἄνδρα μονοφαγίστατον,
ὅστις περιπλεύσας τὴν θυείαν ἐν κύκλῳ
ἐκ τῶν πόλεων τὸ σκῖρον ἐξεδήδοκεν.   925

ΦΙΛΟΚΛΕΩΝ

ἐμοὶ δέ γ' οὐκ ἔστ' οὐδὲ τὴν ὑδρίαν πλάσαι.

ΞΑΝΘΙΑΣ

πρὸς ταῦτα τοῦτον κολάσατ'· οὐ γὰρ ἄν ποτε
τρέφειν δύναιτ' ἂν μία λόχμη κλέπτα δύο·
ἵνα μὴ κεκλάγγω διὰ κενῆς ἄλλως ἐγώ·
ἐὰν δὲ μή, τὸ λοιπὸν οὐ κεκλάγξομαι.   930

ΦΙΛΟΚΛΕΩΝ

ἰοὺ ἰού.
ὅσας κατηγόρησε τὰς πανουργίας.
κλέπτον τὸ χρῆμα τἀνδρός· οὐ καὶ σοὶ δοκεῖ,

923 ἄνδρα μονοφαγίστατον.] 'Beyond all dogs a man of selfish greed.' The inconsistency of κυνῶν ἄνδρα is intentionally ridiculous. The superlative in -ίστατος from μονόφαγος is analogous to λαλίστατος from λάλος, Eur. *Cycl.* 315; cf. Ar. *Ran.* 91.

924 θυείαν.] The mortar means Sicily or the Sicilian sea, as the Scholiast says. A mortar was round (στρογγύλη): cf. *Pac.* 228.

925 σκῖρον.] Eupolis, in his *Golden Age*, has the phrase τροφαλὶς βαδίζει σκῖρον ἠμφιεσμένη. There is a play on the double meaning. Of the cheese, it is the hard under crust; of the cities, the gypsum or stucco of their buildings. And in the next line Philocleon takes it as equivalent to γῆ σκιρράς, with which they used to mend broken pitchers.

928 μία λόχμη.] There was a proverb μία λόχμη δύο ἐριθάκους οὐ τρέφει, 'one bush does not support two redstarts'. Here Xanthias means 'one house can't keep two thieves': he himself (as the dog or

Cleon) being of course one.

929 κεκλάγγω.] Some read κεκλάγχω: but the better editors and MS. R are for κεκλάγγω.

διὰ κενῆς.] This phrase is used adverbially by Thuc. IV. 126, ἡ διὰ κενῆς ἐπανάσεισις τῶν ὅπλων. And the Greeks often put together adverbs of nearly the same meaning. Another instance of διὰ κενῆς ἄλλως is quoted from Plato the comic writer: and Bergler quotes ἄλλως μάτην as combined. To which might be added αὖθις αὖ πάλιν, and similar phrases. It would be easy here to suggest a noun feminine as understood; but probably the speaker had no such definite noun in his mind, and was hardly conscious of any ellipse.

933 κλέπτον τὸ χρῆμα τἀνδρός] = ἀνήρ ἐστι κλέπτης. For τὸ χρῆμα cf. *Nub.* 2, τὸ χρῆμα τῶν νυκτῶν, and the note there.

οὐ καὶ σοί.] The dicast turns round to the cock perched up above him.

ὠλεκτρυόν; νὴ τὸν Δί', ἐπιμύει γέ τοι.
ὁ θεσμοθέτης. ποῦ 'σθ' οὗτος; ἁμίδα μοι δότω.   935

ΒΔΕΛΤΚΛΕΩΝ
αὐτὸς καθελοῦ· τοὺς μάρτυρας γὰρ ἐσκαλῶ.
Λάβητι μάρτυρας παρεῖναι, τρυβλίον,
δοίδυκα, τυρόκνηστιν, ἐσχάραν, χύτραν,
καὶ τἄλλα τὰ σκεύη τὰ προσκεκαυμένα.
ἀλλ' ἔτι σύ γ' οὐρεῖς καὶ καθίζεις οὐδέπω   940

ΦΙΛΟΚΛΕΩΝ
τοῦτον δέ γ' οἶμ' ἐγὼ χεσεῖσθαι τήμερον.

ΒΔΕΛΤΚΛΕΩΝ
οὐκ αὖ σὺ παύσει χαλεπὸς ὢν καὶ δύσκολος,
καὶ ταῦτα τοῖς φεύγουσιν, ἀλλ' ὀδὰξ ἔχει;

ΦΙΛΟΚΛΕΩΝ
ἀνάβαιν', ἀπολογοῦ. τί σεσιώπηκας; λέγε.

934 ἐπιμύει.] 'He winks assent': and a wink from a cock is as good as a nod.
937—9 The dish, cheese-scraper, &c., are called to witness in Labes' favour. The ἐσχάρα was a portable brazier; cf. *Ach.* 887, δμῶες ἐξενέγκατε τὴν ἐσχάραν μοι δεῦρο καὶ τὴν ῥιπίδα. All the kitchen vessels might have seen the theft, and seen also what the thief did with the cheese; whether he gave any to others. The ἐσχάρα was perhaps used for the toasting of the cheese.
939 προσκεκαυμένα.] 'burnt at the fire' as such utensils would be: cf. above v. 828. Dobree and Hermann read προσκεκλημένα 'subpoenaed as witnesses'; an ingenious change: but hardly needed.
942 οὐκ αὖ σὺ κ.τ.λ.] This is addressed to the old man. Bdelycleon had before asked him not to be too hasty in condemning (v. 819): he now asks it again, οὐκ αὖ σὺ 'will you not, I again ask, cease &c.' Florens takes it as addressed to the prosecutor; but there is not much sense in rebuking him for severity; severity would be reasonable in him.
943 καὶ ταῦτα τοῖς φεύγουσιν.] 'And that too against the poor defendants.' Bdelycleon wants him to have some wrath for the prosecutors. Cf. above v. 880, τοὺς φεύγοντάς τ' ἐλεεῖν μᾶλλον τῶν γραψαμένων, κ.τ.λ.
ἀλλ' ὀδὰξ ἔχει.] 'But do you hold on to them with griping teeth?' One of the expected advantages in this law-court at home was, that the dicast being not starved, but having his porridge, would cease δάκνων τὸν ἀπολογούμενον (v. 778). The αὐτοδὰξ τρόπος was a characteristic of the Athenians, cf. *Pac.* 607. The Scholiast strangely mistakes the meaning of this passage; and those who propose ἔχεις for ἔχει propose no improvement. The sense of the middle voice suits quite well: 'you hold fast to, cling to': it appears just the word for a bulldog tenacity.
944 ἀνάβαιν'.] He turns to the defendant here.

ΣΦΗΚΕΣ.

ΦΙΛΟΚΛΕΩΝ

ἀλλ' οὐκ ἔχειν οὑτός γ' ἔοικεν ὅ τι λέγῃ. 945

ΒΔΕΛΥΚΛΕΩΝ

οὔκ, ἀλλ' ἐκεῖνό μοι δοκεῖ πεπονθέναι,
ὅπερ ποτὲ φεύγων ἔπαθε καὶ Θουκυδίδης·
ἀπόπληκτος ἐξαίφνης ἐγένετο τὰς γνάθους.
πάρεχ', ἐκποδών. ἐγὼ γὰρ ἀπολογήσομαι.
χαλεπὸν μὲν, ὦνδρες, ἐστὶ διαβεβλημένου 950
ὑπεραποκρίνεσθαι κυνός· λέξω δ' ὅμως.
ἀγαθὸς γάρ ἐστι καὶ διώκει τοὺς λύκους.

ΦΙΛΟΚΛΕΩΝ

κλέπτης μὲν οὖν οὑτός γε καὶ ξυνωμότης.

ΒΔΕΛΥΚΛΕΩΝ

μὰ Δί', ἀλλ' ἄριστός ἐστι τῶν νυνὶ κυνῶν,
οἷός τε πολλοῖς προβατίοις ἐφεστάναι. 955

ΦΙΛΟΚΛΕΩΝ

τί οὖν ὄφελος, τὸν τυρὸν εἰ κατεσθίει;

ΒΔΕΛΥΚΛΕΩΝ

ὅτι σοῦ προμάχεται καὶ φυλάττει τὴν θύραν

---

945 ἀλλ' οὐκ.] Philocleon maintains his conclusion against the defendant: thinking that he has not a word to say. His son says that it is not conscious guilt, but a sudden paralysis of the tongue.

947 Θουκυδίδης.] Son of Melesias, opponent of Pericles, accused of some misdoings in Thrace, and ostracised, B.C. 444, cf. *Ach.* 703, 708, where Aristophanes appears to pity him, as hardly dealt with. The policy of Pericles our poet does not approve of: cf. *Ach.* 530 sqq., and therefore naturally sympathizes with his rival.

949 πάρεχ', ἐκποδών.] Reiske seems to be right in thus punctuating. For πάρεχε can hardly mean 'take yourself off', or, with ἐκποδών, be equivalent to ἴθι ἐκπ., ἄπαγε ἐκπ., as L. and S. say. πάρεχε is rather 'allow me, give place, let me come', and ἐκποδών 'out of the way with you!' The Scholiast confirms this by his note λακτίσας τὸν κύνα φησὶν ἀναχώρει. Bdelycleon pushes aside the dog and takes the place of defendant.

952 λύκους.] τοὺς συκοφάντας. Schol. It seems rather meant that Laches was an active soldier against his country's enemies.

953 κλ. μὲν οὖν οὑτός γε.] Cf. *Nub.* 1112, ὠχρὸν μὲν οὖν ἔγωγε καὶ κακοδαίμονα.

955 προβατίοις.] Cf. v. 32, πρόβατα συγκαθήμενα. No doubt here too there is an idea of the Athenians being silly sheep.

957 ὅτι σοῦ.] 'The good of him is that he fights for you &c.'

καὶ τἄλλ' ἄριστός ἐστιν· εἰ δ' ὑφείλετο,
ξύγγνωθι. κιθαρίζειν γὰρ οὐκ ἐπίσταται.

ΦΙΛΟΚΛΕΩΝ
ἐγὼ δ' ἐβουλόμην ἂν οὐδὲ γράμματα, 960
ἵνα μὴ κακουργῶν ἐνέγραφ' ἡμῖν τὸν λόγον.

Philocleon had asked ! What is the good of him?' and the answer is natural enough. Dobree reads it ὅ τι; σοῦ 'you ask what good? Why he fights &c.' Either of these seems far preferable to Meineke's conjectural change in his notes, οὐ σοῦ κ.τ.λ. 'Does he not &c.'

959 κιθαρίζειν κ.τ.λ.] A curious excuse for non-appreciation of the difference between 'meum' and 'tuum'. But ignorance of the elements of music implies utter illiterateness; therefore it is as if Bdelycleon had said 'poor fellow! he's had no schooling—knows nothing— what is he to turn his hand to but thieving?' And below at v. 989, Philocleon retorts that he knows no trade but judging and condemning. In *Av.* 1432, τί γὰρ πάθω; σκάπτειν γὰρ οὐκ ἐπίσταμαι, is a similar excuse, given by the informer who knows no trade but his own. The scholiast quotes a proverb, to which there may be allusion, πεζῇ βαδίζω, νεῖν γὰρ οὐκ ἐπίσταμαι, 'I trudge afoot because I cannot swim.' In the *Knights* (v. 188) the sausage-seller objects οὐδὲ μουσικὴν ἐπίσταμαι πλὴν γραμμάτων: but he is told that that is rather odds in his favour for being a statesman now-a-days; and therefore for being a thief perhaps, in Aristophanes' view of his country's statesmen at that time.

960 γράμματα.] Cf. γραμμάτων in *Eq.* 189, quoted above. After ἐβουλόμην ἂν understand ἐπίστασθαι αὐτόν.

961 ἵνα μὴ...ἐνέγραφ'.] A thorough discussion of this construction is to be found in Hermann's notes on Viger, *de Idiotismis*. ἵνα, ὅπως, ὡς, with past indicative, express a consequence now impossible: 'adhibentur quum indicatur consilium, quod quis habuit, nec tamen effectum reddidit.' ' Cum indicativo praeteritorum temporum junguntur, quum significatur aliquid, quod futurum fuisset, si quid aliud actum esset, sed nunc non factum est.' Herm. They indicate something which would have been sure to follow, had something else been done, but which, as it is, has not followed, since that antecedent 'something else' was not done. Examples are, Aristoph. *Pac.* 135, Eur. *Hipp.* 645, Soph. *Oed. Tyr.* 1389—93. This last passage gives a double illustration, one for the imperfect, one for the aorist tense. οὐκ ἂν ἐσχόμην τὸ μὴ 'ποκλεῖσαι τοὐμὸν ἄθλιον δέμας, ἵν' ἦ τυφλός τε καὶ κλύων μηδέν...τί μ' οὐ λαβὼν ἔκτεινας εὐθύς, ὡς ἔδειξα μήποτε ἐμαυτὸν ἀνθρώποισιν ἔνθεν ἦν γεγώς; This past tense of the indicative may be aorist or imperfect: aorist, if a result is expressed not as lasting, but done once for all; imperfect, if lasting. Thus, ἵν' ἦ τυφλός κ.τ.λ., 'that so I might be not only blind but deaf,' the blindness and deafness being results lasting up to the time of speaking; but ὡς ἔδειξα μήποτε ' that so I might never have shewn,' the shewing being but once for all, and now over and done. 'That so' seems the closest English reading. Monk (on the *Hippolytus*) suggested ' in which case.' But this rather loses the notion of intent, purpose, &c. in ἵνα, ὅπως, ὡς. True it is that ἵνα sometimes = ' where,' with a simple relative force; but then it should be followed by οὐ (with ἄν) not by μή. The English 'that' keeps the notion of purpose, &c., while the 'so' = 'in that (now impossible) case,' and

ΣΦΗΚΕΣ.

ΒΔΕΛΥΚΛΕΩΝ

ἄκουσον ὦ δαιμόνιέ μου τῶν μαρτύρων.
ἀνάβηθι, τυρόκνηστι, καὶ λέξον μέγα·
σὺ γὰρ ταμιεύουσ' ἔτυχες. ἀπόκριναι σαφῶς,
εἰ μὴ κατέκνησας τοῖς στρατιώταις ἅλαβες. 965
φησὶ κατακνῆσαι.

ΦΙΛΟΚΛΕΩΝ

νὴ Δί', ἀλλὰ ψεύδεται.

ΒΔΕΛΥΚΛΕΩΝ

ὦ δαιμόνι', ἐλέει τοὺς ταλαιπωρουμένους.
οὗτος γὰρ ὁ Λάβης καὶ τραχήλι' ἐσθίει
καὶ τὰς ἀκάνθας, κοὐδέποτ' ἐν ταὐτῷ μένει.
ὁ δ' ἕτερος οἷός ἐστιν οἰκουρὸς μόνον. 970
αὐτοῦ μένων γὰρ ἅττ' ἂν εἴσω τις φέρῃ,
τούτων μεταιτεῖ τὸ μέρος· εἰ δὲ μή, δάκνει.

thus gives the right shade of meaning. Hermann observes that the Latins have no exactly equivalent construction, but that the Germans have; *e.g.* in Sophocles he well translates, '*damit* ich blind und taub wäre,' and '*damit* ich nie gezeigt hätte wer ich bin.' At the same time 1 would urge, in favour of Monk and his followers, that such conjunctions as ἵνα ὡς ὅπως partake of the character of relatives, and indeed were possibly relatives originally: compare the Latin 'quo,' which comes to be = 'that.' And the more common English way of putting such a sentence is, 'why didst thou not receive me? (or, 'would thou hadst &c.' or, 'thou shouldest have &c.') so had I never shewn.' Cf. note on *Nub.* 1158, 669 for this difference of Greek and English idiom. Shakspeare's, 'I would I were a glove upon that hand, *That* I might touch that cheek,' is a case for this construction, and is so rendered in a Porson exercise.

964 ταμιεύουσ'.] As a political term this would be a dispenser of moneys, provisions, &c. 'treasurer,'

Mitch. In a house it would be 'housekeeper, steward,' or perhaps here 'pantler, buttery-man.'

967 ἐλέει.] This must be a dissyllable in pronunciation, unless, as Dindorf in his notes proposes, we throw out τούς. In one edition Dindorf writes ἔλει, 'recte, ut videtur,' says Meineke. And ἐλεινὸς for ἐλεεινὸς rests on good authority. But possibly some of these combinations were monosyllabically pronounced, and yet not monosyllabically written. Cf. νεανικὴν in v. 1067, and (if the vulg. be retained) ἀπεωσάμεσθα in v. 1085.

968—72. Labes can eat odds and ends and fish bones, and is here, there, and everywhere: the other stops at home, and wants to be well fed. The activity of Laches and the lazy greediness of Cleon are contrasted.

970 οἰκουρὸς.] Κλέωνά φησιν ἐνδομυχοῦντα τὰ τῆς πόλεως κατεσθίειν. Schol. Brunck, followed by Hirschig and Meineke, reads οἰκουρεῖν: which seems better, but the MS. reading is not indefensible: 'is a sort of stay-at-home-merely.'

ΦΙΛΟΚΛΕΩΝ.
αἰβοῖ, τί κακόν ποτ' ἔσθ' ὅτῳ μαλάττομαι;
κακόν τι περιβαίνει με, κἀναπείθομαι.

ΒΔΕΛΤΚΛΕΩΝ.
ἴθ', ἀντιβολῶ σ', οἰκτείρατ' αὐτόν, ὦ πάτερ, 975
καὶ μὴ διαφθείρητε. ποῦ τὰ παιδία;
ἀναβαίνετ', ὦ πονηρά, καὶ κνυζούμενα
αἰτεῖτε κἀντιβολεῖτε καὶ δακρύετε.

ΦΙΛΟΚΛΕΩΝ.
κατάβα κατάβα κατάβα κατάβα.

ΒΔΕΛΤΚΛΕΩΝ.
καταβήσομαι.
καίτοι τὸ κατάβα τοῦτο πολλοὺς δὴ πάνυ 980
ἐξηπάτηκεν. ἀτὰρ ὅμως καταβήσομαι.

ΦΙΛΟΚΛΕΩΝ.
ἐς κόρακας. ὡς οὐκ ἀγαθόν ἐστι τὸ ῥοφεῖν.
ἐγὼ γὰρ ἀπεδάκρυσα νῦν γνώμην ἐμὴν
οὐδέν ποτ' ἀλλ' ἢ τῆς φακῆς ἐμπλήμενος.

973 **αἰβοῖ.**] Philocleon is disgusted to find that he is softening. Bdelycleon takes advantage of this, and produces the little ones of the accused, to whine and excite commiseration. It was a common custom both with Greeks and Romans to bring the family into court, that their tears might move the judges. Cf. Dem. *c. Mid.* 574. Racine takes this idea, 'Venez, famille désolée, Venez, pauvres enfans, qu'on veut rendre orphelins, Venez, faire parler vos esprits enfantins. Oui, Monsieur, vous voyez ici notre misère. Nous sommes orphelins, rendez-nous notre père, &c.'

975 **οἰκτείρατ'.**] Plural, because Philocleon was but one of many dicasts.

979 **κατάβα.**] The customary word for the dicasts to say, when they had heard enough to convince them, and bade the pleader come down from his place and say no more. But they sometimes deceived the hope of acquittal thus raised.

982 **ἐς κόρακας.**] A curse on either the defendant or the porridge; perhaps on both, as Mitchell takes it, 'Curse on yourself and curse upon this pottage!'

983, 4 **ἐγὼ γάρ...ἐμπλήμενος.**] 'For I wept freely but now, as I think, for no earthly reason but because I was full of the lentil porridge;' the heat of which brought tears to his eyes. For γνώμην ἐμὴν cf. *Pac.* 232, καὶ γὰρ ἐξιέναι γνώμην ἐμὴν μέλλει. The old interpretation, 'I wept away my judgment, lost my cool judgment in my tears,' is certainly wrong. Meineke's ἐπεδάκρυσα is confirmed by the Scholiast's ἐπιδακρύσας τῷ τῶν παίδων ὀδυρμῷ, but is against all MSS.

ΒΔΕΛΥΚΛΕΩΝ.
οὐκοῦν ἀποφεύγει δῆτα;

ΦΙΛΟΚΛΕΩΝ.
χαλεπὸν εἰδέναι.   985

ΒΔΕΛΥΚΛΕΩΝ.
ἴθ᾽, ὦ πατρίδιον, ἐπὶ τὰ βελτίω τρέπου.
τηνδὶ λαβὼν τὴν ψῆφον ἐπὶ τὸν ὕστερον
μύσας παρᾷξον κἀπόλυσον, ὦ πάτερ.

ΦΙΛΟΚΛΕΩΝ
οὐ δῆτα· κιθαρίζειν γὰρ οὐκ ἐπίσταμαι.

ΒΔΕΛΥΚΛΕΩΝ
φέρε νύν σε τῃδὶ τὴν ταχίστην περιάγω.   990

ΦΙΛΟΚΛΕΩΝ
ὅδ᾽ ἔσθ᾽ ὁ πρότερος;

987 τηνδί.] He gives him a pebble to vote with, a pebble 'condemnatory,' καταδικάζουσαν. This he wishes him to put into the urn called ἄκυρος and also ὕστερος. The consequence would be the acquittal of the prisoner. Philocleon refuses to do that, but is so led round that he in the end mistakes the urn into which he puts his condemnatory vote, and unintentionally acquits. There were, it appears, two urns, the one called κύριος, of brass, the other ἄκυρος, of wood. There were also two kinds of voting pebble, one bored through with a hole, the other entire and solid (τετρυπημένη, πληρής), or sometimes one black, the other white. The perforated or black were for condemnation, the solid or white for acquittal. That a vote might be used effectually it had to be dropped into the 'valid' urn (κύριος): the other vote was then put into the 'invalid' urn, and had no effect. The votes found in the 'valid' urn were counted, and the result was according to the excess or defect of one or the other. The urns were from their position called πρότερος and ὕστερος: but what this position was exactly, is uncertain. Richter thinks the πρότερος was close to the tribunal, the ὕστερος further off, beyond where the advocate, witnesses, &c., stood, so that the dicasts put their useless vote into this just before leaving the court.

988 μύσας κ. τ. λ.] 'Shut your eyes and pass on hastily to the further urn and acquit him.' This Philocleon refuses to do, retorting on his own words at v. 959, 'that he is no scholar,' and knows but one trade, viz. that of condemning.

990 φέρε νύν σε.] Bdelycleon pretends to be resigned, and offers to conduct him to the πρότερος κάδισκος; but in some way so misleads him that he finds the ὕστερος where the πρότερος should, according to his idea, be, and into it he drops his condemning vote. This amounts to an acquittal; for the other vote, that of acquittal, of course goes into the 'valid' urn.

7—2

ΒΔΕΛΤΚΛΕΩΝ
οὗτος.

ΦΙΛΟΚΛΕΩΝ
αὕτη 'νταῦθ' ἔνι.

ΒΔΕΛΤΚΛΕΩΝ
ἐξηπάτηται, κἀπολέλυκεν οὐχ ἑκών.

ΦΙΛΟΚΛΕΩΝ
φέρ' ἐξεράσω.

ΒΔΕΛΤΚΛΕΩΝ
πῶς ἄρ' ἠγωνίσμεθα;

ΦΙΛΟΚΛΕΩΝ
δείξειν ἔοικεν.

ΒΔΕΛΤΚΛΕΩΝ
ἐκπέφευγας, ὦ Λάβης.
πάτερ πάτερ, τί πέπονθας;

ΦΙΛΟΚΛΕΩΝ
οἴμοι, ποῦ 'σθ' ὕδωρ; 995

ΒΔΕΛΤΚΛΕΩΝ
ἔπαιρε σαυτόν.

ΦΙΛΟΚΛΕΩΝ
εἰπέ νυν ἐκεῖνό μοι,
ὄντως ἀπέφυγεν;

993 ἐξεράσω.] Cf. Aesch. *Eum.* 742, ΑΘ. ἐκβάλλεθ' ὡς τάχιστα τευχέων πάλους, ὅσοις δικαστῶν τοῦτ' ἐπέσταλται τέλος. ΟΡ. ὦ Φοῖβ' Ἄπολλον, πῶς ἀγὼν κριθήσεται; This makes for Dindorf's text against Meineke's; for the dicast Philocleon should empty out and count the votes. But πῶς ἄρ' ἠγωνίσμεθα; does look rather as if it were an impatient question thrown in during the counting; and in the passage of Aeschylus Orestes, the defendant, puts the question. Hence I have slightly altered the arrangement of the dialogue, which now runs thus: 'PHI. Come, let me turn out the votes. BD. How have we sped in the trial?

PHI. 'Twill soon be shewn. BD. Labes, you are acquitted!' Bdelycleon, interested for the accused, asks, 'how have we sped?' and then sees at once the result and tells it to the defendant before the old dicast, in his astonishment and disgust, can get out a word.

994 δείξειν ἔοικε.] Sc. τοὔργον. Cf. *Lys.* 375, τοὔργον τάχ' αὐτὸ δείξει.

995 ποῦ 'σθ' ὕδωρ.] The old man is fainting: cf. *Ran.* 481, ἀλλ' ὡρακιῶ· ἀλλ' οἶσε πρὸς τὴν καρδίαν μου σπογγίαν.

996 ἔπαιρε σαυτόν.] Cf. Eur. *Androm.* 1076, ἆ ἆ, τί δράσεις, ὦ γεραιέ; μὴ πέσῃς· ἔπαιρε σαυτόν. ΠΗ. οὐδέν εἰμ'· ἀπωλόμην.

ΒΔΕΛΤΚΛΕΩΝ
νὴ Δί.

ΦΙΛΟΚΛΕΩΝ
οὐδέν εἰμ' ἄρα.

ΒΔΕΛΤΚΛΕΩΝ
μὴ φροντίσῃς, ὦ δαιμόνι', ἀλλ' ἀνίστασο.

ΦΙΛΟΚΛΕΩΝ
πῶς οὖν ἐμαυτῷ τοῦτ' ἐγὼ ξυνείσομαι,
φεύγοντ' ἀπολύσας ἄνδρα; τί ποτε πείσομαι;   1000
ἀλλ', ὦ πολυτίμητοι θεοὶ, ξύγγνωτέ μοι·
ἄκων γὰρ αὔτ' ἔδρασα κοὺ τοὐμοῦ τρόπου.

ΒΔΕΛΤΚΛΕΩΝ
καὶ μηδὲν ἀγανάκτει γ'. ἐγὼ γάρ σ', ὦ πάτερ,
θρέψω καλῶς, ἄγων μετ' ἐμαυτοῦ πανταχοῖ,
ἐπὶ δεῖπνον, ἐς ξυμπόσιον, ἐπὶ θεωρίαν,   1005
ὥσθ' ἡδέως διάγειν σε τὸν λοιπὸν χρόνον·
κοὐκ ἐγχανεῖταί σ' ἐξαπατῶν Ὑπέρβολος.

999 ξυνείσομαι.] 'How shall I be conscious of this deed with myself,' *i.e.* 'how can I yet live and know that I have done this deed,' which almost = 'how can I pardon myself for this?' To share in the knowledge of a deed (if criminal), and to make no effort to expose it, is in effect to consent to it, or to pardon it; hence the common meaning of συγγιγνώσκειν. The Latins took a different compound to express the same thing, '*ignoscere*' 'to (apparently) *not* know, to refuse to know, ignore, wink at,' and so 'to pardon.' The one language expresses pardon by inward acquiescence in the knowledge of a crime; the other by outward denial of such knowledge.

1002 κοὺ τοὐμοῦ τρόπου.] 'And not (as a deed) fitting my character, not after my wont.' The genitive is the same as that in the common phrases ἀγαθοῦ ἐστιν ἀγαθὰ πράττειν and the like. It was not δικαστικοῦ τρόπου to acquit. 'Not such my wont, as those who know me know' (Tennyson) Philocleon might have said.

1003 καὶ μηδὲν ἀγανάκτει γ'.] 'Yes, yes, and don't be so overmuch grieved.' The γε gives assent to Philocleon's excuse.

1005 θεωρίαν.] Philocleon is to give up law and do nothing but enjoy himself at feasts and theatres. The same kind of retirement is proposed for Cratinus in *Eq.* 536. The 'reformed' life which the old man is to lead is not of the highest order, and is no doubt a satire on the follies and excesses in that direction which were prevalent at Athens in our poet's age.

1007 Ὑπέρβολος.] Cf. *Nub.* 551, 623, 876, 1065.

ἀλλ' εἰσίωμεν.

ΦΙΛΟΚΛΕΩΝ

ταῦτά νυν, εἴπερ δοκεῖ.

ΧΟΡΟΣ

ἀλλ' ἴτε χαίροντες ὅποι βούλεσθ'.
ὑμεῖς δὲ τέως, ὦ μυριάδες   1010
ἀναρίθμητοι,
νῦν μὲν τὰ μέλλοντ' εὖ λέγε-
σθαι μὴ πέσῃ φαύλως χαμᾶζ'
εὐλαβεῖσθε.
τοῦτο γὰρ σκαιῶν θεατῶν
ἐστὶ πάσχειν, κοὐ πρὸς ὑμῶν.
νῦν αὖτε λεῴ πρόσσχετε τὸν νοῦν, εἴπερ καθαρόν τι φιλεῖτε.

1008 Philocleon resigns himself to the change, and they go in to prepare for it, leaving the stage clear for the parabasis.

1009. The parts of this parabasis are: κομμάτιον, 1009—1014, parabasis proper (or anapaests) 1015—1050, μακρὸν, 1051—1059, στροφὴ, 1060—1070, ἐπίρρημα, 1071—1090, ἀντιστροφὴ, 1091—1100, ἀντεπίρρημα, 1101—1121.

ἀλλ' ἴτε χαίροντες.] Cf. *Eq.* 498, *Nub.* 510, ἀλλ' ἴθι χαίρων, κ.τ.λ.

1010 **μυριάδες.**] To be taken rather vaguely of multitudes. Strictly speaking the 'myriads' of the audience would not be many, as Richter reminds us; but each myriad of itself may be ἀναρίθμητος. Plato uses μυριάδες ἀναρίθμητοι, of the numerous generations of forefathers that have preceded us, *Theaet.* 175, A.

1012 **πέσῃ.**] As did the *Clouds*, to the first exhibition of which he refers here and further on in this parabasis.

1013 **σκαιῶν.**] The exact opposite is δεξιός, a favourite word of compliment to the Athenians. Cf. *Nub.* 524—27, ἀνεχώρουν ὑπ' ἀνδρῶν φορτικῶν...ταῦτ' οὖν ὑμῖν μέμφομαι τοῖς σοφοῖς...ἀλλ' οὐδ' ὣς ὑμῶν...προδώσω τοὺς δεξιούς: cf. also *Nub.* 521, θεατὰς δεξιούς. Euripides opposes σκαιὸς and σοφός: *Med.* 190, σκαιοὺς δὲ λέγων κοὐδέν τι σοφοὺς τοὺς πρόσθε βροτοὺς οὐκ ἂν ἁμάρτοις.

1015—1050. The poet complains of unjust treatment. He has done the Athenian public good service: first in the name of other poets, then in his own. He has not debased his Muse to gratify others, nor has he attacked the small; but has boldly withstood the great and powerful, Cleon especially. Also he has exposed other plagues and corrupters of public morals. But the Athenians, though they honoured him at first, gave him up last year, and rejected the best play he had ever given them: entirely through their want of understanding, and through no fault of the poet.

1015 **πρόσσχετε.**] Cf. *Nub.* 575, *Eq.* 504.

καθαρόν.] Cf. above v. 631, καθαρῶς λέγοντος. The word means here 'genuine, pure,' the real thing, as opposed to what is specious but of no real worth.

ΣΦΗΚΕΣ.

μέμψασθαι γὰρ τοῖσι θεαταῖς ὁ ποιητὴς νῦν ἐπιθυμεῖ. 1016
ἀδικεῖσθαι γάρ φησιν πρότερος πόλλ' αὐτοὺς εὖ πεποιηκώς,
τὰ μὲν οὐ φανερῶς, ἀλλ' ἐπικουρῶν κρύβδην ἑτέροισι ποιη-
ταῖς,
μιμησάμενος τὴν Εὐρυκλέους μαντείαν καὶ διάνοιαν,
εἰς ἀλλοτρίας γαστέρας ἐνδὺς κωμῳδικὰ πολλὰ χέασθαι·
μετὰ τοῦτο δὲ καὶ φανερῶς ἤδη κινδυνεύων καθ' ἑαυτόν, 1021
οὐκ ἀλλοτρίων, ἀλλ' οἰκείων Μουσῶν στόμαθ' ἡνιοχήσας.
ἀρθεὶς δὲ μέγας καὶ τιμηθεὶς ὡς οὐδεὶς πώποτ' ἐν ὑμῖν,
οὐκ ἐκτελέσαι φησὶν ἐπαρθεὶς οὐδ' ὀγκῶσαι τὸ φρόνημα,

1017 ἀδικεῖσθαι...... πρότερος.] 'That he is the first to suffer wrong.' not only having done the public no wrong himself, but having done it much good.

1018 ἐπικουρῶν κ.τ.λ.] Philonides and Callistratus were the poets under whose names Aristophanes' earliest plays came out : viz. the *Babylonians*, *Banqueters*, *Acharnians*. For another mention of this, cf. *Nub.* 530, sqq.

1019 Εὐρυκλέους.] A ventriloquist and diviner at Athens, from whom others of the same trade were afterwards called Euryclidae. Schol.

1020 εἰς ἀλλοτρίας.] As Eurycles throws his voice into others, so did I with my plays. Others seemed the utterers; I was the real source of the words which flowed out.

χέασθαι.] Infin. dependent on μιμησάμενος. ἐνδὺς χέασθαι = ἐνδῦναι καὶ χέασθαι: so that the syntax will be μιμησάμενος Εὐρυκλέα (ὥστε) ἐνδῦναι εἰς ἀλλ. γ. καὶ χέασθαι.

1021 καθ' ἑαυτόν.] The *Knights* was Aristophanes' first play exhibited in his own name. And the Scholiast remarks that none would run the risk of acting Cleon's part, hence Aristophanes had to act it himself. This would give peculiar force to 'κινδυνεύων καθ' ἑαυτόν; but it is not necessary here to understand anything more than

the risk of failure before the audience. And καθ' ἑαυτόν, 'by himself,' in his own name, is merely opposed to the ἐπικουρῶν ἑτέροις. Cf. *Eq.* 513, ὡς οὐχὶ πάλαι χορὸν αἰτοίη καθ' ἑαυτόν.

1022 ἡνιοχήσας.] 'Having taken on him to rein the mouths of his own and no others' muses.' The poet, when he had entered as it were into others who were to utter his thoughts, might be termed the charioteer or controller of their mouths, or of the strains to issue from them. For a bold metaphorical use of ἡνίοχος, cf. *Nub.* 602, αἰγίδος ἡνίοχος.

1023 ἀρθεὶς δὲ μέγας.] Cf. Dem. *Olynth.* II. 20, ὥσπερ οὖν διὰ τούτων ἤρθη μέγας, οὕτως ὀφείλει διὰ τῶν αὐτῶν τούτων καὶ καθαιρεθῆναι πάλιν.

1024 οὐκ ἐκτελέσαι κ.τ.λ.] There is a difficulty here, which Reiske saw, and thought ἐκτελέσαι corrupt; but the other commentators seem to pass it over. οὐκ ἐκτ. φ. ἐπ., must mean 'he does not—elated by his honours—say he has attained perfection, done everything that there is to do.' And so the Scholiast says : οὐκ ἐπὶ τέλος ἔδοξεν αὐτῷ ἐλθεῖν οὔτε τῆς ποιήσεως οὔτε τῶν ἐπαίνων. For that ἐκτελέσαι ἐπαρθεὶς = τελέως ἐπαρθῆναι, 'to be completely elated,' as Florens says, following the earlier (and not very intelligible) part of the Scholium, is hardly possible. But οὐδ' ὀγκῶ-

104 ΑΡΙΣΤΟΦΑΝΟΥΣ [1025

οὐδὲ παλαίστρας περικωμάζειν πειρῶν· οὐδ' εἴ τις ἐραστὴς
κωμῳδεῖσθαι παιδίχ' ἑαυτοῦ μισῶν ἔσπευδε πρὸς αὐτόν, 1026
οὐδενὶ πώποτέ φησι πιθέσθαι, γνώμην τιν' ἔχων ἐπιεικῆ,
ἵνα τὰς Μούσας αἷσιν χρῆται μὴ προαγωγοὺς ἀποφήνῃ.
οὐδ' ὅτε πρῶτόν γ' ἤρξε διδάσκειν, ἀνθρώποις φῆσ' ἐπιθέσθαι,
ἀλλ' Ἡρακλέους ὀργήν τιν' ἔχων τοῖσι μεγίστοις ἐπιχειρεῖν,

σαι τ. φ., does not follow with any good sense the clause οὐκ ἐκτ. φ. ἐπ. 'he does not profess to have done everything, nor to be puffed up.' What is wanted is, 'He de-nies that he...or was puffed up.' And the phrase ἐκτελέσαι ἐπαρθεὶς cannot be reasonably explained of anything that the poet would deny. If there is corruption in the text and a change needed (as it seems to me there is), I would propose ὀγκώσας and περικωμάζει. 'He does not—elated or puffed up in thought —profess to have done everything, nor does he go round &c.' Or we might read ὀγκοῦται, 'He does not profess perfection, nor is he puffed up, nor does he &c.' For ὀγκοῦ-σθαι, cf. Ran. 703, ὀγκωσόμεσθα κά-ποσεμνυνούμεθα.
1025 παλαίστρας περικωμάζειν πειρῶν.] Cf. Pac. 762, καὶ γὰρ πρό-τερον πράξας κατὰ νοῦν οὐχὶ παλαί-στρας περινοστῶν παῖδας ἐπείρων. Brunck's correction of the MSS. περιιὼν or περιών to πειρῶν here seems certain. There is a hit at Eupolis, the Scholiast tells us, who περιῄει τὰς παλαίστρας σεμνυνόμενος καὶ τοῖσιν παισὶν ἑαυτὸν δῆλον ποιῶν τῆς νίκης ἕνεκα.
1025—28. Nor would he hold his tongue to screen any, and so connive at their wickedness.
1029. πρῶτόν γ'.] As it was now certainly known that the earlier plays, exhibited under the names of others, were written by Aristopha-nes, this probably refers to those earlier plays. Some have explained ἤρξε διδάσκειν to refer to the *Knights*, because αἱ διδασκαλίαι φέρουσι τοὺς

Ἱππεῖς πρώτους ὑπ' αὐτοῦ καθίεσθαι. But the *Babylonians* was concerned in attacking Cleon, and can hardly be excluded from the θρασέως ξυ-στὰς εὐθὺς ἀπ' ἀρχῆς αὐτῷ τῷ καρ-χαρόδοντι.
ἀνθρώποις.] 'Mere men' as op-posed to τοῖσι μεγίστοις (θηρίοις, κνωδάλοις) 'mighty monsters'. The changes proposed ἀνθρωπίσκοις (from Pac. 751), ἀνδραρίοις ἐπιθ. seem hardly needed. Hercules' labours and contests were generally with such as were more than man. And the Scholiast evidently comments on ἀνθρώποις, saying: ἀλλὰ τέρασι καὶ δαίμοσιν. 'When first the scenic trade of instruction he essay'd, monsters not men were his game, sirs; Strange Leviathans that ask'd strength and mettle, and had task'd Alcides their fury to tame, sirs.' Mitchell.
1030. ἐπιχειρεῖν.] Meineke reads ἐπεχείρει on no MS. authority: to avoid (I suppose) the infinitive pre-sent following upon the infinitive aorist. But as in direct graphic narrative the present indicative is used of past events, so the infinitive of the present may be put in oblique narration, Cf. *Eq.* 514, φησὶ γὰρ ἀνὴρ οὐχ ὑπ' ἀνοίας...διατρίβειν, where the delay meant is a delay in past time, though expressed by the present infinitive; and further on v. 541, ταῦτ' ὀρρωδῶν διέτριβεν ἀεί shows plainly that it is so. We might translate here 'he set not (he says) on mere men, but with noble Herculean wrath he goes at mighty monsters'.

ΣΦΗΚΕΣ.

θρασέως ξυστὰς εὐθὺς ἀπ' ἀρχῆς αὐτῷ τῷ καρχαρόδοντι,
οὗ δεινόταται μὲν ἀπ' ὀφθαλμῶν Κύννης ἀκτῖνες ἔλαμπον,
ἑκατὸν δὲ κύκλῳ κεφαλαὶ κολάκων οἰμωξομένων ἐλιχμῶντο
περὶ τὴν κεφαλήν, φωνὴν δ' εἶχεν χαράδρας ὄλεθρον τετοκυίας,
ῥώκης δ' ὀσμήν, Λαμίας δ' ὄρχεις ἀπλύτους, πρωκτὸν δὲ κα-
μήλου.   1035
τοιοῦτον ἰδὼν τέρας οὔ φησιν δείσας καταδωροδοκῆσαι,

1031. **καρχαρόδοντι.**] Cf. *Eq.* 1017, σώζεσθαί σ' ἐκέλευσ' ἱερὸν κύνα καρχαρόδοντα, in the oracle quoted by Cleon about himself. In *Pac.* 752—758, this passage is repeated. The word καρχαρόδους is applied by Homer to dogs (*Il.* κ. 360), by Theocritus to a wolf, (*Id.* XXIV. 86). Aristotle distinguishes it especially from χαυλιόδους, and explains it thus τὰ μὲν χαυλιόδοντας ἔχει, ὥσπερ ὗς· τὰ δ' ὀξεῖς καὶ ἐπαλλάσσοντας, ὅθεν καρχαρόδοντα καλεῖται, ἐπεὶ γὰρ ἐν τοῖς ὀδοῦσιν ἡ ἰσχὺς αὐτῶν, οἱ χρήσιμοι πρὸς τὴν ἀλκὴν ἐναλλὰξ ἐμπίπτουσιν ὅπως μὴ ἀμβλύνωνται τριβόμενοι πρὸς ἀλλήλους.

1032. **Κύννης.**] In *Eq.* 765, Cleon professes himself to be the best 'after Lysicles, Cynna and Salabaccho.' These two last were courtezans. There is reference to κυνὸς in Κύννης. Bergler compares Homer's κυνὸς ὄμματ' ἔχων (*Il.* α. 225): to which add the use of κυνῶπις and κυνώπης, and κυνοθαρσής (Theocr. *Id.* XV. 53).

1033 **ἑκατὸν δὲ κύκλῳ κ. κ.**] Note the intentional alliteration; which would be impaired, were we to accept Bentley's conjecture γλῶτται, as Meineke is inclined to do. Surely in a description of this kind κεφαλαὶ ἐλιχμῶντο is not too bold a phrase. Cleon is now a hundred-headed hydra: each head is a flatterer's head, and his own, the arch-flatterer's, in the middle. Or indeed he may still be in his old character of Cerberus (*Eq.* 1030), the number of whose heads is variously told,

cf. Hor. *Od.* III. 16, Cessit immanis tibi blandienti Janitor aulae Cerberus, quamvis furiale centum Muniant angues caput ejus, atque Spiritus teter saniesque manet Ore trilingui. **οἰμωξομένων.**] 'Whom perdition seize.' Some phrase like this seems the best rendering of the participle; which, strictly taken, asserts, that that grief will seize them which the speaker devoutly wishes may do so.

1034 **φωνὴν...χαράδρας.**] Cf. *Eq.* 137, κυκλοβόρου φωνὴν ἔχων. A loud voice was a great advantage before the Athenian multitude. In *Eq.* 218, φωνὴ μιαρά is specified as a qualification for a demagogue. Demosthenes more than once charges Aeschines with possessing a loud and coarse voice, as if it were a fault; being himself, as is known, at a disadvantage in this physical quality, cf. Dem. *F. L.* p. 415, βιάσονται τοίνυν ἴσως, μεγαλόφωνοι καὶ ἀναιδεῖς ὄντες.

1035 **φώκης.**] Cf. Hom. *Od.* δ. 406, φῶκαι... πικρὸν ἀποπνείουσαι ἁλὸς πολυβενθέος ὀδμήν, 441, τείρε γὰρ αἰνῶς φωκάων ἁλιοτρεφέων ὀλοώτατος ὀδμή. Cleon's unsavoury trade is frequently attacked in the *Knights*.

Λαμίας.] Lamia was a sort of female hob-goblin wherewith they terrified children.

1036 **καταδωροδοκῆσαι.**] Not, as Bergler says, 'to give bribes:' but, as elsewhere, 'to take bribes.' The poet is not frightened into taking a bribe and holding his tongue, but boldly assails Cleon.

106   ΑΡΙΣΤΟΦΑΝΟΥΣ   [1037

ἀλλ' ὑπὲρ ὑμῶν ἔτι καὶ νυνὶ πολεμεῖ· φησίν τε μετ' αὐτοῦ
τοῖς ἠπιάλοις ἐπιχειρῆσαι πέρυσιν καὶ τοῖς πυρετοῖσιν,
οἳ τοὺς πατέρας τ' ἦγχον νύκτωρ καὶ τοὺς πάππους ἀπέ-
    πνιγον,
κατακλινόμενοί τ' ἐπὶ ταῖς κοίταις ἐπὶ τοῖσιν ἀπράγμοσιν
    ὑμῶν   1040
ἀντωμοσίας καὶ προσκλήσεις καὶ μαρτυρίας συνεκόλλων,

1037 **μετ' αὐτοῦ.**] 'With him;' *i.e.* not only Cleon did he assail, but other plagues as well. μετ' αὐτόν 'after him' Bentley. And the change is very slight, the confusion between υ and ν being frequent. Cf. above v. 416, and *Eq.* 798. This would give more precisely the order of the two attacks; that on Cleon in the *Knights*, that on the 'agues &c.' in the *Clouds*.
1038 **ἠπιάλοις.**] Explained in the Scholiast by ῥιγοπύρετοι, and τὸ πρὸ τοῦ πυρετοῦ κρύος. Didymus rather identifies the word with ἠπιάλης and ἐφιάλτης 'the nightmare;' whereas Ruhnken (on Timaeus' Lexicon) quotes from Phrynichus this distinction: ἠπιάλης. ὁ ἐπιπίπτων καὶ ἐφέρων τοῖς κοιμωμένοις δαίμων· τὸ δὲ ἠπίαλος διὰ τοῦ ὀ μικροῦ ἕτερόν τι σημαίνει, τὸ καλούμενον ῥιγοπύρετον. But whether ἠπιάλοις mean here 'shivering fits, agues,' or 'night-mares,' matters little. Either might be precursors of fever, and be naturally joined with πυρετοῖσιν. What is more important is the general bearing of the passage. And there can be no doubt that it refers to the *Clouds*, and that the ἠπίαλοι mean the sophists. Yet whether all the details can be explained from the *Clouds*, as we have the play, is doubtful. The Scholiast says ἠπιάλους αὐτοὺς ὠνόμασεν ὡς ὠχρότητα περισκώπτων, but he also notes that Aristophanes in the *Clouds* uses the phrase ἅμα δ' ἠπίαλος πυρετοῦ πρόδρομος. Now this phrase is not found in our edition of the *Clouds*, but it may have been in the first edition; and there may have been other passages and scenes also which would explain more satisfactorily the allusions in the four following lines, which do not appear to me to be explicable from the *Clouds* as it has come down to us. Fritzsche thinks the first *Clouds* was very different from our play, relying much on this passage; and without determining how far it differed, I should agree that the expressions here are too definite to refer only to the scenes which Aristophanes' text now gives.
1039 **οἳ τοὺς πατέρας κ. τ. λ.**] 'Throttling fathers by night,' 'choking grandfathers,' finds no sufficient explanation in Phidippides' beating of his father. The 'agues and fevers' (sophists) might be said indeed to commit these enormities, if they persuaded men so to do, but a more definite reference is wanted.
1040 **κατακλινόμενοι κ. τ. λ.**] This, again, finds no warrant in our *Clouds*. The devices of Socrates, or his disciples, or of Strepsiades, when made to wrap himself up and think, do not suit with this passage. Shifts to evade payment of debt are mentioned, but not legal traps for the simple and unwary. Richter renders κατακλ. 'incubantes tamquam incubi in cubilibus.' But 'night-mares framing legal subtleties' is an odd idea. Perhaps it is rather that the sophists were represented as lying on their beds and devising such things.
ἀπράγμοσιν.] Cf. *Eq.* 261, κἄν τιν' αὐτῶν γνῷς ἀπράγμον' ὄντα καὶ κεχηνότα, κ.τ.λ.
1041 **ἀντωμοσίας, κ.τ.λ.**] 'Affi-

ἄστ' ἀναπηδᾶν δειμαίνοντας πολλοὺς ὡς τὸν πολέμαρχον.
τοιόνδ' εὑρόντες ἀλεξίκακον, τῆς χώρας τῆσδε καθαρτήν,
πέρυσιν καταπρούδοτε καινοτάταις σπείραντ' αὐτὸν διανοίαις,
ἃς ὑπὸ τοῦ μὴ γνῶναι καθαρῶς ὑμεῖς ἐποιήσατ' ἀναλδεῖς·
καίτοι σπένδων πόλλ' ἐπὶ πολλοῖς ὄμνυσιν τὸν Διόνυσον
μὴ πώποτ' ἀμείνον' ἔπη τούτων κωμῳδικὰ μηδέν' ἀκοῦσαι.
τοῦτο μὲν οὖν ἔσθ' ὑμῖν αἰσχρὸν τοῖς μὴ γνοῦσιν παραχρῆμα,
ὁ δὲ ποιητὴς οὐδὲν χείρων παρὰ τοῖσι σοφοῖς νενόμισται,
εἰ παρελαύνων τοὺς ἀντιπάλους τὴν ἐπίνοιαν ξυνέτριψεν.
ἀλλὰ τὸ λοιπὸν τῶν ποιητῶν, 1051

davits, summonses, depositions;' legal terms explained in *Dict. Antiq.* p. 335, 336, under Δίκη.

1042 **ἀναπηδᾶν.**] 'So that they jumped up,' as if suddenly startled from sleep: the word rather suits the 'nightmare' explanation of ἠπίαλος.

πολέμαρχον.] The polemarch was the protector of strangers and resident aliens. Such would be these ἀπράγμονες: see the passage from the *Knights*, referred to on v. 1040.

1043 **ἀλεξίκακον.**] Applied to Hermes in *Pac.* 422; but oftener as an epithet of Hercules; and Aristophanes above, at v. 1030, is compared to him. Hercules was a 'purger of the earth' from all monsters &c.; so was the poet to Attica.

1044 **πέρυσιν.**] When the *Clouds* was exhibited, and gained no prize.

καινοτάταις.] Cf. *Nub.* 546, οὐδ' ὑμᾶς ζητῶ 'ξαπατᾶν δὶς καὶ τρὶς ταῦτ' εἰσάγων, ἀλλ' ἀεὶ καινὰς ἰδέας ἐσφέρων σοφίζομαι, οὐδὲν ἀλλήλαισιν ὁμοίας καὶ πάσας δεξιάς.

σπείραντ'.] The metaphor is continued in ἀναλδεῖς. He had sowed good seed, but not reaped a good harvest. Bothe prefers to read διανοίας; which is simpler; Meineke mentions with approval a conjecture of Hecke, αὐτήν, 'having sown it,' *i. e.* the land. But it seems as well for this accusative to be understood, and to keep αὐτόν, 'you sacrificed him when he sowed (the field) with

most novel ideas.'

1045 **τοῦ μὴ γνῶναι.**] He upbraids them with want of judgment in not appreciating his best play. The same complaints are made in the parabasis of the *Clouds*, which certainly belongs to the second edition of that play.

1046 **σπένδων πόλλ' ἐπὶ πολλοῖς.**] Sc. βώμοις or ἱεροῖς. With many a libation, and many a vow, he will swear that never was a better play. Cf. *Nub.* 518, κατερῶ πρὸς ὑμᾶς ἐλευθέρως τἀληθῆ νὴ τὸν Διόνυσον τὸν ἐκθρέψαντά με. οὕτω νικήσαιμί τ' ἐγὼ καὶ νομιζοίμην σοφός, ὡς ...ἡγούμενος...ταύτην σοφώτατ' ἔχειν τῶν ἐμῶν κωμῳδιῶν πρώτους ἠξίωσ' ἀναγεῦσ' ὑμᾶς.

1048 **τοῦτο μὲν οὖν κ.τ.λ.**] It is a discredit to some of you not to have appreciated me; but no discredit whatever to me in the eyes of the wise. So in *Nub.* 527 he appeals to the δεξιοί.

1050 **εἰ παρελαύνων.**] The metaphor is from a chariot race. If the poet's chariot has failed to win, and has been broken in the race, it was while nobly striving to beat his rivals. τὴν ἐπίνοιαν, 'the thoughts, devices, wit, &c. of the play.' τὰ ἐπινοήματα τῶν δραμάτων. Schol.

1051—59. Therefore for the future you must take better care of your good poets and their happy thoughts, if you want to be thought clever fellows.

108   ΑΡΙΣΤΟΦΑΝΟΥΣ   [1052

ὦ δαιμόνιοι, τοὺς ζητοῦντας
καινόν τι λέγειν κἀξευρίσκειν
στέργετε μᾶλλον καὶ θεραπεύετε,
καὶ τὰ νοήματα σώζεσθ' αὐτῶν·   1055
ἐσβάλλετε δ' ἐς τὰς κιβωτοὺς
μετὰ τῶν μήλων.
κἂν ταῦτα ποιῆθ', ὑμῖν δι' ἔτους
τῶν ἱματίων
ὀζήσει δεξιότητος.
ὦ πάλαι ποτ' ὄντες ὑμεῖς ἄλκιμοι μὲν ἐν χοροῖς,   1060
ἄλκιμοι δ' ἐν μάχαις,
καὶ κατ' αὐτὸ δὴ μόνον τοῦτ' ἄνδρες ἀλκιμώτατοι,

1052 ζητοῦντας...λέγειν.] 'Those who seek out something new to say.' The construction seems rather ζητοῦντάς τι (ὥστε) λέγειν than ζητ. λέγειν τι. A parallel from *Av.* 465 is quoted by Bergler; λέγειν ζητῶ τρίπαλαι μέγα καὶ λαρινὸν ἔπος τι.
1055 τὰ νοήματα σώζεσθ'.] Do not let them fail, as our poet's ἐπίνοια did (v. 1050): cf. above, 1012, μὴ πέσῃ φαύλως χαμᾶζ' εὐλαβεῖσθε.
1057 μετὰ τῶν μήλων.] εἰώθασι γὰρ εἰς τὰ κιβώτια μῆλα βάλλειν δι' εὐοσμίαν. Schol. By 'putting them into their clothes' chests, that their garments might smell of cleverness,' it is meant that they should lay them well to heart and so store them up, which would give them a savour of cleverness all the year through. Mitchell quotes from Chaucer a compliment to breath as sweet as 'hord of apples laid in hay or heth.'
1059 τῶν ἱμ. ὀζήσει δεξιότητος.] Cf. *Pac.* 529, τοῦ μὲν γὰρ ὄζει κρομμυοξερυγμίας, ταύτης δ' ὀπώρας, and *Ach.* 852, ὄζων τῶν μασχαλῶν πατρὸς τραγασαίου.
1060—1120. In the strophe the Chorus lament that their youth is gone, but think that they are still better than the foppish striplings of the modern days. They then (in the epirrhema) explain their wasp-like garb, describing their deeds in battle against the barbarian, which gained for them the appellation of wasps. Again (in the antistrophe) they recal their youthful deeds; how they won what the younger men now steal: and (in the antepirrhema) shew that there is a waspish element in their behaviour at home; that they freely use their stings; but that there are idle drones among them, and that this rule ought to be enforced: 'no work, no pay.'
1060 ὦ πάλαι.] With allusion to the proverb quoted in *Plut.* 1002, πάλαι ποτ' ἦσαν ἄλκιμοι Μιλήσιοι, of which the Scholiast on that place gives the reported origin. It was at any rate a proverb of those who had formerly flourished but now did so no longer.
1062 καὶ κατ' αὐτὸ κ.τ.λ.] This line is corrupt in MSS., ending with ἄνδρες μαχιμώτατοι. ἀλκιμώτατοι or ἀνδρικώτατοι, Bentley. ἀλκιμώτατοι, Porson; and the repetition of the same adjective seems better, and is rather nearer in termination to the MS. μαχιμώτατοι.
τοῦτ'.] In fighting and dancing, as opposed to law-suits, which are now their only strong point. Seager thinks τοῦτο is said δεικτικῶς, pointing to their κέντρον. But this sting is the weapon that they have taken to in their old age.

πρίν ποτ' ἦν, πρὶν ταῦτα· νῦν δ'
οἴχεται κύκνου τ' ἔτι πολιώτεραι δὴ
αἵδ' ἐπανθοῦσιν τρίχες. 1065
ἀλλὰ κἀκ τῶν λειψάνων δεῖ τῶνδε ῥώμην
νεανικὴν σχεῖν· ὡς ἐγὼ τοὐμὸν νομίζω
γῆρας εἶναι κρεῖττον ἢ πολλῶν κικίννους νεανιῶν καὶ
σχῆμα κεὐρυπρωκτίαν. 1070
εἴ τις ὑμῶν, ὦ θεαταί, τὴν ἐμὴν ἰδὼν φύσιν
εἶτα θαυμάζει μ' ὁρῶν μέσον διεσφηκωμένον,
ἢ τίς ἡμῶν ἐστιν ἡ 'πίνοια τῆς ἐγκεντρίδος,
ῥᾳδίως ἐγὼ διδάξω, κἂν ἄμουσος ᾖ τὸ πρίν.
ἐσμὲν ἡμεῖς, οἷς πρόσεστι τοῦτο τοὐρροπύγιον, 1075
Ἀττικοὶ μόνοι δικαίως ἐγγενεῖς αὐτόχθονες,

1063 πρίν ποτ' ἦν.] Didymus says this is parodied from Timocreon of Rhodes. It is a commonplace for all poets: cf. Catullus in the dedication of the barque 'Sed haec prius fuere'; Virgil's 'Fuit Ilium', &c.
1064 κύκνου...πολιώτεραι.] Cf. Ov. Tr. 4. 8. 1, Jam mea cycneas imitantur tempora plumas. The chorus in Aesch. Agam. 72—82, lament their age in a similar way.
1066 λειψάνων.] The most must be made of what remains, though it be but an ἰσχὺς ἰσόπαις, an ὄναρ ἡμερόφαντον, as Aeschylus terms it.
1069 κικίννους.] 'Cincinnos.' The long and carefully dressed hair of the Athenian youth is continually a mark for Aristophanes' ridicule. He had not much to boast of in that way himself.
1070 σχῆμα.] 'dress,' cf. Eq. 1331, ἀρχαίῳ σχήματι λαμπρός, and below, v. 1170. But it almost includes affectation in gait; indeed it might be here 'the mien, postures, attitudinizing.'
1072 μέσον διεσφ.] 'Waspwaisted.' Probably the chorus were tightly girded round the waist, so as to give them a waspish contour,

cf. Plut. 561, ἰσχνοί καὶ σφηκώδεις, opposed to fat aldermanic well-to-do fellows.
1073 ἢ τίς.] ἥτις Bentley, Porson, and others. But 'if any wonders at our waspish waists, whatever is the meaning of our sting' would identify the waist with the sting, whereas it should rather be, 'If any wonders at our waists, or (wonders) what means our sting.' An 'or' or 'and' seems wanted. Richter reads χῆτις. Unless indeed ἐγκεντρίς were taken to mean that in which the κέντρον was fastened, and so were to include the girdle which compressed the waist.
ἡμῶν ἐστιν.] ἡμῶν ἐστιν ἡ 'πίνοια τῆσδε τῆς, vulg. Some omit ἡμῶν, some ἐστιν, some τῆσδε.
1074 διδάξω, κἂν ἄμ.] Eur. Stheneboea (Fr. 664), μουσικὴν δ' ἄρα ἔρως διδάσκει κἂν ἄμουσος ᾖ τὸ πρίν.
1076 Ἀττικοὶ κ.τ.λ.] Meineke omits this line with a 'delevit Hamakerus' in his note. He omits v. 1115, οὐκ ἔχοντες...φόρου in the antepirrhema.
ἐγγενεῖς.] So MSS. R, V. and it is rather preferable to εὐγενεῖς. The exaggerated self-praise in ἡμεῖς

ΑΡΙΣΤΟΦΑΝΟΤΣ [1077

ἀνδρικώτατον γένος καὶ πλεῖστα τήνδε τὴν πόλιν
ὠφελῆσαν ἐν μάχαισιν, ἡνίκ᾽ ἦλθ᾽ ὁ βάρβαρος,
τῷ καπνῷ τύφων ἅπασαν τὴν πόλιν καὶ πυρπολῶν,
ἐξελεῖν ἡμῶν μενοινῶν πρὸς βίαν τἀνθρήνια, 1080
εὐθέως γὰρ ἐκδραμόντες σὺν δόρει σὺν ἀσπίδι
ἐμαχόμεσθ᾽ αὐτοῖσι, θυμὸν ὀξίνην πεπωκότες,
στὰς ἀνὴρ παρ᾽ ἄνδρ᾽, ὑπ᾽ ὀργῆς τὴν χελύνην ἐσθίων·
ὑπὸ δὲ τῶν τοξευμάτων οὐκ ἦν ἰδεῖν τὸν οὐρανόν.
ἀλλ᾽ ὅμως ἀπεωσάμεσθα ξὺν θεοῖς πρὸς ἑσπέρα. 1085
γλαῦξ γὰρ ἡμῶν πρὶν μάχεσθαι τὸν στρατὸν διέπτατο.

ἐσμὲν μόνοι 'Α. need not be urged as an objection to the line: for praise of themselves and of their poet is with the Aristophanic chorus quite the rule. The epirrhema in the *Knights* is in a similar spirit.

1078 ἡνίκ᾽ ἦλθ᾽ ὁ βάρβαρος.] Isocrates describes at some length the services of Athens against the barbarian, *Paneg.* p. 58—90.

1079 πυρπολῶν.] Cf. Herod. VIII. 50, ταῦτα τῶν ἀπὸ Πελοποννήσου στρατηγῶν ἐπιλεγομένων ἐληλύθεε ἀνὴρ Ἀθηναῖος ἀγγέλλων ἥκειν τὸν βάρβαρον ἐς τὴν Ἀττικὴν καὶ πᾶσαν αὐτὴν πυρπολέεσθαι. This is of what took place after the abandonment of Athens, before the battle of Salamis. But here τύφων and πυρπολῶν may be merely of the attempt and wish to burn, for what follows refers to Marathon, which was fought ten years earlier than Salamis.

1080 τἀνθρήνια.] τὰ τῶν σφηκῶν κηρία, ἀνθρήνας δὲ οἱ μὲν τὰς μελίττας, οἱ δὲ ἕτερον ζῷον κηροποιὸν παραπλήσιον σφηκί. Schol. Cf. *Nub.* 947. The words ἐξελεῖν, τύφειν, are specially applicable to taking wasps' or bees' nests. Cf. above v. 457, where the wasp chorus are smoked out.

1082 ὀξίνην.] Cf. *Eq.* v. 1304, ὀξίνην Ὑπέρβολον. Florens finds a reference to θύμον 'thyme,' a favourite food of bees, in θυμοῦ. Bergler thinks it may be so, but that it is a comic deviation from θυμὸς ὀξὺς, a common phrase.

πεπωκότες.] 'Having drunk' and so imbibed the spirit of. Cf. above v. 462, βεβρωκότες, and the note there.

1083 χελύνην ἐσθίων.] Bergler illustrates from Tyrtaeus, ἀλλά τις εὖ διαβὰς μενέτω ποσὶν ἀμφοτέροισι στηριχθεὶς ἐπὶ γῆς χεῖλος ὀδοῦσι δακών, Hom. *Od.* a. 381, ὀδὰξ ἐν χείλεσι φύντες.

1084 οὐκ ἦν ἰδεῖν.] It was before Thermopylae, according to Herodotus (VIII. 226), that 'Dieneces a Spartan, hearing from a Trachinian that, when the barbarians discharge their shafts, they hide the sun by reason of the multitude of their arrows, so numerous are they, replied undismayed—making of no account the numbers of the Medes—that the Trachinian stranger's tidings were entirely in their favour, since, should the Medes hide the sun, then would the Greeks fight in the shade.' The saying is given by others to Leonidas.

1085 ἀπεωσάμεσθα.] ἐσωζόμεσθα, V. ἐπαυσάμεσθα, R: the latter can hardly stand: the former is taken by Meineke. ἐωσάμεσθα Bergk. ἀπωσάμεσθα. Dind.

1086 γλαῦξ.] The bird of Athene, and of Athens. Cf. *Eq.* 1092, μοὐδόκει ἡ θεὸς αὐτὴ ἐκ πόλεως ἐλθεῖν, καὶ γλαῦξ αὐτῇ 'πικαθῆσθαι. The Scholiast says that the owl bore the news of victory to the Athenians.

[1101] ΣΦΗΚΕΣ. 111

εἶτα δ' εἰπόμεσθα θυννάζοντες ἐς τοὺς θυλάκους,
οἱ δ' ἔφευγον τὰς γνάθους καὶ τὰς ὀφρῦς κεντούμενοι·
ὥστε παρὰ τοῖς βαρβάροισι πανταχοῦ καὶ νῦν ἔτι
μηδὲν 'Αττικοῦ καλεῖσθαι σφηκὸς ἀνδρικώτερον. 1090
ἆρα δεινὸς ἦ τόθ' ὥστε πάντα μ' ἂν δεδοικέναι,
καὶ κατεστρεψάμην
τοὺς ἐναντίους, πλέων ἐκεῖσε ταῖς τριήρεσιν,
οὐ γὰρ ἦν ἡμῖν ὅπως
ῥῆσιν εὖ λέξειν ἐμέλλομεν τότ', οὐδὲ 1095
συκοφαντήσειν τινὰ
φροντίς, ἀλλ' ὅστις ἐρέτης ἔσοιτ' ἄριστος.
τοιγαροῦν πολλὰς πόλεις Μήδων ἑλόντες,
αἰτιώτατοι φέρεσθαι
τὸν φόρον δεῦρ' ἐσμέν, ὃν κλέ-
πτουσιν οἱ νεώτεροι. 1100
πολλαχοῦ σκοποῦντες ἡμᾶς εἰς ἄπανθ' εὑρήσετε

Tacitus (*Ann.* II. 17) mentions a similar omen before an engagement with some German tribes, 'Interea pulcherrimum augurium octo aquilae petere silvas et intrare visae imperatorem advertere. exclamat, irent, sequerentur Romanas aves, propria legionum numina.'
1087 **εἶτα δ' εἰπόμεσθα.**] Cf. Herod. VII. 113, φεύγουσι δὲ τοῖσι Πέρσῃσι εἴποντο κόπτοντες.
θυννάζοντες.] κεντοῦντες ὡς τοὺς θύννους τοῖς τριοδοῦσι. Schol. Eels are now speared in a similar way, and whales harpooned. There is an evident remembrance of Aesch. *Pers.* 424, τοὶ δ' ὥστε θύννους, ἤ τιν' ἰχθύων βόλον, ἀγαῖσι κωπῶν θραύσμασίν τ' ἐρειπίων ἔπαιον ἐρράχιζον.
1089 **ὥστε κ.τ.λ.**] And thus we proved ourselves very wasps in the way in which we worried them, and have quite justified ourselves in assuming for our old age this waspish attire.
1091 **πάντα μ' ἄν.**] The vulg. πάντα μή is hardly defensible, for πάντα μὴ δ. must = μηδένα (or μηδὲν) δεδοικέναι. But πάντας ἐμέ, Hirschig's correction, is not quite satis-

factory. The text is Dobree's, accepted by Holden. πάντα μ' ἐκδ. might also do.
1093 **ἐκεῖσε.**] To Asia Minor.
1094 **οὐ γὰρ ἦν ἡμῖν ὅπως.**] 'The question with us was not how.'
1095—7 **λέξειν ἐμέλλομεν...ἔσοιτ'**] 'We were likely to speak or to accuse, but who should come to be the best rower.' μέλλω λέξειν, as nearly equal to λέξω, would answer to ἔσομαι in direct speech: hence in oblique relation ἐμέλλομεν λέξειν is tolerably parallel to the .optat. fut. ἔσοιτο.
1098 **πόλεις Μήδων.**] Cities belonging to the Athenians, but subjected to the Medes, and now recovered, says the Scholiast. Richter understands it of allied or tributary cities now gained, which had before been under Persian dominion. No strict accuracy need be expected in this account of 'the many cities taken from the Medes,' but the mention of the φόρος immediately afterwards countenances Richter's view.
1101 **πολλαχοῦ σ. ἡ.**] 'If you look at us under various circum-

τοὺς τρόπους καὶ τὴν δίαιταν σφηξὶν ἐμφερεστάτους.
πρῶτα μὲν γὰρ οὐδὲν ἡμῶν ζῷον ἠρεθισμένον
μᾶλλον ὀξύθυμόν ἐστιν οὐδὲ δυσκολώτερον· 1105
εἶτα τἄλλ' ὅμοια πάντα σφηξὶ μηχανώμεθα.
ξυλλεγέντες γὰρ καθ' ἐσμούς, ὥσπερεὶ τἀνθρήνια,
οἱ μὲν ἡμῶν οὕπερ ἄρχων, οἱ δὲ παρὰ τοὺς ἕνδεκα,
οἱ δ' ἐν ᾠδείῳ δικάζουσ', οἱ δὲ πρὸς τοῖς τειχίοις
ξυμβεβυσμένοι, πυκνὸν νεύοντες ἐς τὴν γῆν, μόλις 1110
ὥσπερ οἱ σκώληκες ἐν τοῖς κυττάροις κινούμενοι.
ἔς τε τὴν ἄλλην δίαιταν ἐσμὲν εὐπορώτατοι.
πάντα γὰρ κεντοῦμεν ἄνδρα κἀκπορίζομεν βίον.
ἀλλὰ γὰρ κηφῆνες ἡμῖν εἰσιν ἐγκαθήμενοι,
οὐκ ἔχοντες κέντρον· οἳ μένοντες ἡμῶν τοῦ φόρου 1115

stances,' lit. 'in many places.' Their likeness to wasps on the battle-field has been shewn: it has now to be shewn at home.

1107 ἐσμούς.] Cf. *Lys.* 353, ἐσμὸς γυναικῶν οὑτοσί.

1108—1111 We swarm like wasps to our several courts. For the respective jurisdiction of the archon, the eleven, &c. see *Dict. Antiq.*, but where each court was held cannot now be fully determined.

1109 ᾠδείῳ.] In this building, which was properly intended for the reciting of poems, the Scholiast doubts whether courts were actually held; but it seems likely enough that the place was sometimes used for this purpose.

πρὸς τοῖς τειχίοις. It is doubtful whether this refers to any definite place, or (as Richter thinks) merely means that wherever there is anything like a wall or enclosure, dicasts are ready to sit and constitute a court, εἰς πάντα τόπον εὑρήσει τις δικαστὰς ἐν 'Αττικῇ. Schol. Cf. *Nub.* 208, οὐ πείθομαι, ἐπεὶ δικαστὰς οὐκ ὁρῶ καθημένους. Holden, followed by Meineke, changes πυκνὸν in the next line to πυκνὸς, an ingenious alteration, thus getting a definite place of meeting. The Pnyx (cf. *Dict. Ant.* p. 362) had 'a boun-

dary wall, part rock, part masonry,' which would be here meant.

1110 ξυμβεβυσμένοι.] 'Crammed together' so that they could hardly move. Cf. the description of the crowds in *Nub.* 1203, ἀμφορῆς νενησμένοι.

1111 σκώληκες ἐν τοῖς κυττάροις.] 'Like wasp-grubs in their cells.' κύτταροι δὲ αἱ τῶν κηρίων κοιλότητες. Schol. Several other kinds of holes are given to which the word may be applied: a curious use is in *Pac.* 199, ὑπ' αὐτὸν ἀτεχνῶς οὐρανοῦ τὸν κύτταρον, explained by τὸ κοιλότατον καὶ μυχαίτατον.

1114 κηφῆνες.] The orators who stop at home and do only the talking are the drones. The Scholiast quotes from Hesiod (*Op.* 302) κηφήνεσσι κοθούροις ἴκελος ὁρμήν οἵτε μελισσάων κάματον τρύχουσιν ἀεργοὶ ἔσθοντες.

1115 οὐκ ἔχοντες κ.τ.λ.] Meineke omitting this line takes πόνον for γόνον in the next. Twenty lines (the number as it now stands) is a number for the epirrhema, supported by the *Clouds* and *Frogs:* but there is enough variety in the number in different plays to prevent any strong argument either way on the score of the probable number of lines in an epirrhema.

[1124] ΣΦΗΚΕΣ. 113

τὸν γόνον κατεσθίουσιν, οὐ ταλαιπωρούμενοι.
τοῦτο δ' ἔστ' ἄλγιστον ἡμῖν, ἤν τις ἀστράτευτος ὢν
ἐκροφῇ τὸν μισθὸν ἡμῶν, τῆσδε τῆς χώρας ὕπερ
μήτε κώπην μήτε λόγχην μήτε φλύκταιναν λαβών.
ἀλλ' ἐμοὶ δοκεῖ τὸ λοιπὸν τῶν πολιτῶν ἐμβραχὺ   1120
ὅστις ἂν μὴ 'χῃ τὸ κέντρον, μὴ φέρειν τριώβολον.

ΦΙΛΟΚΛΕΩΝ

οὔ τοι ποτὲ ζῶν τοῦτον ἀποδυθήσομαι,
ἐπεὶ μόνος μ' ἔσωσε παρατεταγμένον,
ὅθ' ὁ βορέας ὁ μέγας ἐπεστρατεύσατο.

1117 ἀστράτευτος.] Cf. *Nub.*
692, ἥτις οὐ στρατεύεται of Amynias: also *Eq.* 443, where the
sausage-seller threatens Cleon with
twenty indictments for ἀστρατεία.
1119 φλύκταιναν.] Cf. *Ran.*
236, ἐγὼ δὲ φλυκταίνας ἔχω. And
for other sufferings in rowing cf.
Eq. 785, ἵνα μὴ τρίβῃς τὴν ἐν Σαλαμῖνι.
1120 ἐμβραχύ.] καθάπαξ ἢ παντάπασι. Schol. Equivalent, the Scholiast says, to βραχύ, the preposition
having no force; but that it has
none, as he says, in the verb. ἐνδυ-
στυχῆσαι in Eur. *Phoen.* 727 will
not easily be granted.
1121 μὴ 'χῃ τὸ κέντρον.] Whoever is an idle drone, sting-less, and
does no work.
Mitchell notes that 'this comedy
ought to have ended immediately
with these addresses of the chorus
or even before them. The action
was complete; and whatever else is
added must be a mere superfeta-
tion.' And he treats the rest as
a separate piece, giving to it a separate name, 'the Dicast turned gen-
tleman.' There is certainly a strongly marked difference between the
two parts. But undoubtedly they
were one play: nor would the
latter half have had much force
except in contrast to the former.
And the representation of the Dicast converted is analogous to that
of Demus restored to youth in the
Knights. He has passed, it is true,
from one extreme to another, giving
Aristophanes occasion for satire
upon the follies of luxury and pro-
fligacy. Phidippides' conversion
from one bad course to another is a
parallel.
1122—1173 Father and son return: a discussion ensues about a
change in the old man's dress; he is
with difficulty persuaded to discard
his old doublet for a mantle of
newer fashion. Then there is a
similar dispute about shoes; which
ends in his complying, and strutting
about with the gait of the wealthy
men of the time.
1123 παρατεταγμένον] properly
of the man 'next in line.' His
cloak proved his best and trustiest
comrade in the field, when the north
wind swept down upon them.
1124 βορέας.] The Scholiast understands this of the north wind
that caused loss to the Persian fleet
at Artemisium. Probably it is
rather the whole Persian invasion
that is called 'Boreas' as coming
down from the north, while at the
same time any stormy weather that
happened then would be a reason for
Philocleon's gratitude to his trusty
cloak. Conzius thinks that βασι-
λεύς, the great king, is especially
meant by Βορέας, and quotes in
illustration of ἐπεστρατεύσατο, 'Di-

8

ΒΔΕΛΥΚΛΕΩΝ
ἀγαθὸν ἔοικας οὐδὲν ἐπιθυμεῖν παθεῖν.

ΦΙΛΟΚΛΕΩΝ
μὰ τὸν Δί', οὐ γὰρ οὐδαμῶς μοι ξύμφορον.
καὶ γὰρ πρότερον ἐπανθρακίδων ἐμπλήμενος
ἀπέδωκ' ὀφείλων τῷ κναφεῖ τριώβολον.

ΒΔΕΛΥΚΛΕΩΝ
ἀλλ' οὖν πεπειράσθω γ', ἐπειδήπερ γ' ἅπαξ
ἐμοὶ σεαυτὸν παραδέδωκας εὖ ποιεῖν.   1130

ΦΙΛΟΚΛΕΩΝ
τί οὖν κελεύεις δρᾶν με;

ΒΔΕΛΥΚΛΕΩΝ
τὸν τρίβων' ἄφες·
τηνδὶ δὲ χλαῖναν ἀναβαλοῦ τριβωνικῶς.

ΦΙΛΟΚΛΕΩΝ
ἔπειτα παῖδας χρὴ φυτεύειν καὶ τρέφειν,
ὅθ' οὑτοσί με νῦν ἀποπνῖξαι βούλεται;

ΒΔΕΛΥΚΛΕΩΝ
ἔχ', ἀναβαλοῦ τηνδὶ λαβών, καὶ μὴ λάλει.   1135

rus per urbes Afer ut Italas Ceu flamma per taedas vel Eurus Per Siculas equitavit undas.' Hor. *Od.* IV. 4. 44. And a comparison of v. 11 of this play, κἀμοὶ γὰρ ἀρτίως ἐπεστρατεύσατο Μῆδός τις...ὕπνος, confirms this interpretation.

1127 καὶ γάρ κ.τ.λ.] For I spoilt my cloak once with some fish-sauce, and had to pay for its cleaning; so I do not want a more valuable one, lest I may spoil that. ἐπανθρακίδων.] λεπτοὶ ἰχθύες ὀπτοί. Schol. Cf. *Ach.* 670, ἡνίκ' ἂν ἐπανθρακίδες ὦσι παρακείμεναι, οἱ δὲ Θασίαν ἀνακυκῶσι λιπαράμπυκα. It was with this Thasian fish-sauce (ἅλμη) that the garment was spoilt.

1132 τριβωνικῶς.] The Scholiast appears to have had a various reading γεροντικῶς: but τρ. seems right. The τρίβων however we find constantly worn by the older men.

1133 ἔπειτα.] 'After this,' marking astonishment and indignation: cf. *Ach.* 126, κἄπειτ' ἐγὼ δῆτ' ἐνθαδὶ στραγγεύομαι. It is not altogether unlike πρὸς ταῦτα in the tragedians, *e.g.* in Aesch. *Prom. Vinct.* 992, πρὸς ταῦτα ῥιπτέσθω μὲν αἰθαλοῦσσα φλόξ. The Latins use 'nunc' with the same ironical force; 'I nunc et versus tecum meditare canoros' says Horace, after describing the din of the Roman streets.

1134 ἀποπνῖξαι.] The χλαῖνα was evidently soft, woolly, and warm, whereas the old man's τρίβων, however good a defence against Boreas in days past, was probably, the worse for wear.

ΣΦΗΚΕΣ.

ΦΙΛΟΚΛΕΩΝ
τουτὶ τὸ κακὸν τί ἐστι πρὸς πάντων θεῶν;

ΒΔΕΛΥΚΛΕΩΝ
οἱ μὲν καλοῦσι Περσίδ', οἱ δὲ καυνάκην.

ΦΙΛΟΚΛΕΩΝ
ἐγὼ δὲ σισύραν ᾠόμην Θυμαιτίδα.

ΒΔΕΛΥΚΛΕΩΝ
κοὐ θαῦμά γ'· ἐς Σάρδεις γὰρ οὐκ ἐλήλυθας.
ἔγνως γὰρ ἄν· νῦν δ' οὐχὶ γιγνώσκεις.

ΦΙΛΟΚΛΕΩΝ
       ἐγώ;   1140
μὰ τὸν Δί' οὐ τοίνυν· ἀτὰρ δοκεῖ γέ μοι
ἐοικέναι μάλιστα Μορύχου σάγματι.

ΒΔΕΛΥΚΛΕΩΝ
οὔκ, ἀλλ' ἐν Ἐκβατάνοισι ταῦθ' ὑφαίνεται.

ΦΙΛΟΚΛΕΩΝ
ἐν Ἐκβατάνοισι γίγνεται κρόκης χόλιξ;

1137 Περσίδ'...καυνάκην.] χλαῖνα Περσικὴ ἀλεεινή, Schol. That καυνάκη has anything to do with καῦμα is not very likely. Conzius gives a Persian word for a silken texture, which he thinks may be cognate. But this garment appears to have been of wool, or at all events woolly on one side, ἔχον ἐκ τοῦ ἑτέρου μέρους μαλλούς. Philocleon takes it for a rough sheepskin blanket or wrapper, called σισύρα or βαίτη.
1138 Θυμαιτίδα.] From a deme of the tribe of Hippothoon, where such βαῖται were made. Schol.
1139 ἐς Σάρδεις.] Where such Persian apparel is for sale. Cf. Ach. 112, βάμμα Σαρδιανικόν.
1142 ἐοικέναι.] Meineke reads προσεικέναι (a form found in Eccl. 1161) in deference to a rule of Cobet's, that the old Attic writers always said εἴξασιν (Nub. 341, 343, Av. 96, 383) εἰκέναι (Nub. 185) εἰκώς. There are not enough instances to ground a rule upon; convenience for the metre may have determined the form: and there is no strong reason against ἐοικέναι from ἔοικα (cf. below 1171), when all MSS. give it.
Μορύχου.] For whom cf. Ach. 887, Pac. 1008, and above v. 506. It is in keeping with his character that he should muffle himself up. μαλλωτῷ σάγῳ ἐχρῆτο, ὡς τρυφερὸς πλείονι θάλπει χρώμενος. Schol.
1144 κρόκης χόλιξ.] 'A tripe of the woof or thread,' i.e. a tripe-like texture: a curious comparison. 'Laneos floccos in panno exstantes comparat bovis intestino, quod crispum est, et velut pellitum.' Fl. Chr. The same commentator suggests that the texture must have been 'friza, frieze'.

8—2

ΒΔΕΛΤΚΛΕΩΝ

πόθεν, ὠγάθ'; ἀλλὰ τοῦτο τοῖσι βαρβάροις
ὑφαίνεται πολλαῖς δαπάναις. αὕτη γέ τοι
ἐρίων τάλαντον καταπέπωκε ῥᾳδίως.

ΦΙΛΟΚΛΕΩΝ

οὔκουν ἐριώλην δῆτ' ἐχρῆν αὐτὴν καλεῖν
δικαιότερον ἢ καυνάκην;

ΒΔΕΛΤΚΛΕΩΝ

ἔχ ὠγαθέ,
καὶ στῆθί γ' ἀμπισχόμενος.

ΦΙΛΟΚΛΕΩΝ

οἴμοι δείλαιος·
ὡς θερμὸν ἡ μιαρά τί μου κατήρυγεν.

ΒΔΕΛΤΚΛΕΩΝ

οὐκ ἀναβαλεῖ;

ΦΙΛΟΚΛΕΩΝ

μὰ Δί' οὐκ ἔγωγ'. ἀλλ', ὠγαθέ,
εἴπερ γ' ἀνάγκη, κρίβανόν μ' ἀμπίσχετε.

ΒΔΕΛΤΚΛΕΩΝ

φέρ', ἀλλ' ἐγώ σε περιβαλῶ· σὺ δ' οὖν ἴθι.

ΦΙΛΟΚΛΕΩΝ

παράθου γε μέντοι καὶ κρεάγραν.

1145 πόθεν.] 'how so?' or 'nonsense!' He does not see, or pretends not to see, what his father means by the comparison, or what there is amiss with the mantle.

1148 ἐριώλην.] Properly a violent wind: cf. *Eq.* 511, where Cleon is compared to it. Here he puns, and derives it from ἔριον and ὀλύναι. A pronunciation of '*wool*wind' to resemble '*whirl*-wind' might be a fair equivalent.

1149 ἔχ' ὠγαθέ, κ.τ.λ.] 'Steady, my good sir! and stand still while put it on you.' He puts the cloak round his father, but the old man will make no effort to throw i gracefully over his shoulder (ἀναβάλλεσθαι), but rather throws it off; so the putting on has to be done en tirely by the son.

1155—6. Well if I am to b baked or roasted (says Philocleon) let there be a flesh-hook ready t pull me out before I am done all t pieces.

ΣΦΗΚΕΣ.

ΒΔΕΛΤΚΛΕΩΝ
τιὴ τί δή;   1155

ΦΙΛΟΚΛΕΩΝ
ἵν' ἐξέλῃς με πρὶν διερρυηκέναι.

ΒΔΕΛΤΚΛΕΩΝ
ἄγε νυν, ἀποδύου τὰς καταράτους ἐμβάδας,
τασδὶ δ' ἀνύσας ὑπόδυθι τὰς Λακωνικάς.

ΦΙΛΟΚΛΕΩΝ
ἐγὼ γὰρ ἂν τλαίην ὑποδύσασθαί ποτε
ἐχθρῶν παρ' ἀνδρῶν δυσμενῆ καττύματα;   1160

ΒΔΕΛΤΚΛΕΩΝ
ἔνθες ποτ', ὦ τᾶν, κἀπόβαιν' ἐρρωμένως
ἐς τὴν Λακωνικὴν ἀνύσας.

ΦΙΛΟΚΛΕΩΝ
ἀδικεῖς γέ με
ἐς τὴν πολεμίαν ἀποβιβάζων τὸν πόδα.

1155 **τιὴ τί δή.**] Cf. *Nub.* 755, *Thesm.* 84.
1156 **διερρυηκέναι.**] πρὶν συμπεσεῖν ἀπὸ τῆς ὀπτήσεως τὰ κρέα μου. Schol.
1157 **ἀποδύου.**] Hirschig proposes ὑπολύου. As MSS. R, V, have ὑποδύου, this reading is not without some warrant; but we must then take in vv. 1158, 59, 68 ὑποδοῦ, ὑποδήσασθαι, ὑποδησάμενος; the two last Scaliger's readings. However, the present text may stand. The Greeks were not bound to use, in tying on and loosing off shoes, no words save the ordinary ὑποδεῖσθαι and ὑπολύεσθαι. Richter even goes so far as to say that ἐμβάδες and Λακωνικαί were of the kind of foot covering called κοῖλα ὑποδήματα, not so much sandals as low shoes or slippers, and that ἀποδύεσθαι, ὑποδύεσθαι, suit them better than the common words. ἀποδύεσθαι 'to put off,' ὑποδύεσθα 'to get into, slip the feet into.'

1158 **ὑπόδυθι τὰς.**] ὑποδοῦ λαβὼν Hirschig; ὑποδοῦ τι τὰς Meineke. In this last the τι is awkward; in the former λαβὼν a violent change. ὑποδοῦ σὺ τὰς would be as likely, if it were necessary to change at all.
Λακωνικάς.] ἀστειότεραι γὰρ αὗται. Schol. They were men's shoes, as is plain from *Thesm.* 142, where they are mentioned along with χλαῖνα as a distinctive mark of a man.
1160 **ἐχθρῶν κ.τ.λ.**] Cf. Eur. *Heracl.* 1006, ἐχθροῦ λέοντος δυσμενῆ βλαστήματα.
1161 **ἔνθες ποτ'.**] ἔνθες πόδ' is Brunck's reading. 'Do pray at last put (your foot) in' is satisfactory, the ellipse being easy.
1161, 62 **κἀπόβαιν'...ἐς τὴν Λακωνικήν.**] 'Step out (of your own shoe) into the Laconian (shoe),' says the son: but the father understands χώραν Λ. and replies accordingly.
1163 **πολεμίαν.**] The ellipse of

118   ΑΡΙΣΤΟΦΑΝΟΥΣ   [1164

ΒΔΕΛΥΚΛΕΩΝ
φέρε καὶ τὸν ἕτερον.

ΦΙΛΟΚΛΕΩΝ
μηδαμῶς τοῦτόν γ', ἐπεὶ
πάνυ μισολάκων αὐτοῦ 'στιν εἷς τῶν δακτύλων.   1165

ΒΔΕΛΥΚΛΕΩΝ
οὐκ ἔστι παρὰ ταῦτ' ἄλλα.

ΦΙΛΟΚΛΕΩΝ
                                    κακοδαίμων ἐγώ,
ὅστις ἐπὶ γήρᾳ χίμετλον οὐδὲν λήψομαι.

ΒΔΕΛΥΚΛΕΩΝ
ἄνυσόν ποθ' ὑποδυσάμενος· εἶτα πλουσίως
ὡδὶ προβὰς τρυφερόν τι διασαλακώνισον.

ΦΙΛΟΚΛΕΩΝ
ἰδού· θεῶ τὸ σχῆμα, καὶ σκέψαι μ' ὅτῳ   1170
μάλιστ' ἔοικα τὴν βάδισιν τῶν πλουσίων.

ΒΔΕΛΥΚΛΕΩΝ
ὅτῳ; δοθιῆνι σκόροδον ἠμφιεσμένῳ.

γῆ or χώρα with the adjective is very common.

1164. Philocleon puts one foot in, probably the right (says Florens), according to the Pythagorean precept, 'dextrum pedem in calceum praemitte, laevum in ποδάνιπτρον.'

1166 οὐκ ἔστι κ.τ.λ.] Repeated from *Nub.* 698.

1167 χίμετλον.] ' A chilblain ;' it is put (says the Scholiast) by way of surprise for ἀγαθὸν οὐδὲν λήψομαι. τὰ τῶν γερόντων οὐ λήψομαι, 'I shall not enjoy the privileges of old men,' chilblains being among them. It may mean, 'I shall have no chilblains, since these more luxurious shoes will defend my feet,' as Richter says; or, 'I am not to have any chilblains, and so be allowed the privilege of an old man, shabby slippers, but more comfortable than these smart ones.' Philocleon's assertion above, that he had one toe on his left foot a decided Laconian-hater, rather suggests a chilblain already present on that toe, which he is not to indulge.

1169 διασαλακώνισον.] From a certain Salacon. Schol. There is also reference to λακωνίζειν. A reading διαλυκώνισον is mentioned by the Scholiast, and derived from Lycon. These derivations seem but guesses. Dindorf from Hesychius and Photius discovers a word, διασαικώνισον, which Meineke adopts here. The meaning is the same.

1170 σχῆμα.] Appears to include posture, bearing, gait, &c., as well as dress. Cf. above, v. 1070.

1172 δοθιῆνι κ.τ.λ.] An absurd comparison, which it seems vain to analyze. If Δοθιῆνι be read, and if

ΣΦΗΚΕΣ.

ΦΙΛΟΚΛΕΩΝ
καὶ μὴν προθυμοῦμαί γε σαυλοπρωκτιᾶν.

ΒΔΕΛΥΚΛΕΩΝ
ἄγε νυν, ἐπιστήσει λόγους σεμνοὺς λέγειν
ἀνδρῶν παρόντων πολυμαθῶν καὶ δεξιῶν; 1175

ΦΙΛΟΚΛΕΩΝ
ἔγωγε.

ΒΔΕΛΥΚΛΕΩΝ
τίνας δῆτ᾽ ἂν λέγοις;

ΦΙΛΟΚΛΕΩΝ
πολλοὺς πάνυ.
πρῶτον μὲν ὡς ἡ Λάμι᾽ ἁλοῦσ᾽ ἐπέρδετο,
ἔπειτα δ᾽ ὡς ὁ Καρδοπίων τὴν μητέρα.

ΒΔΕΛΥΚΛΕΩΝ
μή μοί γε μύθους, ἀλλὰ τῶν ἀνθρωπίνων
οἵους λέγομεν μάλιστα τοὺς κατ᾽ οἰκίαν. 1180

ΦΙΛΟΚΛΕΩΝ
ἐγῷδα τοίνυν τῶν γε πάνυ κατ᾽ οἰκίαν
ἐκεῖνον, ὡς οὕτω ποτ᾽ ἦν μῦς καὶ γαλῆ.

ΒΔΕΛΥΚΛΕΩΝ
ὦ σκαιὲ κἀπαίδευτε, Θεογένης ἔφη

---

he were a person of known gait, it would only remain to find why the mantle was likened to garlic.

1174—1264. Being now dressed properly, Philocleon is further instructed in the art of fashionable talk, of deportment at a banquet. A feast is imagined: the song is to pass round: he shews how he would bear his part, and succeeds tolerably well. Both father and son then go off to a supper at Philoctemon's house.

1176 τίνας.] From the preceding λόγους, and the following πολλοὺς, this seems almost necessary. But most editors retain τίνα of MSS. R, V.

1178 μητέρα.] λείπει ἔτυψεν. Schol.

1179, 80. No long-winded tales or fables, but common 'household' stories are to be the rule. Richter gives 'Kinder-und Hausmärchen' in illustration. Philocleon at once starts off with the most familiar and household word he knows.

1182 οὕτω.] Cf. Plat. *Phaedr.* 237, ἦν οὕτω δὲ παῖς. And the Scholiast gives ἦν οὕτω γέρων καὶ γραῦς, as another fable beginning in this way. Germ. 'Es war also einmal.'

1183—85. Apparently Theogenes (for whom cf. *Pac.* 928, *Av.* 822,

τῷ κοπρολόγῳ, καὶ ταῦτα λοιδορούμενος,
μῦς καὶ γαλᾶς μέλλεις λέγειν ἐν ἀνδράσιν;   1185

ΦΙΛΟΚΛΕΩΝ
ποίους τινὰς δὲ χρὴ λέγειν;

ΒΔΕΛΥΚΛΕΩΝ
μεγαλοπρεπεῖς,
ὡς ξυνεθεώρεις Ἀνδροκλεῖ καὶ Κλεισθένει.

ΦΙΛΟΚΛΕΩΝ
ἐγὼ δὲ τεθεώρηκα πώποτ' οὐδαμοῖ
πλὴν ἐς Πάρον, καὶ ταῦτα δύ' ὀβολὼ φέρων.

ΒΔΕΛΥΚΛΕΩΝ
ἀλλ' οὖν λέγειν χρή σ' ὡς ἐμάχετό γ' αὐτίκα   1190
Ἐφουδίων παγκράτιον Ἀσκώνδᾳ καλῶς,
ἤδη γέρων ὢν καὶ πολιός, ἔχων δέ τοι

1127, 1295), though of swinish habits, used fine words. Hence they quote his rebuke of the scavenger (perhaps for bringing something 'between the wind and his nobility') as suitable to Philocleon for venturing on such an unsavoury subject as mice and weasels in polite society. ὦ σκαιὲ κἀπαίδευτε is of course a tragic style to begin a rebuke of a κοπρολόγος.

1184 καὶ ταῦτα λ.] 'And that too when abusing him,' and when accordingly you would expect coarser words from such a man, especially as the Greek language is not poor in such expressions.

1185 ἐν ἀνδράσιν.] Such being 'old wives' fables.' Cf. Horace's 'garrit aniles ex re fabellas' of just this style of fable.

1187 ξυνεθεώρεις.] Sacred embassies, which should be given to the honourable and noble, are mentioned in connexion with these worthless men, to reprove the Athenians for placing such rascals in high office.

Androcles appears to have been attacked as a beggar and profligate by other comic writers; Cleisthenes is often assailed by Aristophanes.

1189 ἐς Πάρον.] What expedition to Paros is meant, is uncertain. It was not, at any rate, a θεωρία; but he went merely as a μισθωτὸς στρατιώτης, as the Scholiast says. Richter interprets τεθεώρηκα ἐς Π. 'stipendium merui ad Parum otiose spectando, non fortiter pugnando.'

1191 Ἐφουδίων...Ἀσκώνδᾳ.] It is not necessary that these should be real persons: but it is more likely that they were real pancratiasts, or fictitious names for such, than that they were effeminate persons thus ridiculed, as Richter thinks. What Aristophanes' satire is pointed at is the trifling nature of the conversation, when they could find nothing better to talk of than the details of such athletic contests. Horace gives 'Hora quota est? Thrax est Gallina Syro par?' as an instance of small talk.

ΣΦΗΚΕΣ.

πλευρὰν βαθυτάτην καὶ χέρας λαγόνας τε καὶ
θώρακ' ἄριστον.

ΦΙΛΟΚΛΕΩΝ
παῦε παῦ', οὐδὲν λέγεις.
πῶς δ' ἂν μαχέσαιτο παγκράτιον θώρακ' ἔχων;   1195

ΒΔΕΛΥΚΛΕΩΝ
οὕτως διηγεῖσθαι νομίζουσ' οἱ σοφοί.
ἀλλ' ἕτερον εἰπέ μοι· παρ' ἀνδράσι ξένοις
πίνων, σεαυτοῦ ποῖον ἂν λέξαι δοκεῖς
ἐπὶ νεότητος ἔργον ἀνδρικώτατον;

ΦΙΛΟΚΛΕΩΝ
ἐκεῖν' ἐκεῖν' ἀνδρειότατόν γε τῶν ἐμῶν,   1200
ὅτ' Ἐργασίωνος τὰς χάρακας ὑφειλόμην.

ΒΔΕΛΥΚΛΕΩΝ
ἀπολεῖς με. ποίας χάρακας; ἀλλ' ὡς ἢ κάπρον
ἐδιώκαθές ποτ', ἢ λαγών, ἢ λαμπάδα
ἔδραμες, ἀνευρὼν ὅ τι νεανικώτατον.

ΦΙΛΟΚΛΕΩΝ
ἐγᾦδα τοίνυν τό γε νεανικώτατον·   1205

1194 θώρακ'.] 'The chest,' a signification of the word which is found in later Greek, but, we may infer, was fashionable in a certain class at this earlier time. Philocleon does not understand it, and takes θώραξ to mean 'breastplate.' The pancration only included wrestling and boxing, for neither of which would a breastplate be needed or allowed.
1196 οὕτως.] Such was the style of narrative among the clever young fellows of the time. Bdelycleon then goes on to instruct him that he must be prepared with some boastful story about himself.
1197 ξένοις.] ἔθος γὰρ ἐπὶ τοῖς ξένοις καυχᾶσθαι. Schol.
1201 Ἐργασίωνος.] Some countryman. Deeds of thieving are not unfrequently boasted of: cf. above,
v. 236.
1203 λαμπάδα.] They used to run bearing torches in the Ceramicus. Schol. Cf. *Ran.* 129—133. The torch-race is frequently mentioned by Attic writers, and gives rise to some striking metaphorical expressions: *e.g.* Plato's καθάπερ λαμπάδα τὸν βίον παραδιδόντες ἄλλοις ἐξ ἄλλων; whence Lucretius, 'quasi cursores vitai lampada tradunt.' But the precise rules of the race are difficult to ascertain.
1204 νεανικώτατον.] The word from the sense of 'youthful, vigorous, mettlesome,' comes to mean 'violent, overbearing;' as below at v. 1307. νεανιεύεσθαι has similar meanings.
1205—7 ἐγᾦδα.] If races and chaces are to be the order of the

122   ΑΡΙΣΤΟΦΑΝΟΥΣ   [1206

ὅτε τὸν δρομέα Φάϋλλον, ὢν βούπαις ἔτι,
εἷλον διώκων λοιδορίας ψήφοιν δυοῖν.

ΒΔΕΛΤΚΛΕΩΝ
παῦ'· ἀλλὰ δευρὶ κατακλινεὶς προσμάνθανε
ξυμποτικὸς εἶναι καὶ ξυνουσιαστικός.

ΦΙΛΟΚΛΕΩΝ
πῶς οὖν κατακλινῶ; φράζ' ἀνύσας.

ΒΔΕΛΤΚΛΕΩΝ
                                εὐσχημόνως.   1210

ΦΙΛΟΚΛΕΩΝ
ἀεὶ κελεύεις κατακλινῆναι;

ΒΔΕΛΤΚΛΕΩΝ
           μηδαμῶς.

ΦΙΛΟΚΛΕΩΝ
πῶς δαί;

ΒΔΕΛΤΚΛΕΩΝ
τὰ γόνατ' ἔκτεινε, καὶ γυμναστικῶς
ὑγρὸν χύτλασον σεαυτὸν ἐν τοῖς στρώμασιν.
ἔπειτ' ἐπαίνεσόν τι τῶν χαλκωμάτων,
ὀροφὴν θέασαι, κρεκάδι' αὐλῆς θαύμασον·   1215

day, then, thinks the old dicast, my prosecuting Phayllus is the right sort of exploit. He puns on the double meaning of διώκειν, as in *Ach.* 700, *Eq.* 969, διώξει Σμικύθην καὶ κύριον. Phayllus is mentioned as a great runner in *Ach.* 215, οὐκ ἂν ἐπ' ἐμῆς γε νεότητος ὅτ' ἐγὼ φέρων ἀνθράκων φόρτιον ἠκολούθουν Φαΰλλῳ τρέχων. See note and Scholiast there. And even if this be another Phayllus (for the Scholiast on the *Acharnians* says there were three, and the third a λωποδύτης), yet there is plainly some reference to the Olympian namesake, when it is said of him that 'for all he ran so fast, he was (pur)sued and caught at last.'

1210 κατακλινῶ.] Aor. 2. conj. of the passive voice: cf. κατακλινεὶς above.

εὐσχημόνως.] Bergler quotes from Euripides Silenus' directions to the Cyclops (*Cycl.* 563), θὲς δὴ τὸν ἀγκῶν' εὐρύθμως, κᾆτ' ἔκπιε ὥσπερ μ' ὁρᾷς πίνοντα.

1213 ὑγρὸν χύτλασον.] 'Throw yourself in loose easy posture.' L. and S. refer to Hippocrates for ὑγρὸς κεῖσθαι. Cf. Pindar's ὑγρὸν νῶτον αἰωρεῖ of the eagle (*Pyth.* I. 17). About χύτλασον the Scholiast appears to be wrong, taking it of anointing. The context here shews that it must be a description of a certain way of lying.

1214. ἐπαίνεσον.] Complimentary remarks on the plate, tapestry, &c. would be usual. But the parasite in Diphilus (quoted by Athenaeus) holds a rather different view:
ὅταν με καλέσῃ πλούσιος δεῖπνον

ΣΦΗΚΕΣ.

ὕδωρ κατὰ χειρός· τὰς τραπέζας ἐσφέρειν·
δειπνοῦμεν· ἀπονενίμμεθ'· ἤδη σπένδομεν.
ΦΙΛΟΚΛΕΩΝ
πρὸς τῶν θεῶν, ἐνύπνιον ἐστιώμεθα;
ΒΔΕΛΥΚΛΕΩΝ
αὐλητρὶς ἐνεφύσησεν. οἱ δὲ συμπόται
εἰσὶν Θέωρος, Αἰσχίνης, Φανὸς, Κλέων,   1220
ξένος τις ἕτερος πρὸς κεφαλῆς Ἀκέστορος.
τούτοις ξυνὼν τὰ σκόλια πῶς δέξει;
ΦΙΛΟΚΛΕΩΝ
καλῶς.

ποιῶν, οὐ κατανοῶ τὰ τρίγλυφ' οὐδὲ τὰς στέγας· οὐδὲ δοκιμάζω τοὺς Κορινθίους κάδους· ἀτενὲς δὲ τηρῶ τοῦ μαγείρου τὸν καπνόν.
1216. ὕδωρ κατὰ χειρός.] Cf. Av. 463, καταχεῖσθαι κατὰ χειρὸς ὕδωρ φερέτω ταχύ τις. Ε. δειπνήσειν μέλλομεν; ἤ τί;
ἐσφέρειν] imperatively used. The tables were actually brought in in ancient times. See Dict. Ant. p. 613.
1217. ἀπονενίμμεθ'.] μετὰ τὸ δειπνῆσαι ἔθος λέγειν· ἀπονίψασθαι δός, ὦ παῖ. Schol.
1219. αὐλητρίς.] Music and dancing were usual after a banquet. Cf. Homer's μολπή τ' ὀρχηστύς τε τὰ γάρ τ' ἀναθήματα δαιτός. (Od. a. 152). In Ach. 1090—93 many details of a banquet are enumerated, dancing girls among them.
1220. Θέωρος κ.τ.λ.] Phanus, a dependant of Cleon's, is mentioned in Eq. 1256. Cf. note there. For Theorus and Aeschines cf. vv. 42, 325.
1221. ξένος τις...Ἀκέστορος.] Another foreigner lying above Acestor. Acestor appears from the Scholiast here and on Av. 431 to have been of Thracian extraction, and called Σάκας 'the Sacian.' In Av. 31, νόσον νοσοῦμεν τὴν ἐναντίαν Σάκᾳ· ὁ μὲν γὰρ οὐκ ὢν ἀστὸς ἐσβιάζεται· ἡμεῖς δὲ...ἀνεπτόμεθ' ἐκ τῆς πατρίδος.

1222—3. There are different ways of arranging the dialogue. The text is Richter's: Dindorf's (in the Poetae Scenici) hardly makes sense, καλῶς is better given to Philocleon, and ἀληθες, to Bdelycleon. Meineke further puts οὐδ' εἰ Δ. for οὐδεὶς Δ., meaning Diacrion to be a proper name, I suppose, and his reading would mean 'I shall take up the song well, so that not even if Diacrion were to take it could he take it better.'
1222. σκόλια.] It was the old custom at a banquet for the guests to follow whoever led off first with the song, continuing the song where he left it. For the leader held a branch of bay or myrtle and sang a song of Simonides or Stesichorus, as far as he pleased, and then passed it on to whom he would, in no particular order; and he who received it from the first continued the song and then again passed it on. Schol. Various explanations are given of the word σκόλιον: that the songs were so called from the irregular nature of the metre and music; from the zig-zag manner in which the song might pass this way and that way about the table; from the irregular arrangement of the couches. The fact that the song passed according to no rule seems to shew that it is lost labour in this passage to attempt to arrange the guests, to

124 ΑΡΙΣΤΟΦΑΝΟΥΣ [1223

ΒΔΕΛΤΚΛΕΩΝ
ἄληθες;
ΦΙΛΟΚΛΕΩΝ
ὡς οὐδεὶς Διακρίων δέξεται.
ΒΔΕΛΤΚΛΕΩΝ
ἐγὼ εἴσομαι· καὶ δὴ γάρ εἰμ᾽ ἐγὼ Κλέων,
ᾄδω δὲ πρῶτος Ἁρμοδίου· δέξει δὲ σύ.   1225
οὐδεὶς πώποτ᾽ ἀνὴρ ἐγένετ᾽ Ἀθηναῖος
ΦΙΛΟΚΛΕΩΝ
οὐχ οὕτω γε πανοῦργος κλέπτης
ΒΔΕΛΤΚΛΕΩΝ
τουτὶ σὺ δράσεις; παραπολεῖ βοώμενος·
φήσει γὰρ ἐξολεῖν σε καὶ διαφθερεῖν
καὶ τῆσδε τῆς γῆς ἐξελᾶν.
ΦΙΛΟΚΛΕΩΝ
ἐγὼ δέ γε,   1230

account for some not singing, to suppose (as one commentator does) that the text is corrupt or deficient on that account. It is plain that Aristophanes might take just as many singers as suited his purpose.
1223. **Διακρίων.**] The old division of the Athenians was into Diacrians, Pediaeans, Paralians. Richter observes that Marathon was in the Diacrian district, and Philocleon has termed himself Μαραθωνομάχας: so of the old-fashioned divisions, which, as a lover of old customs, he keeps to, he chooses that.
1224. **ἐγὼ εἴσομαι.**] Cf. above v. 416, and *Nub.* 901.
καὶ δή.] 'For now *suppose* me Cleon:' as in Eur. *Med.* 386, καὶ δὴ τεθνᾶσι. He begins with Cleon, as the most important person at table, and giving a ready handle for a parody.
1225. **Ἁρμοδίου**] sc. μέλος. Cf. *Ach.* 980, τὸν Ἁρμόδιον ᾄσεται, whence Reiske inferred Ἁρμόδιον should be read here. But in *Lysistr.* 1237 ᾄδοι Τελαμῶνος seems a genitive of the same kind.

1226. **οὐδείς...Ἀθηναῖος.**] This line does not suit well with the ἐν μύρτου κλαδὶ τὸ ξίφος φορήσω κ.τ.λ. in metre. Meineke's change improves it, but is uncertain. Bergk and Dindorf propose ἐγέντ᾽ Ἀθήναις, which Holden adopts. In the next line something is wanted before κλέπτης. Bentley supplies ὡς σύ, Bergk οὐδέ. This first line was apparently to end in praise of Harmodius, but is turned off to abuse of Cleon.
1227. **κλέπτης.**] By Cleon's own confession (*Eq.* 1252) his successor would be κλέπτης μὲν οὐκ ἂν μᾶλλον εὐτυχὴς δ᾽ ἴσως.
1228 **τουτὶ σὺ δράσεις;**] Porson reads τοῦτ᾽ εἰ σ. δ. παραπολεῖ· βοώμενος φήσει γάρ. Dobree takes this, but punctuates after βοώμενος. But the separate short sentences of the common text are satisfactory. βοώμενος is to be taken passively 'bawled down.' Cleon's loud voice is constantly spoken of.
1228. **παραπολεῖ.**] 'You will be ruined by the way, into the bargain,' you will get with your song more than you ever bargained for.

ΣΦΗΚΕΣ.

ἐὰν ἀπειλῇ, νὴ Δί' ἕτερον ᾄσομαι.
ἄνθρωφ', οὗτος ὁ μαιόμενος τὸ μέγα κράτος,
ἀντρέψεις ἔτι τὰν πόλιν· ἁ δ' ἔχεται ῥοπᾶς.   1235

ΒΔΕΛΤΚΛΕΩΝ
τί δ', ὅταν Θέωρος πρὸς ποδῶν κατακείμενος
ᾄδῃ Κλέωνος λαβόμενος τῆς δεξιᾶς,
'Ἀδμήτου λόγον, ὦταῖρε, μαθὼν τοὺς ἀγαθοὺς φίλει,
τούτῳ τί λέξεις σκόλιον;

ΦΙΛΟΚΛΕΩΝ
ᾠδικῶς ἐγώ,   1240
οὐκ ἔστιν ἀλωπεκίζειν,
οὐδ' ἀμφοτέροισι γίγνεσθαι φίλον.

ΒΔΕΛΤΚΛΕΩΝ
μετὰ τοῦτον Αἰσχίνης ὁ Σέλλου δέξεται
ἀνὴρ σοφὸς καὶ μουσικός· κᾆτ' ᾄσεται·
χρήματα καὶ βίαν   1245

1231. **ἕτερον ᾄσομαι.**] As the MSS. have ἑτέραν ᾄσομαι Dobree corrects to ἕτερ' ἀντᾴσομαι. With ἕτερον must be supplied μέλος or σκόλιον.

1232. **ἄνθρωφ'.**] From Alcaeus, the Scholiast tells us. The lines as he gives them are rather different and hardly intelligible: μαινόμενος stands in place of μαιόμενος. They are meant here as a rebuke to Cleon's grasping ambition.

1235. **ἔχεται ῥοπᾶς**] 'is near the turning of the scale,' wants but little to decide its fall.

1236. **πρὸς ποδῶν**] 'at the feet of,' next below.' Cf. above v. 1221.

1238. **'Ἀδμήτου.**] The Scholiast supplies another line of this song: τῶν δειλῶν ἀπέχου γνοὺς ὅτι δειλῶν ὀλίγα χάρις. But whether this praise of bravery, and caution against cowardice, is concerned with Admetus' spiritless conduct, or with his wife's bravery, and who is supposed to speak it, is uncertain. Here it gives occasion for a hit at Theorus' cowardice and flattery. The metre of this song is that of Horace's 'Tu ne quaesieris (scire nefas) quem mihi, quem tibi.'

1240. **ᾠδικῶς.**] Dindorf's proposed reading in his notes ὠδί πως is apparently as good. The MSS. and old edd. have ᾀδικὸς or ἀδικός. Meineke (with Hamaker) ejects the line.

1240. **ἀλωπεκίζειν.**] The fox was the emblem of cunning and flattery, of old, as now. Cf. Pind. *Pyth.* 11. 141, where such persons are called ἀλωπέκων ἴκελοι.

1245. **χρήματα κ.τ.λ.**] There was a well-known song of Clitagora: cf. *Lys.* 1237, Κλειταγόρας ᾄδειν δέον. She was a poetess, and a Thessalian acc. to one Scholiast, a Laconian acc. to another. But what the original bearing of the song was does not appear. The Thessalians helped the Athenians in the war against their tyrants. βίον is read for βίαν by some editors. As concluded by Philocleon, the song is

Κλειταγόρᾳ τε κἀ-
μοὶ μετὰ Θετταλῶν

ΦΙΛΟΚΛΕΩΝ

πολλὰ δὴ διεκόμισας σὺ κἀγώ.

ΒΔΕΛΥΚΛΕΩΝ

τουτὶ μὲν ἐπιεικῶς σύ γ' ἐξεπίστασαι·
ὅπως δ' ἐπὶ δεῖπνον ἐς Φιλοκτήμονος ἴμεν.   1250
παῖ παῖ, τὸ δεῖπνον, Χρυσέ, συσκεύαζε νῷν,
ἵνα καὶ μεθυσθῶμεν διὰ χρόνου.

ΦΙΛΟΚΛΕΩΝ

μηδαμῶς.
κακὸν τὸ πίνειν· ἀπὸ γὰρ οἴνου γίγνεται
καὶ θυροκοπῆσαι καὶ πατάξαι καὶ βαλεῖν,
κἄπειτ' ἀποτίνειν ἀργύριον ἐκ κραιπάλης.   1255

ΒΔΕΛΥΚΛΕΩΝ

οὔκ, ἢν ξυνῇς γ' ἀνδράσι καλοῖς τε κἀγαθοῖς.
ἢ γὰρ παρῃτήσαντο τὸν πεπονθότα,
ἢ λόγον ἔλεξας αὐτὸς ἀστεῖόν τινα,
Αἰσωπικὸν γέλοιον ἢ Συβαριτικόν,

meant to ridicule Aeschines for his boasting: especially his boasting of wealth which he never had. Cf. *Av.* 921, ἆρ' ἐστὶν αὑτηγὶ Νεφελοκοκκυγία, ἵνα καὶ τὰ Θεογένους τὰ πολλὰ χρήματα τά τ' Αἰσχίνου γ' ἅπαντα; Hence Burges' διεκόμπασας for διεκόμισας has great probability, and is approved by several editors. Thus, whatever the song was going to say about the wealth &c., Philocleon retorts that Aeschines had nothing to do with wealth, save in bragging of it.

1250 **Φιλοκτήμονος.**] ἄσωτος οὗτος. Schol.

1251 **τὸ δεῖπνον συσκ.**] εἰ δέ πού τις ἐκαλεῖτο εἰς ἄριστον ἢ εἰς δεῖπνον, τὸ ἄριστον ἢ τὸ δεῖπνον ἑαυτοῦ ἔφερε. Schol.

1253—55. The old dicast retains as yet his old caution, and thinks that drinking leads to brawls and damages to pay next morning.

1257. **παρῃτήσαντο.**] As in Eur. *Heracl.* 1025, κτεῖν', οὐ παταιτοῦμαί σε, and Herod. v. 33, VI. 24. Cf. also *Eq.* 37, ἓν δ' αὐτοὺς παραιτησώμεθα: and this double acc. construction is common. The verb also takes simply the accusative of the penalty, *e.g.* παραιτεῖσθαι ζημίαν: as well as the acc. of that which you rescue, παραιτεῖσθαι τὴν ψυχήν: resembling in this the Lat. 'deprecari'.

1259 **Αἰσωπικόν.**] Cf. above v. 566. The Aesopic were (acc. to the Scholiast) about beasts, the Sybaritic about men. The father follows his son's advice below at v. 1401.

ὧν ἔμαθες ἐν τῷ συμποσίῳ· κᾆτ' ἐς γέλων 1260
τὸ πρᾶγμ' ἔτρεψας, ὥστ' ἀφείς σ' ἀποίχεται.

ΦΙΛΟΚΛΕΩΝ

μαθητέον τἄρ' ἐστὶ πολλοὺς τῶν λόγων,
εἴπερ ἀποτίσω μηδέν, ἤν τι δρῶ κακόν.
ἄγε νυν ἴωμεν· μηδὲν ἡμᾶς ἰσχέτω.

ΧΟΡΟΣ

πολλάκις δὴ 'δοξ' ἐμαυτῷ δεξιὸς πεφυκέναι, 1265
καὶ σκαιὸς οὐδεπώποτε·
ἀλλ' Ἀμυνίας ὁ Σέλλου μᾶλλον οὐκ τῶν Κρωβύλου,
οὗτος ὅν γ' ἐγώ ποτ' εἶδον ἀντὶ μήλου καὶ ῥοᾶς
δειπνοῦντα μετὰ Λεωγόρου.
πεινῇ γὰρ ᾗπερ Ἀντιφῶν. 1270

1260 **ἐς γέλων κ.τ.λ.**] 'Solvuntur risu tabulae: tu missus abibis.' Hor.
1261 **ἀφείς**.] sc. ὁ πεπονθώς.
1262—3. Philocleon's spirit here is rather like Strepsiades' in the *Clouds*.

1265—1291 Here follows a kind of second short parabasis, consisting of a strophe and epirrhema, and an antepirrhema: the antistrophe being lost. There are second parabases in the *Knights*, *Peace*, *Birds*, each of four parts: in the *Acharnians* there is only a commation with strophe and antistrophe. The Chorus here attack and ridicule certain worthless charaƈters, and explain the poet's conduƈt with respeƈt to Cleon.

1267 **Ἀμυνίας κ.τ.λ.**] Amynias was the son of Pronapus really, but is called son of Sellus, that he may be made out brother to Aeschines son of Sellus, and as poor as was Aeschines. He was an effeminate coward (*Nub.* 691—92), and was foppish in his way of dressing his hair (cf. v. 466, κομηταμυνίας), hence he is called οὐκ τῶν Κρωβύλου. The general sense of the passage (which is rather obscure) seems to be 'I thought myself dexterous and clever, but that poor beggar Amynias beats me; whom I saw, instead of his frugal meal, enjoying a feast with the epicure Leogoras. But then he did go on an embassy to Thessaly, and there held conference with the Penestans, being himself a Penestan (beggar-man) equal to any.' The ἀλλὰ γάρ seems to be put as if to account for the sudden change in Amynias' meals and mode of living; but, as the sentence is turned off with a pun which implies they were all poor together; we are left to conclude that his δεξιότης was but that of a hungry parasite, and what began as praise is thus turned to satire. The Scholiast says we ought to supply σκαιός ἐστιν after μᾶλλον: but what then is the bearing of the whole passage?

οὐκ τῶν Κρωβύλου.] 'Of the family of *Chignon*.' For this mode of dressing the hair cf. *Thuc.* I. 6: and *Eq.* 1331, note on τεττιγοφόρας. The Scholiast here describes it εἶδος πλοκῆς ἐπ' ἀνδρῶν εἰς ὀξὺ ληγούσης.

1269 **Λεωγόρου**.] Cf. *Nub.* 109, and note there.

1270 **Ἀντιφῶν.**] An orator of

ἀλλὰ πρεσβεύων γὰρ ἐς Φάρσαλον ᾤχετ᾽· εἶτ᾽ ἐκεῖ
μόνος μόνοις
τοῖς Πενέσταισι ξυνῆν τοῖς
Θετταλῶν, αὐτὸς πενέστης ὢν ἐλάττων οὐδενός.
ὦ μακάρι᾽ Αὐτόμενες, ὥς σε μακαρίζομεν,   1275
παῖδας ἐφύτευσας ὅτι χειροτεχνικωτάτους,
πρῶτα μὲν ἅπασι φίλον ἄνδρα τε σοφώτατον,
τὸν κιθαραοιδότατον, ᾧ χάρις ἐφέσπετο·
τὸν δ᾽ ὑποκριτὴν ἕτερον, ἀργαλέον ὣς σοφόν·
εἶτ᾽ Ἀριφράδην, πολύ τι θυμοσοφικώτατον,   1280
ὅντινά ποτ᾽ ὤμοσε μαθόντα παρὰ μηδενός,
ἀλλ᾽ ἀπὸ σοφῆς φύσεος αὐτόματον ἐκμαθεῖν
γλωττοποιεῖν ἐς τὰ πορνεῖ᾽ εἰσιόνθ᾽ ἑκάστοτε.

. . . .

εἰσί τινες οἵ μ᾽ ἔλεγον ὡς καταδιηλλάγην,

some note. He was attacked by the comic writers as receiving money for speeches written for others.

1271 πρεσβεύων.] The Scholiast tells us that Eupolis mentioned this embassy, and attacked Amynias as παραπρεσβευτήν. Perhaps some bribery is hinted at here as the possible reason of his sudden luxury.

1272 μόνος μόνοις.] A favourite Greek collocation, ξυνῆν μόνος μόνῳ = 'he had a tête-a-tête:' here perhaps it means 'he had some private talk with them,' he and they laid their heads together.

1273 Πενέσταισι. The lower class among the Thessalians. δέον οὖν εἰπεῖν μετὰ τῶν πολιτευομένων ξυνῆν, εἶπε μετὰ τῶν Πενεστῶν. Schol. and there is a play on πένης and Πενέστης.

1278 τὸν κιθαραοιδότατον.] Arignotus, spoken of in *Eq.* 1277, as ἀνὴρ φίλος, as well known to all, and as *not* a brother in nature though in name to Ariphrades (τοὺς τρόπους οὐ ξυγγενής). Why Richter includes Arignotus as 'turpissimis usus moribus' in the face of these two passages is inexplicable.

1279 ὑποκριτήν.] The name of this actor is unknown.
ἀργαλέον ὡς σοφόν.] Compare the phrases θαυμαστὸν ὅσον, ἀμήχανον ὅσον.

1280 θυμοσοφικώτατον.] Cf. *Nub.* 877, θυμόσοφός ἐστιν φύσει.

1281 ὤμοσε.] Supply ὁ πατήρ, says the Scholiast: but it is awkward to do so. ὤμοσα Bentley. ὃν ὁ πατήρ ποτ᾽ ὤμοσε Bergk.

1284—91 The transactions between Cleon and Aristophanes, to which this antepirrhema alludes, are not known. Apparently Cleon had attacked the poet—perhaps had brought him into court—*after* the exhibition of the *Knights*, as we know he did on an earlier occasion referred to in *Ach.* 376. The antistrophe is lost after v. 1283; perhaps this might have explained something. Bergk thinks that it consisted of a violent attack on Cleon, to make up for any previous leniency, and to justify the proverb in v. 1291. This antepirrhema is short by one line.

1284 καταδιηλλάγην.] In the *Clouds* Cleon had been spared; or

ἡνίκα Κλέων μ' ὑπετάραττεν ἐπικείμενος
καί με κακίαις ἔκνισε· κᾀθ' ὅτ' ἀπεδειρόμην,
ἐκτὸς ἐγέλων μέγα κεκραγότα θεώμενοι,
οὐδὲν ἄρ' ἐμοῦ μέλον, ὅσον δὲ μόνον εἰδέναι
σκωμμάτιον εἴποτέ τι θλιβόμενος ἐκβαλῶ.
ταῦτα κατιδὼν ὑπό τι μικρὸν ἐπιθήκισα·
εἶτα νῦν ἐξηπάτησεν ἡ χάραξ τὴν ἄμπελον.

ΞΑΝΘΙΑΣ

ἰὼ χελῶναι μακάριαι τοῦ δέρματος,
καὶ τρισμακάριαι τοῦ 'πὶ ταῖς πλευραῖς τέγους.
ὡς εὖ κατηρέψασθε καὶ νουβυστικῶς

1285

1290

at all events was not the principal object of attack; for *Nub.* 586, 591, are not complimentary to him.

1287 ἐκτός.] This seems to rest on better MS. authority than the common reading οὐκτός. Indeed what can οὐκτός mean? 'Those who were without,' *i.e.* those who were out of the scrape themselves?

1288 οὐδὲν ἄρ' ἐμοῦ μέλον.] The absolute use of the participle μέλον is analogous to that of ἐξόν, παρόν, and the like.

1290—91. When Aristophanes saw that he received no help from those who only cared for the amusement to be got out of him, he played the flatterer awhile, but afterwards turned on Cleon.

1290 ἐπιθήκισα.] The ape is often the emblem of flattery. Cf. Pind. *Pyth.* II. 132, καλός τοι πίθων παρὰ παισίν· ὁ δὲ Ῥαδάμανθυς... φρενῶν ἔλαχε καρπόν... οὐδ' ἀπάταισι τέρπεται.

1291 ἡ χάραξ.] This was a proverb of those deceived in what they believed to be their prop or stay. Thus Cleon rested secure that Aristophanes would not, after once giving in, return to the attack, but was quite deceived in this hope. Cleon is the vine, Aristophanes the vine-prop. To trust in a reed, which breaks and pierces the hand of him that leans on it, is a similar expression. Cf. 2 Kings xviii. 21.

1292—1449. Xanthias comes in smarting from blows, and tells how Philocleon bore him at the banquet; how he outdid all in tipsy revelry, and is laying about him with his staff. Philocleon soon enters, tolerably drunk, and with a flute-girl. His son follows, and tries to check him; but to little purpose, the father retorting on him some of his own instructions. A baker-woman demands compensation for spoilt loaves, a man assaulted threatens law-proceedings; but they only get mocked at, and absurdly put off with fables: till at last the son prepares to take his father indoors out of harm's way.

1292 χελῶναι.] Cf. above, v. 429, ὀστρακόδερμα is given by the Scholiast as applied to animals protected by such shells.

1293 τέγους.] This correction (for MS. ἐμαῖς and στέγειν) is due to Bentley. The general sense of the passage and the following κατηρέψασθε κεράμῳ leave hardly any doubt that Aristophanes wrote τέγους.

1294 νουβυστικῶς.] νοῦ πεπληρωμένως. Schol. This curious compound occurs again in *Eccl.* 441, γυναῖκα δ' εἶναι πρᾶγμ' ἔφη νουβυστικόν.

ΑΡΙΣΤΟΦΑΝΟΥΣ

κεράμῳ τὸ νῶτον ὥστε τὰς πληγὰς στέγειν.   1295
ἐγὼ δ' ἀπόλωλα στιζόμενος βακτηρίᾳ.

ΧΟΡΟΣ
τί δ' ἔστιν, ὦ παῖ; παῖδα γάρ, κἂν ᾖ γέρων,
καλεῖν δίκαιον ὅστις ἂν πληγὰς λάβῃ.

ΞΑΝΘΙΑΣ
οὐ γὰρ ὁ γέρων ἀτηρότατον ἄρ' ἦν κακὸν
καὶ τῶν ξυνόντων πολὺ παροινικώτατος;   1300
καίτοι παρῆν Ἵππυλλος, Ἀντιφῶν, Λύκων,
Λυσίστρατος, Θούφραστος, οἱ περὶ Φρύνιχον.
τούτων ἁπάντων ἦν ὑβριστότατος μακρῷ.
εὐθὺς γὰρ ὡς ἐνέπλητο πολλῶν κἀγαθῶν,
ἐνήλατ', ἐσκίρτα, πεπόρδει, κατεγέλα,   1305
ὥσπερ καχρύων ὀνίδιον εὐωχήμενον·
κἄτυπτεν ἐμὲ νεανικῶς, παῖ παῖ καλῶν.
εἶτ' αὐτὸν ὡς εἶδ', ἤκασεν Λυσίστρατος·
ἔοικας, ὦ πρεσβῦτα, νεοπλούτῳ τρυγὶ

1295 στέγειν.] This is commonly used of water, 'to keep it out, or in,' to be water-proof or water-tight. Here it is of the cudgel-proof shell of the tortoise.
1297 τί δ' ἔστιν, ὦ παῖ.] Cf. *Thesm.* 582, τί δ' ἔστιν, ὦ παῖ; παῖδα γάρ σ' εἰκὸς καλεῖν, ἕως ἂν οὕτω τὰς γνάθους ψιλὰς ἔχῃς.
1300 παροινικώτατος.] In *Ach.* 981 παροίνιος is given by MSS. Some change that to παροινικός. It is quite possible there were two forms.
1301 Ἵππυλλος κ.τ.λ.] Of three of these guests we know nothing. For Antiphon cf. above, v. 1270; for Lysistratus, v. 787; *Ach.* 855, *Eq.* 1265. There seem to have been several of the name of Phrynichus: a tragic poet, a comic poet, and an actor. For analogous forms to Thuphrastus (=Theophrastus) cf. *Eq.* 1103, Θουφάνης, 1267, Θούμαντις.
1303 ὑβριστότατος.] The regular comparative and superlative of this word are confirmed by several examples. See L. and S. But Cobet, Meineke, and others adopt ὑβρίστατος.
1305 ἐνήλατ'.] Some MSS. have ἐνήλλατ': whence Meineke reads ἐνήλλετ', Lenting ἀνήλλετ'. Certainly ἐνάλλεσθαι rather requires an object, and the imperfect tense suits with the other verbs. But it may be ἐνήλατό (μοι), of the first insulting attack, followed by the imperfects, to describe the rest of his tipsy frolic.
1306 ὥσπερ κ.τ.λ.] Like a full-fed donkey he began to frisk. Bergler compares Xen. *Anab.* v. 8. 3, εἰ ἐν τοιούτῳ καιρῷ ὕβριζον ὁμολογῶ καὶ τῶν ὄνων ὑβριστότερος εἶναι, οἷς φασιν ὑπὸ τῆς ὕβρεως κόπον οὐκ ἐγγίνεσθαι.
1307 νεανικῶς.] Cf. below, v. 1333, νεανίας; and above, note on v. 1204.
1309 ἔοικας.] Absurd and hardly intelligible comparisons: cf. those

ΣΦΗΚΕΣ.

κλητῆρί τ' εἰς ἀχυρὸν ἀποδεδρακότι.
ὁ δ' ἀνακραγὼν ἀντήκασ' αὐτὸν πάρνοπι
τὰ θρῖα τοῦ τρίβωνος ἀποβεβληκότι,
Σθενέλῳ τε τὰ σκευάρια διακεκαρμένῳ.
οἱ δ' ἀνεκρότησαν, πλήν γε Θουφράστου μόνου·
οὗτος δὲ διεμύλλαινεν ὡς δὴ δεξιός.
ὁ γέρων δὲ τὸν Θούφραστον ᾖρετ', εἰπέ μοι,
ἐπὶ τῷ κομᾷς καὶ κομψὸς εἶναι προσποιεῖ,
κωμῳδολοιχῶν περὶ τὸν εὖ πράττοντ' ἀεί;
τοιαῦτα περιύβριζεν αὐτοὺς ἐν μέρει,
σκώπτων ἀγροίκως καὶ προσέτι λόγους λέγων
ἀμαθέστατ', οὐδὲν εἰκότας τῷ πράγματι.
ἔπειτ' ἐπειδὴ 'μέθυεν, οἴκαδ' ἔρχεται
τύπτων ἅπαντας, ἤν τις αὐτῷ ξυντύχῃ.
ὁδὶ δὲ δὴ καὶ σφαλλόμενος προσέρχεται.
ἀλλ' ἐκποδὼν ἄπειμι πρὶν πληγὰς λαβεῖν.

1310

1315

1320

1325

of Bdelycleon at v. 1172. The compliments exchanged between Sarmentus and Messius in Horace (*Sat.* I. 5. 56) are somewhat similar.

νεοπλούτῳ τρυγί.] Δίδυμός φησιν ὅτι ἀδιανόητα σκώπτει. Schol. And indeed it seems so. 'Solent recens ditati esse insolentes.' Bergler. Richter thinks it means 'one newly made rich,' but adds 'loquuntur bene poti.'

1310 **κλητῆρί κ.τ.λ.**] κλητῆρι is put where ὄνῳ should be (cf. above, v. 189); for the Scholiast gives a proverb ὄνος εἰς ἄχυρον. The ass that had made its way to the strawyard would (probably) pick up a good feed there, and wax skittish. And 'bailiff' is put for 'ass' with reference to the dicast's employment.

1312 **τὰ θρῖα τ. τ. ἀ.**] 'That has lost the leaves of its cloak,' *i. e.* its leaf-like covering, or its wings. Lysistratus (a poor man) is reproached with his threadbare cloak, and compared to a locust which has cast or lost its wings. The outer wings of locusts are sufficiently leaf-like to make θρῖα τ. τ. intelligible, though of course the simile is meant to be ridiculous.

1313 **Σθενέλῳ.**] Sthenelus was a tragic actor, who from his poverty had to sell all his stage dress and furniture. Schol.

1315 **διεμύλλαινεν.**] ὑπερηφάνως τὰ χείλη διέστρεφεν ὡς χλευάζων καὶ μὴ ἡσθεὶς τῷ λελεγμένῳ. Schol.

δεξιός.] As if such rude common jests were beneath him.

1318 **κωμῳδολοιχῶν.**] Cf. *Nub.* 451, ματτυολοιχός, for the termination of this compound. It must mean 'playing the fool to amuse, and so earning a dinner;' 'punster and parasite.'

1319 **περιύβριζεν.**] L. and S. give only the sense 'to insult exceedingly;' but both here and in *Thesm.* 535, τοιαῦτα περιυβρίζειν ἡμᾶς ἁπάσας, it perhaps means 'to insult all round.'

1321 **οὐδὲν εἰκότας.**] Of which we have specimens 1309—10.

ΑΡΙΣΤΟΦΑΝΟΥΣ [1326

ΦΙΛΟΚΛΕΩΝ
ἄνεχε, πάρεχε·
κλαύσεταί τις τῶν ὄπισθεν
ἐπακολουθούντων ἐμοί·
οἷον, εἰ μὴ 'ρρήσεθ', ὑμᾶς,
ὦ πονηροὶ, ταυτηὶ τῇ   1330
δᾳδὶ φρυκτοὺς σκευάσω.

ΚΑΤΗΓΟΡΟΣ
ἦ μὴν σὺ δώσεις αὔριον τούτων δίκην
ἡμῖν ἅπασι, κεἰ σφόδρ' εἶ νεανίας.
ἀθρόοι γὰρ ἥξομέν σε προσκαλούμενοι.

ΦΙΛΟΚΛΕΩΝ
ἰὴ ἰεῦ, καλούμενοι.   1335
ἀρχαῖά γ' ὑμῶν· ἆρά γ' ἴσθ'
ὡς οὐδ' ἀκούων ἀνέχομαι
δικῶν; ἰαιβοῖ αἰβοῖ.
τάδε μ' ἀρέσκει· βάλλε κημούς.
οὐκ ἄπει σύ; . . ποῦ 'στιν   1340

1326 ἄνεχε, πάρεχε.] Cf. Av. 1720, ἄναγε, δίεχε, πάραγε, πάρεχε. In Eur. Troad. 308, ἄνεχε, πάρεχε is said by Cassandra, and in Eur. Cycl. 202, ἄνεχε, πάρεχε by Silenus. Plainly it is an exclamation of excitement and of drunkenness; 'stop there! make way!' Philocleon is making tipsy demonstrations to those who are following him to get redress for insults. And for πάρεχε cf. note above on v. 949.
1329 οἷον.] Cf. Eq. 367, οἷόν σε δήσω 'ν τῷ ξύλῳ.
1331 φρυκτούς.] οἱ φουκτοί or τὰ φρυκτὰ were specially small fish for frying. The Scholiast says ὡς ἰχθύδια πεφρυγμένα φρυκτοὺς σκευάσω ὀπτήσας.
1332 ἦ μὴν κ.τ.λ.] These lines should be given to one of those following Philocleon, as Bergk and Lenting suggest. Bdelycleon, to whom they were given, should not come in till v. 1363: nor have they much force in the mouth of the chorus, who have been on the stage while Philocleon has been feasting.
1333 νεανίας.] 'Insolent.' Cf. above, v. 1307.
1335—9. Philocleon scorns the idea of a summons, and cannot bear even the word.
1336 ἀρχαῖά γ' ὑμῶν.] '''tis out of date—your plan.'
1339 τάδε.] 'this,' viz. the life I now lead, one of mirth and jollity.
βάλλε κημούς.] βάλλε ἐς κόρακας τὰ δικαστικὰ σκεύη. Schol.
1340 οὐκ ἄπει σύ.] Addressed to the departing κατήγορος. Meineke in his notes proposes ἀπολεῖς: the MSS. have ἄπεισι. After ἄπει σύ something is wanted to complete the line. Meineke reads ποῦ 'στιν ἡμῖν. Dindorf in his notes ποῦ 'στι, ποῦ 'στιν, which may be acquiesced in.

ἡλιαστής; ἐκποδών.
ἀνάβαινε δεῦρο χρυσομηλολόνθιον,
τῇ χειρὶ τουδὶ λαβομένη τοῦ σχοινίου.
ἔχου· φυλάττου δ', ὡς σαπρὸν τὸ σχοινίον·
ὅμως γε μέντοι τριβόμενον οὐκ ἄχθεται.
ὁρᾷς ἐγώ σ' ὡς δεξιῶς ὑφειλόμην   1345
μέλλουσαν ἤδη λεσβιεῖν τοὺς ξυμπότας·
ὧν οὕνεκ' ἀπόδος τῷ πέει τῳδὶ χάριν.
ἀλλ' οὐκ ἀποδώσεις οὐδὲ φιαλεῖς, οἶδ' ὅτι,
ἀλλ' ἐξαπατήσεις κἀγχανεῖ τούτῳ μέγα·
πολλοῖς γὰρ ἤδη χἀτέροις αὔτ' εἰργάσω.   1350
ἐὰν γένῃ δὲ μὴ κακὴ νυνὶ γυνή,
ἐγώ σ', ἐπειδὰν οὑμὸς υἱὸς ἀποθάνῃ,
λυσάμενος ἕξω παλλακήν, ὦ χοιρίον.
νῦν δ' οὐ κρατῶ 'γὼ τῶν ἐμαυτοῦ χρημάτων.
νέος γάρ εἰμι καὶ φυλάττομαι σφόδρα.   1355
τὸ γὰρ υἵδιον τηρεῖ με, κἄστι δύσκολον
κἄλλως κυμινοπριστοκαρδαμόγλυφον.
ταῦτ' οὖν περί μου δέδοικε μὴ διαφθαρῶ.
πατὴρ γὰρ οὐδείς ἐστιν αὐτῷ πλὴν ἐμοῦ.
ὁδὶ δὲ καὐτός· ἐπὶ σὲ κἄμ' ἔοικε θεῖν.   1360

1341 **ἡλιαστής.**] He calls the man by this name perhaps in a tipsy confusion of ideas. 'Where's our heliast? our man who is for the courts and for summoning.' 'Oh! I see now he's taken himself off.' Philocleon then turns to the girl.
1342 **χρυσομηλολόνθιον.**] Cf. *Nub.* 763 for the μηλολόνθη, and the practice of letting it fly by a string.
1348 **φιαλεῖς.**] Cf. *Pac.* 432 for this rare word.
1352 **ἐπειδὰν κ.τ.λ.**] He speaks of his son as a son might speak of his father: as expecting his death, and as under strict tutelage. But when his own master, then he will (he says) free this girl from slavery and make her his mistress.
1354 **κρατῶ 'γώ.**] Elmsley proposed κρατῶ πω: 'rightly,' says Meineke: but it is questionable whether such change is needed. The pronoun is naturally enough expressed 'but at present I am not master myself of my own property.'
1357 **κυμινοπρ.**] Alexis in Athenaeus has κυμινοπρίστης ὁ τρόπος ἐστί σου πάλαι. Hesychius explains κυμινοπρίσται· οἱ φειδωλοί· ὁμοίως καὶ οἱ καρδαμογλύφοι.
1359 **πατὴρ γάρ.**] A ridiculous reversal of the usual order of things: 'he has no son but me' would be ordinary enough from a son to a father.
1360 **ὁδὶ δὲ καὐτός.**] This 'and here comes his very self' shews that Bdelycleon did not return with his father at v. 1326; therefore the lines 1332—4 cannot be rightly assigned to him.

134   ΑΡΙΣΤΟΦΑΝΟΥΣ   [1361

ἀλλ' ὡς τάχιστα στῖθι τάσδε τὰς δετὰς
λαβοῦσ', ἵν' αὐτὸν τωθάσω νεανικῶς,
οἵως ποθ' οὗτος ἐμὲ πρὸ τῶν μυστηρίων.

ΒΔΕΛΤΚΛΕΩΝ
ὦ οὗτος οὗτος, τυφεδανὲ καὶ χοιρόθλιψ,
ποθεῖν ἐρᾶν τ' ἔοικας ὡραίας σοροῦ.   1365
οὔ τοι καταπροίξει μὰ τὸν Ἀπόλλω τοῦτο δρῶν.

ΦΙΛΟΚΛΕΩΝ
ὡς ἡδέως φάγοις ἂν ἐξ ὄξους δίκην.

ΒΔΕΛΤΚΛΕΩΝ
οὐ δεινὰ τωθάζειν σε, τὴν αὐλητρίδα
τῶν ξυμποτῶν κλέψαντα;

1361—2 δετὰς λαβοῦσ'. The girl is to take the torch, that the old man may make his absurd assertions, vv. 1371—7.
1363 οἵως.] Better, as following νεανικῶς, than οἵοις of MSS. R. V.
πρὸ τῶν μ.] It appears to have been the custom for those already initiated to frighten those who were preparing to be so. Schol. 'When I was simple and ignorant, my son played on my fears and made a fool of me: now that I am grown wiser, I will pay him in kind.' I was, as it were, a child and minor then: now I am come of age.
1364 τυφεδανὲ.] The Scholiast explains this as equivalent to τυφογέρων, a word used twice by Aristophanes (Nub. 908, Lys. 335), with a possible play on the similarity in sound to τυμβογέρων. But the Scholiast's further comment ἄξιος τετύφθαι is curious. The word cannot surely have anything to do with τύπτειν. Richter suggests that the Scholiast wrote ἄξιος τεθάφθαι: but, though that suits the context here, τυφεδανὸς cannot be connected with θάπτω. Might not τυφεδανὸς mean 'inflamed with passion, or love, amorous'? Compare Lys. 221, ὅπως

ἂν ἀνὴρ ἐπιτυφῇ μάλιστά μου: and Plat. Phaedr. 230 A, θηρίον Τυφῶνος πολυπλοκώτερον καὶ μᾶλλον ἐπιτεθυμμένον. The opposite is denoted by ἄτυφος, ἀτυφία, 'modest, modesty.' See Thompson's note on the passage in the Phaedrus. This sense of τυφεδανὸς suits the context far better than that given by L. and S., 'smoky-witted, a dullard.' And indeed τυφογέρων may as well mean 'puffed up, excited, inflamed,' as 'stupified, dull.'
1365 ὡραίας σοροῦ.] By surprise for ὡραίας κόρης: but also with the sense of 'an early bier.' Cf. Lys. 601, σὺ δὲ δὴ τί μαθὼν οὐκ ἀποθνῄσκεις;...σορὸν ὠνήσει.
1367 ὡς ἡδέως φάγοις ἄν.] He tells his son that no doubt he would like to sue and punish his father, a suit would be a sweet morsel to him. Bdelycleon is now twitted as φιλόδικος, Philocleon is μισόδικος. For description of pleasures as eatables cf. above, v. 511, and Eq. 706, φέρε τί δῶ σοι καταφαγεῖν; ἐπὶ τῷ φάγοις ἥδιστ' ἄν; ἐπὶ βαλλαντίῳ; Also we have a fragment of the Gerytades (Fr. 92), καὶ πῶς ἐγὼ Σθενέλου φάγοιμ' ἂν ῥήματα, εἰς ὄξος ἐμβαπτόμενος ἢ ξηροὺς ἅλας;

ΦΙΛΟΚΛΕΩΝ
ποίαν αὐλητρίδα;
τί ταῦτα ληρεῖς, ὥσπερ ἀπὸ τύμβου πεσών;   1370
ΒΔΕΛΥΚΛΕΩΝ
νὴ τὸν Δί', αὕτη πού 'στί σοί γ' ἡ Δαρδανίς.
ΦΙΛΟΚΛΕΩΝ
οὐκ, ἀλλ' ἐν ἀγορᾷ τοῖς θεοῖς δᾷς κάεται.
ΒΔΕΛΥΚΛΕΩΝ
δᾷς ἥδε;
ΦΙΛΟΚΛΕΩΝ
δᾷς δῆτ'. οὐχ ὁρᾷς ἐστιγμένην;
ΒΔΕΛΥΚΛΕΩΝ
τί δὲ τὸ μέλαν τοῦτ' ἐστὶν αὐτῆς τοὐν μέσῳ;
ΦΙΛΟΚΛΕΩΝ
ἡ πίττα δήπου καομένης ἐξέρχεται.   1375
ΒΔΕΛΥΚΛΕΩΝ
ὁ δ' ὄπισθεν οὐχὶ πρωκτός ἐστιν οὑτοσί;
ΦΙΛΟΚΛΕΩΝ
ὄζος μὲν οὖν τῆς δᾳδὸς οὗτος ἐξέχει.
ΒΔΕΛΥΚΛΕΩΝ
τί λέγεις σύ; ποῖος ὄζος; οὐκ εἶ δεῦρο σύ;
ΦΙΛΟΚΛΕΩΝ
ἆ ἆ, τί μέλλεις δρᾶν;

1370 **ἀπὸ τύμβου πεσών.**] This is a variation on *Nub.* 1273, τί δῆτα ληρεῖς ὥσπερ ἀπ' ὄνου καταπεσών; where the fall ἀπ' ὄνου is meant to suggest a fall ἀπὸ νοῦ, 'from the wits, mind, sense.' ἀπὸ τύμβου here seems put for the same. Philocleon is making out himself to be young, his son an old τυμβογέρων, everything being now reversed. But the phrase is very curious, 'fallen from a tomb.' The general meaning is 'Why have you come out of your grave (in which you ought to be) to talk such rubbish?' He ridicules the idea of its being a flute-player, and would fain persuade his son that his eyes deceive him. In the Jacobite song 'Hame came our gudeman at een' the wife says to her lord, 'Ye're an auld doited carle, and unco blind ye be,' when trying to make him believe that the horse, plume, and sword of the concealed cavalier are a milch-cow, hen, and parritch-stick.

1371 **Δαρδανίς.**] Phrygia was noted for its flute-players.

ΑΡΙΣΤΟΦΑΝΟΥΣ

ΒΔΕΛΤΚΛΕΩΝ
ἄγειν ταύτην λαβὼν
ἀφελόμενός σε καὶ νομίσας εἶναι σαπρὸν
κοὐδὲν δύνασθαι δρᾶν.

ΦΙΛΟΚΛΕΩΝ
ἄκουσόν νυν ἐμοῦ.
Ὀλυμπίασιν ἡνίκ' ἐθεώρουν ἐγώ,
Ἐφουδίων ἐμαχέσατ' Ἀσκώνδᾳ καλῶς,
ἤδη γέρων ὤν· εἶτα τῇ πυγμῇ θενὼν
ὁ πρεσβύτερος κατέβαλε τὸν νεώτερον.
πρὸς ταῦτα τηροῦ μὴ λάβῃς ὑπώπια.

ΒΔΕΛΤΚΛΕΩΝ
νὴ τὸν Δί' ἐξέμαθές γε τὴν Ὀλυμπίαν.

ΑΡΤΟΠΩΛΙΣ
ἴθι μοι παράστηθ', ἀντιβολῶ πρὸς τῶν θεῶν.
ὁδὶ γὰρ ἀνήρ ἐστιν ὅς μ' ἀπώλεσεν
τῇ δᾳδὶ παίων, κἀξέβαλεν ἐντευθενὶ
ἄρτους δέκ' ὀβολῶν κἀπιθήκην τέτταρας.

ΒΔΕΛΤΚΛΕΩΝ
ὁρᾷς ἃ δέδρακας; πράγματ' αὖ δεῖ καὶ δίκας
ἔχειν διὰ τὸν σὸν οἶνον.

ΦΙΛΟΚΛΕΩΝ
οὐδαμῶς γ', ἐπεὶ

1382 **Ὀλυμπίασιν κ.τ.λ.**] He begins to put in practice his son's precepts on polite conversation. Cf. above, v. 1190.
1388—91. The baker-woman comes in to recover compensation for her lost loaves.
1390 **ἐντευθενί.**] Perhaps she points to her basket.
1391 **ἄρτους δέκ' ὀβολῶν.**] 'ten loaves worth as many obols:' or 'loaves—ten obols' worth,' the number of loaves being left indefinite. Dobree's and Cobet's τεττάρων would make this last rendering necessary, though indeed it may be so taken even with the common text.
κἀπιθήκην τέτταρας.] 'And four given in:' ἐπιθήκη is explained as 'additamentum, superpondium.' It seems a large proportional addition, a liberal 'baker's ten.' But ἐπ. τεττάρων, 'a further lot worth four,' after ἀ. δ. ὀ. is a clumsy way of expressing fourteen obols' worth.
1392 **πράγματ' αὖ.**] Again they will have trouble, lawsuits, &c., from which Bdelycleon hoped he had set them both free.

1408]   ΣΦΗΚΕΣ.   137

λόγοι διαλλάξουσιν αὐτὰ δεξιοί·
ὥστ' οἶδ' ὁτιὴ ταύτῃ διαλλαχθήσομαι.   1395

ΑΡΤΟΠΩΛΙΣ

οὔ τοι μὰ τὼ θεὼ καταπροίξει Μυρτίας
τῆς Ἀγκυλίωνος θυγατέρος καὶ Σωστράτης,
οὕτω διαφθείρας ἐμοῦ τὰ φορτία.

ΦΙΛΟΚΛΕΩΝ

ἄκουσον, ὦ γύναι· λόγον σοι βούλομαι
λέξαι χαρίεντα.

ΑΡΤΟΠΩΛΙΣ

μὰ Δία μή μοί γ', ὦ μέλε.   1400

ΦΙΛΟΚΛΕΩΝ

Αἴσωπον ἀπὸ δείπνου βαδίζονθ' ἑσπέρας
θρασεῖα καὶ μεθύση τις ὑλάκτει κύων.
κᾄπειτ' ἐκεῖνος εἶπεν, ὦ κύον κύον,
εἰ νὴ Δί' ἀντὶ τῆς κακῆς γλώττης ποθὲν
πυροὺς πρίαιο, σωφρονεῖν ἄν μοι δοκοῖς.   1405

ΑΡΤΟΠΩΛΙΣ

καὶ καταγελᾷς μου; προσκαλοῦμαί σ' ὅστις εἶ,
πρὸς τοὺς ἀγορανόμους βλάβης τῶν φορτίων,
κλητῆρ' ἔχουσα Χαιρεφῶντα τουτονί.

1394 **λόγοι κ.τ.λ.**] Cf. above, 1258.
1396 **μὰ τὼ θεώ.**] An oath much used by women; and therefore of most frequent occurrence in the Lysistrata, Thesmophoriazusae, Ecclesiazusae: *e.g. Lys.* 51, 112, 148, *Thesm.* 383, 566, *Eccl.* 155, 156, 158.
1399. He begins upon fables: cf. above, v. 1260.
1402 **ὑλάκτει.**] Note the ῡ long in an augmented tense: whereas at v. 904 ἀγαθός γ' ὑλακτεῖν begins a verse; the υ is therefore short.
1405 **πυροὺς.**] To make bread with, and so repair the loss of her loaves. Schol. Such will be the force of πυροὺς in the intended application of the story. In the story itself it is not quite clear whether the κύων is a literal one or not. The μεθύση does not suit the animal: but the tale is of course intentionally absurd.
1406 **καὶ καταγελᾷς.**] 'Do you also (or even) laugh at me;' do you add insult to injury? Cf. *Eq.* 274, καὶ κέκραγας.
1407 **ἀγορανόμους.**] Cf. *Ach.* 723, τοὺς ἐπισκοποῦντας τὰ τῆς πόλεως ὤνια καὶ διοικοῦντας αὐτά. Schol.
1408 **Χαιρεφῶντα.**] One of the pale scholars of Socrates in the *Clouds.* Cf. *Nub.* 103, 504, τοὺς ὠχρι-

138   ΑΡΙΣΤΟΦΑΝΟΥΣ   [1409

ΦΙΛΟΚΛΕΩΝ
μὰ Δί', ἀλλ' ἄκουσον, ἤν τί σοι δόξω λέγειν.
Λᾶσός ποτ' ἀντεδίδασκε καὶ Σιμωνίδης· 1410
ἔπειθ' ὁ Λᾶσος εἶπεν, ὀλίγον μοι μέλει.
ΑΡΤΟΠΩΛΙΣ
ἄληθες, οὗτος;
ΦΙΛΟΚΛΕΩΝ
καὶ σὺ δή μοι, Χαιρεφῶν,
γυναικὶ κλητεύειν ἔοικας θαψίνῃ,
Ἰνοῖ κρεμαμένῃ πρὸς ποδῶν Εὐριπίδου,
ΒΔΕΛΥΚΛΕΩΝ
ὁδί τις ἕτερος, ὡς ἔοικεν, ἔρχεται 1415
καλούμενός σε· τόν γέ τοι κλητῆρ' ἔχει.
ΚΑΤΗΓΟΡΟΣ
οἴμοι κακοδαίμων. προσκαλοῦμαί σ', ὦ γέρον,
ὕβρεως.

ὤντας...λέγεις, and ΣΩ: οὐδὲν διοίσεις Χαιρεφῶντος τὴν φύσιν. ΣΤ. οἴμοι κακοδαίμων, ἡμιθνὴς γενήσομαι.
1409—12. Lasus and Simonides were rivals, and had a contest. Lasus said he cared little for his opponent: nor do I care for your summons and lawsuit. This is apparently the application, if it has any. Lasus of Hermione was an early writer on music, and originator of the Dithyrambic contest. Simonides, the lyric poet of Ceos, is well known.
1411 ὀλίγον μοι μέλει.] τοῦ Σιμωνίδου δηλονότι. Schol.
1412 ἄληθες οὗτος.] Cf. *Eq.* 89.
1413 κλητεύειν.] Meineke follows Dobree in reading κλητεύων. Chaerephon would then be compared to a sallow woman: cf. note on v. 1408. But προσπολῶν, in the next line, does not suit so well with this as with κλητεύειν.
θαψίνῃ.] Cf. Theocr. *Id.* 11. 88, καὶ μευ χρὼς μὲν ὁμοῖος ἐγίνετο πολλάκι θάψῳ. One Scholiast thinks there is an allusion to θάπτειν.

1414 Ἰνοῖ, κ.τ.λ.] Ino threw herself from a rock, and was (the Scholiast says) ὠχρὰ ὑπὸ τῆς κακοπαθείας. How Ino in Euripides' play was κρεμαμένη πρὸς ποδῶν is not clear: but προσπολῶν, an alteration of Hermann's, accepted by some editors, does not make such undoubted good sense as to be unhesitatingly taken: 'attending on the hanging Ino of Euripides.' κρ. ἐκ ποδῶν (or κρ.) must refer apparently to Ino when about to throw herself over. Euripides (*Med.* 1288) describes her as ἀκτῆς ὑπερτείνασα ποντίας πόδα, and in the play of *Ino* there may have been some phrase justifying κρ. ἐκ ποδῶν here. That the *Ino* was a play full of distress, tears, &c. we may infer from *Ach.* 434, where Ino's and Thyestes' rags have between them those of Telephus.
1417 οἴμοι κακοδαίμων.] Holden gives this to Bdelycleon. But after an assault (ὕβριν) the plaintiff might well say the words. See the behaviour of the old man described at v. 1323.

ΒΔΕΛΥΚΛΕΩΝ

ὕβρεως; μὴ, μὴ καλέσῃς πρὸς τῶν θεῶν.
ἐγὼ γὰρ ὑπὲρ αὐτοῦ δίκην δίδωμί σοι,
ἢν ἂν σὺ τάξῃς, καὶ χάριν προσείσομαι.   1420

ΦΙΛΟΚΛΕΩΝ

ἐγὼ μὲν οὖν αὐτῷ διαλλαχθήσομαι
ἑκών· ὁμολογῶ γὰρ πατάξαι καὶ βαλεῖν.
ἀλλ' ἐλθὲ δευρὶ πρότερον, ἐπιτρέπεις ἐμοί,
ὅ τι χρή μ' ἀποτίσαντ' ἀργύριον τοῦ πράγματος,
εἶναι φίλον τὸ λοιπόν, ἢ σύ μοι φράσεις;   1425

ΚΑΤΗΓΟΡΟΣ

σὺ λέγε. δικῶν γὰρ οὐ δέομ' οὐδὲ πραγμάτων.

ΦΙΛΟΚΛΕΩΝ

ἀνὴρ Συβαρίτης ἐξέπεσεν ἐξ ἅρματος,
καί πως κατεάγη τῆς κεφαλῆς μέγα σφόδρα·
ἐτύγχανεν γὰρ οὐ τρίβων ὢν ἱππικῆς.
κἄπειτ' ἐπιστὰς εἶπ' ἀνὴρ αὐτῷ φίλος·   1430
ἔρδοι τις ἣν ἕκαστος εἰδείη τέχνην.
οὕτω δὲ καὶ σὺ παράτρεχ' ἐς τὰ Πιττάλου.

ΒΔΕΛΥΚΛΕΩΝ

ὅμοιά σου καὶ ταῦτα τοῖς ἄλλοις τρόποις.

1420 προσείσομαι.] Better thus than separately, πρὸς εἴσομοι, as Dindorf's earlier editions have it. Richter compares Soph. *Oed. Tyr.* 232, τὸ γὰρ κέρδος τελῶ 'γώ, χἠ χάρις προσκείσεται.
1421—26. Philocleon gets the man to come and listen quietly in hopes of compensation, and then puts him off with a Sybaritic fable: following in this to the letter his son's precept at v. 1260.
1423 ἐπιτρέπεις ἐμοὶ ὅ τι χρή.] 'Do you leave it to me (to name) what sum I am to pay you and be friends, or will you name it?'

1428 κατ. τῆς κεφαλῆς.] Cf. *Ach.* 1180, and *Pac.* 71, ξυνετρίβη τῆς κεφαλῆς.
1430—31. He got no pity, but a proverb. 'Quam quisque norit artem, in hac se exerceat.' Cic. *Tusc.* I. 18.
1432 οὕτω δὲ κ.τ.λ.] And so you, as you will get no pity, had better get a plaister for your head. Meineke, following Hamaker, places this line after v. 1440.
ἐς τὰ Πιττάλου.] Cf. *Ach.* 1222, which Elmsley would reduce to exact correspondence with this phrase; unnecessarily.

ΚΑΤΗΓΟΡΟΣ
ἀλλ' οὖν σὺ μέμνησ' αὐτὸς ἀπεκρίνατο.

ΦΙΛΟΚΛΕΩΝ
ἄκουε, μὴ φεῦγ'· ἐν Συβάρει γυνή ποτε   1435
κατέαξ' ἐχῖνον.

ΚΑΤΗΓΟΡΟΣ
ταῦτ' ἐγὼ μαρτύρομαι.

ΦΙΛΟΚΛΕΩΝ.
οὑχῖνος οὖν ἔχων τιν' ἐπεμαρτύρατο·
εἶθ' ἡ Συβαρῖτις εἶπεν, εἰ ναὶ τὰν κόραν
τὴν μαρτυρίαν ταύτην ἐάσας ἐν τάχει
ἐπίδεσμον ἐπρίω, νοῦν ἂν εἶχες πλείονα.   1440

ΚΑΤΗΓΟΡΟΣ
ὕβριζ', ἕως ἂν τὴν δίκην ἄρχων καλῇ.

ΒΔΕΛΤΚΛΕΩΝ.
οὔ τοι μὰ τὴν Δήμητρ' ἔτ' ἐνταυθὶ μενεῖς,
ἀλλ' ἀράμενος ἐγώ σε

ΦΙΛΟΚΛΕΩΝ.
τί ποιεῖς;

ΒΔΕΛΤΚΛΕΩΝ.
ὅ τι ποιῶ;
εἴσω φέρω σ' ἐντεῦθεν· εἰ δὲ μή, τάχα
κλητῆρες ἐπιλείψουσι τοὺς καλουμένους.   1445

ΦΙΛΟΚΛΕΩΝ
Αἴσωπον οἱ Δελφοί ποτ'

1434 ἀλλ' οὖν.] Addressed to the κλητήρ.
1436 ἐχῖνον.] The Scholiast tells us this word meant at Athens a vessel for holding depositions of witnesses. It is not likely that here it means more than 'a pot, pitcher,' or the like.
1437 ἐπεμαρτύρατο.] Philocleon continues his story, but neatly adopts the other's word.

1438 τὰν κόραν.] δωρίζει ἐπιτηδες. Schol. The Sybaritic woman would use some such dialect: and the oath was specially a Sicilian one.
1443 ἐγώ σε.] ἔγωγε Brunck. οἴσω σε vulg. εἴσω σε Reisig, Richter.
1446 Αἴσωπον κ.τ.λ.] The Delphians were going to throw Aesop down from a rock for his

ΣΦΗΚΕΣ.

ΒΔΕΛΤΚΛΕΩΝ
ὀλίγον μοι μέλει.

ΦΙΛΟΚΛΕΩΝ
φιάλην ἐπητιῶντο κλέψαι τοῦ θεοῦ·
ὁ δ' ἔλεξεν αὐτοῖς ὡς ὁ κάνθαρός ποτε

ΒΔΕΛΤΚΛΕΩΝ
οἴμ' ὡς ἀπολεῖ σ' αὐτοῖσι τοῖσι κανθάροις.

ΧΟΡΟΣ
ζηλῶ γε τῆς εὐτυχίας   1450
τὸν πρέσβυν, οἱ μετέστη
ξηρῶν τρόπων καὶ βιοτῆς·
ἕτερα δὲ νῦν ἀντιμαθὼν
ἢ μέγα τι μεταπεσεῖται
ἐπὶ τὸ τρυφῶν καὶ μαλακόν.   1455

supposed theft, when he told them the fable of the beetle. How it saved him does not appear, nor how Philocleon meant to apply it here, for his fabling is cut short. This fable is again spoken of in *Pac.* 129.

1449 ἀπολεῖ σ'.] 'He (this plaintiff) will ruin you, you and your beetles.' The MSS. have ἀπολεῖς: whence the above text may be inferred. 'Your tale of a beetle will not save you though it saved Aesop.' It is perhaps more usual to omit the definite article in this use of αὐτοῖς, but cf. above, v. 170, τὸν ὄνον ἄγων αὐτοῖσι τοῖς κανθηλίοις. The other readings of the editions ἀπόλοι', ἀπολῶ σ' are further from the MSS. And the son did not want to destroy, but to save, his father. Richter suggests ἀπολεῖς μ', 'you will ruin me.' But this would require as a continuation 'with your beetles,' not 'beetles and all.' Meineke's τοῖς σοῖς for τοῖσι is unnecessary, if it is to avoid the def. art. with κανθάροις: if it be thought that τοῖσι crept in wrongly because of αὐτοῖσι preceding, then we might as well fill it up αὐτοῖσι κανθάροις ὅδε, to gain a subject to ἀπολεῖ.

1450—1473. The chorus, having now quite changed their views (compare the conduct of the chorus in the *Acharnians*, *Clouds*, and *Peace*), praise the old man for his altered mode of life, and his son for his cleverness in bringing about this result. The song is antistrophic: vv. 1450—1461 = 1462—1473. The metre of most of the lines is a monometer iambic followed by a choriambus; but the last lines of strophe and antistrophe have a cretic in place of a choriambus. The reading and metre of v. 1454 are uncertain.

1452 ξηρῶν.] The old man certainly was well moistened by liquor now.

1454 μεταπεσεῖται.] This reading is fairly satisfactory both for sense and metre. The MSS. vary much. Dobree proposed ἀντιμαθὼν ἤθη μεταπ. The line seems to be a sort of Anacreontic. It should correspond to v. 1466. Strophe and antistrophe seem thus to be broken up into two parts of five and seven lines.

τάχα δ' ἂν ἴσως οὐκ ἐθέλοι.
τὸ γὰρ ἀποστῆναι χαλεπὸν
φύσεος, ἣν ἔχοι τις ἀεί.
καίτοι πολλοὶ ταῦτ' ἔπαθον·
ξυνόντες γνώμαις ἑτέρων   1460
μετεβάλλοντο τοὺς τρόπους.
πολλοῦ δ' ἐπαίνου παρ' ἐμοὶ
καὶ τοῖσιν εὖ φρονοῦσιν
τυχὼν ἄπεισιν διὰ τὴν
φιλοπατρίαν καὶ σοφίαν   1465
ὁ παῖς ὁ Φιλοκλέωνος.
οὐδενὶ γὰρ οὕτως ἀγανῷ
ξυνεγενόμην, οὐδὲ τρόποις
ἐπεμάνην, οὐδ' ἐξεχύθην.
τί γὰρ ἐκεῖνος ἀντιλέγων   1470
οὐ κρείττων ἦν βουλόμενος
τὸν φύσαντα σεμνοτέροις
κατακοσμῆσαι πράγμασι;

ΞΑΝΘΙΑΣ

νὴ τὸν Διόνυσον, ἄπορά γ' ἡμῖν πράγματα

1456 **τάχα δ' ἄν.**] Perhaps he may not complete the change: nature is difficult to overcome, 'expellas furca, tamen usque recurret.' Hor..

1462 **παρ' ἐμοί.**] 'With me,' in my estimation, in my mind. Passages constantly occur where we should in English say 'from' rather than 'with;' but of course the strict meaning of παρά with dative is 'with.'

1469 **ἐπεμάνην.**] Cf. above, v. 744. πράγμαθ' οἷς τότ' ἐπεμαίνετο.

ἐξεχύθην.] No exact Greek parallel is quoted. 'Effundi,' effuse laetari in Latin is common. Colloquially we use 'to gush, gushing.'

1473 **κατακοσμῆσαι.**] Meineke's κατακομῆσαι (to suit with μετεβάλλοντο in v. 1461, which seems right, as no reason can be given for the imperfect tense μετεβάλλοντο) is very doubtful. The word κατακομᾶν is given by L. and S. intransitive, 'to wear long hair.' But κατακομῆσαι σ. π., 'to plume himself on grander things,' is not very good: τὸν φύσαντα is more naturally the object than the subject of the verb. And κατακοσμῆσαι is satisfactory in sense: nor is it certain that the first part of such a line might not consist of anapaest and spondee. For the general meaning compare *Nub.* 515, νεωτέροις τὴν φύσιν αὐτοῦ πράγμασιν χρωτίζεται. A various reading κατακηλῆσαι, 'to charm,' is proposed by one Scholiast.

1474—1537. Xanthias enters with an account of the wonderful pranks his master is now playing. He is gone mad upon dancing. Philocleon follows, and begins his wild measures, challenging all the world of tragic dancers. The challenge is

ΣΦΗΚΕΣ.

δαίμων τις ἐσκεκύκληκεν ἐς τὴν οἰκίαν.
ὁ γὰρ γέρων ὥς ἔπιε διὰ πολλοῦ χρόνου
ἤκουσέ τ' αὐλοῦ, περιχαρὴς τῷ πράγματι
ὀρχούμενος τῆς νυκτὸς οὐδὲν παύεται
τἀρχαῖ' ἐκεῖν' οἷς Θέσπις ἠγωνίζετο·
καὶ τοὺς τραγῳδοὺς φησιν ἀποδείξειν κρόνους
τοὺς νῦν, διορχησάμενος ὀλίγον ὕστερον.

ΦΙΛΟΚΛΕΩΝ
τίς ἐπ' αὐλείοισι θύραις θάσσει;

ΞΑΝΘΙΑΣ
τουτὶ καὶ δὴ χωρεῖ τὸ κακόν.

ΦΙΛΟΚΛΕΩΝ
κλῇθρα χαλάσθω τάδε. καὶ δὴ γὰρ
σχήματος ἀρχὴ

taken up by three sons of Carcinus successively, who come on and dance, their name being made the subject of various punning allusions. Philocleon joins them, and the chorus, after a brief song, depart escorted by the dancers, and probably dancing off the stage themselves. This 'ballet' was quite a novelty: introduced to make as strong a contrast as possible between Philocleon's present habits and his former judicial life. At the same time a travesty of certain tragic dancing was probably intended.

1475 ἐσκεκύκληκεν.] Properly ἐσκυκλεῖν is the opposite of ἐκκυκλεῖν: to bring in by means of the machine called ἐκκύκλημα. Thus in *Thesm.* 265 the man who had been wheeled out says, εἴσω τις ὡς τάχιστά μ' ἐσκυκλησάτω. A word of rather tragic sound is chosen, as a fit prelude to Philocleon's heroics.

1476 διὰ πολλοῦ χρόνου.] Wrongly translated in the Latin version 'diu multumque,' and by Mitchell, 'had given long time to his cups.' It means 'after a long time:' *i.e.* after long abstinence from such drinking, for his habits had been ξηροί (v. 1452). Cf. *Plut.* 1045, διὰ πολλοῦ χρόνου ἑορακέναι, and above at v. 1252, ἵνα μεθυσθῶμεν διὰ χρόνου, cf. *Pac.* 570, 710. Florens remarks 'videntur facilius inebriari qui contra morem bibunt.'

1479 τἀρχαῖ' ἐκεῖν'.] As an old man his dances would be old-fashioned: those in use with Thespis. But this does not prevent him from charging others with being κρόνοι, for which word cf. *Nub.* 398, 929. No other Thespis than the well-known founder of tragedy need be supposed.

1481 διορχησάμενος.] So MSS. R. V. vulg. διορχησόμενος. Either may be satisfactorily rendered : the aorist by 'he will prove them fools by dancing a match with them;' the future by 'he will prove them fools, for he means to dance, &c.' For the sense of διὰ in the compound compare διαπίνειν, to which there is allusion in *Ach.* 751, διαπειναμες.

1482. τίς κ.τ.λ.] Tragic style: and below κλῇθρα χαλάσθω is illustrated from Eur. *Hipp.* χαλᾶτε κλῇθρα, πρόσπολοι, πυλωμάτων, and *Hel.* 1196, *Iph. Taur.* 1304.

ΞΑΝΘΙΑΣ
μᾶλλον δέ γ' ἴσως μανίας ἀρχή.

ΦΙΛΟΚΛΕΩΝ
πλευρὰν λυγίσαντος ὑπὸ ῥώμης,
οἷον μυκτὴρ μυκᾶται καὶ
σφόνδυλος ἀχεῖ.

ΞΑΝΘΙΑΣ
πῖθ' ἐλλέβορον.

ΦΙΛΟΚΛΕΩΝ.
πτήσσει Φρύνιχος ὥς τις ἀλέκτωρ,   1490

ΞΑΝΘΙΑΣ
τάχα βαλλήσεις.

ΦΙΛΟΚΛΕΩΝ
σκέλος οὐράνιόν γ' ἐκλακτίζων.
πρωκτὸς χάσκει.

ΞΑΝΘΙΑΣ
κατὰ σαυτὸν ὅρα.

1487 **λυγίσαντος.**] Cf. Theocr. *Id.* I. 96, τὺ θὴν τὸν ἔρωτα κατεύχεο, Δάφνι, λυγιξεῖν; where it is of one wrestler bending down by force and so throwing the other. Here the dance is said to bend or twist the side. 'The twisted side the forceful motion owns; Lows the wide nostril, and the back-bone groans.' Mitchell.

1489 **πῖθ' ἐλλέβορον.**] The common cure for madness. Philocleon continues his speech, regardless of Xanthias' interruptions.

1490 **πτήσσει Φρύνιχος.**] The old commentators seem in the wrong to take πτήσσει here of fear. Whether this Phrynichus be the well-known tragic poet, as is probable enough (for the old man uses the measures of Thespis (v. 1479), and so, naturally enough, those of Phrynichus), or a dancer of the name, it it is plain that there was some dance called Phrynichean (v. 1524), in which the leg was kicked out. This fling the old man begins to execute, and describes himself as 'Phrynichus throwing out his leg heaven-high,' to the imminent danger of Xanthias, who interpolates τάχα βαλλήσεις. This throwing out the leg is compared to the stroke of a cock when fighting. But πτήσσει need not be discarded for πλήσσει, as Bentley and Porson wished; πτήσσει means 'crouches, gathers himself up,' in act to spring. Cf. Eur. *Andr.* 753, for πτήξαντες of such crouching: ὅρα δὲ μὴ νῷν εἰς ἐρημίαν ὁδοῦ πτήξαντες οἵδε πρὸς βίαν ἄγωσί με. But Dindorf's note is 'fingitur trepidare Phrynichus, quippe victus a meliore saltatore, Philocleone.' Of course there are abundant examples to illustrate πτήσσει used of a bird crouching in fear; but I do not see that this interpretation makes good sense in connexion with v. 1492 compared with v. 1524.

1493 **κατὰ σαυτὸν ὅρα.**] 'Do look where you're going.'

1503] ΣΦΗΚΕΣ. 145

ΦΙΛΟΚΛΕΩΝ
νῦν γὰρ ἐν ἄρθροις τοῖς ἡμετέροις
στρέφεται χαλαρὰ κοτυληδών. 1495
οὐκ εὖ;

ΒΔΕΛΤΚΛΕΩΝ
μὰ Δί᾽ οὐ δῆτ᾽, ἀλλὰ μανικὰ πράγματα.

ΦΙΛΟΚΛΕΩΝ
φέρε νυν ἀνείπω κἀνταγωνιστὰς καλῶ.
εἴ τις τραγῳδός φησιν ὀρχεῖσθαι καλῶς,
ἐμοὶ διορχησόμενος ἐνθάδ᾽ εἰσίτω.
φησίν τις, ἢ οὐδείς;

ΒΔΕΛΤΚΛΕΩΝ
εἷς γ᾽ ἐκεινοσὶ μόνος. 1500

ΦΙΛΟΚΛΕΩΝ
τίς ὁ κακοδαίμων ἐστίν;

ΒΔΕΛΤΚΛΕΩΝ
                    υἱὸς Καρκίνου
ὁ μέσατος.

ΦΙΛΟΚΛΕΩΝ
ἀλλ᾽ οὗτός γε καταποθήσεται·
ἀπολῶ γὰρ αὐτὸν ἐμμελείᾳ κονδύλου.

1495 κοτυληδών.] τὸ δὲ ἐν ᾧ στρέφεται ὁ μηρός, κοτυληδών. Aristot.
1496 οὐκ εὖ;] This is Dobree's arrangement: better than the common one.
1498—9 εἴ τις κ.τ.λ.] Contrast with this εἴ τις θύρασιν ἡλιαστὴς, εἰσίτω, v. 891.
1501 Καρκίνου.] He had three (some say four) sons: their names are rather variously given; cf. *Nub.* 1263. They were dancers; but one of them wrote tragedy. They are ridiculed in *Pac.* 781—9, ὄρτυγας οἰκογενεῖς γυλιαύχενας ὀρχηστὰς ναννοφυεῖς, σφυράδων ἀποκνίσματα, μηχανοδίφας.
1502 ὁ μέσατος.] This implies that there were but three: though the Scholiast on this passage asserts there were four: three dancers, one, Xenocles, a poet. But plainly the poet was one of the dancers, v. 1511: so that we may content ourselves with three, Xenocles, Xenotimus, and Xenarchus. The other names, Demotimus and Xenoclitus, perhaps are in some way mistakes for Xenotimus and Xenocles.
1503 ἐμμελείᾳ κονδύλου.] ἐμμέλεια τραγικὴ ὄρχησις. Schol. But destroying him in the 'knuckle measure' also means correcting him with blows. Cf. *Eq.* 1236, κονδύλοις ἡρμοττόμην.

10

146 ΑΡΙΣΤΟΦΑΝΟΥΣ [1504
ἐν τῷ ῥυθμῷ γὰρ οὐδέν ἐστ'.

ΒΔΕΛΥΚΛΕΩΝ
ἀλλ' ὤζυρέ,
ἕτερος τραρῳδὸς Καρκινίτης ἔρχεται,   1505
ἀδελφὸς αὐτοῦ.

ΦΙΛΟΚΛΕΩΝ
νὴ Δί' ὠψώνηκ' ἄρα.

ΒΔΕΛΥΚΛΕΩΝ
μὰ τὸν Δί' οὐδέν γ' ἄλλο πλήν γε καρκίνους.
προσέρχεται γὰρ ἕτερος αὖ τῶν Καρκίνου.

ΦΙΛΟΚΛΕΩΝ
τουτὶ τί ἦν τὸ προσέρπον; ὀξίς, ἢ φάλαγξ;

ΒΔΕΛΥΚΛΕΩΝ
ὁ πιννοτήρης οὗτός ἐστι τοῦ γένους,   1510
ὁ σμικρότατος, ὃς τὴν τραγῳδίαν ποιεῖ.

ΦΙΛΟΚΛΕΩΝ
ὦ Καρκίν', ὦ μακάριε τῆς εὐπαιδίας·
ὅσον τὸ πλῆθος κατέπεσεν τῶν ὀρχίλων.
ἀτὰρ καταβατέον γ' ἐπ' αὐτούς μ', ὤζυρέ·
ἅλμην κύκα τούτοισιν, ἣν ἐγὼ κρατῶ.   1515

1504 **ἐν τῷ ῥυθμῷ κ.τ.λ.**] 'For he is not at all in rhythm:' he does not keep time or measure in his dancing, and therefore requires a regular knuckle-rapping to keep him in order.
1505 **ἕτερος.**] Number two of Carcinus' sons.
1506 **ὠψώνηκ' ἄρα.**] 'I'm well found, methinks, in fish:' the κάρκινοι coming under the class ὄψον.
1507 **μὰ Δί'...καρκίνους.**] Xanthias objects that all the ὄψον he has got is crabs, for now enters number three.
1509 **ὀξίς.**] Some variety of crab is thought to be meant; or a shrimp. Brunck quotes *Av.* 1203, ὄνομα δέ σοι τί ἐστι, πλοῖον ἢ κυνῆ; as an analogous passage. It is not clear how a vinegar-cruet and a spider could be suggested by the same person. The smallest of the three Carcinites, who were perhaps in some way put on the stage so as to resemble crabs, might be something like a spider, by a stretch of imagination.
1510 **πιννοτήρης.**] A small kind of crab. Some write the word πινοτήρης.
1511 **ὃς τ. τραγῳδίαν π.**] Xenocles. Cf. note at v. 1502.
1513 **ὀρχίλων.**] 'Wrens' probably: cf. *Av.* 568. As being of diminutive stature these sons of Carcinus are so called: but there is reference to ὀρχηστῶν, 'dancers.'
1515 **ἅλμην.**] In which they are to be dressed; ἐπειδὴ ἅλμην

ΣΦΗΚΕΣ.

ΧΟΡΟΣ

φέρε νυν ἡμεῖς αὐτοῖς ὀλίγον ξυγχωρήσωμεν ἅπαντες,
ἵν' ἐφ' ἡσυχίας ἡμῶν πρόσθεν βεμβικίζωσιν ἑαυτούς.
ἄγ', ὦ μεγαλώνυμα τέκνα
τοῦ θαλασσίοιο,
πηδᾶτε παρὰ ψάμαθον   1520
καὶ θῖν' ἁλὸς ἀτρυγέτοιο.
καρίδων ἀδελφοί·
ταχὺν πόδα κυκλοσοβεῖτε,
καὶ τὸ Φρυνίχειον
ἐκλακτισάτω τις, ὅπως   1525
ἰδόντες ἄνω σκέλος ὤ-
ζωσιν οἱ θεαταί.
στρόβει, παράβαινε κύκλῳ καὶ γαστρισον σεαυτὸν,
ῥῖπτε σκέλος οὐράνιον· βέμβικες ἐγγενέσθων.   1530
καὐτὸς γὰρ ὁ ποντομέδων ἄναξ πατὴρ προσέρπει
ἡσθεὶς ἐπὶ τοῖσιν ἑαυτοῦ παισὶ, τοῖς τριόρχοις.

παρασκευάζουσιν ἐπὶ τὸ φαγεῖν ἰχθύδια ἢ καρκίνους. Schol.
1516 **φέρε νυν**] The Chorus clear a space for this Phrynichean ballet, in which they perhaps join, but the Carcinites were the chief performers.
1517 **βεμβικίζωσιν.**] Cf. Av. 1465, βεμβικιᾶν. And these same dancers are called Καρκίνου στρόβιλοι Pac. 864. The Scholiast quotes the well-known epigram οἱ δ' ἄρ' ὑπὸ πληγῇσι θοὰς βέμβικας ἔχοντες ἔστρεφον εὐρείη παῖδες ἐνὶ τριόδῳ.
1518—23. Rather epic in style and language: hence the termination -οιο in v. 1519.
1519 **θαλασσίοιο.**] Vulg. θαλασσίου: to which many editors add θεοῦ, to be scanned as a monosyllable. But the Scholiast on Pac. 792 quotes from Plato Com. Ξενοκλῆς ὁ δωδεκαμήχανος, ὁ Καρκίνου ταῖς τοῦ θαλαττίου. 'Children of him of the sea' seems rather better than specifying that he was θεός. Besides the epic form is quite in place.
1521 **ἀτρυγέτοιο.**] It does not

appear well to change this to ἀτρυγέτου that it may correspond metrically with v. 1526: for it seems likely that the Homeric phrase would have been taken as it was. Richter reads ὦ ᾠζωσιν at v. 1526; where MS. Rav. has ᾠζωσιν, which Bergk approves. We cannot be quite certain that this song is antistrophic.
1524 **Φρυνίχειον.**] Cf. note on v. 1490. δῆλον ὡς σημειῶδές τι ἦν τὸ Φρυνίχειον, τὸ εἰς ὕψος ἐν τῇ ὀρχήσει ἐκλακτίζειν. Schol.
1530 **βέμβικες ἐγγ.**] 'Let there be pirouettes,' top-like spinnings round and round. The Scholiast rather implies that a certain dance was called βέμβιξ or βεμβικισμός.
1534 **τριόρχαις.**] 'His dancing triad of sons.' Whether the other sense of τριόρχης (a kind of falcon, cf. Av. 1181, 1206) is played upon, is doubtful. But as ὄρχιλος above means a bird, perhaps it is so. These dancers might be falcons in their gyrations.

148   ΑΡΙΣΤΟΦΑΝΟΥΣ ΣΦΗΚΕΣ.   [1535

ἀλλ' ἐξάγετ', εἴ τι φιλεῖτ' ὀρχούμενοι, θύραζε   1535
ἡμᾶς ταχύ· τοῦτο γὰρ οὐδείς πω πάρος δέδρακεν,
ὀρχούμενον ὅστις ἀπήλλαξεν χορὸν τρυγῳδῶν.

1535—7. The Chorus request the Carcinites, if they like dancing so much, to conduct them off the stage with a dance: an unheard of novelty, for the Chorus entered indeed with a dance, but did not make their exit so.
1536 ἡμᾶς.] I can see no reason for preferring ὑμᾶς, Bentley's alteration.
1537 ὀρχούμενον ὅστις.] Whether ὀρχούμενον or ὀρχούμενος be taken, matters little. ὀρχούμενός τις MSS. The Chorus are conducted off the stage by the dancers, but it seems probable they in some sort joined the dance themselves. The whole line is explanatory of οὐδείς πω δέδρακεν. 'This no man ever yet did. I mean—no man has there been who took his chorus off with a dance.' And the accusative is perhaps rather preferable. Bentley's rendering, 'no-one (who has escaped with impunity for such innovation) ever took off his chorus dancing,' seems awkward.

INDEX TO THE CHIEF MATTER OF THE NOTES.

ἀγαθοῦ δαίμονος, 525
ἀγοραί, 659
ἀγοράνομοι, 1407
Αἴσωπος, 566, 1259, 1446
ἀκαλήφη, 884
ἀκαρῆ, 541
Ἀκέστωρ, 1221
ἄκρατον, 525
ἀλεξίκακος, 1043
ἅλμη, 1515
ἀλοκίζειν, 850
ἀλωπεκίζειν, 1240
Ἀμυνίας, 74, 1267
ἄν with infinitive, 160
  with indicative, 709
ἀναμασᾶσθαι, 783
ἀναπηδᾶν, 1042
ἄνεων, 369
ἀνθρήνιον, 1080
ἀνιέναι, 574
ἀνιῶν, 565
Ἀντιφῶν, 1270, 1301
ἀντωμοσία, 545, 1041
ἀνυπεύθυνος, 587
ἄξιος, 491
ἀπάγχειν, 686
ἀπαλλάσσεσθαι, 484
ἀπέλου, 118
ἀπεωσάμεσθα, 1085
ἀποδύεσθαι, 1157
ἀπομερμηρίσαι, 5
ἀπομορχθείς, 560
ἀποσκλῆναι, 160
ἀπὸ τύμβου πεσών, 1370
ἀποφυσᾶν, 330
ἀπράγμων, 1040
ἆρα, 460
ἀργέλοφοι, 672
Ἁρμόδιος, 1225
ἀρύστιχοι, 855
ἀρχαιομελισιδωνοφρυνιχήρατα, 220
Ἀσκληπιός, 123
αὐξάνεσθαι, 636
αὐτοῖσι τοῖς, 170, 1449
αὐτὸς αὑτοῦ ἰσχύειν, 357
ἄφυαι, 496

βακτηρίαι, 33
βάλανος, 155, 200
βαλβῖδες, 548
βάλλε, 1340
βατίς, 510
βεμβικίζειν, 1517

βέμβιξ, 1530
βλέπειν κάρδαμα, 455
σκύτη, 643
τιμᾶν, 847
κλέπτον, 900
βόρβορος, 259
βορέας, 1124
βουκολεῖν, 10
Βρασίδας, 475
βρωμᾶσθαι, 618
Βυζάντιον, 236

γνώμην ἐμήν, 984
γράμματα, 960
γρῖφος, 20
γωνία, 910

δεινός, 27, 551
δεξιός, 65
δημιόπρατα, 659
δημίζειν, 699
δημός, δῆμος, 40
Δημολογοκλέων, 342
διὰ κενῆς, 929
διὰ χρόνου, 1252
διακρίνειν, 763
Διάκριοι, 1223
διαλείχειν, 904
διαλέξαι, 350
διαμυλλαίνειν, 1315
διασαλακωνίσαι, 1315
διατινθάλεος, 329
δυστάναι, 41
Διοπείθης, 380
διορύξαι, 350
διορχεῖσθαι, 1481
δοθιήν, 1172
δοκός, 201
δοκῶ with pres. inf., 177
δορπηστός, 103
Δρακοντίδης, 438
δριμύς, 146, 278
δρύφακτοι, 386

ἐάν quantity of, 228
ἐγκάπτειν, 791
ἐγκυκλεῖν, 699
ἐγκυκλοῦσθαι, 395
ἐγχυτρίζειν, 289
εἰρεσιῶναι, 399
εἰσάγειν, 825, 840
εἰσελθεῖν, 560
Ἑκάτειον, 864

INDEX

ἑκατοσταί, 659
ἐκκαλαμᾶσθαι, 609
ἐκτελέσαι, 1024
ἐκφρεῖν, 125
ἐκχεῖσθαι, 1469
ἐλαολόγος, 712
ἐλεεῖν, 967
Ἑλλας πόρος, 308
ἐλλέβορος, 1489
ἐμβραχύ, 1120
ἐμμέλεια, 1503
ἐμπεπρησμένη, 36
ἐμπλήμενος, 424
ἐνάλλεσθαι, 1305
ἐνασελγαίνεσθαι, 61
ἐν δίκῃ, 421
ἐντετοκώς, 651
ἐξάγειν, 175
ἐξερᾶν, 993
ἔξοδος, 582
ἐξωμίς, 444
ἐοικέναι, 1142
ἐπανθρακίς, 1127
ἔπειτα, 1133
ἐπιθήκη, 1391
ἐπίκληρος, 583
ἐπιμαίνεσθαι, 744, 1469
ἐπιρρύζειν, 704
ἐπισίζειν, 704
ἐπιστρατεύεσθαι, 11
ἐπίχαλκος, 18
ἐπτάμην, ἐπτόμην, 16
ἔριον, 701
ἐριώλη, 1148
ἐς κόρακας, 51
ἐσκαλαμᾶσθαι, 381
ἐσκυκλεῖν, 1475
ἐσμός, 1107
ἔσπασεν ταύτῃ, 175
Εὔαθλος, 592
Εὐριπίδης, 61
εὐτράπελος, 469
Εὐφήμιος, 599
ἴφεξις, 338
ἐφολκός, 268
ἔχεσθαι, 943
ἐχῖνος, 1436

ἡλιάζεσθαι, 772
ἡλιαστής, 1341
ἡ μακρά, 106
ἡνιοχεῖν, 1022
ἠπίαλος, 1038
Ἡρακλῆς, 60

θατέρῳ, 497
θάψινος, 1413

θεοισεχθρία, 418
θερμός, 917
Θέωρος, 45, 418, 599, 1220
θῖνα ταράττειν, 696
Θουκυδίδης, 947
θρῖον, 1312
θρίων ψόφος, 436
Θυμαιτίς, 1138
θυμοσοφικός, 1280
θυννάζειν, 1087
θώραξ, 1194

ἰδέσθαι, 183
ἰμάς, 231
ἵνα, 188
ἵνα μή with indic. 961
ἰπνός, 139, 837
Ἱππίας, 502
ἰχθύες, 789

κάδισκοι, 321
καθαρός, 631, 1015
καθέψειν, 795
καθίζειν δικαστήριον, 305
καθιέναι, 174
Καινόν, 120
καινοτομεῖν, 876
καλεῖν, 825
κάνναι, 394
Καπνίας, 151
Κάρκινος, 1501, 1502
Καρκινίτης, 1505
κάρυα, 58
καρχαρόδους, 1031
κατάβα, 979
κατακλείς, 154
κατακοσμῆσαι, 1473
καταλύειν φυλακήν, 2
καταπτάμενον, 16
καταχήνη, 575
κατεαγέναι, 1428
κατερεῖξαι, 649
καυνάκη, 1137
κεκραξιδάμας, 596
κέκραχθι, 198
κέλυφος, 545
κεφαλή, 584
κηθάριον, 674
κημός, 99
κηφήν, 1114
κιθαρίζειν, 959, 989
κίκιννος, 1069
κίων, 105
Κλέων, 62, 759
κλητεύειν, 1413
κλητήρ, 189, 1310

INDEX. 151

κλῳός, 897
κνεφαῖος, 124
κνώδαλον, 4
κόγχη, 585
κολάζεσθαι, 406
κολακώνυμος, 592
κόλλοψ, 574
κολοιός, 129
κολόσυρτος, 666
κολώμενος, 244
κομηταμυνίας, 466
κόνδυλος, 254
Κόννου ψῆφος, 675
κόρκορος, 239
κορυβαντιᾶν, 8
κορυβαντίζειν, 119
κοτυληδών, 1495
κρόκης χό'λιξ, 1144
Κυδαθηναιεύς, 895
κύκλῳ, 1033
κύκνος, 1064
κυμινοπριστοκαρδαμόγλυφος, 1357
Κύννα, 1032
κύτταρος, 1111
κωλαγρέτης, 695
κωμῳδολοιχεῖν, 1318

λαγαρίζεσθαι, 674
λαγῷον, 709
Λακωνική, 1158
Λαμία, 1035
λαμπάδα δραμεῖν, 1204
Λᾶσος, 1409
Λάχης, 240, 836
Λεωγόρας, 1269
λιβανωτός, 96
λίθον ἕψειν, 280
λιμένες, 659
λοπίς, 790
λυγίζειν, 1487
Λύκος, 389
Λυσίστρατος, 787, 1302

μὰ τὼ θεώ, 1396
με, Attic use of, 776
Μεγαρόθεν, 57
μεθιέναι, μεθίεσθαι, 416, 437
μέλον, 1288
Μῆδος, 12
μῆλα, 1057
μισθάριον, 300
μισθοί, 659
μόνος μόνοις, 1272
μονοφαγίστατος, 923
Μόρυχος, 506, 1142
μοχλός, 155, 200

μύκητες, 262
μυσπολεῖν, 140
μυττωτεύειν, 63

ναὶ τὰν κόραν, 1438
Νάξος, 355
ναυμαχεῖν, 479
νεανικός, 1204, 1307, 1333
νεόπλουτος τρύξ, 1309
Νιόβη, 580
νουβυστικός, 1294
νουμηνία, 171

ξυμβεβυσμένοι, 1110
ξυνειδέναι, 999
ξυνωμότης, 345, 483
ξυσταλείς, 423

ὀδάξ, 943
ὄζειν with double gen. 1059
οἰκουρός, 970
οἰμωξόμενος, 1033
οἷον, 1329
ὄνου σκιά, 191
ὀξίνης, 1082
ὀξίς, 1509
ὀπίας, 353
ὀρνίθων γάλα, 508
ὀροφίας, 206
ὅσον ὅσον, 213
ὅτι, 22
οὐ πάνυ, 797
οὔτις, οὔτι, 186

παθεῖν τι, 387
πακτοῦν, 128
πανδοκεύτρια, 35
παρακύπτειν, 178
παρατάσσεσθαι, 1123
πάρεχε, 949, 1326
πάροινος, παροινικός, 1300
πασπάλη, 91
παχύς, 288
Πένεσται, 1273
πεπνιγμένος, 511
πεπωκώς, 1082
περικωμάζειν, 1025
περικωνεῖν, 600
περιπέττειν, 668
περιυβρίζειν, 1319
πεσεῖν, 1012
πιθηκίζειν, 1290
πινάκιον, 167
πιννοτήρης, 1510
πιτυλεύειν, 678
πολέμαρχος, 1042

INDEX.

πόλλ' ἐπὶ πολλοῖς, 1046
ποππύζειν, 623
πόρρω, 192
πρινώδες, πρίνινος, 383, 877
πρίων, 694
προβάτια, 32, 955
Προξενίδης, 325
προσέχεσθαι, 105
προσίεσθαι, 742
προσκαύσασα, 828
προσκεκαυμένος, 939
προσσχεῖν, 1015
πρυτανεία, 659
πρώφειλες, 3
πρῶτον ξύλον, 90
πτήσσειν, 1490
πύελος, 141
πυός, 710
πυριάτης, 710
Πυριλάμπης, 98

ῥῆσις, 580
ῥυππαπαῖ, 909

Σαβάζιος, 10
Σάμος, 283
σανίδες, 349, 848
σέλινος, 480
σεσηρώς, 901
σημεῖον, 690
σήσαμα, 676
Σθένελος, 1313
σίμβλος, 241
σίραιος, 878
σκαιός, 1013
σκάφος, 29
σκῖρον, 925
Σκιώνη, 210
σκόλια, 1222
σκορδινᾶσθαι, 642
σορός, 1365
σοῦ σοῦ, 209, 458
σπουδάζειν, 694
στέγειν, 1295
στομφάζειν, 721
στράτιον, 618
στρυφνός, 877
συνηγορικόν, 691
σύρφαξ, 673

ταμιεύειν, 964
τὰ Πιττάλου, 1432
τέγος, 1293
τείχια, 1109

τέλη, 659
τετραπῆχυς, 553
τηλία, 147
τιθασευτής, 704
τὸ δεῖνα, 524
τὸ χρῆμα, 933
τοιοῦτος, 25
τολμᾶν, 327
τόνος, 337
τραυλίζειν, 44
τριβώνιον, 33
τριβωνικῶς, 1132
τριόρχης, 1534
τριχοίνικος, 481
τροφαλίς, 838
τυραννίς, 488
τυφεδανός, 1364

ὑγρός, 1213
ὑδρορρόα, 126
ὑπακούειν, 318
ὑπειπεῖν, 4
Ὑπέρβολος, 1007
ὑποκρίνεσθαι, 53
ὕρχη, 676

φακῆ, 811, 813
φαύλως, 656
φέψαλος, 227
φιαλεῖν, 1348
φιληλιαστής, 88
φιλοθύτης, 82
Φιλοκλέης, 462
φλύκταινα, 1119
φορβειά, 582
φρυαγμοσεμνάκους, 135
φρυκτοί, 1331
Φρύνιχος, 220, 269, 1302, 1490
φυστή, 610
φώκη, 1035

Χαιρεφῶν, 1408
χαράδρα, 1034
χάραξ, 1291
χελύνη, 1083
χελώνη, 1292
χίμετλος, 1167
χοῖνιξ, 440
χοιρίνη, 332
χόνδρος, 738
χυτλάζειν, 1213

ψευδαμάμαξυς, 326

ᾠδεῖον, 1109

3, WATERLOO PLACE, PALL MALL.
April, 1878.

Books for Schools and Colleges
PUBLISHED BY
MESSRS. RIVINGTON

ENGLISH
SELECT PLAYS OF SHAKSPERE
RUGBY EDITION

With Introduction and Notes to each Play.
Small 8vo.

AS YOU LIKE IT. 2*s.*

MACBETH. 2*s.* HAMLET. 2*s.* 6*d.*

KING LEAR. 2*s.* 6*d.* ROMEO AND JULIET.
With Notes at the end of   [*In preparation.*
the Volume.

Edited by the Rev. CHARLES E. MOBERLY, M.A., *Assistant-Master at Rugby School, and formerly Scholar of Balliol College, Oxford.*

CORIOLANUS. 2*s.* 6*d.*
Edited by ROBERT WHITELAW, M.A., *Assistant-Master at Rugby School, formerly Fellow of Trinity College, Cambridge.*

THE TEMPEST. 2*s.*
Edited by J. SURTEES PHILLPOTTS, M.A., *Head-Master of Bedford Grammar School, formerly Fellow of New College, Oxford.*
With Notes at the end of the Volume.

THE MERCHANT OF VENICE.
Edited by R. W. TAYLOR, M.A., *Head-Master of Kelly College, Tavistock, and late Fellow of St. John's College, Cambridge.*
With Notes at the end of the Volume.
[*In preparation.*

LONDON, OXFORD, AND CAMBRIDGE.

ENGLISH SCHOOL-CLASSICS

With Introductions, and Notes at the end of each Book.

Edited by FRANCIS STORR, B.A.,

CHIEF MASTER OF MODERN SUBJECTS AT MERCHANT TAYLORS' SCHOOL, LATE SCHOLAR OF TRINITY COLLEGE, CAMBRIDGE, AND BELL UNIVERSITY SCHOLAR.

Small 8vo.

THOMSON'S SEASONS: Winter.
With Introduction to the Series, by the Rev. J. FRANCK BRIGHT, M.A., Fellow of University College, and Historical Lecturer at Balliol, New, and University Colleges, Oxford; late Master of the Modern School at Marlborough College. 1s.

COWPER'S TASK.
By FRANCIS STORR, B.A., Chief Master of Modern Subjects at Merchant Taylors' School. 2s.
Part I. (Book I.—The Sofa; Book II.—The Timepiece) 9d. Part II. (Book III. —The Garden; Book IV.—The Winter Evening) 9d. Part III. (Book V.—The Winter Morning Walk; Book VI.—The Winter Walk at Noon) 9d.

SCOTT'S LAY OF THE LAST MINSTREL.
By J. SURTEES PHILLPOTTS, M.A., Head Master of Bedford School, formerly Fellow of New College, Oxford. 2s. 6d.
Part I. (Canto I., with Introduction, &c.) 9d. Part II. (Cantos II. and III.) 9d. Part III. (Cantos IV. and V.) 9d. Part IV. (Canto VI.) 9d.

SCOTT'S LADY OF THE LAKE.
By R. W. TAYLOR, M.A., Assistant-Master at Rugby School. 2s.
Part I. (Cantos I. and II.) 9d. Part II. (Cantos III. and IV.) 9d. Part III. (Cantos V. and VI.) 9d.

NOTES TO SCOTT'S WAVERLEY.
By H. W. EVE, M.A., Head-Master of University College School, London. 1s., or with the Text, 2s. 6d.

TWENTY OF BACON'S ESSAYS.
By FRANCIS STORR, B.A., Chief Master of Modern Subjects at Merchant Taylors' School. 1s.

SIMPLE POEMS.
Edited by W. E. MULLINS, M.A., Assistant-Master at Marlborough College. 8d.

SELECTIONS FROM WORDSWORTH'S POEMS.
By H. H. TURNER, B.A., late Scholar of Trinity College, Cambridge. 1s.

WORDSWORTH'S EXCURSION: The Wanderer.
By H. H. TURNER, B.A., late Scholar of Trinity College, Cambridge. 1s.

MILTON'S PARADISE LOST.
By FRANCIS STORR, B.A., Chief Master of Modern Subjects at Merchant Taylors' School.
Book I. 9d. Book II. 9d.

MILTON'S L'ALLEGRO, IL PENSEROSO, AND LYCIDAS.
By EDWARD STORR, M.A., late Scholar of New College, Oxford. 1s. .

SELECTIONS FROM THE SPECTATOR.
By OSMUND AIRY, M.A., Assistant-Master at Wellington College. 1s.

LONDON, OXFORD, AND CAMBRIDGE.

ENGLISH SCHOOL-CLASSICS—continued.

BROWNE'S RELIGIO MEDICI.
By W. P. Smith, M.A., Assistant-Master at Winchester College. 1s.

GOLDSMITH'S TRAVELLER AND DESERTED VILLAGE.
By C. Sankey, M.A., Assistant-Master at Marlborough College. 1s.

EXTRACTS FROM GOLDSMITH'S VICAR OF WAKEFIELD.
By C. Sankey, M.A., Assistant-Master at Marlborough College. 1s.

POEMS SELECTED FROM THE WORKS OF ROBERT BURNS.
By A. M. Bell, M.A., Balliol College, Oxford. 2s.

MACAULAY'S ESSAYS.
MOORE'S LIFE OF BYRON. By Francis Storr, B.A. 9d.
BOSWELL'S LIFE OF JOHNSON. By Francis Storr, B.A. 9d.
HALLAM'S CONSTITUTIONAL HISTORY. By H. F. Boyd, late Scholar o Brasenose College, Oxford. 1s.

SOUTHEY'S LIFE OF NELSON.
By W. E. Mullins, M.A., Assistant-Master at Marlborough College.

* *The General Introduction to the Series will be found in* Thomson's Winter.

(*See Specimen on Pages* 4 *and* 5.)

OPINIONS OF TUTORS AND SCHOOLMASTERS.

"Nothing can be better than the idea and the execution of the English School-Classics, edited by Mr. Storr. Their cheapness and excellence encourage us to the hope that the study of our own language, too long neglected in our schools, may take its proper place in our curriculum, and may be the means of inspiring that taste for literature which it is one of the chief objects of education to give, and which is apt to be lost sight of in the modern style of teaching Greek and Latin Classics with a view to success in examinations."—*Oscar Browning, M.A., Fellow of King's College, Cambridge.*

"I think the plan of them is excellent; and those volumes which I have used I have found carefully and judiciously edited, neither passing over difficulties, nor preventing thought and work on the pupil's part by excessive annotation."—*Rev. C. B. Hutchinson, M.A., Assistant-Master at Rugby School.*

"I think that these books are likely to prove most valuable. There is great variety in the choice of authors. The notes seem sensible, as far as I have been able to examine them, and give just enough help, and not too much; and the size of each volume is so small, that in most cases it need not form more than one term's work.

Something of the kind was greatly wanted."—*E. E. Bowen, M.A., Master of the Modern Side, Harrow School.*

"I have used some of the volumes of your English School-Classics for several months in my ordinary form work, and I have recommended others to be set as subjects for different examinations for which the boys have to prepare themselves. I shall certainly continue to use them, as I have found them to be very well suited to the wants of my form."—*C. M. Bull, M.A., Master of the Modern School at Marlborough College.*

"I have no hesitation in saying that the volumes of your Series which I have examined appear to me far better adapted for school use than any others which have come under my notice. The notes are sufficiently full to supply all the information which a boy needs to understand the text without superseding the necessity of his thinking. The occasional questions call the learner's attention to points which he can decide from his own resources. The general plan, and the execution of the volumes which have come before me, leave little to be desired in a School Edition of the English Classics."—*The Rev. Chas. Grant Chittenden, M.A., The Grange, Hoddesdon, Herts.*

LONDON, OXFORD, AND CAMBRIDGE.

44   COWPER'S TASK.

I say the pulpit (in the sober use
Of its legitimate peculiar pow'rs)
Must stand acknowledg'd, while the world shall stand,
The most important and effectual guard,
Support and ornament of virtue's cause.
There stands the messenger of truth: there stands
The legate of the skies; his theme divine,
His office sacred, his credentials clear.
By him, the violated law speaks out   340
Its thunders, and by him, in strains as sweet
As angels use, the Gospel whispers peace.
He stablishes the strong, restores the weak,
Reclaims the wand'rer, binds the broken heart,
And, arm'd himself in panoply complete
Of heav'nly temper, furnishes with arms
Bright as his own, and trains, by ev'ry rule
Of holy discipline, to glorious war,
The sacramental host of God's elect.
Are all such teachers? would to heav'n all were!   350
But hark—the Doctor's voice—fast wedged between
Two empirics he stands, and with swoln cheeks
Inspires the news, his trumpet. Keener far
Than all invective is his bold harangue,
While through that public organ of report
He hails the clergy; and, defying shame,
Announces to the world his own and theirs.
He teaches those to read, whom schools dismiss'd,
And colleges, untaught; sells accent, tone,
And emphasis in score, and gives to pray'r   360
Th' *adagio* and *andante* it demands.
He grinds divinity of other days
Down into modern use; transforms old print
To zigzag manuscript, and cheats the eyes
Of gall'ry critics by a thousand arts.—
Are there who purchase of the Doctor's ware?
Oh name it not in Gath!—it cannot be,
That grave and learned Clerks should need such aid.
He doubtless is in sport, and does but droll,
Assuming thus a rank unknown before,   370
Grand caterer and dry-nurse of the church.

I venerate the man whose heart is warm,
Whose hands are pure, whose doctrine and whose life.

[ENGLISH SCHOOL CLASSICS. *See* page 2.]

NOTES TO THE TIMEPIECE. 87

gether as with a close seal. . . . . The flakes of his flesh are joined together: they are firm in themselves; they cannot be moved."

Hobbes, in his famous book to which he gave the title *Leviathan*, symbolised thereby the force of civil society, which he made the foundation of all right.

315-325 Cowper's limitation of the province of satire—that it is fitted to laugh at foibles, not to subdue vices—is on the whole well-founded. But we cannot forget Juvenal's famous "facit indignatio versum," or Pope's no less famous—

"Yes, I am proud: I must be proud to see
Men not afraid of God, afraid of me:
Safe from the bar, the pulpit, and the throne,
Yet touched and shamed by ridicule alone."

326-372 *The pulpit, not satire, is the proper corrector of sin. A description of the true preacher and his office, followed by one of the false preacher, " the reverend advertiser of engraved sermons."*

330 *Strutting and vapouring.* Cf. *Macbeth*, v. 5.

" Life's but a walking shadow, a poor player,
That struts and frets his hour upon the stage,
And then is heard no more; it is a tale
Told by an idiot, full of sound and fury,
Signifying nothing."

" And what in real value's wanting,
Supply with vapouring and ranting."—HUDIBRAS.

331 *Proselyte.* προσήλυτος, a new comer, a convert to Judaism.

338 *His theme divine.* Nominative absolute.

343 *Stablishes.* Notice the complete revolution the word has made—stabilire, établir, establish, stablish; cf. state, &c.

346 *Of heavenly temper.* Cf. *Par. Lost*, i. 284, " his ponderous shield etherial temper." See note on *Winter Morning Walk*, l. 664.

349 *Sacramental.* Used in the Latin sense. Sacramentum was the oath of allegiance of a Roman soldier. The word in its Christian sense was first applied to baptism—the vow to serve faithfully under the banner of the cross. See *Browne on the Thirty-nine Articles*, p. 576.

350 *Would to heaven.* A confusion between " would God " and " I pray to heaven."

351 A picture from the life of a certain Dr Trusler, who seems to have combined the trades of preacher, teacher of elocution, writer of sermons, and literary hack.

352 *Empirics.* ἐμπειρικός, one who trusts solely to experience or practice instead of rule, hence a quack. The accent is the same as in Milton (an exception to the rule. See note on *Sofa*, l. 52).

The Rudiments of English Grammar and Composition.

By J. HAMBLIN SMITH, M.A., *of Gonville and Caius College, and late Lecturer at St. Peter's College, Cambridge.*

Crown 8vo. 2s. 6d.

"Though prepared specially for the requirements of the University of Cambridge in the local examinations, this grammar is well worthy of the attention of all who are engaged in the teaching of English."
Glasgow Herald.

"The book is simply and intelligently written; it contains nearly all that a young student should know, and it is full of well chosen examples from English classics to illustrate the different subjects treated."
Spectator.

"This work is very elementary, but, like all Mr. Hamblin Smith's useful books, wonderfully lucid. It should well fulfil its design as a text-book for the local examinations. We are pleased to note the varied and tasteful selection of the illustrative quotations." — *Oxford and Cambridge Undergraduates' Journal.*

"We have here the most difficult study in the English language and what is usually the dryest reduced to language so simple that the smallest child, even before it learns to read can understand the parts of speech of the tongue it articulates, and rendered so interesting as entirely to remove the stigma of dullness."
Cambridge Chronicle.

Dictionary of the English Language.

By R. G. LATHAM, M.A., M.D., *late Fellow of King's College, Cambridge.*

Abridged from Dr. Latham's Edition of Johnson's English Dictionary.

Medium 8vo. 24s.

The Beginner's Drill-book of English Grammar.

Adapted for Middle Class and Elementary Schools.

By JAMES BURTON, T.C.D., *First English Master in the High School of the Liverpool Institute.* [*In the Press.*

"The aim of this book is simply to conduct pupils as far as the analysis and parsing of ordinary constructions, at which point the pursuit of grammar becomes a special study. Up to this point, however, grammar is necessary for every person, since the due analysis of speech lies at the root both of all intelligent reading of the thoughts of others and also of any adequate expression of our own.

"There is no sounder way of leading learners to apprehend grammatical distinctions and relations than, after concise instruction has been given on any point, to enforce and illustrate it by examples from standard authors. Hence it has been the writer's aim to prepare a book which should serve as a means of grammatical drill, consisting of a bare framework of instruction and a large body of really workable exercises.

"The exercises are framed to illustrate great principles rather than over-refined distinctions, and the sentences in them have been chosen from acknowledged literature, first for the sake of authority, and then with the purpose of at once stimulating the learner's mind by aptness or beauty of expression, and relieving the teacher's labour by recalling the pleasures of previous reading."—*Extract from the Preface.*

LONDON, OXFORD, AND CAMBRIDGE.

HISTORICAL HANDBOOKS

Edited by

OSCAR BROWNING, M.A.,

FELLOW OF KING'S COLLEGE, CAMBRIDGE.

Crown 8vo.

ENGLISH HISTORY IN THE XIVTH CENTURY.
By CHARLES H. PEARSON, M.A., *Head-Master of the Presbyterian Ladies' College, Melbourne, late Fellow of Oriel College, Oxford.*
3s. 6d.

THE REIGN OF LEWIS XI.
By P. F. WILLERT, M.A., *Fellow of Exeter College, Oxford.*
With Map. 3s. 6d.

THE ROMAN EMPIRE. A.D. 395–800.
By A. M. CURTEIS, M.A., *Assistant-Master at Sherborne School, late Fellow of Trinity College, Oxford.*
With Maps. 3s. 6d.

HISTORY OF THE ENGLISH INSTITUTIONS.
By PHILIP V. SMITH, M.A., *Barrister-at-Law; Fellow of King's College, Cambridge.*
Second Edition. 3s. 6d.

HISTORY OF MODERN ENGLISH LAW.
By Sir ROLAND KNYVET WILSON, Bart., M.A., *Barrister-at-Law; late Fellow of King's College, Cambridge.*
3s. 6d.

HISTORY OF FRENCH LITERATURE.
Adapted from the French of M. DEMOGEOT, *by* C. BRIDGE.
3s. 6d.

LONDON, OXFORD, AND CAMBRIDGE.

With numerous Maps and Plans. Crown 8vo.

A History of England.

By the Rev. J. FRANCK BRIGHT, M.A., *Fellow of University College, and Historical Lecturer at Balliol, New, and University Colleges, Oxford; late Master of the Modern School at Marlborough College.*

This work is divided into three Periods of convenient and handy size, adapted for use in Schools, as well as for Students reading special portions of History for local and other Examinations.

Period I.—MEDIÆVAL MONARCHY: The departure of the Romans, to Richard III. From A.D. 449 to A.D. 1485. 4s. 6d.

Period II.—PERSONAL MONARCHY: Henry VII. to James II. From A.D. 1485 to A.D. 1688. 5s.

Period III.—CONSTITUTIONAL MONARCHY: William and Mary, to the present time. From A.D. 1689 to A.D. 1837. 7s. 6d.

"It is a relief to meet with a piece of sterling, careful work like this first instalment of Mr. Bright's English History... A careful examination of its pages can hardly fail to suggest that it has cost the compiler a great deal of trouble, and is likely, in consequence, to save both teacher and learner a proportionate amount. For the use for which it is especially designed —that of a text-book in our public schools —it is excellently adapted."—*Academy.*

"An air of good common sense pervades it; the style is entirely free from affectation or inflation, and is at the same time tolerably clear and easy to follow."
Athenæum.

"We do not know a book more suitable for school use, or one more likely to stimulate in boys an intelligent interest in constitutional and social history. We confess to having read the greater part of it with a very real pleasure."—*Educational Times.*

"It is written in a clear, straightforward, sensible way, and contains as much instruction as possible, put in a way that can be easily understood."—*Examiner.*

"It is a critical and thoughtful examination of the growth of this great nation; and while the facts are given always with clearness and force, the student is led to understand and to reflect not merely upon the events themselves, but upon a number of interesting and important considerations arising out of these events."
School Board Chronicle.

"A model of what a clear, attractive, well-arranged, and trustworthy manual of historical information ought to be."
Glasgow Herald.

"We can speak with entire satisfaction of the style in which the work is done. Mr. Bright's is a lucid, steady, vigorous style, which leaves nothing in doubt, and is comprehensive and thoroughly practical."
Liverpool Albion.

"Admirably adapted for the purpose intended, and should rank high as a text-book in all educational establishments."
Civil Service Gazette.

"Mr. Bright has done his work, as it seems to us, in a very careful manner."
Scotsman.

"The narrative is clear and concise, and illustrated by useful plans and maps."
Notes and Queries.

"Written with remarkable grace and fluency, and free, as far as we have been able to judge, from prejudice and intolerance, it is eminently worthy to attain the high position which Mr. Bright ventures to claim for it."—*Liverpool Mail.*

"The work deserves great praise; indeed our only fear is that it is too good, and that its thoroughness may tempt the student to do without consulting the original authorities."—*London Quarterly Review.*

"On the whole, our judgment assigns it the first place among text-books on English history, a study which is becoming increasingly popular, and most wonderfully instructive to American youth."—
National Journal of Education (Boston).

LONDON, OXFORD, AND CAMBRIDGE.

1825] *THE TURKISH QUESTION* 1397

state of things was for the moment crossed by the death of Alexander (Dec. 1, 1825). The view which his successor Nicholas would take became in the last degree important; Canning, with great wisdom, chose Wellington—opposed indeed to his policy, but personally acceptable to the Russian Czar—as his special ambassador to take the royal congratulations upon the new Emperor's accession, and to continue the negotiations if possible. The appointment met with universal approbation ; even Metternich believed that in the hands of Wellington the question must be settled in accordance with his views. It was with much surprise and anger that the Turks and Austrians heard that, on the 4th of April, an arrangement had been arrived at between the Courts of England and Russia. Taking advantage of the very moderate claims of the Greeks, who demanded no more than to be placed on the same footing as the Danubian Principalities, remaining as self-governing but dependent vassals of the Turkish Government, the English minister had succeeded in procuring the signature ʻof a protocol embodying a plan for peaceful intervention. *Protocol between England and Russia. April 1826.*

The cause of Greek independence had already excited enthusiasm in England, many volunteers had joined the armies, and money had been subscribed for them. In this enthusiasm Canning in his heart fully joined ; from early youth one of his favourite dreams had been the independence of that race to which as an ardent lover of the classics he felt he owed so much. But, true to his principles, and determined to maintain the strict neutrality of England, he had done his best to check any active assistance to the insurgents. According to his view it was necessary that England should intervene with clean hands, and as the friend of both parties. He was also in constant dread of the watchfulness of his Tory enemies, fearing lest any sign of too great favour to Russia should enable them entirely to thwart his plans. Nevertheless the knowledge of the approaching intervention gave a great impetus to the feeling in favour of Greece in England, and men and money were poured in considerable quantities into the peninsula. Lord Cochrane, the most dashing and adventurous of English sailors, had joined the insurgents with an American frigate, General Churchill took command of their armies. vet their destruction seemed immi- *Enthusiasm for Greek independence in England.*

[ENGLISH HISTORY—J. F. BRIGHT. *See* p. 8.]

HISTORICAL BIOGRAPHIES

Edited by

THE REV. M. CREIGHTON, M.A.,

LATE FELLOW AND TUTOR OF MERTON COLLEGE, OXFORD.

With Maps and Plans. Small 8vo.

The most important and the most difficult point in Historical Teaching is to awaken a real interest in the minds of Beginners. For this purpose concise handbooks are seldom useful. General sketches, however accurate in their outlines of political or constitutional development, and however well adapted to dispel false ideas, still do not make history a living thing to the *young*. They are most valuable as maps on which to trace the route beforehand and show its direction, but they will seldom allure any one to take a walk.

The object of this series of Historical Biographies is to try and select from English History a few men whose lives were lived in stirring times. The intention is to treat their lives and times in some little detail, and to group round them the most distinctive features of the periods before and after those in which they lived.

It is hoped that in this way interest may be awakened without any sacrifice of accuracy, and that personal sympathies may be kindled without forgetfulness of the principles involved.

It may be added that round the lives of individuals it will be possible to bring together facts of social life in a clearer way, and to reproduce a more vivid picture of particular times than is possible in a historical handbook.

By reading short Biographies a few clear ideas may be formed in the pupil's mind, which may stimulate to further reading. A vivid impression of one period, however short, will carry the pupil onward and give more general histories an interest in their turn. Something, at least, will be gained if the pupil realises that men in past times lived and moved in the same sort of way as they do at present.

Now ready.

1. SIMON DE MONTFORT. 2s. 6d. 2. THE BLACK PRINCE. 2s. 6d.
3. SIR WALTER RALEGH. 3s.

In preparation.

4. OLIVER CROMWELL.
5. THE DUKE OF MARLBOROUGH. 6. THE DUKE OF WELLINGTON.

(*See Specimen Page opposite.*)

History of the Church under the Roman Empire, A.D. 30-476. *By the* Rev. A. D. CRAKE, B.A., *Chaplain of All Saints' School, Bloxham.*
Crown 8vo. 7s. 6d.

A History of England for Children.
By GEORGE DAVYS, D.D., *formerly Bishop of Peterborough.*
New Edition. 18mo. 1s. 6d.

LONDON, OXFORD, AND CAMBRIDGE.

fellow-countrymen, there was need of some outward mark to distinguish friend from foe. All had entire confidence in the wisdom and military skill of their leader, whose exploits in Gascony had marked him out as being one of the foremost soldiers of the age.

Before sunrise, on the morning of May 14th, the Barons' army was ordered to march through the woods across the summit of the ridge of down which lay between Fletching and Lewes. Such was the care of Earl Simon in the disposition and ordering of his forces that, although many of them were novices to war, the march was accomplished in perfect order and discipline. Before starting Earl Simon dubbed as knights the young Gilbert de Clare, Earl of Gloucester; Robert de Vere, Earl of Oxford; and John de Burgh.

The army advanced within two miles of Lewes when they ascended the slope of a hill, from which they soon caught sight of the bell-tower of the priory. Then dismounting from his horse, Earl Simon addressed his soldiers: "Beloved comrades and followers, we are about to enter upon battle to-day in behalf of the Government of the kingdom, to the honour of God, of the blessed Mary, of all the saints, and of our mother Church, and moreover for the maintenance of our faith. Let us pray to the King of all, that, if what we now undertake pleases Him, He would grant us vigour and help, so that we may do a pleasing service, and overpower the malice of our enemies. Since

[HISTORICAL BIOGRAPHIES—SIMON DE MONTFORT. *See* p. 10.]

MATHEMATICS
RIVINGTONS' MATHEMATICAL SERIES

The following Schools, amongst many others, use this Series:—Eton: Harrow: Rugby: Winchester: Charterhouse: Marlborough: Shrewsbury: Cheltenham: Clifton: City of London School: Haileybury: Tonbridge: Fettes College, Edinburgh: H.M.'s Dockyard Schools, Sheerness and Devonport: Hurstpierpoint: King William's College, Isle of Man: Bradfield College, Reading: St. Peter's, Clifton, York: Birmingham: Bedford: Felsted: Christ's College, Finchley: Liverpool College: Windermere College: Eastbourne College: Competitive College, Bath: Brentwood: Perse School, Cambridge: Queen's College, Cork. Also in use in the Royal Naval College, Greenwich: H.M. Training Ships: the Owen's College, Manchester: Harvard College, U.S.: the Grammar and High Schools of Canada: Melbourne University, Australia: the other Colonies: and some of the Government Schools in India.

OPINIONS OF TUTORS AND SCHOOLMASTERS.

"A person who carefully studies these books will have a thorough and accurate knowledge of the subjects on which they treat."—*H. A. Morgan, M.A., Tutor of Jesus College, Cambridge.*

"We have for some time used your Mathematical books in our Lecture Room, and find them well arranged, and well calculated to clear up the difficulties of the subjects. The examples also are numerous and well-selected."—*N. M. Ferrers, M.A., Fellow and Tutor of Gonville and Caius College, Cambridge.*

"I have used in my Lecture Room Mr. Hamblin Smith's text-books with very great advantage."—*James Porter, M.A., Master of St. Peter's College, Cambridge.*

"For beginners there could be no better books, as I have found when examining different schools."—*A. W. W. Steel, M.A., Fellow and Assistant-Tutor of Gonville and Caius College, Cambridge.*

"I consider Mr. Hamblin Smith's Mathematical Works to be a very valuable series for beginners. His Algebra in particular I think is the best book of its kind for schools and for the ordinary course at Cambridge."—*F. Pattrick, M.A., Fellow and Tutor of Magdalen College, Cambridge.*

"The series is a model of clearness and insight into possible difficulties."—*Rev. J. F. Blake, St. Peter's College, Clifton, York.*

"I can say with pleasure that I have used your books extensively in my work at Haileybury, and have found them on the whole well adapted for boys."—*Thomas Pitts, M.A., Assistant Mathematical Master at Haileybury College.*

"I can strongly recommend them all."—*W. Henry, M.A., Sub-Warden, Trinity College, Glenalmond.*

"I consider Mr. Smith has supplied a great want, and cannot but think that his works must command extensive use in good schools."—*J. Henry, B.A., Head-Master, H.M. Dockyard School, Sheerness, and Instructor of Engineers, R.N.*

"We have used your Algebra and Trigonometry extensively at this School from the time they were first published, and I thoroughly agree with every mathematical teacher I have met, that, as school text-books, they have no equals. We are introducing your Euclid gradually into the School."—*Rev. B. Edwards, sen., Mathematical Master at the College, Hurstpierpoint, Sussex.*

"I consider them to be the best books of their kind on the subject which I have yet seen."—*Joshua Jones, D.C.L., Head-Master, King William's College, Isle of Man.*

"I have very great pleasure in expressing an opinion as to the value of these books. I have used them under very different circumstances, and have always been satisfied with the results obtained."—*C. H. W. Biggs, Editor of the 'Educational Times,' and the 'Monthly Journal of Education.'*

LONDON, OXFORD, AND CAMBRIDGE.

RIVINGTONS' MATHEMATICAL SERIES

ELEMENTARY ALGEBRA. *By* J. HAMBLIN SMITH, M.A., *of Gonville and Caius College, and late Lecturer at St. Peter's College, Cambridge.*
Small 8vo. 3s. Without Answers, 2s. 6d.   A KEY. Crown 8vo. 9s.

EXERCISES ON ALGEBRA. *By* J. HAMBLIN SMITH, M.A.
Small 8vo. 2s. 6d. (Copies may be had without the Answers.)

ALGEBRA. Part II. *By* E. J. GROSS, M.A., *Fellow of Gonville and Caius College, Cambridge, and Secretary to the Oxford and Cambridge Schools Examination Board.*
Crown 8vo. 8s. 6d.

"We have to congratulate Mr. Gross on his excellent treatment of the more difficult chapters in Elementary Algebra. His work satisfies not only in every respect the requirements of a first-rate text-book on the subject, but is not open to the standing reproach of most English mathematical treatises for students, a minimum of teaching and a maximum of problems. The hard work and considerable thought which Mr. Gross has devoted to the book will be seen on every page by the experienced teacher; there is not a word too much, nor is the student left without genuine assistance where it is needful. The language is precise, clear, and to the point. The problems are not too numerous, and selected with much tact and judgment. The range of the book has been very rightly somewhat extended beyond that assigned to simpler treatises, and it includes the elementary principles of Determinants. This chapter especially will be read with satisfaction by earnest students, and the mode of exposition will certainly have the approval of teachers. Altogether we think that. this *Algebra* will soon become a general text-book, and will remain so for a long time to come." — *Westminster Review.*

KINEMATICS AND KINETICS. *By* E. J. GROSS, M.A.
Crown 8vo. 5s. 6d.

GEOMETRICAL CONIC SECTIONS.
By G. RICHARDSON, M.A., *Assistant-Master at Winchester College, and late Fellow of St. John's College, Cambridge.*
Crown 8vo. 4s. 6d.

A TREATISE ON ARITHMETIC. *By* J. HAMBLIN SMITH, M.A.
Small 8vo. 3s. 6d. (Copies may be had without the Answers.)
A KEY. Crown 8vo. 9s.

EXAMINATION FOR TEACHERS' CERTIFICATES: SUGGESTIONS FROM DR. MCLELLAN.—"I therefore recommend all intending candidates to read carefully Hamblin Smith's Arithmetic. Some of this Author's works are already well and favourably known in Ontario; the Arithmetic is one of the most valuable of the series. It explains and illustrates the Unitary Method, showing how the elementary principles of pure science, without being disguised. in multitudinous perplexing 'Rules,' can be applied to the solution of all classes of questions.
"If then candidates master (as they can easily do) the method of this book, and apply it to the excellent examples which the Author has supplied, and to those questions set from time to time by the Central Committee, there will be fewer failures at the next examination."—*Extract from Letter of Dr. J. A. McLellan, Senior High School Inspector for Canada, to the* "*Toronto Mail,*" *November* 22, 1876.

LONDON, OXFORD, AND CAMBRIDGE.

RIVINGTONS' MATHEMATICAL SERIES—continued.

ELEMENTS OF GEOMETRY.
By J. HAMBLIN SMITH, M.A.
Small 8vo. 3s. 6d.
Containing Books 1 to 6, and portions of Books 11 and 12, of EUCLID, with Exercises and Notes, arranged with the Abbreviations admitted in the Cambridge University and Local Examinations.

Books 1 and 2, limp cloth, 1s. 6d., may be had separately.

" Euclid's Axioms will be required, and no proof of any proposition will be admitted which assumes the proof of anything not proved in preceding propositions in Euclid."—*Extract from the Regulations for the Cambridge Local and Schools Examinations for* 1877.

The effect of the above regulation is that the method of proof given in Mr. Hamblin Smith's Geometry satisfies the requirements of these Examinations.

(*See Specimen Page opposite.*)

TRIGONOMETRY. By J. HAMBLIN SMITH, M.A.
Small 8vo. 4s. 6d. A KEY. Crown 8vo. 7s. 6d.

ELEMENTARY STATICS. By the same. Small 8vo. 3s.

ELEMENTARY HYDROSTATICS. By the same. Small 8vo. 3s.

A KEY TO STATICS AND HYDROSTATICS.
[*In preparation.*

BOOK OF ENUNCIATIONS FOR HAMBLIN SMITH'S GEOMETRY, ALGEBRA, TRIGONOMETRY, STATICS, AND HYDROSTATICS. Small 8vo. 1s.

The Principles of Dynamics. An Elementary Text-book for Science Students. By R. WORMELL, D.Sc., M.A., *Head-Master of the City of London Middle-Class School.*
Crown 8vo. 6s.

Arithmetic, Theoretical and Practical.
By W. H. GIRDLESTONE, M.A., *of Christ's College, Cambridge, Head-Master of Sunningdale Preparatory School, and formerly Principal of the Theological College, Gloucester.*
Crown 8vo. 6s. 6d. Also a School Edition. Small 8vo., 3s. 6d.

LONDON, OXFORD, AND CAMBRIDGE.

Proposition XLI. Theorem.

If a parallelogram and a triangle be upon the same base, and between the same parallels, the parallelogram is double of the triangle.

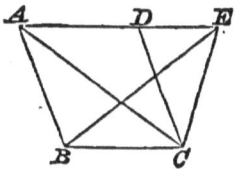

Let the ▱ *ABCD* and the △ *EBC* be on the same base *BC* and between the same ∥s *AE*, *BC*.

Then must ▱ *ABCD* be double of △ *EBC*.

Join *AC*.

Then △ *ABC* = △ *EBC*, ∵ they are on the same base and between the same ∥s ;   I. 37.

and ▱ *ABCD* is double of △ *ABC*, ∵ *AC* is a diagonal of *ABCD* ;   I. 34.

∴ ▱ *ABCD* is double of △ *EBC*.

Q. E. D.

Ex. 1. If from a point, without a parallelogram, there be drawn two straight lines to the extremities of the two opposite sides, between which, when produced, the point does not lie, the difference of the triangles thus formed is equal to half the parallelogram.

Ex. 2. The two triangles, formed by drawing straight lines from any point within a parallelogram to the extremities of its opposite sides, are together half of the parallelogram.

[RIVINGTONS' MATHEMATICAL SERIES—GEOMETRY. *See* p. 14.]

SCIENCE

A Year's Botany. Adapted to Home and School Use.
By FRANCES ANNA KITCHENER.
Illustrated by the Author. Crown 8vo. 5s.
(*See Specimen Page opposite.*)

Contents.

General Description of Flowers—Flowers with Simple Pistils—Flowers with Compound Pistils — Flowers with Apocarpous Fruits — Flowers with Syncarpous Fruits—Stamens and Morphology of Branches—Fertilisation—Seeds—Early Growth and Food of Plants—Wood, Stems, and Roots—Leaves—Classification—Umbellates, Composites, Spurges, and Pines—Some Monocotyledonous Families—Orchids—Appendix of Technical Terms—Index.

"One and only one English book do I know that might almost make a stupid man teach one science well; and that is Mrs. Kitchener's 'A Year's Botany' (Rivingtons). That happily does not teach facts only; but is the expression of the method of a first-rate teacher in such a form as to enable any one to follow it."—*J. M. Wilson, M.A., in "Nature" of April* 13, 1876.

An Easy Introduction to Chemistry.
For the use of Schools. *Edited by the* Rev. ARTHUR RIGG, M.A., *late Principal of The College, Chester, and* WALTER T. GOOLDEN, B.A., *late Science Scholar of Merton College, Oxford; and Lecturer in Natural Science at Tonbridge School.*
New Edition, revised. With Illustrations. Crown 8vo. 2s. 6d.

Notes on Building Construction.
Arranged to meet the requirements of the syllabus of the Science and Art Department of the Committee of Council on Education, South Kensington Museum. Medium 8vo.

PART I.—FIRST STAGE, OR ELEMENTARY COURSE.
    With 325 woodcuts, 10s. 6d.

PART II.—COMMENCEMENT OF SECOND STAGE, OR ADVANCED COURSE. With 277 woodcuts, 10s. 6d.

PART III.—ADVANCED COURSE. [*Nearly Ready.*

REPORT ON THE EXAMINATION IN BUILDING CONSTRUCTION, HELD BY THE SCIENCE AND ART DEPARTMENT, SOUTH KENSINGTON, IN MAY, 1875.—"The want of a text-book in this subject, arranged in accordance with the published syllabus, and therefore limiting the students and teachers to the prescribed course, has lately been well met by a work published by Messrs. Rivingtons, entitled '*Notes on Building Construction*, arranged to meet the requirements of the Syllabus of the Science and Art Department of the Committee of Council on Education, South Kensington.'
June 18, 1875. (Signed) H. C. SEDDON, Major, R.E."

"Something of the sort was very much needed. The whole series when published will be a great boon to young students."
Builder.
"The text is prepared in an extremely simple and consecutive manner, advancing from rudimental and general statements to those which are comparatively advanced; it is a thoroughly coherent, self-sustained account."—*Athenæum.*

LONDON, OXFORD, AND CAMBRIDGE.

A YEAR'S BOTANY.

of all of them open by two slits turned towards the centre of the flower. Their stalks have expanded and joined together, so as to form a thin sheath round the central column (fig. 12). The dust-spikes are so variable in length in this flower, that it may not be possible to see that one short one comes between two long ones, though this ought to be the case.

Fig. 12.
Dust-spikes of gorse (enlarged).

The *seed-organ* is in the form of a longish rounded pod, with a curved neck, stretching out beyond the dust-spikes. The top of it is sticky, and if you look at a bush of gorse, you will see it projecting beyond the keel in most of the fully-blown flowers, because the neck has become more curved than in fig. 12. Cut open the pod; it contains only one cavity (not, as that of the wall-flower, two separated by a thin partition), and the grains are suspended by short cords from the top (fig. 13). These grains may be plainly seen in the seed-organ of even a young flower. It is evident that they are the most important part of the plant, as upon them depends its diffusion and multiplication. We have already seen how carefully their well-being is considered in the matter of their perfection, how even insects are pressed into their service for this purpose! Now let us glance again at our flower, and see how wonderfully contrivance is heaped upon contrivance for their protection!

Fig. 13.
Split seed-pod of gorse.

First (see fig. 10, p. 14), we have the outer covering, so covered with hairs, that it is as good for keeping out rain as a waterproof cloak; in the buttercup, when you pressed the bud, it separated into five leaves; here there are five leaves, just the same, but they are so tightly joined that you may press till the whole bud is bent without making them separate at all, and when the bud

' [A YEAR'S BOTANY—KITCHENER. *See* p. 16.]

LATIN

A First Latin Writer.

Comprising Accidence, the Easier Rules of Syntax illustrated by copious Examples, and progressive Exercises in Elementary Latin Prose, with Vocabularies.

By G. L. BENNETT, M.A., *Head-Master of the High School, Plymouth; formerly Assistant-Master at Rugby School, and Scholar of St. John's College, Cambridge.*

Crown 8vo. [*In the Press.*
A KEY for the use of Tutors only. Crown 8vo.

Easy Latin Stories for Beginners.

With Vocabulary and Notes. Forming a First Latin Reading Book for Junior Forms in Schools.

By G. L. BENNETT, M.A., *Head-Master of the High School, Plymouth; formerly Assistant-Master at Rugby School, and Scholar of St. John's College, Cambridge.*

Crown 8vo. 2*s.* 6*d.*
A KEY for the use of Tutors only. [*In Preparation.*

(*See Specimen Page at the end of this Catalogue.*)

The aim of this book is to supply easy stories illustrating the elementary principles of the Simple and Compound sentence. Short selections from the Public School Primer (for permission to use which I am indebted to the Rev. Canon Kennedy) are printed at the head of the Notes to each Part: explanation of these is left to the master. The Geographical and Historical Notes are very brief, as they are intended for boys who are not likely to be acquainted with Ancient History. I am greatly indebted to my friend Mr. Arthur Sidgwick for most valuable and constant help, and for his kindness in revising the whole work. I have also to thank the Rev. F. D. Morice for corrections in the text, and Mr. J. S. Phillpotts, Head-Master of Bedford School, for some most useful suggestions. Most of these stories are adapted from an old translation of Herodotus by Schweighaeuser.—*Preface.*

" These stories are various and amusing, and the grammatical, geographical, and historical notes on them are, as far as we have tested them, careful and judicious."
Saturday Review.
" The choice of extracts has been skilfully made, and each is presented with an attractive heading. What is even more to the purpose, the passages are arranged in sections devoted respectively to the illustration of simple sentences, compound sentences, adverbial clauses, and substantive clauses; and all needful aids to construing are supplied in concise notes and a well-digested vocabulary. A more attractive book for very young Latinists we do not remember to have seen."—*Scotsman.*

" The stories are necessarily brief, but they are such as young students will take great interest in. A vocabulary and notes are furnished, and altogether Mr. Bennett's work will, we should think, prove a most useful one."—*Civil Service Gazette.*
" We can most cordially recommend Mr. Bennett's little book to all who are engaged in imparting a knowledge of the elements of Latin."
Liverpool Weekly Albion.
" Chosen with great judgment; and the happy headings of the various stories, which are printed in neat and clear type, are such as almost of themselves to induce boys to an effort to unravel their meanings."
Glasgow Herald.

LONDON, OXFORD, AND CAMBRIDGE.

Elementary Rules of Latin Pronunciation.
By ARTHUR HOLMES, M.A., *late Senior Fellow and Dean of Clare College, Cambridge.*
Crown 8vo. On a card, 9*d.*

Outlines of Latin Sentence Construction.
By E. D. MANSFIELD, M.A., *Assistant-Master at Clifton College.*
Demy 8vo. On a card, 1*s.*

Easy Exercises in Latin Prose.
By CHARLES BIGG, D.D., *Principal of Brighton College.*
Small 8vo. 1*s.* 4*d.*

Latin Prose Exercises.
For Beginners, and Junior Forms of Schools.
By R. PROWDE SMITH, B.A., *Assist.-Master at Cheltenham College.*
New Edition. Crown 8vo. 2*s.* 6*d.*

An Elementary Latin Grammar.
By J. HAMBLIN SMITH, M.A., *of Gonville and Caius College, and late Lecturer at St. Peter's College, Cambridge.*
Crown 8vo. 3*s.* 6*d.*
(*See Specimen Page at the end of this Catalogue.*)

Exercises on the Elementary Principles of Latin Prose Composition.
With Examination Papers on the Elementary Facts of Latin Accidence and Syntax.
By J. HAMBLIN SMITH, M.A., *of Gonville and Caius College, and late Lecturer in Classics at St. Peter's College, Cambridge.*
Crown 8vo. 3*s.* 6*d.*
A KEY for the use of Tutors only. Crown 8vo. 5*s.*

LONDON, OXFORD, AND CAMBRIDGE.

Henry's First Latin Book.
By THOMAS KERCHEVER ARNOLD, M.A.
Twenty-fourth Edition. 12mo. 3*s*.
A KEY for the use of Tutors only. 1*s*.
Recommended in the *Guide to the Choice of Classical Books* by J. B. Mayor, M.A., Professor of Classical Literature at King's College, late Fellow and Tutor of St. John's College, Cambridge.

Arnold's Henry's First Latin Book.
A New and Revised Edition. 12mo.
By C. G. GEPP, M.A., *late Junior Student of Christ Church, Oxford, and formerly Assistant-Master at Tonbridge School; Author of "Progressive Exercises in Latin Elegiac Verse."* [*In the Press.*
A KEY for the use of Tutors only. [*In the Press.*

A Practical Introduction to Latin Prose Composition.
By THOMAS KERCHEVER ARNOLD, M.A.
Seventeenth Edition. 8vo. 6*s*. 6*d*. TUTOR'S KEY. 1*s*. 6*d*.

Arnold's Practical Introduction to Latin Prose Composition.
A New and Revised Edition. 8vo.
By GEORGE G. BRADLEY, M.A., *Master of University College, Oxford, and late Head-Master of Marlborough College.* [*In the Press.*
A KEY for the use of Tutors only. [*In the Press.*

A First Verse Book.
Being an Easy Introduction to the Mechanism of the Latin Hexameter and Pentameter.
By THOMAS KERCHEVER ARNOLD, M.A.
Eleventh Edition. 12mo. 2*s*. TUTOR'S KEY, 1*s*.

Progressive Exercises in Latin Elegiac Verse.
By C. G. GEPP, M.A., *late Junior Student of Christ Church, Oxford, and formerly Assistant-Master at Tonbridge School.*
Third Edition, Revised. Crown 8vo. 3*s*. 6*d*. TUTOR'S KEY, 5*s*.

LONDON, OXFORD, AND CAMBRIDGE.

Materials and Models for Latin Prose Composition.

Selected and arranged by J. Y. SARGENT, M.A., *Fellow and Tutor of Hertford College, Oxford;* and T. F. DALLIN, M.A., *Tutor, late Fellow, of Queen's College, Oxford.*

New Edition, re-arranged, with fresh Pieces and additional References.

Crown 8vo. 6s. 6d.

Latin Version of (60) Selected Pieces from Materials and Models.

By J. Y. SARGENT, M.A.

Crown 8vo. 5s.

May be had by Tutors only, on direct application to the Publishers.

The Æneid of Vergil.

Edited, with Notes at the end, by FRANCIS STORR, B.A., *Chief Master of Modern Subjects at Merchant Taylors' School.*

Crown 8vo.

BOOKS I. and II. 2s. 6d.
BOOKS XI. and XII. 2s. 6d.

Classical Examination Papers.

Edited, with Notes and References, by P. J. F. GANTILLON, M.A., *Classical Master at Cheltenham College.*

Crown 8vo. 7s. 6d.

Or interleaved with writing-paper, half-bound, 10s. 6d.

Ecloga Ovidianæ.

From the Elegiac Poems. With English Notes.

By THOMAS KERCHEVER ARNOLD, M.A.

Fourteenth Edition, Revised. 12mo. 2s. 6d.

"The best known introduction to the study of Ovid."—*School Board Chronicle.*
"A student of Ovid's charming poetry could scarcely find a better introduction to his work than in these carefully edited pages, with their grammatical notes, and their explanations of all obscure allusions and difficult constructions of the syntax."—*Public Opinion.*

"No better edition of the Eclogues than this for school purposes could be wished. The notes are numerous, and are admirably adapted to give the pupil an intelligent understanding of the numerous obscure topographical and other references in the text."—*Scotsman.*

LONDON, OXFORD, AND CAMBRIDGE.

Stories from Ovid in Elegiac Verse.

With Notes for School Use and Marginal References to the PUBLIC SCHOOL LATIN PRIMER.
By R. W. TAYLOR, M.A., *Head-Master of Kelly College, Tavistock, and late Fellow of St. John's College, Cambridge.*
Crown 8vo. 3s. 6d.
(*See Specimen Pages at the end of this Catalogue*).

"We have seldom met with a book which we can more thoroughly recommend to schoolmasters."—*Academy.*
"A collection of legends calculated to prove attractive in respect of their subject-matter, while the beautiful Latinity in which they are clothed must exert a wholesome influence in the formation of literary taste . . . Ample notes supply illustrative information and elucidate grammatical difficulties."—*Scotsman.*
"The passages selected are short, and the story is told by a few introductory paragraphs. The notes contain a fund of information fully illustrative and explanatory of the text, and solve all real grammatical difficulties, and obscure allusions to manners, customs, laws, and mythology. The myths are very often very correctly explained. . . . Another special merit of the work is the fund of illustrations it supplies from Milton, Tennyson, Chaucer, and Spenser, who are largely quoted. This will be a twofold advantage to the student, as enlarging his knowledge and deepening his interest in English literature, as well as in classical knowledge."
School Board Chronicle.

Selections from Livy, Books VIII. and IX.

With Notes and Map.
By E. CALVERT, LL.D., *St. John's College, Cambridge; and* R. SAWARD, M.A., *Fellow of St. John's College, Cambridge; Assistant-Master at Shrewsbury School.*
Small 8vo. 2s.

Cornelius Nepos.

With Critical Questions and Answers, and an Imitative Exercise on each Chapter.
By THOMAS KERCHEVER ARNOLD, M.A.
Fifth Edition. 12mo. 4s.

Terenti Comoediae.

Edited *by* T. L. PAPILLON, M.A., *Fellow of New College, and late Fellow of Merton, Oxford.*
ANDRIA ET EUNUCHUS. With Introduction on Prosody. 4s. 6d.
Or separately,
ANDRIA. With Introduction on Prosody. 3s. 6d.
EUNUCHUS. 3s.
Crown 8vo.
Forming Parts of the "Catena Classicorum."

LONDON, OXFORD, AND CAMBRIDGE.

Juvenalis Satirae.
Edited by G. A. SIMCOX, M.A., *Fellow of Queen's College, Oxford.*
THIRTEEN SATIRES.
Second Edition. Crown 8vo. 5s.
Forming a Part of the "Catena Classicorum."

Persii Satirae.
Edited by A. PRETOR, M.A., *of Trinity College, Cambridge, Classical Lecturer of Trinity Hall, Composition Lecturer of the Perse Grammar School, Cambridge.*
Crown 8vo. 3s. 6d.
Forming a Part of the "Catena Classicorum."

Horati Opera.
By J. M. MARSHALL, M.A., *Under-Master at Dulwich College.*
VOL. I.—THE ODES, CARMEN SECULARE, AND EPODES.
Crown 8vo. 7s. 6d.
Forming a Part of the "Catena Classicorum."

Taciti Historiae. BOOKS I. and II.
Edited by W. H. SIMCOX, M.A., *Fellow of Queen's College, Oxford.*
Crown 8vo. 6s.
Forming a Part of the "Catena Classicorum."

Taciti Historiae. BOOKS III. IV. and V.
Edited by W. H. SIMCOX, M.A., *Fellow of Queen's College, Oxford.*
Crown 8vo. 6s.
Forming a Part of the "Catena Classicorum."

LONDON, OXFORD, AND CAMBRIDGE.

GREEK

A Primer of Greek Accidence for the Use of Schools.

By EVELYN ABBOTT, M.A., *Fellow and Tutor of Balliol College, Oxford*; and E. D. MANSFIELD, M.A., *Assistant-Master at Clifton College*. With a Preface by JOHN PERCIVAL, M.A., LL.D., *Head-Master of Clifton College*.

Crown 8vo. 2*s.* 6*d.*

(*See Specimen Page opposite.*)

"A glance at the book will show that the Editors, remembering how important it is that the early training should run on the same lines as the higher studies that are to follow, have kept steadily in view its preparatory character. They have at the same time bestowed much pains on making it as clear and intelligible as possible, whilst they have given special prominence to the laws that regulate the changes of sound. The learner's attention is also specially drawn to the Stem-theory, particularly in dealing with the various parts of the Verb and their relation to each other, and in the classification of the Irregular Verbs.

"It only remains for me to add that the book, being already in use here, comes before the public not altogether untested by experience, and that it has been subjected to the criticism of masters in other schools.

"At a time of educational change like the present, it is of peculiar importance that the grammatical foundations should be laid firmly and surely, and in such a manner that there shall be no lingering feeling in the mind of the learner that perhaps they are not quite sound. This 'Primer' will, as I believe, contribute in some degree towards making this process an easier one for those who have to teach the elements of Greek; and if so, all Schoolmasters will agree that the labour spent upon it by the Editors has been well bestowed."—*Extract from the Preface.*

A Short Greek Syntax.

By the same Editors. [*In preparation.*

Elements of Greek Accidence.

By EVELYN ABBOTT, M.A., *Fellow and Tutor of Balliol College, Oxford, and late Assistant-Master at Clifton College*.

Crown 8vo. 4*s.* 6*d.*

"This is an excellent book. The compilers of elementary Greek Grammars have not before, so far as we are aware, made full use of the results obtained by the labours of philologists during the last twenty-five years. Mr. Abbott's great merit is that he has; and a comparison between his book and the *Rudimenta* of the late Dr. Donaldson—a most excellent volume for the time at which it was published—will show how considerable the advance has been; while a comparison with the works in ordinary use, which have never attained anything like the standard reached by Dr. Donaldson, will really surprise the teacher."—*Athenæum.*

LONDON, OXFORD, AND CAMBRIDGE.

DECLENSION OF SUBSTANTIVES.

36. SECOND DECLENSION.

O STEMS.

	SIMPLE.			CONTRACTED.	
STEM. ENGL.	λογο, speech.	νησο, island.	ζυγο, yoke.	νοο, mind.	όστεο, bone.
Sing.					
Nom.	ὁ λόγος	ἡ νῆσος	τὸ ζυγόν	ὁ νόος νοῦς	τὸ ὀστέον ὀστοῦν
Voc.	λόγε	νῆσε	ζυγόν	νόε νοῦ	ὀστέον ὀστοῦν
Acc.	λόγον	νῆσον	ζυγόν	νόον νοῦν	ὀστέον ὀστοῦν
Gen.	λόγου	νήσου	ζυγοῦ	νόου νοῦ	ὀστέου ὀστοῦ
Dat.	λόγῳ	νήσῳ	ζυγῷ	νόῳ νῷ	ὀστέῳ ὀστῷ
Dual					
N.V.A.	λόγω	νήσω	ζυγώ	νόω νώ	ὀστέω ὀστώ
G. D.	λόγοιν	νήσοιν	ζυγοῖν	νόοιν νοῖν	ὀστέοιν ὀστοῖν
Plur.					
N. V.	λόγοι	νῆσοι	ζυγά	νόοι νοῖ	ὀστέα ὀστᾶ
Acc.	λόγους	νήσους	ζυγά	νόους νοῦς	ὀστέα ὀστᾶ
Gen.	λόγων	νήσων	ζυγῶν	νόων νῶν	ὀστέων ὀστῶν
Dat.	λόγοις	νήσοις	ζυγοῖς	νόοις νοῖς	ὀστέοις ὀστοῖς

EXAMPLES.

SIMPLE.—ἄνθρωπος, ὁ, man; οἶκος, ὁ, house; ξύλον, τό, wood.
CONTR. —πλοῦς, ὁ, voyage; κανοῦν, τό, basket.

Obs. 1. In the neuters, nom., acc., and voc. are always the same; and in the plural these cases always end in α. The contraction of ὀστέα into ὀστᾶ is irregular, cp. 11.

Obs. 2. The following words are feminine :—ὁδός, *way*; νῆσος, *island*; νόσος, *disease*; δρόσος, *dew*; σποδός, *ashes*; ψῆφος, *pebble*; ἄμπελος, *vine*; γνάθος, *jaw*; ἤπειρος, *continent*; and some others.

[PRIMER OF GREEK ACCIDENCE—ABBOTT. *See* p. 24.]

A First Greek Writer.
By ARTHUR SIDGWICK, M.A., *Assistant-Master at Rugby School, and formerly Fellow of Trinity College, Cambridge.*

[*In preparation.*]

An Introduction to Greek Prose Composition, with Exercises.
By ARTHUR SIDGWICK, M.A., *Assistant-Master at Rugby School, and formerly Fellow of Trinity College, Cambridge.*
Crown 8vo. 5s.
A KEY for the use of Tutors only. 5s.
(*See Specimen Page opposite.*)

"A most masterly and complete summary of the chief rules for writing Greek, and of the difficulties which the student will encounter in his task, is the feature of the work. In arrangement, in exhaustiveness, and in lucidity, it is a model of what such a treatise should be. There is no royal road to the art of writing Greek prose, or indeed to any other art, yet we have seen learners acquire no inconsiderable skill with a celerity that seemed almost magical."
Spectator.

"Very few, if any, University candidates for classical honours could fail to derive benefit from a careful study of Mr. Sidgwick's notes and lists, which occupy about half the book; so that we anticipate a great success for this valuable and novel publication."—*Athenæum.*

"Students of all grades, from the fifth form to the aspirant after first-class honours, will find the work most useful. . . . The arrangement is excellent, the 'Notes on Construction and Idiom' are full and clear, and the whole volume is redolent of sound and elegant scholarship. Its publication is a new departure in the teaching of Greek composition."—*Examiner.*

"The hints on Greek idiom are not only invaluable in themselves, but the order and clearness with which they are stated make them still more invaluable. It is one of the most useful books we have seen for a considerable time on the difficult subject of Greek prose composition."—*Standard.*

"One of the best and most useful books of its kind that we remember to have seen. The 'Notes on Construction and Idiom,' which occupy the first 100 pages, are admirably clear and suggestive, and useful not only for beginners, but for advanced scholars and teachers; while the Exercises (175 in number) are well selected and graduated to suit different stages of attainment, with just sufficient assistance at the foot of each towards some of the more difficult idioms, and a good English-Greek vocabulary at the end of the book."
Guardian.

"The rules are clear, and abundantly illustrated. The exercises are not short detached sentences, but complete tales or narratives. The book is, of its kind, the best we have ever seen."—*Nonconformist.*

"Schoolmasters will no longer have the excuse of the want of a good book to put into the hands of their pupils. . . . The notes on idiom are particularly useful."
John Bull.

Stories in Attic Greek.
Forming a Greek Reading Book for the use of Junior Forms in Schools. With Notes and Vocabulary.
By FRANCIS DAVID MORICE, M.A., *Assistant-Master at Rugby School; and Fellow of Queen's College, Oxford.*

[*In the Press.*]

LONDON, OXFORD, AND CAMBRIDGE.

trace of anything artificial, except perhaps in the orators: and even there the art is shown as much in the *extreme naturalness* of the order as in anything else.

The considerations therefore that determine the order of words are chiefly the following: clearness: emphasis: neatness and euphony.

Clearness is the chief thing. Let the words come out in their natural order, but so that there be no ambiguity. In a Latin sentence you have to think about balance and point and marshalling of verbs and so forth: in Greek it is best to be not hampered by rules for order, but to strive simply to say what you mean, and let it come out in the most natural way; and above all, to be clear.

An extremely good test for Greek prose composition is to leave it for a bit after writing, and then read it all over like a new piece. If you are stopped for an instant by not seeing the meaning, or are for an instant misled, then be sure there is a blemish in the order or clearness of the writing.

A common mistake for beginners to make in Greek is to be *artificial* in the arrangement of sentences: to start with some theory, as for example that notion (derived from Latin) that all verbs must be at the ends of the clauses. And so if they get a sentence to translate like this:—

'He said he would kill all who did not do what he ordered,'

They will produce the following obscure passage:

οὗτος, ὅτι πάντας, οἳ μὴ ὅπερ κελεύοι δρῷεν, ἀποκτενοῖ, ἔφη, which is perfectly correct in Grammar, but the order is dreadful, with that heavy *sediment* of verbs at the end.

[INTRODUCTION TO GREEK PROSE—SIDGWICK. *See* p. 26.]

Selections from Lucian.
With English Notes.
By EVELYN ABBOTT, M.A., *Fellow and Tutor of Balliol College, Oxford, and late Assistant-Master at Clifton College.*
Small 8vo. 3s. 6d.

Alexander the Great in the Punjaub.
Adapted from Arrian, Book V. An easy Greek Reading Book.
Edited, with Notes and a Map, by the Rev. CHARLES E. MOBERLY, M.A., *Assistant-Master at Rugby School, and formerly Scholar of Balliol College, Oxford.*
Small 8vo. 2s.

Stories from Herodotus.
The Tales of Rhampsinitus and Polycrates, and the Battle of Marathon and the Alcmæonidae. *In Attic Greek.*
Edited by J. SURTEES PHILLPOTTS, M.A., *Head-Master of Bedford Grammar School; formerly Fellow of New College, Oxford.*
Crown 8vo. 1s. 6d.

Iophon: an Introduction to the Art
of Writing Greek Iambic Verses.
By the WRITER of "*Nuces*" and "*Lucretilis.*"
Crown 8vo. 2s.

The First Greek Book.
On the plan of *Henry's First Latin Book.*
By THOMAS KERCHEVER ARNOLD, M.A.
Sixth Edition. 12mo. 5s. TUTOR'S KEY, 1s. 6d.

A Practical Introduction to Greek Accidence.
By THOMAS KERCHEVER ARNOLD, M.A.
Ninth Edition. 8vo. 5s. 6d.

A Practical Introduction to Greek Prose Composition.
By THOMAS KERCHEVER ARNOLD, M.A.
Twelfth Edition. 8vo. 5s. 6d. TUTOR'S KEY, 1s. 6d.

LONDON, OXFORD, AND CAMBRIDGE.

SCENES FROM GREEK PLAYS
RUGBY EDITION
Abridged and adapted for the use of Schools, by
ARTHUR SIDGWICK, M.A.,
ASSISTANT-MASTER AT RUGBY SCHOOL, AND FORMERLY FELLOW OF TRINITY COLLEGE, CAMBRIDGE.

Small 8vo. 1s. 6d. each.

ARISTOPHANES.
THE CLOUDS. THE FROGS. THE KNIGHTS. PLUTUS.

EURIPIDES.
IPHIGENIA IN TAURIS. THE CYCLOPS. ION.
ELECTRA. ALCESTIS. BACCHÆ. HECUBA.

Recommended in the *Guide to the Choice of Classical Books*, by J. B. Mayor, M.A., Professor of Classical Literature at King's College, late Fellow and Tutor of St. John's College, Cambridge.

Homer's Iliad.
Edited, with Notes at the end for the Use of Junior Students, by ARTHUR SIDGWICK, M.A., *Assistant-Master at Rugby School, and formerly Fellow of Trinity College, Cambridge.*

Small 8vo.
Books I. and II. 2s. 6d.
Books III. and IV. *[In preparation.*

Homer for Beginners.
ILIAD, Books I.—III. With English Notes.
By THOMAS KERCHEVER ARNOLD, M.A.
Fifth Edition. 12mo. 3s. 6d.

Homer without a Lexicon, for Beginners.
ILIAD, Book VI.
Edited, with Notes giving the meanings of all the less common words, by J. SURTEES PHILLPOTTS, M.A., *Head Master of Bedford Grammar School, formerly Fellow of New College, Oxford.*
Small 8vo, 2s.

LONDON, OXFORD, AND CAMBRIDGE.

The Iliad of Homer.
From the Text of Dindorf. With Preface and Notes.
By S. H. REYNOLDS, M.A., *Fellow and Tutor of Brasenose College, Oxford.*
Books I.—XII. Crown 8vo. 6s.
Forming a Part of the " Catena Classicorum."

The Iliad of Homer.
With English Notes and Grammatical References.
By THOMAS KERCHEVER ARNOLD, M.A.
Fifth Edition. 12mo. 12s.

A Complete Greek and English Lexicon for the Poems of Homer and the Homeridæ.
By G. CH. CRUSIUS. *Translated from the German.* Edited by T. K. ARNOLD, M.A.
New Edition. 12mo. 9s.

The Anabasis of Xenophon.
Edited, with Preface, Introduction, Historical Sketch, Itinerary, Syntax Rules, Notes, Indices, and Map, by R. W. TAYLOR, M.A., *Head-Master of Kelly College, Tavistock, and late Fellow of St. John's College, Cambridge.*
Crown 8vo.
Books I. and II. 3s. 6d.
Books III. and IV. 3s. 6d.
(*See Specimen Pages at the end of this Catalogue.*)

A Short Greek Syntax.
Extracted from "XENOPHON'S ANABASIS, WITH NOTES."
By R. W. TAYLOR, M.A., *Head-Master of Kelly College, Tavistock; late Fellow of St. John's College, Cambridge.*
Crown 8vo. 9d.

Xenophon's Memorabilia.
Book I., with a few omissions. *Edited, with an Introduction and Notes,* by the Rev. C. E. MOBERLY, *Assistant-Master at Rugby School, and formerly Scholar of Balliol College, Oxford.*
Small 8vo. 2s.

LONDON, OXFORD, AND CAMBRIDGE.

Materials and Models for Greek Prose Composition.

Selected and arranged by J. Y. SARGENT, M.A., *Fellow and Tutor of Hertford College, Oxford;* and T. F. DALLIN, M.A., *Tutor, late Fellow, of Queen's College, Oxford.*
Second Edition, containing Fresh Pieces and additional References.
Crown 8vo. 5s.

Greek Version of Selected Pieces from Materials and Models.

By J. Y. SARGENT, M.A.
Crown 8vo. 7s. 6d.
May be had by Tutors only, on direct application to the Publishers.

Zeugma; or, Greek Steps from Primer to Author.

By the Rev. LANCELOT SANDERSON, M.A., *Principal of Elstree School, late Scholar of Clare College, Cambridge;* and the Rev. F. B. FIRMAN, M.A., *Assistant-Master at Elstree School, late Scholar of Jesus College, Cambridge.*
Small 8vo. 1s. 6d.

Demosthenes.

Edited, *with English Notes and Grammatical References,* by THOMAS KERCHEVER ARNOLD, M.A.
12mo.
OLYNTHIAC ORATIONS. Third Edition. 3s.
PHILIPPIC ORATIONS. Third Edition. 4s.
ORATION ON THE CROWN. Second Edition. 4s. 6d.

Demosthenis Orationes Privatae.

Edited by ARTHUR HOLMES, M.A., *late Senior Fellow and Dean of Clare College, Cambridge, and Preacher at the Chapel Royal, Whitehall.*
Crown 8vo.
DE CORONA. 5s.
Forming a Part of the "*Catena Classicorum.*"

Demosthenis Orationes Publicae.

Edited by G. H. HESLOP, M.A., *late Fellow and Assistant-Tutor of Queen's College, Oxford; Head-Master of St. Bees.*
Crown 8vo.
OLYNTHIACS, 2s. 6d. } or, in One Volume, 4s. 6d.
PHILIPPICS, 3s.
DE FALSA LEGATIONE, 6s.
Forming Parts of the "*Catena Classicorum.*"

LONDON, OXFORD, AND CAMBRIDGE.

Classical Examination Papers.

Edited, with Notes and References, by P. J. F. GANTILLON, M.A., sometime Scholar of St. John's College, Cambridge; Classical Master at Cheltenham College.

Crown 8vo. 7s. 6d.
Or interleaved with writing-paper, half-bound, 10s. 6d.

Recommended in the *Guide to the Choice of Classical Books*, by J. B. Mayor, M.A., Professor of Classical Literature at King's College, late Fellow and Tutor of St. John's College, Cambridge.

Sophocles.

Edited by T. K. ARNOLD, M.A., ARCHDEACON PAUL, and HENRY BROWNE, M.A.

12mo.

AJAX. 3s.   PHILOCTETES. 3s.   ŒDIPUS TYRANNUS. 4s.

Isocratis Orationes.

Edited by JOHN EDWIN SANDYS, M.A., Fellow and Tutor of St. John's College, Cambridge, and Public Orator of the University.

Crown 8vo.
AD DEMONICUM ET PANEGYRICUS. 4s. 6d.
Forming a Part of the "Catena Classicorum."

Sophoclis Tragoediae.

Edited by R. C. JEBB, M.A., Professor of Greek at the University of Glasgow, late Fellow and Assistant-Tutor of Trinity College, Cambridge.

Crown 8vo.
ELECTRA. 3s. 6d.   AJAX. 3s. 6d.
Forming Parts of the "Catena Classicorum."

Aristophanis Comoediae.

Edited by W. C. GREEN, M.A., late Fellow of King's College, Cambridge; Assistant-Master at Rugby School.

Crown 8vo.
THE ACHARNIANS and THE KNIGHTS. 4s.
THE CLOUDS. 3s. 6d.   THE WASPS. 3s. 6d.
THE ACHARNIANS and THE KNIGHTS, revised for Schools. 4s.
Forming Parts of the "Catena Classicorum."

Herodoti Historia.
Edited by H. G. WOODS, M.A., *Fellow and Tutor of Trinity College, Oxford.*
Crown 8vo.
BOOK I. 6s. BOOK II. 5s.
Forming Parts of the "Catena Classicorum."

A Copious Phraseological English-Greek Lexicon.
Founded on a work prepared by J. W. FRÄDERSDORFF, Ph.D., *late Professor of Modern Languages, Queen's College, Belfast.*
Revised, Enlarged, and Improved by the late THOMAS KERCHEVER ARNOLD, M.A., and HENRY BROWNE, M.A.
Fifth Edition. 8vo. 21s.

Thucydidis Historia. Books I. and II.
Edited by CHARLES BIGG, D.D., *late Senior Student and Tutor of Christ Church, Oxford; Principal of Brighton College.*
Crown 8vo. 6s.
Forming a Part of the "Catena Classicorum."

Thucydidis Historia. Books III. and IV.
Edited by G. A. SIMCOX, M.A., *Fellow of Queen's College, Oxford.*
Crown 8vo. 6s.
Forming a Part of the "Catena Classicorum."

An Introduction to Aristotle's Ethics.
Books I.—IV. (Book X., c. vi.—ix. in an Appendix). With a Continuous Analysis and Notes. Intended for the use of Beginners and Junior Students.
By the Rev. EDWARD MOORE, B.D., *Principal of S. Edmund Hall, and late Fellow and Tutor of Queen's College, Oxford.*
Second Edition, Revised and Enlarged. Crown 8vo. 10s. 6d.

Aristotelis Ethica Nicomachea.
Edidit, emendavit, crebrisque locis parallelis e libro ipso, aliisque ejusdem Auctoris scriptis, illustravit JACOBUS E. T. ROGERS, A.M.
Small 8vo. 4s. 6d. Interleaved with writing-paper, half-bound. 6s.

LONDON, OXFORD, AND CAMBRIDGE.

Selections from Aristotle's Organon.
Edited by JOHN R. MAGRATH, M.A., *Pro-Provost of Queen's College, Oxford.*
Second Edition. Crown 8vo. 3s. 6d.

Madvig's Syntax of the Greek Language, especially of the Attic Dialect.
For the use of Schools.
Edited by THOMAS KERCHEVER ARNOLD, M.A.
Second Edition. Imperial 16mo. 8s. 6d.
Recommended by the Cambridge Board of Classical Studies for the Classical Tripos.

The Greek Testament.
With a Critically Revised Text; a Digest of Various Readings; Marginal References to Verbal and Idiomatic Usage; Prolegomena; and a Critical and Exegetical Commentary. For the use of Theological Students and Ministers.
By HENRY ALFORD, D.D., *late Dean of Canterbury.*
New Edition. 4 vols. 8vo. 102s.
The Volumes are sold separately, as follows:—
   Vol. I.—The FOUR GOSPELS. 28s.
   Vol. II.—ACTS to 2 CORINTHIANS. 24s.
   Vol. III.—GALATIANS to PHILEMON. 18s.
   Vol. IV.—HEBREWS to REVELATION. 32s.

The Greek Testament.
With Notes, Introductions, and Index.
By CHR. WORDSWORTH, D.D., *Bishop of Lincoln.*
New Edition. 2 vols. Impl. 8vo. 60s.
The Parts may be had separately, as follows:—
   The GOSPELS. 16s.
   The ACTS. 8s.
   St. Paul's EPISTLES. 23s.
   GENERAL EPISTLES, REVELATION, and INDEX. 16s.

Notes on the Greek Testament.
By the Rev. ARTHUR CARR, M.A., *Assistant-Master at Wellington College, late Fellow of Oriel College, Oxford.*
THE GOSPEL ACCORDING TO S. LUKE.
Crown 8vo. 6s.

LONDON, OXFORD, AND CAMBRIDGE.

CATENA CLASSICORUM
Crown 8vo.

Sophoclis Tragoediae. By R. C. Jebb, M.A.
THE ELECTRA. 3s. 6d.   THE AJAX. 3s. 6d.

Juvenalis Satirae. By G. A. Simcox, M.A. 5s.

Thucydidis Historia.—Books I. & II.
By Charles Bigg, D.D. 6s.

Thucydidis Historia.—Books III. & IV.
By G. A. Simcox, M.A. 6s.

Demosthenis Orationes Publicae. By G. H. Heslop, M.A.
THE OLYNTHIACS. 2s. 6d. } or, in One Volume, 4s. 6d.
THE PHILIPPICS. 3s.
DE FALSA LEGATIONE. 6s.

Demosthenis Orationes Privatae.
By Arthur Holmes, M.A.
DE CORONA. 5s.

Aristophanis Comoediae. By W. C. Green, M.A.
THE ACHARNIANS AND THE KNIGHTS. 4s.
THE WASPS. 3s. 6d.   THE CLOUDS. 3s. 6d.
* An Edition of The Acharnians and the Knights, revised and especially adapted for use in Schools. 4s.

Isocratis Orationes. By John Edwin Sandys, M.A.
AD DEMONICUM ET PANEGYRICUS. 4s. 6d.

Persii Satirae. By A. Pretor, M.A. 3s. 6d.

Homeri Ilias. By S. H. Reynolds, M.A.
BOOKS I. TO XII. 6s.

Terenti Comoediae. By T. L. Papillon, M.A.
ANDRIA AND EUNUCHUS. With Introduction on Prosody. 4s. 6d.
Or separately,
ANDRIA. With Introduction on Prosody. 3s. 6d.
EUNUCHUS. 3s.

Herodoti Historia. By H. G. Woods, M.A.
BOOK I., 6s.   BOOK II., 5s.

Horati Opera. By J. M. Marshall, M.A.
Vol. I.—THE ODES, CARMEN SECULARE, AND EPODES. 7s. 6d.

Taciti Historiae. By W. H. Simcox, M.A.
BOOKS I. AND II. 6s.   BOOKS III., IV., and V. 6s.

LONDON, OXFORD, AND CAMBRIDGE.

DIVINITY

MANUALS OF RELIGIOUS INSTRUCTION

Edited by
JOHN PILKINGTON NORRIS, B.D.,
CANON OF BRISTOL, AND EXAMINING CHAPLAIN TO THE BISHOP OF MANCHESTER.

Three Volumes. Small 8vo. 3s. 6d. each.
Or each Book in Five Parts. 1s. each Part.

"Contain the maximum of requisite information within a surprising minimum of space. They are the best and fullest and simplest compilation we have hitherto examined on the subject treated."
Standard.

"Carefully prepared, and admirably suited for their purpose, they supply an acknowledged want in Primary Schools, and will doubtless be in great demand by the teachers for whom they are intended."
Educational Times.

THE OLD TESTAMENT.
By the Rev. E. I. GREGORY, M.A., *Vicar of Halberton.*

PART I. The Creation to the Exodus. PART II. Joshua to the Death of Solomon. PART III. The Kingdoms of Judah and Israel. PART IV. Hebrew Poetry—The Psalms. PART V. The Prophets of the Captivity and of the Return—The Maccabees—Messianic Teaching of the Old Testament.

THE NEW TESTAMENT.
By C. T. WINTER.

PART I. St. Matthew's Gospel. PART II. St. Mark's Gospel. PART III. St. Luke's Gospel. PART IV. St. John's Gospel. PART V. The Acts of the Apostles.

THE PRAYER BOOK.
By JOHN PILKINGTON NORRIS, B.D., *Canon of Bristol, &c.*

PART I. The Catechism to the end of the Lord's Prayer—The Order for Morning and Evening Prayer. PART II. The Catechism, concluding portion—The Office of Holy Baptism—The Order of Confirmation. PART III. The Theology of the Catechism—The Litany—The Office of Holy Communion. PART IV. The Collects, Epistles, and Gospels, to be used throughout the year. PART V. The Thirty-Nine Articles.

LONDON, OXFORD, AND CAMBRIDGE.

Rudiments of Theology.

A First Book for Students.

By JOHN PILKINGTON NORRIS, B.D., *Canon of Bristol; Vicar of St. Mary Redcliffe, and Examining Chaplain to the Bishop of Manchester.*

Crown 8vo. 7s. 6d.

"We can recommend this book to theological students as a useful and compendious manual. It is clear and well arranged. . . . We venture to believe that, on the whole, he is a very fair exponent of the teaching of the English Church, and that his book may be profitably used by those for whom it is chiefly intended—that is, candidates for ordination."—*Spectator.*

"This is a work of real help to candidates for ordination, and to the general student of theology."—*Standard.*

A Manual of Devotion, chiefly for the use of School-boys.

By the Rev. WILLIAM BAKER, D.D., *Head-Master of Merchant Taylors' School.*

With Preface by J. R. WOODFORD, D.D., *Lord Bishop of Ely.*

Crown 16mo. 2s. 6d.

Also a Cheap Edition, limp cloth. 1s. 6d.

A Companion to the Old Testament.

Being a plain Commentary on Scripture History down to the Birth of our Lord.

Small 8vo. 3s. 6d.

Household Theology.

A Handbook of Religious Information respecting the Holy Bible, the Prayer Book, the Church, the Ministry, Divine Worship, the Creeds, &c., &c.

By the Rev. JOHN HENRY BLUNT, M.A.

New Edition. Small 8vo. 3s. 6d.

The Young Churchman's Companion to the Prayer Book.

By the Rev. J. W. GEDGE, M.A., *Diocesan Inspector of Schools for the Archdeaconry of Surrey.*

Part I.—Morning and Evening Prayer and Litany.
Part II.—Baptismal and Confirmation Services.
Part III.—The Holy Communion.

18mo. 1s. each, or in Paper Cover, 6d.

Recommended by the late and present LORD BISHOPS OF WINCHESTER.

LONDON, OXFORD, AND CAMBRIDGE.

Easy Lessons Addressed to Candidates for Confirmation.

By JOHN PILKINGTON NORRIS, B.D., *Canon of Bristol; Vicar of S. Mary Redcliffe, and Examining Chaplain to the Bishop of Manchester.*

18mo. 1*s.* 6*d.*

A Manual of Confirmation.

With a Pastoral Letter instructing Catechumens how to prepare themselves for their First Communion.

By EDWARD MEYRICK GOULBURN, D.D., *Dean of Norwich.*

Ninth Edition. Small 8vo. 1*s.* 6*d.*

The Way of Life.

A Book of Prayers and Instruction for the Young at School. With a Preparation for Holy Communion.

Compiled by a Priest. Edited by *the* Rev. T. T. CARTER, M.A., *Rector of Clewer, Berks.*

Second Edition. 18mo. 1*s.* 6*d.*

Keys to Christian Knowledge.

Cheap Edition. Small 8vo. 1*s.* 6*d.* each.

"Of cheap and reliable text-books of this nature there has hitherto been a great want. We are often asked to recommend books for use in Church Sunday schools, and we therefore take this opportunity of saying that we know of none more likely to be of service both to teachers and scholars than these *Keys.*" — *Churchman's Shilling Magazine.*

"Will be very useful for the higher classes in Sunday schools, or rather for the fuller instruction of the Sunday-school teachers themselves, where the parish Priest is wise enough to devote a certain time regularly to their preparation for their voluntary task."—*Union Review.*

By J. H. BLUNT, M.A., Editor of the *Annotated Book of Common Prayer.*

THE HOLY BIBLE.
THE BOOK OF COMMON PRAYER.
THE CHURCH CATECHISM.
CHURCH HISTORY, ANCIENT.
CHURCH HISTORY, MODERN.

By JOHN PILKINGTON NORRIS, B.D., *Canon of Bristol.*

THE FOUR GOSPELS.
THE ACTS OF THE APOSTLES.

LONDON, OXFORD, AND CAMBRIDGE.

MISCELLANEOUS

At Home and Abroad; or, First Lessons in Geography.
By J. K. LAUGHTON, M.A., F.R.A. and G.S.S., *Mathematical Instructor and Lecturer in Meteorology at the Royal Naval College.*
Crown 8vo. [*In the Press.*

A German Accidence for the Use of Schools.
By J. W. J. VECQUERAY, *Assistant-Master at Rugby School.*
New Edition, Revised. 4to. 3s. 6d.

First German Exercises.
Adapted to Vecqueray's "German Accidence for the Use of Schools."
By E. F. GRENFELL, M.A., *late Assistant-Master at Rugby School.*
Crown 8vo. 2s.

German Exercises. Part II.
With Hints for the Translation of English Prepositions into German. Adapted to Vecqueray's "German Accidence for the Use of Schools."
By E. F. GRENFELL, M.A., *late Assistant-Master at Rugby School.*
Crown 8vo. [*In the Press.*

Lessing's Fables.
Arranged in order of difficulty. With Introduction, Notes, and Vocabulary. A First German Reading Book.
By F. STORR, B.A., *Chief Master of Modern Subjects in Merchant Taylors' School, and late Assistant-Master in Marlborough College.*
Crown 8vo. 2s. 6d.

LONDON, OXFORD, AND CAMBRIDGE.

The Campaigns of Napoleon.

The Text (in French) from M. THIERS' "*Histoire de la Révolution Française*," and "*Histoire du Consulat et de l'Empire.*" Edited, with English Notes, for the use of Schools, by EDWARD E. BOWEN, M.A., Master of the Modern Side, Harrow School.
With Maps. Crown 8vo.

ARCOLA. 4s. 6d.   MARENGO. 4s. 6d.
JENA. 3s. 6d.   WATERLOO. 6s.

Selections from Modern French Authors.

Edited, with English Notes and Introductory Notice, by HENRI VAN LAUN, Translator of Taine's HISTORY OF ENGLISH LITERATURE.
Crown 8vo. 3s. 6d. each.

HONORÉ DE BALZAC.   H. A. TAINE.

La Fontaine's Fables. Books I. and II.

Edited, with English Notes at the end, for use in Schools, by Rev. P. BOWDEN-SMITH, M.A., Assistant-Master at Rugby School.
Small 8vo. 2s.

The First French Book.

By T. K. ARNOLD, M.A.
Sixth Edition. 12mo. 5s. 6d. KEY, 2s. 6d.

The First German Book.

By T. K. ARNOLD, M.A., and J. W. FRÄDERSDORFF, Ph.D.
Seventh Edition. 12mo. 5s. 6d. KEY, 2s. 6d.

The First Hebrew Book.

By T. K. ARNOLD, M.A.
Fifth Edition. 12mo. 7s. 6d. KEY, 3s. 6d.

The Chorister's Guide.

By W. A. BARRETT, Mus. Bac., Oxon., of St. Paul's Cathedral, Author of "*Flowers and Festivals,*" &c.
Second Edition. Crown 8vo. 2s. 6d.

LONDON, OXFORD, AND CAMBRIDGE.

VERBS.

SHALL AND WILL.

98. In the employment of these words to form a future tense, we must distinguish the *unemphatic* from the *emphatic* use.

In ordinary conversation, when *shall* and *will* are merely used as signs to mark future events, custom (or, as some say, courtesy) has decided that *shall* is to be used for the *first* person, and *will* for the *second* and *third* persons : thus we say

> I shall go to London to-morrow.
> You will be too late for the train.
> The Queen will leave Windsor to-day.

But, even in the discourse of common life, when the *intention* marked by the word *will*, or the *compulsion* implied in the word *shall*, is to be made prominent in even a slight degree, *will* is used with the *first* person, and *shall* with the *second* and *third* persons :

Falstaff. You must excuse me, Master Robert Shallow.

Shallow. I will not excuse you : you shall not be excused : excuses shall not be admitted.

99. Next, in the emphatic language of poetry and the higher prose, *will* denotes *free intention*.

Shall denotes *strong compulsion, earnest admonition, firm assurance*, what must be, what ought to be, what is sure to come to pass

Hence *will* is often used with the *first* person :

> I *will* arise and slay thee with my hands.—*Tennyson.*
> And for her sake I do rear up her boy,
> And for her sake I *will* not part with him.—*Shakespeare.*

And *shall* is often used with the *second* and *third* persons :

[ENGLISH GRAMMAR—J. H. SMITH. *See* p. 6.]

EASY LATIN STORIES FOR BEGINNERS.

PART I.

I.—THE STORY OF ARION.

Arion, after travelling abroad, hires a vessel to take him home.

1.—ARION citharista praeclarus erat. Is diu apud Periandrum Corinthiorum regem versatus erat. Tum in Italiam Siciliamque navigare cupivit. Ingentibus opibus ibi comparatis, Corinthum redire voluit. Itaque Tarento, urbe Italiae, profectus est, ubi navigium hominum Corinthiorum conduxerat.

The sailors form a plan to rob and murder him.

2.—Hi autem eum in mare proiicere constituerunt; pecunia enim potiri cupiebant. Tum vero Arion consilium intellexit. Tristis ad preces confugit. Pecunia omni nautis oblata, vitam deprecatus est. Nautae vero precibus viri non commoti, mortem ei statim minati sunt.

Arion sings a beautiful song, and leaps overboard.

3.—In has angustias redactus Arion, in puppi stetit, omni ornatu suo indutus. Tum unum e carminibus canere incepit. Nautae suavi carmine capti e puppi mediam in navem concesserunt. Ille omni ornatu indutus, capta cithara, carmen peregit. Cantu

NOTES.

PART I.

SIMPLE SENTENCES.

EVERY Simple Sentence is either:—
  I. A Statement; as Psittacus loquitur, *The parrot speaks.*
  II. A Command or Request; as Loquere, psittace, *Speak, parrot.*
  III. A Question; as Loquiturne psittacus? *Does the parrot speak?*

1. **apud**—'at the court of.'
   Corinth—a town on the isthmus which separates Northern Greece from the Peloponnesus (island of Pelops).—*Lat. Prim.* § 101.
   ingentibus opibus comparatis.—*Lat. Prim.* § 125.
   Tarentum—now Taranto, the largest Greek city in Italy, on the gulf of the same name.—*Lat. Prim.* § 121, c.
2. **oblata**—from offero.
3. **redactus**—from redigo.
   mediam navem—'the middle of the ship;' so with other adjectives of position, as, summus mons—'the top of the mountain.'
4. **Taenarum**—now Cape Matapan, the most southern promontory of Greece.
   delatus—from defero.
5. **multum pecuniae**—*lit.* 'much of money.'—*Lat. Prim.* § 131.
6. **Massagetae**—a wandering tribe in Central Asia.
   Scythae—a people of S.-E. Europe.
   simili Scytharum—short for 'like *those* of the S.'
   Utor.—*Lat. Prim.* § 119, a.
   Ex equis—'on horseback.'
   ad omnia—'*for* everything.'
   cocta—from coquo.
7. **quisque . . . sepeliunt**—'They bury . . . each in his own.'
8. **ungulis bovinis**—'with the hoofs of an ox.'—*Lat. Prim.* § 115.
   magnitudine.—*Lat. Prim.* § 116.
9. The phoenix was said to live five hundred years, and then to kill itself by fire, its ashes producing a young one.
   ex intervallo—'after an interval.'
   aliorum . . . aliorum—of some . . . of others.—See 91, note.
   circumlitum—from circumlino.
   magni—'at a high price.'—*Lat. Prim.* § 128. a.
   [EASY LATIN STORIES—G. L. BENNETT. *See* p. 18.]

CLEARCHUS IN COLLUSION WITH CYRUS. [BK. L CH. III.

Misled by the absence of allusion to any intention of going against the king, the soldiers applaud. Clearchus' understanding with Cyrus.

7. Ταῦτα εἶπεν· οἱ δὲ στρατιῶται, οἵ τε αὐτοῦ ἐκείνου καὶ οἱ ἄλλοι, ταῦτα ἀκούσαντες, ὅτι οὐ φαίη⁶³ παρὰ βασιλέα πορεύεσθαι, ἐπῄνεσαν· παρὰ δὲ Ξενίου καὶ Πασίωνος πλείους ἢ δισχίλιοι λαβόντες τὰ ὅπλα καὶ τὰ σκευοφόρα ἐστρατοπεδεύσαντο παρὰ Κλεάρχῳ. 8. Κῦρος δὲ τούτοις¹⁹ᵃ ἀπορῶν τε καὶ λυπούμενος μετεπέμπετο τὸν Κλέαρχον· ὁ δὲ ἰέναι μὲν οὐκ ἤθελε, λάθρᾳ δὲ τῶν στρατιωτῶν²⁶ πέμπων αὐτῷ ἄγγελον ἔλεγε θαρρεῖν ὡς καταστησομένων τούτων²⁷,⁵⁸ᵃ εἰς τὸ δέον· μεταπέμπεσθαι δ' ἐκέλευεν αὐτόν· αὐτὸς δ' οὐκ ἔφη ἰέναι. 9. Μετὰ δὲ ταῦτα συναγαγὼν τούς θ' ἑαυτοῦ στρατιώτας καὶ τοὺς προσελθόντας αὐτῷ καὶ τῶν ἄλλων²¹ᵃ τὸν βουλόμενον ἔλεξε τοιάδε·

Clearchus' second speech. 'Plainly the connexion between us and Cyrus is broken off; I am ashamed to face him, for I fear lest he should punish my breach of faith. Indeed we had all better look out for some way of escape, for Cyrus is a stern foe, and has a large force encamped at our side.'

"Ἄνδρες στρατιῶται, τὰ μὲν δὴ Κύρου⁸ᵃ δῆλον ὅτι οὕτως ἔχει πρὸς ἡμᾶς, ὥσπερ τὰ ἡμέτερα πρὸς ἐκεῖνον· οὔτε γὰρ ἡμεῖς ἐκείνου ἔτι στρατιῶται, ἐπεί γε⁵¹ οὐ συνεπόμεθα αὐτῷ, οὔτε ἐκεῖνος ἔτι ἡμῖν μισθοδότης· ὅτι μέντοι ἀδικεῖσθαι⁴³ᵃ νομίζει ὑφ' ἡμῶν, οἶδα· 10. ὥστε καὶ μεταπεμπομένου αὐτοῦ²⁷ οὐκ ἐθέλω⁴⁹ᵃ ἐλθεῖν, τὸ μὲν μέγιστον,¹⁴ᵇ αἰσχυνόμενος, ὅτι σύνοιδα ἐμαυτῷ πάντα ἐψευσμένος⁹ᵇ,⁴³ᶜ αὐτόν, ἔπειτα δὲ καὶ δεδιὼς, μὴ λαβών με δίκην ἐπιθῇ⁴³ᵈ ὧν⁴ᵃ,¹³ νομίζει ὑπ' ἐμοῦ ἠδικῆσθαι. 11. Ἐμοὶ οὖν δοκεῖ οὐχ ὥρα⁴³ᵃ, ᵒᵇˢ· εἶναι ἡμῖν καθεύδειν, οὐδ' ἀμελεῖν ἡμῶν αὐτῶν,²³ ἀλλὰ βουλεύεσθαι, ὅ τι χρὴ⁴⁵ ποιεῖν ἐκ τούτων. Καὶ ἕως γε μένομεν⁵²ᶜ αὐτοῦ, σκεπτέον³¹ᵃ μοι δοκεῖ εἶναι, ὅπως ἀσφαλέστατα μενοῦμεν·⁵⁰ᶜ εἴ τε ἤδη δοκεῖ ἀπιέναι, ὅπως ἀσφαλέστατα ἄπιμεν, καὶ ὅπως τὰ ἐπιτήδεια ἕξομεν· ἄνευ γὰρ τούτων οὔτε στρατηγοῦ²¹ οὔτε ἰδιώτου ὄφελος οὐδέν. 12. Ὁ δ' ἀνὴρ πολλοῦ²⁶ᵃ μὲν ἄξιος φίλος, ᾧ ἂν φίλος ᾖ,⁴⁸ χαλεπώτατος δ' ἐχθρὸς, ᾧ ἂν πολέμιος ᾖ

[XENOPHON'S ANABASIS OF CYRUS—TAYLOR. *See* p. 30.]

ANABASIS OF CYRUS, BOOK I. [III. 7-16]

ἀλεξήσασθαι is not the usual Attic form of the aorist of ἀλέξω, but has here the strongest MS. authority.

7. παρὰ βασιλέα] To the king's court; ἐπί, which would imply hostility, seems purposely avoided. The effect of the speech is plain. Clearchus is not personally popular, but his declaration, that he is not going this long march inland in a strange country, at once brings over some even of Xenias' men, who probably knew what the march was. Ep. i. 1. 2.

8. τούτων] Neuter; that things would right themselves.

9. τὰ μὲν δὴ Κύρου] Cyrus' relations to us must vary with our relation to him. Note the cleverness with which the different points in this speech are put:—1. Of course our pay ceases, and we are thrown on our own resources: 2. we are the aggressors; I cannot face Cyrus, because I know I am treating him shabbily: 3. we shall require all our vigilance to guard our own safety: 4. we cannot neglect the strong force which Cyrus has, and which is sufficient to crush us, for he will be no relenting foe, if foe we make him, and he is close at our doors.

11. ἤδη] At once.
τούτων] *i.e.* τῶν ἐπιτηδείων.

12. ἐχθρὸς] Note the difference between ἐχθρός and πολέμιος. A man may be at war with you without any personal feeling of enmity, but he, if he be your foe, will be a bitter and unrelenting one. Krüger quotes appropriately CURTIUS vii. 10. 8: 'Illi nunquam se *inimicos* ei, sed bello lacessitos *hostes* fuisse, respondent.'

13. ἃ ἐγίγνωσκον] Like the γνώμην ἀποφαίνεσθαι of the Athenian assembly.
γνώμης] Consent.

14. εἷς δὲ δὴ εἶπε] 'One went so far as to say.'
ἡ δὲ ἀγορὰ κ.τ.λ.] It is this that gives point to the recommendation to buy provisions; it reminds them that they could not even get them without Cyrus' permission.
διὰ φιλίας τῆς χώρας] Note that φιλίας is predicate. The presence of a guide from Cyrus might secure their being unmolested.
ὧν πολλοὺς κ.τ.λ.] Another insidious hint of danger.
It was the Greeks mainly who had plundered the country in reprisals for the loss of their comrades.

15. ὡς δέ] *i.e.* ἕκαστος δὲ λεγέτω ὡς. The construction is changed from ὡς πεισόμενον, and a general positive word is understood from the negative μηδείς.

16. ὥσπερ κ.τ.λ.] As if Cyrus would not want his ships to convey back

[XENOPHON'S ANABASIS OF CYRUS—TAYLOR. See p. 30.]

ATTRIBUTIVE EXPRESSIONS.

NOTE 3.—The Objective Genitive in Latin, denoting the object of an action implied in the noun that it qualifies, is often used in phrases where in English we use the Prepositions *for, about, from.*

ENGLISH.	LATIN.
Resentment *for* a wrong.	Dolor injuriae.
Escape *from* danger.	Fuga periculi.
A craving *for* gain.	Fames lucri.
Sleep is a refuge *from* all toils.	Somnus est perfugium omnium laborum.
Anxiety *about* the body.	Cura corporis.

NOTE 4.—The Attributive Adjective is used in Latin in many cases where we use Prepositions, such as *of, in, against;* thus—

Mons summus, *the top of the mountain.*
Sullanus exercitus, *the army of Sulla.*
Media aestas, *the middle of the summer.*
Bellum Africanum, *the war in Africa.*
Bellum Mithridaticum, *the war against Mithridates.*
Reliqua Graecia, *the rest of Greece.*
Italia tota, *the whole of Italy.*

NOTE 5.—Observe carefully the following distinctions:—

LATIN.	ENGLISH.
Urbs Roma.	The city *of* Rome.
Sardinia insula.	The island *of* Sardinia.
Civis Romanus.	A citizen *of* Rome.
Civis Atheniensis.	A citizen *of* Athens.
Graecus homo.	A Greek.
Homo Romanus.	A Roman.
Vir patricius.	A patrician.

NOTE 6.—The Objective Genitive follows many adjectives in Latin to express the object of *desire, knowledge,* etc., implied in the adjective; thus—

[ELEMENTARY LATIN GRAMMAR—J. H. SMITH. *See* p. 19.]

INDEX

	PAGE		PAGE
HISTORY	7	LATIN	18
ENGLISH	1	GREEK	24
MATHEMATICS	12	CATENA CLASSICORUM	35
SCIENCE	16	DIVINITY	36

MISCELLANEOUS 39

	PAGE
ABBOTT (E.), Selections from Lucian	28
—— Elements of Greek Accidence	24
—— and Mansfield's Primer of Greek Accidence	24
—— Short Greek Syntax	24
Alford (Dean), Greek Testament	34
Aristophanes, by W. C. Green	32, 35
—— Scenes from, by Arthur Sidgwick	29
Aristotle's Ethics, by Edward Moore	33
—— by J. E. T. Rogers	33
Aristotle's Organon, by J. R. Magrath	34
Arnold (T. K.), Cornelius Nepos	22
—— Crusius' Homeric Lexicon	30
—— Demosthenes	31
—— Eclogæ Ovidianæ	21
—— English-Greek Lexicon	33
—— First French Book	40
—— First German Book	40
—— First Greek Book	28
—— First Hebrew Book	40
—— First Verse Book	20
—— Greek Accidence	28
—— Greek Prose Composition	28
—— Henry's First Latin Book	20
—————— edited by C.G.Gepp	20
—— Homer for Beginners	29
—— Homer's Iliad	30
—— Latin Prose Composition	20
—————— edited by G. G. Bradley	20
—— Madvig's Greek Syntax	34
—— Sophocles	32
BAKER's (W.) Manual of Devotion for School-boys	37
Barrett (W. A.), Chorister's Guide	40
Bennett (G. L.), Easy Latin Stories	18, 42, 43
—— First Latin Writer	18
Bigg (Ch.), Exercises in Latin Prose	19
—— Thucydides	33, 35
Blunt (J. H.), Household Theology	37
—— Keys to Christian Knowledge: The Holy Bible, The Prayer Book, Church History (Ancient and Modern), Church Catechism	38
Bowen (E.), Napoleon's Campaigns	40
Bradley (G. G.), Arnold's Latin Prose Composition	20
Bridge (C.), French Literature	7
Bright (J. Franck), English History	8
Browning (O.), Hist. Handbooks	7
Building Construction, Notes on	16
Burton's The Beginner's Drill-book of English Grammar	6
CALVERT (E.), Selections from Livy	22
Carr (A.), Notes on Greek Testament	34

	PAGE
Catena Classicorum	35
Companion to the Old Testament	37
Cornelius Nepos, by T. K. Arnold	22
Crake (A.D.), History of the Church	10
Creighton (M.), Hist. Biographies	10
Crusius' Homeric Lexicon, by T. K. Arnold	30
Curteis (A.M.), The Roman Empire	7
DAVYS (Bishop), Hist. of England	10
Demosthenes, by T. K. Arnold	31
—— by G. H. Heslop	31, 33
—— by Arthur Holmes	31, 35
ENGLISH SCHOOL CLASSICS, edited by Francis Storr	1-5
Euclid, by J. Hamblin Smith	14
Euripides, Scenes from, by Arthur Sidgwick	29
FIRMAN (F. B.), and Sanderson (L.), Zeugma	31
Frädersdorff (J. W.) English-Greek Lexicon	33
GANTILLON (P. G. F.), Classical Examination Papers	21, 32
Gedge (J. W.), Young Churchman's Companion to the Prayer Book	37
Gepp (C. G.), Latin Elegiac Verse	20
—— Henry's First Latin Book	20
Girdlestone (W. H.), Arithmetic	14
Goolden (W. T.), and Rigg (A.), Chemistry	16
Goulburn (Dean), Manual of Confirmation	38
Greek Testament, by Dean Alford	34
—— by Chr. Wordsworth	34
Green (W. C.), Aristophanes	32, 35
Grenfell's (E. F.) First German Exercises	39
—— German Exercises, Part II.	39
Gross (E. J.), Algebra, Part II.	13
—— Kinematics and Kinetics	13
HERODOTUS (Stories from), by J. Surtees Phillpotts	28
—— by H. G. Woods	33, 35
Heslop (G. H.), Demosthenes	31, 35
Historical Biographies, edited by M. Creighton	10
Historical Handbooks, edited by Oscar Browning	7
Holmes (Arthur), Demosthenes	31, 35
—— Rules for Latin Pronunciation	19
Homer for Beginners, by T. K. Arnold	29
Homer's Iliad, by T. K. Arnold	30
—— by S. H. Reynolds	30, 35
—— by A. Sidgwick	29
—— Book VI., by J. S. Phillpotts	29

INI

	PAGE
Horace, by J. M. Marshall	23, 35
IOPHON	28
Isocrates, by J. E. Sandys	32, 35
JEBB (R. C.), Sophocles	32, 35
Juvenal, by G. A. Simcox	23, 35
KEYS TO CHRISTIAN KNOWLEDGE	38
Kitchener (F. A.), A Year's Botany	16
LA FONTAINE'S FABLES, by P. Bowden-Smith	40
Latham (R. G.) English Dictionary	6
Laughton's (J. K.) At Home and Abroad	39
Laun (Henri Van), French Selections	40
Lessing's Fables, by F. Storr	39
Livy, Selections from, by R. Saward and E. Calvert	22
Lucian, by Evelyn Abbott	28
MADVIG'S GREEK SYNTAX, by T. K. Arnold	34
Magrath (J.R.), Aristotle's Organon	34
Mansfield (E. D.), Latin Sentence Construction	19
Manuals of Religious Instruction	37
Marshall (J. M.), Horace	23, 35
Materials and Models	21, 31
Moberly (Charles E.), Shakspere	1
—— Arrian's Alexander the Great in the Punjaub	28
—— Xenophon's Memorabilia, Book I.	30
Morice (F.D.), Stories in Attic Greek	26
Moore (Edward), Aristotle's Ethics.	33
NORRIS (J. P.), Key to the Gospels	38
———— to the Acts	38
———— Manuals of Religious Instruction	36
———— Rudiments of Theology	37
———— Confirmation Lessons	38
OVID, Stories from, by R. W. Taylor	22
Ovidianæ Eclogæ, by T. K. Arnold	21
PAPILLON (T. L.), Terence	23, 35
Pearson (Charles), English History in the XIVth Century	7
Persius, by A. Pretor	23, 35
Phillpotts (J. Surtees), Stories from Herodotus	28
———— Shakspere's Tempest.	1
———— Homer's Iliad, Book VI.	29
Pretor (A.), Persii Satiræ	23, 35
REYNOLDS (S. H.), Homer's Iliad	30, 35
Richardson (G.), Conic Sections	13
Rigg (A.), and Goolden (W. T.), Introduction to Chemistry	16
Rivingtons' Mathematical Series	12
Rogers (J. E. T.), Aristotle's Ethics	33
SANDERSON (L.), and Firman (F. B.), Zeugma	31
Sandys (J. E.), Isocrates	32, 35
Sargent (J. Y.) and Dallin (T. F.), Latin Prose	21
———— Latin Selected Pieces	21
———— and Dallin (T. F.), Greek Prose	31
———— Greek Selected Pieces	31

	PAGE
Saward (R.), Selections from Livy	22
Shakspere's As You Like It, Macbeth, Hamlet, King Lear, and Romeo and Juliet, by C. E. Moberly	1
—— Coriolanus, by R. Whitelaw	1
—— Tempest, by J. S. Phillpotts	1
—— Merchant of Venice, by R. W. Taylor	1
Sidgwick (Arthur), Scenes from Greek Plays	29
—— Greek Prose Composition	26
—— Homer's Iliad, Books I.-IV.	29
—— First Greek Writer	26
Simcox (G. A.), Juvenal	23, 35
———— Thucydides	33, 35
Simcox (W. H.), Tacitus	23, 35
Smith (J. H.), Arithmetic	13
—— Key to Arithmetic	13
—— Elementary Algebra	13
—— Key to Algebra	13
—— Enunciations	14
—— Exercises on Algebra	13
—— Hydrostatics	14
—— Geometry	14
—— Statics	14
—— Trigonometry	14
—— Key to Trigonometry	14
—— Latin Grammar	19, 46
—— English Grammar	6, 41
—— Latin Exercises	19
—— Key to Latin Exercises	19
—— (P. B.), La Fontaine's Fables	40
—— (Philip V.), History of English Institutions	7
—— (R. Prowde), Latin Prose Exercises	19
Sophocles, by T. K. Arnold	32
—— by R. C. Jebb	32, 35
Storr (F.), English School Classics	1–5
—— Vergil's Aeneid, Books I. II. and XI. XII.	21
—— Lessing's Fables	39
TACITUS, by W. H. Simcox	23, 35
Taylor (R. W.), Stories from Ovid	22
—— Merchant of Venice	1
—— Anabasis of Xenophon	30, 44, 45
—— A Short Greek Syntax	30
Terence, by T. L. Papillon	23, 35
Thiers' Campaigns of Napoleon, by E. E. Bowen	40
Thucydides, by C. Bigg	33, 35
—— by G. A. Simcox	33, 35
VECQUERAY (J. W. J.), First German Accidence	39
Vergil's Aeneid, by F. Storr	21
WAY OF LIFE	38
Whitelaw (Robert), Coriolanus	1
Willert (F.), Reign of Lewis XI.	7
Wilson (R. K.), History of Modern English Law	7
Woods (H. G.), Herodotus	33, 35
Wordsworth (Bp.), Greek Testament	34
Wormell (R.), Dynamics	14
XENOPHON'S Memorabilia, Book I., by C. E. Moberly	30
—— Anabasis of Cyrus, by R. W. Taylor	30

www.ingramcontent.com/pod-product-compliance
Lightning Source LLC
Chambersburg PA
CBHW021731220426
43662CB00008B/791